Which Side Are You On?

Which Side Are You On?

Seven Social Responsibility Debates in American Librarianship, 1990–2015

Elaine Harger

McFarland & Company, Inc., Publishers
Jefferson, North Carolina

Back cover photograph of Elaine Harger, 2015,
by David Richard Harger

Collage artwork by the author

LIBRARY OF CONGRESS CATALOGUING-IN-PUBLICATION DATA

Names: Harger, Elaine, author.
Title: Which side are you on? : seven social responsibility debates
in American librarianship, 1990–2015 / Elaine Harger.
Description: Jefferson, North Carolina : McFarland & Company, Inc.,
Publishers, 2016 | Includes bibliographical references and index.
Identifiers: LCCN 2016000055 | ISBN 9780786494552
(softcover : acid free paper) ∞
Subjects: LCSH: Libraries and society—United States—History—20th century. |
Library science—Social aspects—United States—History—20th century. |
Library science—Political aspects—United States—History—20th century. |
Librarians—Political activity—United States—History—20th century. |
American Library Association—History—20th century.
Classification: LCC Z716.4 .H367 2016 | DDC 020.973—dc23
LC record available at http://lccn.loc.gov/2016000055

BRITISH LIBRARY CATALOGUING DATA ARE AVAILABLE

ISBN (print) 978-0-7864-9455-2
ISBN (ebook) 978-1-4766-2471-6

© 2016 Elaine Harger. All rights reserved

Front cover images © 2016 iStock

*No part of this book may be reproduced or transmitted in any form
or by any means, electronic or mechanical, including photocopying
or recording, or by any information storage and retrieval system,
without permission in writing from the publisher.*

Edited by Robert Franklin

Printed in the United States of America

*McFarland & Company, Inc., Publishers
Box 611, Jefferson, North Carolina 28640
www.mcfarlandpub.com*

To the memory of

Miriam Braverman
E. J. Josey
Zoia Horn

Helen Harger
sweetness incarnate

and

Edwin Ensign
who taught me my first lesson in social justice

Acknowledgments

One thing learned from writing this book is that a writer could write nothing without all who came before—from the first human to tell a story, scratch a symbol in the sand, to writers who have left countless miles of paper trails for a reader to lose herself in, to those whose eyes and hands mined minerals for ink, manufactured pen and paper, assembled the laptop computer upon which my fingers tap-dance at this very moment. Although they will certainly never receive this acknowledgement, I honor all.

For those who can and will receive my thanks, the first goes to Robbie Franklin (my publisher and an ALA Councillor 1988–2000) for suggesting the book in the first place. My telling of Council stories might not be quite what he envisioned, but these are the stories I have to give.

Thank you to all librarians, archivists, paraprofessionals, clerical workers, shelvers, and student desk attendants at the ALA Archives, University of Illinois–Champaign-Urbana, the University of Washington Suzzallo and Allen Libraries, Gallagher Law Library and Seattle Public Library who directly and indirectly provided the records, articles, books, and databases without which I could not have accomplished this work.

Just as a writer cannot write without tools, food, and inspiration, so too an activist cannot act without comrades, context, and hope. For these thanks go to members of the Progressive Librarians Guild, Social Responsibilities Round Table, ALA Council, and #critlib-Seattle. Without our conversations and activism this book would not exist.

Nor would it exist without the baristas at Zeitgeist, Allegro, Broadcast Coffee, Ballard Coffee Works, and Victrola's who sparked my synapses into action, and provided environments conducive to writing. To RemedyTeas also, for the tranquility that must come after caffeinated brainstorms and writing marathons.

Among colleagues, I must acknowledge by name and give the deepest heartfelt thanks to Al Kagan, Susan Maret, Kathleen de la Peña McCook, Mark Rosenzweig, and last, but not least, Sara Plaza Moreno and Edgardo Civallero, who have seen this project through with me, one word at a time.

Finally, I must acknowledge my family—Mom, for raising me to be adventurous; Dad, for being a model of speaking truth to power…consequences be damned; Natalie, for sharing all kinds of adventures with me; Stephen, for inspiring me to aim toward skillful perfection (and for taking me fishing!); David, for being the magical, magnetic brother who would for sure have received an invitation to Hogwarts if it had been around when we were kids; Keith, for setting the bar high in caring for others and challenging self; and everybody who's connected in blood or spirit to us Hargers. Each and every one of you inspires me with your warmth, ideals, courage, endless capacity for *fun*…and stirring the stew!

Namasté a todos!

Table of Contents

Acknowledgments — vi

Introduction — 1

1. In Denial—Speaking about *The Speaker* — 15
2. Singing (and Silencing) Solidarity—Interrupting Legacies of Racism and the Anti-Apartheid "Book Boycott" — 41
3. Censuring a Censor—The Debate on Censorship in Israel and the Occupied Territories — 75
4. Speaking with One Voice, Strangling Others?—McDonald's and the Boy Scouts of America — 111
5. Abandoning Snowden...*and* Privacy?—Hegemony at Play in ALA — 141
6. Charting a New Course—ALA and Climate Crisis — 175

Works Cited — 203

Index — 215

Introduction

Toward the end of the journey writing this book, I began walking ten or so miles a day on a picket line in front of the middle school where I work in Seattle. By unanimous vote, members of the Seattle Education Association voted on September 3, 2015, to go out on strike if a tentative contract had not been reached by the 9th—the day students were to return to school. When the end of the 8th arrived with no tentative agreement, all the teachers, paraprofessionals, instructional assistants, and office workers gathered in the classroom nearest the S. Jackson Street exit to hear an update on negotiations, and receive instructions from our picket captain, Nurse Palumbo.

My first job as a librarian was at the Harry Van Arsdale, Jr., School of Labor Studies in New York City. Known as the "Labor College" the school was a branch of the State University of New York's Empire State College, and had been founded by New York's labor unions in the 1970s in the belief that workers needed a college where they could learn about working class history, labor law, occupational safety and health, union benefit fund administration, and other related topics. A spirit of labor solidarity was at the heart of the school, and frequent occurrences for Labor College staff and students were activities like marching in New York City's annual Labor Day parade, and walking on picket lines with whoever happened to be on strike—carpenters, stagehands, newspaper workers, public employees. I'd walked many picket lines, but never one of my own. So, the SEA strike was a first for me, and I was bound and determined that we'd all sing that great labor anthem "Solidarity Forever" while tramping on the line.

Being a proactive sort of person, I'd taken the liberty of knowing a strike was possible to e-mail our choir teacher. In the message, I included links to two YouTube videos. The first to Utah Phillips singing "Solidarity Forever," a song written in 1915 by IWW poet-laureate Ralph Chaplin during a coalminers' strike in West Virginia. Rousing lyrics set to the tune of "The Battle Hymn of the Republic" / "John Brown's Body" (Chaplin). For good measure, I added a link to a Billy Bragg rendition of "Union Maid" with a new, 21st century last verse.

And we sang!

At the end of the 5-day strike, everyone was given an "exit ticket" on which to write what they wanted to remember most about the experience. Many noted singing "Solidarity Forever."

Another old union song surfaced during the strike. One of my librarian colleagues from an elementary school was asked by a parent if she had any recommendations for picture books about strikes that could be read to young children. This picket line reference request resulted in a resource list compiled by three striking librarians (Pat Bliquez, Craig

Seasholes, and myself), which we then distributed to other Seattle librarians once the strike was over and we could use district e-mail again. On the list was a picture book written by George Ella Lyon and illustrated by Christopher Cardinale called *Which Side Are You On? The Story of a Song*. A song written during a siege of a coal-company house, amidst a hail of bullets, by the wife of a union organizer, while her seven children hid under the bed. A mother singing to her frightened children during a battle for workers' rights.

For several days I hummed the song, considered its history, and recalled a reference desk experience repeated several times at the Labor College. Suddenly, the purpose of the book you have in your hands crystallized.

The experience from the reference desk, which occurred multiple times over the seven years I worked there, was as follows: A student, always a white male in his early- to mid-twenties, and an apprentice in the electrical workers' union, would come into the library to work on an assignment for a labor history class. He'd be visibly disturbed, and I'd carefully get around to asking him what was on his mind. The answer was inevitably an expression of anger that he'd "never learned any of this stuff in school." Not once did a black or female student express the same anger, possibly because they were familiar enough with whose stories get shortchanged in high school history books.

Countless histories are overlooked, ignored, hidden by that class of people who stand to benefit from being in control of deciding whose stories are considered worthy, which perspectives are legitimate and true. The class of people who accrue power from ignorance and the incapacity of the oppressed to recognize and accept the fact that their oppression is not natural or deserved or inevitable. Although burdened by insufficient, partial, unreliable information, ostracized from decision-making bodies by cults of expertise, incapacitated by fears and doubts generated by cultural elites, oppressed peoples do break through their bondage. They brave fear of ridicule, fear of reputation, fear of losing their position or livelihood, of being ostracized, blacklisted, disappeared, killed. Oppressed peoples begin to question instilled doubts that they actually do know, that their knowledge is legitimate. The Other revolts, demands for "freedom and justice for all" are made, and social change begins.

This book seeks to tell the stories that lay behind several debates within the American Library Association during the years between 1990 and 2015. The debates emerge from concerns and conversations amongst librarians who take seriously ALA's mission regarding the social responsibilities of librarianship and stand in opposition to those who insist that a position of political neutrality is the only legitimate place in the public arena for librarianship.

Nearly every librarian expresses commitment to core values as articulated over the past several decades—access, confidentiality and privacy, democracy, diversity, education and lifelong learning, intellectual freedom, preservation, the public good, professionalism, service, and social responsibility. One need only attend half-a-dozen programs at a local, state, regional, national, or international library conference to hear appeals to any or all of these values. As is often said, however, talking the talk is one thing, walking the walk is another.

A level of commitment deeper than the norm is on display in the stories presented in this book. Just as the students at the Labor College learned to search beyond the mainstream for a comprehensive understanding of who makes history, the librarian activists who brought to ALA's attention the issues at the center of debates described here are people who bridge mere expressions of solidarity, and dare to risk putting reputations and jobs on the line in the desire to actualize our profession's values. These librarians are fully cognizant of the connection between one's own life and the lives of others, librarians who acknowledge the complicity of the privileged with systems of injustice and oppression, who refuse the edict that they remain neutral in the face of human suffering, and instead engage in dialogue, debate and action for change. These are librarians who know that a hail of bullets directed at a mother and her children in order to maximize coal company profitability was not, and is not, an isolated incident, but a regular, ongoing occurrence. Place, circumstance, and specifics change but the overall dynamic remains—privilege maintained by ignorance, distraction, violence. These are librarians who know which side they are on.

The individuals involved in identifying and realizing the social responsibilities of librarianship in each of the cases presented here were motivated by the belief that *every* human needs and deserves an environment free of violence, a place that nurtures potential, free of political intimidation, economic exploitation, emotional and spiritual repression, ecological degradation. Each firmly believes in the social responsibilities of librarianship as articulated in ALA's mission statement,

> ALA recognizes its broad social responsibilities. The broad social responsibilities of the American Library Association are defined in terms of the contribution that librarianship can make in ameliorating or solving the critical problems of society; support for efforts to help inform and educate the people of the United States on these problems and to encourage them to examine the many views on and the facts regarding each problem; and the willingness of ALA to take a position on current critical issues with the relationship to libraries and library service set forth in the position statement [ALA A.1.1].

In your hands then is a collection of stories about seven debates engaged on the floor of ALA's governing Council. Each focused on a critical social problem. In telling these stories my purpose is to describe the debates; explain the reasons why those who brought each issue to the table considered it worthy of attention; use each debate as an illustration of the manner in which hegemonies of power are challenged, reproduced, reinforced, and altered within a professional association; and make a small contribution to the historic record of the American Library Association.

In these seven debates, I was either an observer or a participant. With one exception, the debates are contained within the years 1990–2015. One debate began in 1978, long before I entered the profession, but was raised again in 2014 on the listserv of Council where I've lurked behind the e-curtains since leaving my seat on Council in 2009. The subjects of the resolutions debated by Council, in the order in which they appear in this book are: the re-release by ALA's Office of Intellectual Freedom of a controversial film, *The Speaker*; ALA's support of anti-apartheid boycotts on behalf of the freedom struggles of black South Africans; censorship by Israeli authorities within Israel and the Occupied Territories; partnerships between ALA and corporations, specifically McDonald's, the fast food giant; ALA's relationship with the Boy Scouts of America, an organization that discriminated against gay scouts and scout leaders; Edward Snowden, the whistleblower who released documents revealing widespread and illegal gathering by the National Security Agency of telephone and internet communications of the U.S. public and others; and, finally, two resolutions focused on the environment—fossil fuel divestment and sustainable libraries—ending with a proposal for a concrete step librarianship could take in the face of climate change.

Change begins in dialogue

Each debate arose from a spark of unknown origin, in the heart and mind of a librarian who saw self connected to the world, and began to engage in an internal dialogue between what is and what could be. An eternal spark, born with the universe, leaps across the void between me-and-you, catching your combustible conditions, spreading through the undergrowth toward others, until our shared world is fully aflame with an idea which, to some, is incendiary, to others enlightening, and a call to action for yet others.

In his contribution to *The Black Librarian in America* (1970), a collection of essays edited by E. J. Josey, a longtime member of ALA Council and onetime president of the Association, Josey pays tribute to such sparks via a quote from Eldridge Cleaver.

> And why does it make you sad to see how everything hangs by such thin and whimsical threads? Because you're a dreamer, an incredible dreamer with a tiny spark hidden somewhere inside you which cannot die, even which you cannot kill or quench and which tortures you horribly because all the odds are against its continual burning. In the midst of the foulest decay and putrid savagery, this spark speaks to you of beauty, of human warmth and kindness, of goodness, of greatness, of heroism, of martyrdom, and it speaks to you of love [297].

We see the blossoming of these sparks of love throughout the history of librarianship. They materialize slowly into ideas, proposals, demands, decisions, and sometimes morph into adjectives becoming the labels we use to qualify our calling, to self-identify, to distinguish, to challenge the status quo, and to prove that change is possible.

Time was that "librarian" (unqualified by any preceding adjective) conjured up the image of a white man. When Melville Dewey began inviting women (!) to attend his newly established school of librarianship at Columbia University the trustees of that kingly institution were so offended that they ran Dewey off campus all the way upstate to Albany. Later came a time when to identify as a *children's* librarian was to declare oneself not only cutting-edge, but downright anti-establishment. Later, not-for-nothin' did Margaret A. Edwards feel moved by her place on the timeline of librarianship to entitle her book on library services to teenagers *The Fair Garden and the Swarm of Beasts* (1969), for the title quite succinctly mirrored attitudes widely held at the time toward teens in the library, and inner city youth in particular. Once abhorred, youth were served by a new breed of *teen* (later YA, i.e., young adult) librarians. Which brings to mind other "beasts" in that fair garden—the black librarian, the working-class librarian, the gay librarian. And then there are the socially responsible librarian, progressive librarian, radical librarian, anarchist librarian, intellectual freedom purist librarian, green eco-librarian. A diversity of adjectives evolving over the years to describe librarians who have followed their conscience in working, as surely as water sculpts stone, to shape a librarianship that is responsive to every member of society.

What constituted radical ideas in the late 19th century or early to mid–20th century doesn't even register as anything but "the norm" in the 21st. But none of this happens without someone engaging first in an internal dialogue, then in discussion with allies, moving into the public arena via debate with opponents where, sometimes, the persuasive powers of intellectual engagement bring about something new via decision-making processes rooted in the ideals of democracy.

The debates: organization of these stories

When a spark of inspiration ignites, spreads, and grows into a coherent demand, proponents take it into the wider public arena for further discussion, debate, and action. The unfolding of every debate reveals multiple perspectives, and debates on Council are no exception. Positions are seldom starkly pro or con, yes or no. However, each story told here generally ends in a decision that is either an affirmation or a rejection of one specific perspective on the matter at hand. Sometimes decisions are reached via compromise, other times compromise is not necessary. Sometimes persuasive arguments that lead to decisions are later deemed unacceptable by someone who then argues that a mistake was made, that Council must revisit its decision, that unintended (negative) consequences might flow from the decision and endanger the Association in some imagined way or another. This is the dynamic at play in these stories.

The issues at the heart of each debate presented here were brought to Council as a challenge to a status quo, and they came to Council often via members of ALA's Social Responsibilities Round Table. One of the resolutions concerning *The Speaker* originated from dialogue between members of the Black Caucus of ALA; the challenge to ALA's support of anti-apartheid movement sanctions came from the American Association of Publishers; the fossil fuel resolution originated from a member of the Progressive Librarians Guild; and the resolution concerning sustainable libraries arose from ALA's newest unit, the Sustainability Round Table.

Each chapter here has three purposes. The first is to simply tell the story of a particular Council debate. The second purpose is to illustrate some aspect of the evolution of the process—from spark of inspiration into ALA policy (or not)—and the mechanisms at play in the process. The third is to utilize the work of various critical theorists to deepen our understanding of the power dynamics at play within each debate.

Chapter 1, "In Denial—Speaking about *The Speaker*," picks up on a debate conducted in 1978 because of the re-release of the film by the Office of Intellectual Freedom in 2014. This re-release and the mounting of the film on YouTube demand a reexamination of racism in librarianship. The issues raised by *and* about the film in 1978 are still relevant, and the repeat of the hurt and outrage caused by the earlier incident provide a powerful incentive for librarians to consider the role denial plays in our work and thinking. Reference is made in this chapter to the work of Stanley Cohen, in his book *States of Denial: Knowing About Atrocities and Suffering*, for the light it sheds on the tendency of people to deny offense and injury, exploitation, disappearances, imprisonment, torture, murder. Cohen's work should inform discussions among librarians in many areas of our work and inquiry. Reference is also made to the work of three other scholars concerned with the concept of "epistemological racism"—Patricia Hill Collins' book *Black Feminist Thought*; James Joseph Scheurich's edited work *Anti-Racist Scholarship*; and Todd Honma's article "Trippin' Over the Colorline." The chapter also includes coverage of the incident at Harvard inspiring the film's storyline, to provide the reader with a fuller picture of the debate than has appeared thus far in the library literature.

Chapter 2, "Singing (and Silencing) Solidarity—Interrupting Legacies of Racism and the Anti-Apartheid 'Book Boycott,'" describes the 1989/90 challenge to ALA's support of anti-apartheid sanctions by the Association of American Publishers and ALA's own Intellectual Freedom Committee. Both the AAP and IFC argued that support of sanctions, which included books, databases, and other information resources, interfered with the "free flow of information" and was an act of censorship. The chapter attempts, via an account of the history of the anti-apartheid movement in the United States, to show how librarians become politicized to the point where they force ALA to take action. This account is my own way of painting a picture of activism in the making. Tensions between intellectual freedom "purists" and social responsibility librarians are discussed. Reference is made to the work of Stephen L. Esquith whose book, *The Political Responsibilities of Everyday Bystanders*, gives an excellent account of how awareness, acknowledgment, and action in the face of severe violence gives rise to people acting from the conviction that they have a responsibility towards harm done to others.

Chapter 3, "Censuring a Censor—The Debate on Censorship in Israel and the Occupied Territories," presents the attention given within ALA, between the years 1983 and 1993, to censorship practices by Israeli authorities both within Israel and the Occupied Territories (as Palestine was called at that time). Again, an attempt is made to provide historical context to facilitate understanding of the debate, and in this instance I refer to the evolution of my own understanding of the conflict that continues to this day between Israeli and Palestinian peoples.

Chapter 4, "Speaking with One Voice, Strangling Others?—McDonald's and the Boy Scouts of America," tells the stories of two debates to illustrate the desire on the part of some within ALA to ensure that the Association "speaks with one voice." The stories include two statements issued by the Social Responsibilities Round Table, one regarding ALA's use of corporate sponsors (in this case McDonald's), and another regarding the Boy Scouts of America (BSA) and their discriminatory policies against gay and atheist scouts. Historical information is provided for the Boy Scout section because the relationship between ALA and the Scouts dates back to the early 20th century, and also because of the ideological elements that produced an emotionally powerful sense of violation when the ALA/BSA relationship was put in question.

Chapter 5, "Abandoning Snowden...*and* Privacy?—Hegemony at Play in ALA," concerns the debate from the 2013 annual conference on the "Resolution in support of whistleblower Edward Snowden." A considerable portion of the audio transcript of the sessions at which the topic was discussed are used to give the reader a full taste of Council floor debates—its give-and-take, formal structure, parliamentary procedures, and the players involved. This detailed presentation of the Snowden debate is used to reveal how ALA Council, Executive Board, and other units often constitute a conduit of hegemonic power within the Association, and via ALA throughout the profession. Certain members of ALA can (and do) utilize their standing within the profession and Association to exercise decision-making influence that is outside the usual operating norms, processes, and expectations. Reference is made to Noam Chomsky's articulation of the manufacture of consent, and to Richard Sennett's work on the sociology of authority. In addition, because the Snowden case has to do with issues of privacy, we look briefly at the historical roots of the 4th Amendment to the United States Constitution, and to the work of philosopher Sissela Bok who writes about secrecy, confidentiality, and privacy.

The last chapter of the book, "Charting a New Course—ALA and Climate Crisis," presents two resolutions, dealt with by Council, and another that veers off into the future. One resolution, on fossil fuel divestment, was rejected by Council, while the second, on sustainable libraries, received Council's support. This issue is of particular concern to me, and so I have taken the liberty of presenting a new resolution, a draft, a proposal, for the consideration of both readers and ALA members. As the economist Naomi Klein notes in her book, *This Changes Everything: Capitalism versus Climate*, climate change is not an issue. Climate change has become the *context* within which humans must address all other issues from this moment on.

Social responsibility debates— what they are, why they matter

Within librarianship, long outdated and debunked theoretical mindsets continue to find safe harbor in LIS curricula, research, journals, conference programs, professional practices, and library services, in conversations throughout the field, and in the very name of the degree we hold. Library and information *science* doesn't just suggest, but lays claim, on behalf of every degree holder, to the mantle of objectivity, the notion of natural order, and the assumed legitimacy of disinterested, incorruptible, truth-seeking authorities as embodied by those calling themselves scientists.

Gloria Leckie and John Buschman, in their introduction to the edited work *Critical Theory for Library and Information Science* (2010), present the other side of the theoretical coin, describing the development of theories that question, challenge, expose the ideological interests of those who claim pristine objectivity and neutrality in their explanations of how the world works. While priests and kings, technologists and CEOs claim for their own edicts and laws the same inviolability and inevitability as those that largely govern the natural world (and enforce man-made laws via ideology and violence), the Other raises questions. Leckie and Buschman give a brief overview of critical theories such as the philosophers of the Frankfurt School in the 1930s who examined social relations during the rise of Hitler and Nazism, and of post–World War II French scholars, all of whom questioned received notions of knowledge, agency, priority, normality. Hegemonic processes that reproduced structures of power from one generation to the next were investigated and uncovered.

About the now rich body of critical theory, Leckie and Buschman write,

> These notions dovetail with the refusal to accept Western privileging of mathematics and scientific definitions of reality at the expense of other ways of knowing. The overall project supports inclusion and democratic justice for persons of color, women, gay men and lesbians in society, bringing about a refreshing poignancy to conceptions of fairness [p. viii].

Ideally, critical theory informs professional practice, allowing the practitioner to understand institutional purposes and functions in a way that empowers those so inclined to question, disrupt, and demand change within power structures that violate basic values of fairness and human equality.

At the juncture where critical theory meets experiences of unjust social relations, and informs the actions of a person willing to ask probing questions, is where one encounters debates described as socially responsible. Over the past century the façade of objectivity within librarianship has been challenged in ways big and small. Diehard assumptions, biases, and claims of neutrality regarding class, race, gender, age, language, ethnicity, sexual orientation, gender identity, and political leanings have determined the direction and form of all levels of practice—collection development, subject headings, and outreach services (to name just a few). Collections exclude ___, library doors have been closed to ___, subject-headings have ___. Socially responsible librarians notice areas in which the profession falls short, question underlying beliefs and processes, investigate them, consider alternatives, and demand change.

Thus, a social responsibility debate is openly, unabashedly, and unapologetically partisan. No pretense of neutrality.

One other area distinguishes the social responsibility debate from others, in relation to matters regarding intellectual freedom. Intellectual freedom "purists" often enough accuse social responsibility advocates with censorship. However, socially responsible librarians fully support freedom of speech, press, association, and religion. Where they differ from the "purists" is in the distinction that must be made between free speech and reckless speech. The act of yelling "Fire!" in a crowded theater, for instance, is not protected speech. Few, if any, intellectual freedom purists would argue that it should be. However, the spectrum of speech is very broad and includes extremes from the prohibited yelling of "Fire!" to the protected protest of government policies regarding climate change on the streets. Within that spectrum are other gradations—hate speech, misleading speech, "fighting words," speech that rallies acts of violence, lies. For those who believe the engagement of social responsibilities to be a central professional duty it is important to make distinctions when matters of free speech arise. Under the rubric of neutrality and intellectual freedom purism, the First Amendment rights of Dr. King are the same as those of the Grand Dragon of the Ku Klux Klan. However, when these two individuals enter the public arena, one preaching love and nonviolence, the other hatred and terror, the questions become "Are their rights still equal? How and how not?" Are they due the same protection under the law, the same access to public stages and airwaves? Without hesitation, the purists would answer in the affirmative. The socially responsible would make the case that because the hatred and racism of the Klan have as their objects the violation of other people's rights, their lives even, this sort of speech is not protected. An individual may hold whatever opinion, belief, nonsensical notion they like, but other people—including librarians—are under no obligation to support or serve as conduit for harmful information.

Why do social responsibility debates matter? Simply because the perspectives put forward within such debates are informed by considerations of the greater good. Social responsibilities matter particularly today because we live in times of increasing imbalances in power across the social spectrum—political power, economic power, military/police power, educational and technological and cultural power. These imbalances have created social tensions throughout the world, and nations, tribes, ethnic and religious groups increasingly turn to violence in order to maintain structures of inequality—whether it be white male hegemony in the United States, or males of any sort and place over women. Each takes advantage of the old tactic of divide-and-conquer for the benefit of the few. The 1 percent in the U.S. can live like kings, while their minions foment discord among the 99 percent.

Humans are social beings, we could not survive without caring for one another. We live in a world today dominated by people whose socially pathological use of violence to maintain power over others has brought our species to the brink of environmental and social collapse and chaos. The only possibility for moving peacefully into the future lies in conversation, in talking through problems, in taking responsibility, making amends, solving problems in a spirit of human solidarity rather than the usual, violent discord. Ultimately, this is why social responsibilities matter, within society and within librarianship. Librarians can help facilitate the process between ourselves and throughout our communities.

Council as a platform for debate

In 1969, ALA was alive with activism opposed to the "old boy" system of governance within the Association. Much has been written of the huge ALA membership meetings, stretching on for hours, with thousands of participants discussing the democratization of ALA. Readers are referred to Toni Samek's *Intellectual Freedom and Social Responsibility in American Librarianship, 1967–1974* (2001); Douglas Raber's article in *Library Trends* (2007) entitled "ACONDA and ANACONDA: Social Change, Social Responsibility, and Librarianship"; and the chapter on ALA's Social Responsibilities Round Table in Al Kagan's book *Progressive Library Organizations: A Worldwide History* (2015). The activism for democratic decision-making described by these authors led to the governance structures and processes described in this book. Of central focus here, of course, is the work of ALA Council, which is the Association's policy making body.

ALA policy is made via two basic avenues. Committees established by Council can recommend a course of action, which Council then considers, and approves (or not). Most often, recommendations from Committees generate little debate or amendment. The process seldom takes much time, as committee members are generally trusted with the charge given them. The other route for making ALA policy is for a resolution to be brought to Council's agenda either via passage at an ALA membership meeting, or through sponsorship by at least two members of Council—the mover and a seconder. In either case, the resolution comes into existence because someone, somewhere, has a concern about which they believe ALA should take action. The individual or group either already knows about the Council resolution process or has been informed about it by someone who does. Often a person new to the process will be shepherded through it by an experienced colleague. The *ALA Policy Manual* (2015), available online, contains guidelines on the resolution process, plus information such as ALA's constitution and bylaws, descriptions of units and their areas of responsibility, and, of course, established policies.

Once a resolution is placed on Council's agenda it is handled according to parliamentary procedures—formal and informal discussion, formal debate, with decisions to table, refer, rule out-of-order, amend, reject, approve. Debate on social responsibility resolutions are seldom dry, pro forma affairs, but animated, impassioned, colorful. Council floor provides a soapbox for every perspective and the room comes alive with a spirit of democracy at work.

Before concluding this introduction, it will be helpful to introduce some of the entities that play a role in the stories that follow. Every story always begins with one person speaking to another. In some cases, these people are known, in others not. Given the nature of documented history, the constraints under which I was working, and my own talents and skills (or lack thereof), very few of the people involved in dialogue that led up to the debates are identified, and only a few of those involved in the debates themselves are named. However, the groups within which people worked are known, and identified as occasion arises. Below is a list of the major units, arranged alphabetically by the acronym with which they were familiarly known within ALA at the time of the debate being described. Thus, for example, I refer to the GLBTF, not the GLBTRT, the later of which is a unit of ALA today—the Gay, Lesbian, Bisexual, and Transgender Round Table—GLBTF having declared its independence from SRRT as a task force in 2011. Do note that what follows is not a comprehensive list of ALA units, but of those that play a role in the debates covered in this book. Interspersed throughout the list also are acronyms frequently used in different chapters that refer to organizations outside ALA. In parentheses are source notes (see Works Cited at the back of the book).

- AAP—Association of American Publishers, founded in 1970, is the trade association for book and journal publishers in the United States.
- ABA—American Booksellers Association, founded in 1900, is a non-profit organization that advocates on behalf of independent booksellers.
- ALA—The American Library Association is the oldest professional organization for librarians in the world. Established in 1876 in Philadelphia, ALA today is headquartered in Chicago and has about 60,000 members. Its mission is "to provide leadership for the development, promotion, and improvement of library and information services and the profession of librarianship in order to enhance learning and ensure access to information for all" (About ALA).
- ALA Council—Council is the Association's governing and policy-making body. Membership consists of 100 members elected at-large, plus members elected from ALA divisions, roundtables, and chapters. Currently there are 185 members (Council Composition).
- ACRL—Association of College and Research Libraries is a division of ALA, "dedicated to enhancing the ability of academic library and information professionals to serve

the information needs of the higher education community and to improve learning, teaching, and research" (About ACRL). Members of ACRL elect one of their colleagues as ACRL Division Councilor to ALA's governing Council.

- ALSC—Association of Library Services to Children is another division of ALA and is "dedicated to the support and enhancement of library service to children" (About ALSC). Like all divisions, ALSC is given policy-making powers in its area of expertise in accordance with ALA's constitution and bylaws, and its members elect one of their own as ALSC Division Councilor.
- ANC—African National Congress, founded in 1912 as an organization for the liberation of black South Africans in the struggle for political, economic, and cultural change.
- BARC—Budget Analysis and Review Committee, a committee of Council responsible for reviewing and making recommendations on actions that impact ALA's finances.
- BCALA—Black Caucus of ALA was founded, in 1970, by black librarians frustrated that the Association was not serving their needs as professionals, or the needs of libraries and library users in black communities. BCALA's mission is to serve "as an advocate for the development, promotion, and improvement of library services and resources to the nation's African American community; and provides leadership for the recruitment and professional development of African American librarians" (Our History). The Black Caucus became an official affiliate of ALA in 1992.
- BSA—Boy Scouts of America, founded in 1910, is a national educational and recreational club for boys.
- Chapters of ALA—Every state has its own library association, and members of each state association elect one of its members to serve a three-year term as Chapter Councilor. Thus, there are 50 chapter councilors representing each state, plus one each from the District of Columbia, and U.S. territories Guam and the Virgin Islands (Council Roster).
- COL—Committee on Legislation is a committee of Council, charged with "full responsibility for the association's total legislative program on all levels: federal, state, and local" (ALA Committee). It recommends legislation, protests any legislation harmful to libraries, assists in interpreting laws, representing ALA before government officials, and providing a forum within ALA on matters of legislation. The Committee acts in an advisory capacity to Council.
- COO—Committee on Organization also is a committee of Council whose purpose is to "advise and assist regarding structural and organizational concerns in ALA" (Committee). COO reviews applications for the establishment of new units to ALA, their names, charges, membership, relations with other units, and makes recommendations to Council in areas covered by its charge.
- Council Forum (no acronym used)—This is an informal, evening gathering during ALA midwinter and annual conferences of members of Council, and interested others, where issues on Council's agenda are discussed informally. Frequently these discussions assist in shaping resolutions, working through sticking points, and clarifying any confusion.
- EB—Executive Board of ALA serves to implement policy as established by Council and is also empowered to carry out the day-to-day functioning of the Association. At the helm of the Board is the ALA Executive Director. The director does not have voting power on the Board, but is employed by and reports to it.
- EMIERT—Ethnic Materials and Information Exchange Round Table, an ALA roundtable devoted to promoting materials from a wide range of ethnic authors and publishers.
- GLBTF—Gay, Lesbian, Bisexual Task Force was a unit of SRRT until it became a

roundtable of ALA. Its purpose is to promote the interests of GLBTQA librarians, library users, libraries and collections (Gay).
- GODORT—Government Documents Round Table is one of ALA's twenty roundtables, and is concerned with issues related to communications within librarianship regarding government documents, and to the education and training of government documents librarians (Government). GODORT began as a task force of SRRT.
- IFLA—International Federation of Library Associations
- IFRT—Intellectual Freedom Round Table, a unit of ALA devoted to intellectual freedom issues.
- IFC—Intellectual Freedom Committee is another committee of Council, whose purpose is "to safeguard the rights of library users, libraries, and librarians, in accordance with the first amendment" of the U.S. Constitution, the Library Bill of Rights, and to work on behalf of the Association in matters concerning censorship and intellectual freedom (Intellectual).
- IHRTF—International Human Rights Task Force, a task force of SRRT.
- IRC—International Relations Committee is also a committee of Council. It has "full responsibility for the association's international relations programs and initiatives" and works internationally on matters concerning librarianship (International). IRC makes recommendations to Council regarding ALA policy.
- IWW—Industrial Workers of the World. A labor union organized in Chicago in 1905 that set about to recruit unskilled and exploited immigrants, people of all colors, women, and migrant workers who were excluded from the craft unions of the American Federation of Labor.
- MDM—Mass Democratic Movement, founded in 1988, as a loose coalition of anti-apartheid organizations in South Africa.
- NSA—National Security Agency is an agency of the U.S. government responsible for collecting foreign intelligence.
- OLDS—Office of Literary and Outreach services. The ALA office with which SRRT has a staff liaison.
- OSSC—Organizational Self Study Committee, a special committee established in 1995 for the purpose of recommending structural changes to ALA.
- PLG—Progressive Librarians Guild is connected to ALA as an affiliate of the Social Responsibilities Round Table. PLG publishes *Progressive Librarian: A Journal for Critical Studies and Progressive Politics in Librarianship*. Founded in 1990, PLG is committed to providing a forum for critical examination of all aspects of librarianship, supporting activist librarians, questioning hierarchies and commercialization within the profession, examining information technologies, and making connections between librarianship and social justice movements (PLG's). Members of PLG have been active in ALA on various levels, including Council.
- Progressive Council Caucus (no acronym used)—Similar to Council Forum, but attended by Councilors who identify with socially responsible, progressive perspectives. Caucus members hold one or more evening meetings, as need arises, during ALA midwinter and annual.
- SRRT—Social Responsibilities Round Table has long been ALA's largest roundtable. Founded in 1969, it has been committed to bringing social justice issues to the attention of the Association for action. SRRT played a leading role in democratizing ALA in the late 60s and early 70s. Currently it consists of six task forces on feminism; hunger, homelessness, and poverty; international responsibilities; the Martin Luther King, Jr., Holiday; the Rainbow Project; and the environment (Social). SRRT members elect a representative to Council, and SRRT is governed by an Action Council, which consists of elected members, the chairs of task forces, and representatives from affiliate groups.

- SustainRT—Sustainability Round Table is the newest unit of ALA, founded "to provide resources for the library community to support sustainability through curriculum development; collections; exhibits; events; advocacy, communication, library buildings and space design" (Sustainability).
- TFoE—Task Force on the Environment, a SRRT task force dedicated to raising issues concerning the state of the planet within ALA through programming, publications, and special projects.
- USIA—United States Information Agency, an agency of the U.S. government established in 1953 to engage in public diplomacy internationally. USIA established libraries, maintained radio stations, engaged in publication of information, conducted student and professional exchange programs, held conferences, and other activities around the globe.
- YALSA—Young Adult Library Services Association is a division of ALA, and has a representative on Council. YALSA's mission is "to expand and strengthen library services for teens, aged 12–18" (About YALSA).

With our organizational cast of characters introduced, it is time to proceed with stories from Council—seven social responsibility debates in U.S. librarianship.

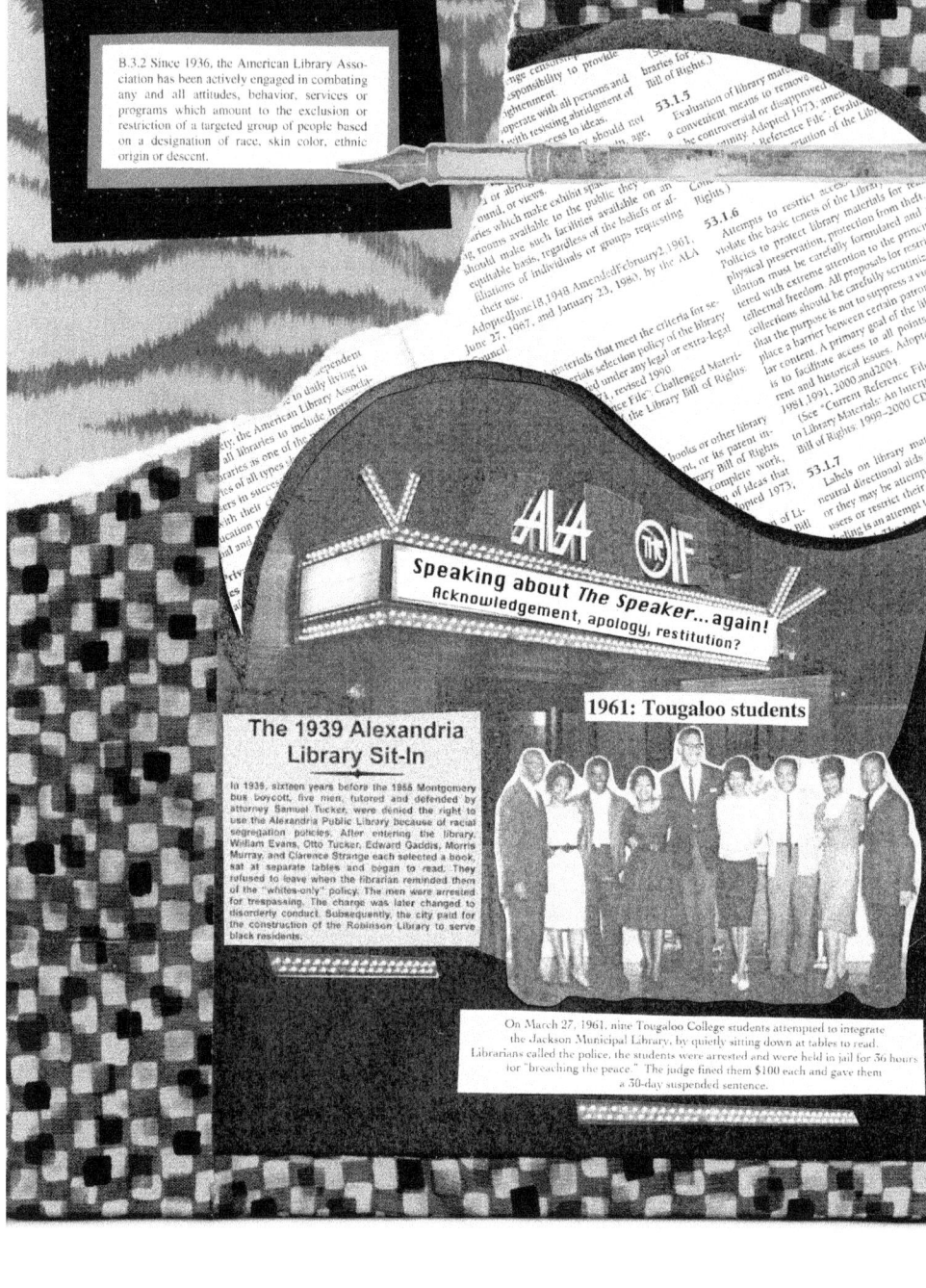

1. In Denial—Speaking about *The Speaker*

... black people feel that their humanity is not debatable.
—Clara Stanton Jones, 1977

It has been almost 40 years since The Speaker *appeared as an explosive and divisive issue within ALA. I still recall the sense of betrayal as I perceived the racist aspect of the film.*
—Mary Biblo, 2014

Our votes were no more for "censorship" than American Libraries *rejecting an article, or ALA Publishing deciding to reject a book that did not meet its standards.*
—Pat Schuman, 2014

The identification and acknowledgement of epistemological racism in LIS is a first step in advancing a theory of race and social responsibility.
—Todd Honma, 2005[1]

In May 2014, the Council listserv erupted in a cascade of e-mail and emotion. Long silent embers of pain fanned back to life, then dropped to smolder alone as those responsible for reviving an old ALA conflict proceeded to make their merry way to Las Vegas for a primetime re-release and panel discussion of a dusty old film called *The Speaker*.

The Speaker's resurrection for the 2014 annual conference was the work of ALA's Office for Intellectual Freedom (OIF), with support from the Association of American Publishers, Library History Round Table, and the Black Caucus of ALA. Announcing the upcoming program, "Speaking About *The Speaker*," in the June issue of *American Libraries*, OIF director Barbara M. Jones wrote,

> *The Speaker* has fractured friendships and professional relationships.... Recently, I was warned by members who attended [the film's 1977 premier] not to bring up the controversy ever again. But some participants and a new generation of librarians want to revisit the film, and they have agreed to discuss it ... [Jones 2014, 13].

In 1977, the inaugural showing of *The Speaker*, at an ALA membership meeting in Detroit, launched a contentious and divisive debate, pitting a majority of ALA's African-American leadership and their allies against the film's makers and their allies. The film was intended to teach viewers about the role of libraries in promoting and defending intellectual freedom. The full title was *The Speaker: A Film about Freedom*. However, the immediate response of not a few viewers was that it was racist, and that its representation of intellectual freedom was such a caricature as to constitute an embarrassment for the Association. At the second membership meeting during the 1977 conference a vote was taken to remove ALA's name from the film, with 318 voting for removal and 334 voting to retain identification of ALA as the film's sponsor. When Council voted on a similar resolution, the vote was 2 to 1 against removal. Clearly, at the grassroots level, although not at the policy-making level, "divisive" was the operational descriptor of the film.

Jones' decision to ignore warnings against reopening old wounds in favor of resurrecting a possibly racist and misleading film demands attention. Although an object of curiosity amongst a new generation of librarians who were neither present at the 1977 showing nor engaged in debates concerning it, the film's revival presented a Pandora's box of insult, outrage, betrayal. Jones' might have heeded cautionary warnings given by those from whom she sought guidance, but an award was to be given in Las Vegas to her predecessor's widower, and what better way to honor the memory of Judith Krug than to try to polish *the* major blemish on Krug's tenure as OIF director—*The Speaker*.

"Speaking About *The Speaker*" would feature two showing of the film, and a panel discussion featuring Beverly Lynch (UCLA Graduate School of Education and Information Studies professor), Robert Wedgeworth (former executive director of ALA), Mark McCallon (associate dean for library services, Abilene Christian University), and Julius Jefferson (Information research specialist at the Library of Congress) moderating. The OIF's website contained links to the digitized film on YouTube (https://www.youtube.com/watch?v=ojFYx52X-Ys), electronic files of the discussion guide that accompanied the film, and links to articles from the library press covering the controversy, and other relevant materials, including a statement issued by the Black Caucus of ALA explaining their opposition to the film. Since being mounted on YouTube, the film has tallied about 1,500 views (as of August 2015).

This chapter seeks to explore the purpose served by the revival of a dated film, one that now stands as an ongoing, permanent, easily accessed and publicly available representation of OIF's, and ALA's, understanding of First Amendment rights. The film has not been edited to include, for the edification of a 21st century audience, any information about the controversy it generated. *The Speaker* is simply presented as it was in 1977. As long as it existed on 16 mm film (or maybe as a video cassette), the film could only be shown purposefully, with intent, within the context of a LIS class or workshop or any other venue where *someone* was likely to know *something* about its history and controversy, knowledge either shared with the audience or not. Today, a YouTube viewer could be a fifth-grader, a grandma, a member of Congress, anybody curious about intellectual freedom, who would most likely take the film at face value.

My contention here is that both the 1977 vote to retain ALA's imprimatur on the film, and the film's 2014 revival constitute a refusal by mainstream librarians to take seriously charges of its underlying racism and misleading portrayal of First Amendment rights. The fact that the 2014 revival received support from the Black Caucus of ALA in no way negates the legitimacy of charges of racism. The film's insistence that the long-discredited theory claiming blacks' genetically determined intellectual inferiority to whites deserves a public platform, and that the theorist's intellectual freedom is denied if not allowed that platform, is faulty and misleading. Furthermore, to present the film to the public without any context or information about the controversy is irresponsible. Today, for instance, most YouTube viewers of *The Speaker* will have no knowledge of

William Shockley (the model for the film's title character), or of his Voluntary Sterilization Bonus Plan, or of the real life controversies generated by this Nobel laureate's scientifically misbegotten dysgenic theory, or the fact that throughout the 1970s Shockley declaimed from stages across the country that every percentage point of "white blood" that a black person had increased his or her IQ by one point.

The film and its revival also serve as an example of epistemological racism, the concept that ways of knowing are culturally determined, and in a racist society what constitutes as knowledge is defined through a racist lens. Decades ago, for instance, feminist scholars discovered epistemological misogyny (although that was not a phrase that emerged from their work), and developed feminist ways of knowing. Just as women, generally speaking, no longer accept male authority to define what is or is not sexist, so too blacks have no reason to let whites decide what theories on race are correct and which practices are racist. In the case of *The Speaker*, white librarians insisted that black librarians were wrong in seeing racist elements in the film. However, as Patricia Hill Collins notes in her book *Black Feminist Thought* (2000),

> Epistemological choices about whom to trust, what to believe, and why something is true are not benign academic issues. Instead, these concerns tap the fundamental question of which versions of truth will prevail [252].

Given unexamined assumptions about what constitutes racism, the racism inherent in *The Speaker* was deeper than the white people who made it had the capacity to notice without engaged reflection. Most of the black librarians, and their allies, had different experiences of racism, and levels of empathy toward those who suffered from it. Blacks' knowledge of what counted as racist was not mainstream white knowledge, and so was immediately discounted, ignored, even ridiculed.

What follows then is a revisiting of an old ALA debate, along with an account of the incident that provided the film's storyline; a look into the role that denial played in both the distant and recent debates; and a suggestion as to what this discussion means for librarianship in today's world of the "new Jim Crow" in terms of acknowledging racist and misleading aspects of the film and, perhaps, making reparations for suffering inflicted.

Birth of The Speaker*—1977*

The summer the nation celebrated the bicentennial of the American Revolution, Mrs. Clara Stanton Jones, director of the Detroit Public Library, was inaugurated as the first black librarian to serve as president of the American Library Association. Jones' election followed by three years the appointment of Robert Wedgeworth as executive director of ALA, the first black to serve in that position. These were watershed developments for a profession that had tolerated racism and racial segregation for most of its history.

At the same time as Jones was preparing to step into her role as president, ALA's Executive Board approved an appropriation of $100,000 to the Intellectual Freedom Committee (IFC) for production of a film on libraries and the First Amendment. Jones later wrote, in a festschrift published in honor of E. J. Josey, of the initial excitement the proposed film engendered among Executive Board members, "The project was launched with enthusiasm and high hope in an atmosphere of trust and cooperation" (Jones 1992, p. 18). Jones also described how Judith Krug, OIF director, requested that she, in her role as ALA President, write a letter to libraries seeking pre-orders for a yet-to-be-made film that would "explain the special role of the library in preserving and disseminating controversial works" (13).

Collaboration was fated to end here. Funding procured, and Jones' letter sent, Krug and the two members of the IFC subcommittee charged with making the film sought no further input from anyone. Furthermore, requests for information about the film's progress met with silence or inadequate responses. The film's script was shared with Board members only two months *after* the film had been made, and when Executive Board members viewed the film their reaction was so negative that the Board voted not to release the film until it had been shown to ALA members. Jones wrote,

> Before reading the script, we had not known that the agreed subject and setting had been changed, much less removed from the library field to another discipline dealing with an entirely different subject. All of this was a great shock, and the added negative racial aspects of the film created a kind of paralyzing awkwardness. Even with the basic good will of the Board members, emotions were highly charged. In searching for a solution, we discussed the possibility of releasing the film without the ALA "imprimatur." A Board member objected, saying that would be censorship. The effect of the word "censorship" was electrifying. Attention was turned away from consideration of the merits of the film and was subsumed by this new threatening idea [14].

Surfacing his own memories of that day in Chicago, in a 2003 article for *American Libraries*, Robert Wedgeworth recalls the reaction of Board members to the screening.

> When the Executive Board preview ended, no one moved. You could hear a pin drop on the carpet. For at least 30 seconds no one even coughed. Finally, the board members began to get up and exit from the room, still with almost no talking. The cocktail reception that followed the preview was very subdued.
> By the next morning it was clear that the board considered the film an embarrassment at best, and at worst completely unacceptable [Wedgeworth 2003, 50].

In preparing for its 2014, "Speaking About *The Speaker*" program in Las Vegas, the IFC compiled information about the film and the controversy, and mounted it on the OIF's website (http://www.oif.ala.org/oif/?p=4985). The information includes the cataloging note from OCLC's record for the film:

> *The Speaker... a Film About Freedom*. Chicago: ALA, 1977, 42 minutes. Originally distributed with 32 p. discussion guide. Summary: A dramatization about a high school current events committee which invites a university professor to speak on a theory of genetic inferiority of Afro-Americans. Controversy develops and spills over into the community and parents and community leaders advise the student committee to reconsider. When the Committee refuses, the school board president cancels the speaker. Intended to evoke discussion of constitutional protection of speech on controversial and unpopular topics [Viewing].

Following links to the YouTube digitized version of the film, are PDFs to the original discussion guide, a chronology of the film's development, a listing of Council actions, and a bibliography of both contemporary and historical reports, opinion pieces, and news coverage regarding it.

Beyond the OCLC summary, salient details regarding the film are the following:

- Film opens with a teacher lecturing on the Lincoln-Douglas debates, vividly describing to a rapt class of students the manner in which the two presidential candidates would arrive in a town for their debate over slavery.
- The high school current events committee consists of both black and white, male and female students, and its white faculty advisor Victoria Dunn, a highly respected social studies teacher on the eve of her retirement.
- The speaker character, given the name Dr. Boyd and based on the real life William Shockley, believes that intelligence is genetically determined and that the genetic make-up of blacks relegates them to intellectual inferiority when compared to whites.
- The film never reveals the origin of the proposal to invite Dr. Boyd. Was he suggested by a white student? A black student? An adult? Does it matter?
- Students on the committee are divided, not along racial or sexual lines, as to the appropriateness of Boyd as a speaker. Over the course of the film two students change their minds, only one student, a black girl remains steadfastly opposed. She eventually resigns from the committee in protest, as does a white student who's been told his involvement in the controversy could endanger his chances of getting into college.
- The only portrayals of libraries and librarians are very brief and show the librarians involved in situations where they discuss censorship and in one scene engage in self-censorship.
- At one point a student on the committee says there is only one choice, either Boyd is invited or he isn't. Not once is the possibility of a debate suggested.
- Black students on campus who object to Boyd as a speaker are visibly angry, intimidating, tearing down posters. The image is stereotypical—emotional, possibly violent black people. Are the whites in the film who express concern about racial relations worried about riots, rampaging blacks?
- Concerns regarding racial relations within the community galvanize public pressure and lead to the cancellation of the student-organized program to invite Boyd.
- Dunn insists throughout and to the conclusion of the film that a decision not to invite Boyd to speak would be a violation of his rights to freedom of speech.

Dunn represents the perspective of the OIF and IFC subcommittee members that the First Amendment demands that citizens of a democracy must tolerate detestable ideas.

Had the film not diverged from the original proposal, had the three-person subcommittee shared the script and sought input from the larger Intellectual Freedom Committee, the momentum of both Jones' presidency and the film's potential might have joined together in a powerful statement of ALA's commitments to both racial equality and intellectual freedom. The filmmakers and OIF overseer, however, redirected the original proposal, refused to provide information to the IFC and members of the Executive Board. Thus, before a year had passed, the two—racial progress within ALA and the film—were set on a collision course, which turned into a massive pile-up of a wreck exactly one year later.

As Jones prepared to host the 1977 annual conference in her hometown of Detroit, the IFC appointed a subcommittee to carry out the film project. The subcommittee consisted of three white people: Judith Krug, OIF director; Florence McMullin, IFC chair;

and Robert Delzell, IFC member. By July 1976, the subcommittee had selected a professional film production company, Vision Associates (VA). In September, Lee Bobker, VA's director, and writer Barbara Eisberg arrived at the main idea for the film.

As an article in the July/August 1977 *American Libraries* later described it, the idea came from

> an interview with Archibald Cox, who said his most difficult First Amendment challenge was not Watergate but his inability to deal with student efforts to prevent a controversial speaker from appearing on campus [Pearson 372].

Archibald Cox, a Harvard Law School professor, had been appointed special prosecutor for the Watergate hearings and was fired from that position on orders from President Nixon on 20 October 1973, in what came to be known as the Saturday Night Massacre. Cox had demanded tape-recordings of Oval Office conversations, which Nixon refused to provide. The student incident to which Cox referred, and gave rise to Bobker and Eisberg's storyline, took place at Harvard Law School and concerned a debate planned by a student organization featuring Roy Innis of the Congress of Racial Equality (CORE) and Stanford University professor William Shockley, a physicist, inventor of the transistor, and Nobel Laureate, whose own business, Shockley Semiconductor, gave birth to what came to be known as Silicon Valley. Shockley was also an amateur "raceologist" (as he called himself), notorious for his lectures on the genetically determined intellectual superiority of whites and inferiority of blacks. In referring to the origins of *The Speaker* storyline, the library press at the time erroneously reported that "although he was given the platform, student hecklers—in an expression of their freedom of speech?—apparently made it impossible for Shockley to be heard" (Berry 1574).

As will be seen, the actual story is much more complex and sheds a revealing light on the controversy within ALA. Cox's opinion on the incident was not the prevailing one, although Bobker and the IFC subcommittee chose to treat it as if it were. The intellectual freedom story Cox considered more important than Watergate was titillating and timely. Bobker and Eisberg found it compelling.

Before proceeding with the story of reactions to the film within ALA, we to turn to the incident on which Bobker and Eisberg based their script, not only for any light it might shed on the ALA controversy or as context for the times in which the controversy raged, but also as a source of support for arguments put forward in 1977–78 by the film's opponents that its treatment of the First Amendment was distorted, misinformed, and inaccurate. What better place to seek historical and legal context for the controversy, but at Harvard Law School, one of the nation's preeminent law schools?

A debate at Harvard Law School—1973

In the fall of 1973, a student organization, the Harvard Law Forum, invited Roy Innis, executive director of the Congress on Racial Equality (CORE), to speak. The Forum had a long history of inviting provocative figures to campus (Fidel Castro, for example, had spoken in 1959), and had sent out 180 letters seeking speakers for the 1973/74 school year. Innis accepted the invitation and suggested a debate, first with Roy Wilkins, executive director of the NAACP. When Wilkins proved either uninterested or unavailable, Innis then proposed William Shockley who agreed to a debate, the title of which was to be "Race Differences in IQ, and Dysgenics." Forum members agreed that this would be a lively topic and announced the event would take place in late October.

Word quickly spread that the infamous proponent of blacks' intellectual inferiority had been invited to speak on the Harvard campus, and was met with strong disapproval from faculty members, the dean of the law school, and students, including the Black Law Student Association (BLSA) and Harvard's chapter of Students for a Democratic Society (SDS).

One Harvard professor, Derrick Bell, was quoted as saying,

> If we want to have a former Nazi come in and debate as to whether the six million Jews should have been killed in Europe, then we can have a debate on whether blacks are genetically inferior to whites. Otherwise, however, there are some matters that are beneath having anything to do with a law school such as Harvard [Kubitz 5].

The BLSA requested a meeting with Forum organizers and presented objections to the planned debate. Their statement, published in the October 19, 1973, issue of *Harvard Law Record*, stated in part, "efforts to bring rational, enlightened, and well-informed speakers to the campus are diametrically opposed to the self-serving demagoguery of speakers like Schockley [*sic*] and Innis" (p. 9). (Please note: Shockley's name was misspelled in several of the *Record*'s articles, not only in this one from the BLSA.) The statement charged that the debate would generate a "Roman circus atmosphere," could exacerbate racial tensions on campus and within the community, and "possibly rend the social fabric of Harvard by infusing elements of racism, genocide and the haunting specter of selective breeding and extermination that stalked Germany not 30 years ago." Calling for the cancellation of the debate, the BLSA addressed the First Amendment aspect of the situation.

> We realize that cogent arguments can be made for the position that Schockley and Innis have the right to express their opinions in a public forum. We do not deny that basic right; we merely think that Harvard Law School and the Forum should take a moral stand and not lend their support and facilities to this kind of inflammatory and derogatory discussion.... It is time that demagogues and racists not be accorded academic respectability for their insidious, ill-proven and dangerous allegations [9].

The statement ended, expressing the hope that "an expeditious and honorable resolution" to the dispute could be reached. Otherwise BLSA was prepared to take their case to the court of public opinion—"the larger community and the press" (*ibid.*). Forum members considered the situation and the Innis-Shockley debate at Harvard was cancelled generating a flurry of both protest and approval.

The reports in the *Harvard Law Record* on the BLSA's statement appeared on the very day that Archibald Cox demanded tape-recordings from the Oval Office, a demand that resulted in the Saturday Night Massacre the next day, when President Nixon demanded that Attorney General Elliot Richardson fire Cox, Richardson resigned rather than carry out the commander-in-chief's orders, Nixon then ordered Deputy Attorney General William Ruckelshaus to fire Cox, and he too refused and resigned, leaving the dirty work to Solicitor General Robert Bork.

Two weeks later, the *Record*'s front page leading headline was "Profs Condemn Firing of Cox" and a below-the-fold headline "NYC Genetics Debate Set" reported on the continuing saga of the cancelled Innis-Shockley forum. Shockley would be facing the associate dean of Harvard Medical School, Alvin F. Poussaint, in a debate moderated by David Susskind, which would be aired on the WNEW television station.

On page 13 of the same issue, the *Record* published the text of a statement from the dean of Harvard Law School, Albert M. Sacks, who sought to clarify rumors circulating throughout the Harvard community as to his own reasons for opposing the Harvard Law School–sponsored Innis-Shockley debate. He first stated, unconditionally, that the student organizers of the Harvard Law Forum were free to invite anyone they wished to speak at the Law School. Next he stated that he found it "quite understandable" that Forum organizers cancelled the debate after hearing the appeal of the BLSA, but noted this would not exclude the possibility of such a debate in the future. Lastly, he addressed the rumor that the debate had been cancelled because of threats or predictions of disruption. Sacks wrote that such threats were rumors only, and that if such threats had, in fact, been made, they could *not* be used to justify cancellation.

> Just as the Forum must be free from pressures from the Law School's Administration, so too must it be free of any other pressures which are expressed through coercion rather than persuasion. Otherwise, the precious tradition of free speech at Harvard is in peril [Sacks 13].

Sacks makes a distinction here that the OIF and IFC subcommittee refused to acknowledge in 1977. First, the free speech issue truly at stake in *The Speaker* was not Boyd's right to a platform, but the student current events committee's right to invite whomever they wanted. Second, that an action to withdraw an invitation to a speaker resulting from the persuasive power of reasoned argument does *not* constitute censorship or a violation of the First Amendment. Whereas coercive acts, especially on the part of those in authority positions, do. Sacks' statement provides a critical nuance that the film's supporters would not allow, despite the fact that those opposing the film did point out that ultimately it was the student committee's rights that were violated.

Sacks was not the only person to say that the Forum was justified in canceling the debate. In a letter to the *Harvard Crimson*, one reader notes that Shockley needed no stage at Harvard from which to exercise his 1st Amendment rights. He had ready access to the mass media. The writer goes on to state that,

> A debate with Innis would not expose Shockley as unscientific, but would give him a kind of legitimacy as a *political opponent* of Innis, as someone proposing social policy who also is an "intellectual." What results is a war of credentials—professor of physics and Nobel winner versus distinguished civil right leader [Shockley's 1].

In another letter to the *Crimson*, members of SDS also noted the political dimension of the controversy,

> We oppose William Shockley because he is using unscientific assertions to suggest genocidal policy. His Nobel Prize in physics gives him no expertise in the field of genetics, although it makes his ideas more influential [Bailey].

The letter goes on to state a point that was obvious to many in *The Speaker* debates, but which, as we shall see, was considered so illegitimate (or feared so irrefutable) by the film's supporters that they consistently refused to acknowledge much less address it:

> ... there is no "right" to speak at the Harvard Law Forum.... Everyone agrees that there are limits to "abstract free speech".... Should a medical professor be allowed to teach that thalidomide [a drug causing birth defects] is a good sleeping drug for pregnant women? Should a scientist of Shockley's prestige be free to suggest genocide as a solution to America's problems? [*ibid.*].

In the 1970s, William Shockley was speaking on campuses across the country telling audiences that the federal government should adopt his Voluntary Sterilization Bonus Plan, which would pay people with "low IQs" $1000 per IQ point below 100 if they would undergo surgery of their reproductive organs.

Even I attended a Shockley debate on February 12, 1976, at Mississippi State University (MSU). My father, a psychology professor at Jackson State University and ardent opponent of Shockley, wanted to hear him speak and so we drove down to Hattisburg with a friend, gay rights activist Eddie Sandifer. MSU, through an organization called the American Program Bureau, had decided to host a debate between Shockley and Richard Goldsby, an African-American biologist. Goldsby argued that, while there certainly are biologically determined aspects to race, intelligence is so largely shaped by social and environmental factors that it would be impossible to find genetic factors (Goldsby 1977). The sparks that flew at MSU were intellectual ones, the mixed-race audience attentive and polite. My father recalls that Shockley was put out when asked a direct question regarding his sterilization plan, references to which he was beginning to drop from public speeches.

Two years earlier, while Shockley was at the height of popularity on lecture circuits, the debate that generated the most controversy took place at Yale University where students disrupted his debate with William Rusher, publisher of the *National Review*. Eleven of a reported 600 protesters were charged with leading the disruption and were suspended (Weker). In 1975, the Yale chapter of Young Americans for Freedom (YAF) rescheduled the disrupted debate.

The 1975 Yale debate is instructive in the political use made of public forums by budding neoliberals. A *Harvard Crimson* report on April 23, 1975, "Shockley's Racism Circus Comes to Yale: Debating Government Interference" by David J. States, describes a debate set up by its organizers, *not* to dispute Shockley's racist theories, but to counter Shockley's "liberal" belief that the government was *capable* of carrying out his sterilization plan. According to States, William Rusher

> charged in his first 20-minute segment that he would oppose the government stepping in and sterilizing allegedly genetically inferior blacks. But his view was not formulated out of human considerations. Rusher simply said he could not, in good conscience, trust the government to run a railroad, let alone do a good job of sterilizing the nation's blacks [States, 1].

States interviewed one of the Young Americans for Freedom (YAF) organizers, a Yale law school student, who said,

Our reasons for bringing Shockley here are three-fold.... We wanted to refute his statist views (on government intervention into private lives); we want to vindicate Yale's students after their performances [i.e. disruptive behavior] last year; and to check Yale's commitment to freedom of speech [ibid.].

Another Yale student interviewed, Eugene Meyer, YAF president, had his own interesting spin on political power and free speech. "The problem of Hitler," he is quoted as saying, "was not that he spoke, but that he was allowed to shut people up" (ibid.).

The "problem of Hitler" was the genocide he promulgated in *both* word and deed. The problem with Meyer's formulation is that Hitler's power to "shut people up" was acquired via his speech, plus the countless platforms given and created for him. Access to mass media amplified Hitler's ideas to such an extent that it engendered a social mindset and milieu that eventually "allowed" him and his collaborators to silence millions of people. Had Hitler been given all the freedom of speech in the world and *no public platform*, he might have babbled himself into old age and senility standing on a soapbox on a corner, rather than pontificating his way into positions of political power from which he launched both World War II and the Holocaust. Platforms, as the BLSA, Sacks, and others pointed out, lend *legitimacy* to the sponsored speakers.

The First Amendment states,

> Congress shall make no law respecting an establishment of religion, or prohibiting the free exercise thereof; or abridging the freedom of speech, or of the press; or the right of the people peaceably to assemble, and to petition the Government for a redress of grievances [Bill].

As the Harvard SDS students' letter pointed out, this does not mean that every Tom, Dick, and Harry (or Eboni, Isabel, and InSoon for that matter) *must be invited* to engage their free speech rights at Harvard, Yale, Mississippi State, or at a nameless high school in Somewhere U.S.A. What it means is that no laws can be enacted that deprive a citizen of any platform they might procure from which to exercise their First Amendment rights, whether it be a Wobbly's soapbox in Spokane in 1909 or a stage for Shockley in Boston, New Haven, or Hattisburg in the 1970s. But, the First Amendment obliges no one, anywhere, to give a platform to anybody.

Speech can mold opinion and public sentiment. According to Abraham Lincoln,

> Public sentiment is everything. With public sentiment, nothing can fail; without it nothing can succeed. Consequently, he who molds public sentiment goes deeper than he who enacts statutes or pronounces decisions. He makes statutes and decisions possible or impossible to be executed [Lincoln].

In the mid- to late-1970s, memories of the old Jim Crow were fresh in the minds of many people. And some, especially blacks, had personal experience not only with being the victims of segregation and racism, but with mustering the courage and literally putting one's *life* on the line to combat both. The fact that William Shockley was invited to tread the floorboards of stages across the country and espouse his genocidal VSBP in an attempt to mold public sentiment and influence government policy, was seen by most blacks and some whites as an institutional legitimization of his ideas. This was the atmosphere prevailing at the very time that Bobker, Eisberg, Krug, McMullin and Delzell decided to make their provocative film.

Debating The Speaker—1977

ALA President Clara Stanton Jones, director of the Detroit Public Library and a black woman, stood at a microphone during the last Council meeting of the 1977 conference and spoke about the impact *The Speaker* and ensuing debate had in the hearts and minds of hundreds of ALA members, black and white alike, "…black people feel that their humanity is not debatable" (Berry 1573). If black librarians and their white allies felt that the humanity of African-Americans was not subject to debate, what might Krug, McMullin, and Delzell have felt as they listened to Jones speak?

- Regret? *We should have sought input.*
- Sorrow? *We had no idea our colleagues would feel this way.*
- Embarrassment? *Maybe we should apologize.*
- Satisfaction? *The film does* exactly *what we hoped it would do.*
- Worry? *What do we do if we can't sell this film?*

We might never know what was in the hearts and minds of these three people, but the library press covered what many people said during the debate in considerable detail. Judith Krug, it seems, said little, letting others defend the film. Krug probably considered that the preface to the film's discussion guide said all that needed saying. Coauthored by McMullin and Krug, the preface informed readers,

> We are proud of *The Speaker*, but we are also aware that it addresses one of the most sensitive—but doubtless one of the most important—aspects of freedom of expression: toleration of ideas we find offensive or repugnant. Ultimately, such tolerance derives from a complicated process involving both our reason and our emotions. It is our hope that *The Speaker* will make a major contribution to this process [McMullin n.p.].

At the very least, one can assume that both McMullin and Krug felt some level of satisfaction as they listened to Jones and everyone else who participated in the debate, for the film certainly did engage both reason and emotion.

The controversy, as mentioned earlier, began at an Executive Board meeting. One Executive Board member defended the film on grounds that the suggestion to remove ALA's name from it constituted an act of censorship. Another charge made against opponents of the film was that they were "hysteric" or overly "sensitive" in their reactions to racial elements of the film. Jones addressed the later characterization in an article "Reflections on *The Speaker*" published in the September 1977 issue of *Wilson Library Bulletin*.

> The importance of the overwhelming rejection of *The Speaker* by black ALA members should not be underestimated. This judgment indicates the film's score on a crucial test [Jones gave it an "F"]. The significance of this failure cannot be circumvented by characterizing the reaction as "super-sensitive" or "touchy" on the subject of race. These are responsible, concerned practitioners, many of whom have been outstanding leaders of the profession for years. Racism is sometimes unintentional, as in this instance, but that can be likened to the pleas of ignorance of the law—*no excuse!* [Jones 1977, 55].

In 2014, during discussion at OIF's program "Speaking About *The Speaker*," an unidentified African-American librarian is reported as asking an essential question, "The big question was why ALA at this moment in history, when blacks had just become an equal part of the organization by joining committees, would turn around and publicly humiliate them?" (Morehart).

While it is doubtful that the conscious intention of Bobker, Eisberg, Krug, McMullin, and Delzell was public humiliation of black librarians, the insidious racism pervading U.S. society evidenced in the notion that the intellectual inferiority of blacks was worthy of public debate, wove its way through the incident at Harvard Law School, into Archibald Cox's reaction, Vision Associate's script, and, ultimately, into OIF's film. Krug must have suspected there would be objections to the script and film. Why else keep details of both a secret from October 1976 through February 1977 despite requests for information from at least one IFC member, incoming chair Zoia Horn.

In her memoirs (1995), Zoia Horn devotes an entire chapter to her service on the Intellectual Freedom Committee, which began just as the IFC was approving production of the film that would become *The Speaker*. As a new committee member, Horn found its workings a bit odd, its members seemingly uninterested in asking questions about the film, being kept up-to-date with details of its progress, or in being consulted about a project for which the entire Committee was responsible. Horn herself wondered "why there had been no working librarian among the consultants, particularly someone who had direct experience with censorship conflicts" (Horn 202). "As a neophyte," she wrote,

> It never occurred to me that the members of the committee would not be informed of the progress in choosing the subject, focus, or treatment and would not be consulted and given an opportunity to comment [203–4].

Concerned that she was "missing something" Horn wrote to Krug in November 1976 asking for information about the film. Krug replied about a month later, with no answers to Horn's direct questions, except to say, "The script agreed upon by the subcommittee and Vision Associates focuses on the everyday potential for a bit-by-bit erosion of First Amendment guarantees" (*ibid.*, p. 204). Horn judged Krug's letter "evasive" and she "perceived a cavalier disregard of my interest in being informed and active as a committee member" (*ibid.*).

Members of the IFC did not see the film script until February 1977, *after* filming had been completed. In keeping IFC members in the dark, Krug prevented any debate from occurring during the film's development. She could not, however, prevent the explosion of dialogue unleashed by its release, although the loyalty she enjoyed among many IFC members almost guaranteed that her will would prevail.

The debate within ALA about *The Speaker* evolved over the course of approximately one year, involving individuals in several groups: members of the ALA Executive Board, the library press, at least two intellectual freedom committees (ALA's and that of the Young Adult Services Division—YASD), the Black Caucus of ALA (BCALA), at least three social responsibility groups (ALA's, and local ones in the San Francisco Bay area and New York), plus general members of ALA, and the national press in the form of the popular news program *60 Minutes*.

Prior to January 30, 1977, no information regarding the content of script or film had been shared by the film subcommittee. On that day, members of the Executive Board and the Intellectual Freedom Committee met with Bobker, who shared still images from the film in the form of a slide presentation. A request was made for copies of the script to be distributed to those present. Jones reports that she received a copy of the script in mid–April, about two weeks before she saw the film (Jones 1992, 13).

The film was given its premier showing to an audience of the public in May in Sunnyvale, California, at the school were the filming took place. In the audience were students, parents, and teachers who played roles in the film. The film preview for the Executive Board was April 26. Members of the IFC also previewed the film, and it was shown at an ALA Membership meeting on June 19 during the annual conference in Detroit.

Zoia Horn attended the Sunnyvale showing, and describes reactions of teachers and students as "elated." Horn herself, however, was "furious, resentful, and ashamed." She reports containing her anger when speaking with Bobker, but quietly sharing with him her objections to the film. He became "very defensive," and informed her that, given the obvious enthusiastic reception *The Speaker* had just received, she would be "a very lonely minority of one" (Horn 207).

IFC members saw the film prior to its presentation at the June 19 ALA membership meeting. In his August 1977 *Library Journal* article, "The Debate Nobody Won," John Berry details IFC discussion and action over the course of two meetings during the conference. Miriam Braverman, a professor at Columbia University's School of Library Service, presented a resolution at the beginning of the first IFC meeting, moving that the Committee officially disassociate itself from the film, and recommending that ALA do the same. Braverman cited several reasons in support of this action.

- *The Speaker*'s depiction of librarians and libraries was simplistic and negative;
- black characters were portrayed as stereotypically emotional;
- the community in which the film was set was unrealistic (i.e. without any bigots); and
- the controversy chosen to represent First Amendment challenges was unrepresentative of the majority of attacks on freedom of expression that regularly confronted libraries, schools, and communities.

IFC member Grace Slocum is reported to have said that Braverman's resolution read "like a book review," and suggested that if the film were a book published by ALA, no one would complain. To which Braverman responded that this was a false analogy—the ideas, perspectives, arguments, and contents of a book are attributed to its author, not to the publisher, whereas *The Speaker* was attributed directly to the IFC and ALA. Viewers would consider the film to represent the views of the Association, not those of Bobker, Eisberg, Krug, McMullin, and Delzell as individuals.

Judith Krug was asked to restate the purpose of the film. IFC members, after all, had approved production of a film that was to "explain the special role of the library in preserving and disseminating controversial works," and *The Speaker* clearly did not reflect that intent. Berry reports that Krug

> ... stated the purposes much as they read in the *Discussion Guide*, but emphasized that the film was not intended for libraries, but to promote discussion with other audiences. "Most people don't understand the First Amendment," she said. "It is too complicated to try to

explain the library role viz-a-viz the First Amendment. We hope to follow up with productions on the library role" [Berry 1575].

How Krug could justify her claim that the film was "not intended for libraries" when it was marketed—solely—to libraries, is anyone's guess. While her opinion that "most people don't understand the First Amendment" might be true, the whole idea of educational films is to *assist* the viewers in understanding. *The Speaker*'s formulation that the First Amendment *means* that people in a democracy must tolerate intolerable ideas *and* provide an audience for them does not clarify, but compounds misunderstanding. In all likelihood, Krug herself had a more nuanced understanding of the First Amendment. For instance, she must have assisted with the discussion guide accompanying the film, which contains a lengthy article by Northwestern University professor of communications, Franklyn S. Haiman, who had been president of the Illinois division of the American Civil Liberties Union from 1964 to 1975. The article, an abridged version of the original published in an ACLU publication, covers evolving legal interpretations of the First Amendment. Haiman quite cogently describes for lay readers some complicated legal opinions. For example:

- Supreme Court Justice Black "consistently opposed all restrictions on allegedly obscene and libelous speech, and was the Court's most vigorous spokesman for the rights of dissenters against a variety of national security claims." But Black had his limits, dissenting, for instance, from the majority opinion in a landmark case "that upheld the right of students to wear antiwar armbands in public school."
- Zechariah Chafee, Jr., a leading legal authority on free speech in the 1940s, was a proponent of the view "later accepted by the U.S. Supreme Court, that some expression, like profanity, is so devoid of ideas and akin to a physical blow against its target that any possible value it may have is ... not protected by the First Amendment."
- Supreme Court Justice Oliver Wendell Holmes put forward the notion that speech may lose First Amendment protection if it presented a "clear and present danger."
- Philosopher Alexander Meiklejohn was of the opinion that as long as speech had anything to do with self-governance that it should be given "the absolute protection he felt the First Amendment required."
- Another free speech scholar, Thomas Emerson, "proposes that everything which is defined as 'expression' be absolutely free, and that only 'action' be subject to government control."
- In the 1960s yet another scholar, Leonard Levy, argued that "each generation be free to adapt the provisions of the Constitution to the needs of its own day" [Haiman 17–19].

Haiman goes on to write about "speech without ideas," "symbolic speech," and, as mass media developed, interpretations of the First Amendment in regard to "access" to speech. He sums up, for a reader in the 1970s, four points from Emerson that constitute what was then the prevailing interpretation of the First Amendment in regard to free speech. The function of freedom of expression in a democracy is to serve as

(1) "a means of assuring individual self-fulfillment,"
(2) "an essential process for advancing knowledge and discovering truth,"
(3) "to provide for participation in decision making by all members of society," and
(4) "a method of achieving a more adaptable and hence a more stable community, of

maintaining the precarious balance between healthy cleavage and necessary consensus" [24].

Interestingly, nowhere in the discussion guide's abridged version of Haiman's essay is the filmmakers' formulation that the First Amendment means "toleration of ideas we find offensive or repugnant," a perspective that did have proponents within the community of legal scholars. Supreme Court Justice Oliver Wendell Holmes once wrote, "we should be eternally vigilant against attempts to check the expression of opinions that we loathe" (Holmes), although the context of the dissenting opinion within which Holmes made this statement is quite different than that of *The Speaker*. Holmes was writing about a case involving the publication of antiwar leaflets during World War I, by a relatively isolated individual. Shockley's sphere of influence was much more extensive.

Putting complexities of scholarship on the First Amendment aside, part of the job of scriptwriters of educational films (and of high school social studies teachers) is to take complexity, such as that presented by Haiman, and mold it into a form that makes it understandable to audiences and students. Over simplification such at that in *The Speaker* is not helpful; indeed, it can be counter-productive, rendering a concept, which citizens *should* understand—the right to freedom of speech—into a cartoon. Audiences and students are not guided into an understanding of the First Amendment by formulas like "tolerate the intolerable."

Returning to the IFC's discussion in June 1977, committee member Elliott Shelkrot declared that "the debate about the film proves its effectiveness." Berry adds that the person next to whom he was seated whispered, "He [Shelkrot] may be right, but there's a hell of a lot better and cheaper ways to start an argument" (Berry 1575).

Zoia Horn, who would be taking over the position of IFC chair from McMullin at conference end, informed the committee of her efforts in prior months to get information about the film from Krug, and of Krug's far from adequate response. Horn concluded her objections to the film, countering Shelkrof's remarks, by saying

> The film, as a whole, (quite apart from its subject focus), is defeatist and feeds cynicism. The young teacher won't speak up to save his job. The retiring teacher, however, can afford to take a stand.... The student, afraid of a "trouble-maker" label that might hamper college entrance, backs down. The high school principal is embarrassed and knuckles under in anticipation of community pressure almost before it comes. And finally, and above all, the complete defeat of the students by powerful adults in both unofficial and official capacities, against all democratic procedures, leads to the conclusion that the cards are stacked and nothing is worth fighting for. Is that the message we want to send—to anyone? What is to be learned from such a film? [*ibid.*].

The IFC postponed a vote on Braverman's resolution until after the showing of the film at the membership meeting. When IFC reconvened, chair McMullin was missing, called home due to an illness in her family, and Horn asked Shelkrot to preside over resumption of discussion on *The Speaker*. Before a vote on Braverman's resolution was taken, the following points were made:

Horn: ALA sponsorship of the film made advance sales possible, as an IFC member she was not allowed to share any responsibility for the film, left completely in the dark.

> ... there was no democracy in the selection of the subject of the film, no debate on the choice ... and the result is an image of librarians as frightened, timid; it is a caricature. The film offers a depressing and cynical story, set in an unrealistic community. The *Discussion Guide* is of little help, since you can't force people to use it.... The film is the stacked deck in this affair [1577].

Ella Yates, the IFC's only black member: "for me [the film] provides a personal reliving of experiences I had in a school library in Montclair, New Jersey ... the deed is done ... and I couldn't have greater pride" (*ibid.*).

Rabbi Karl Weiner: "When I heard that Nazis were coming to Skokie, my own conscience was disturbed.... I was challenged in my opposition to Nazis.... I was willing to accept what came ... but I was troubled and torn.... The film is stronger than reality.... I saw myself in everybody in it..." (*ibid.*).

Last to speak was a new IFC member, Tyrone Emerick, who said: "The film is defeatist, it ought to provide a little encouragement ... it doesn't alert the viewer to every course of action ... but it has merit in spite of its weakness.... I reluctantly go along with ALA sponsorship" (*ibid.*).

A vote was called, and Braverman's resolution to dissociate IFC from *The Speaker* was defeated, 7 against, 2 in favor.

In between Braverman's presentation of her resolution and the IFC's defeat of it, *The Speaker* was shown at the ALA membership meeting on June 19. As people entered the meeting hall, each received a form on which to evaluate the film. The survey asked for input in five categories: content (choice of subject, concept, pertinence); treatment (authenticity, acting, script); technical qualities (photography, sound track, editing); utilization (viewer interest, usefulness with individuals and groups); and an overall rating.[2]

After the showing, ratings were tallied and the results published in Berry's August 1977 article. At the 2014 "Speaking About *The Speaker*" program in Las Vegas, Professor McCallon presented data tallies regarding viewers' ratings of content. In an e-mail, McCallon stated that he believed Berry's numbers to have been of the overall rating.

	1977 Detroit, overall rating	*2014 Las Vegas, content rating*
	108 superior	154 superior
	141 good	131 good
	109 fair	92 fair
	235 poor	189 poor
	121 didn't vote	
TOTAL	614	566

Before ALA Executive Director Robert Wedgeworth presented the evaluation results on the evening of June 19, 1977, discussion on the film was launched when the membership meeting, following parliamentary procedure, converted to a "committee of the whole" for debate. President Jones, anticipating the possibility that discussion might need encouragement, had asked three librarians to begin with three-minute remarks—Geraldine Clark, director of libraries for New York City Board of Education; Ervin Gaines from the

Cleveland Public Library; and Gerald Shields, a library school professor at the State University of New York–Buffalo.

According to Berry's report, Clark objected to the film's stereotyping of "every character in the film"; of leading viewers to believe that blacks neither relate to nor support the First Amendment; and of conveying a very negative image of both school and public librarians. Gaines shared a personal story of protests directed against a review he had written that recommended for library collections a book promoting a theory similar to Shockley's. While he had no regrets, and would not reverse his recommendation, he objected to *The Speaker* on the grounds that it was the equivalent of shouting fire in a crowded theater—an irresponsible use of free speech. Shields was disturbed that the film didn't "explore the relationship of libraries and free expression" and charged that ALA had missed an opportunity to inform and inspire the public about the role libraries and librarians do, in fact, play in supporting the First Amendment.

In selecting these three librarians to share on-the-spot, personal reactions to the film, Jones had no idea they would all react negatively. However, as soon as discussion was opened on the floor, the charge was made by Dorothy Broderick that "it was wrong to load the platform!!!" (Berry 1576).

ALA members lined up at the microphones. One can imagine the tension filling the room. E. J. Josey denounced the film for racism; Sam Whitten called it "great"; Connie Dunlap called it "courageous"; Mary K. Chelton, head of the Young Adult Services Division, considered the portrayal of librarians accurate, "all too familiar"; an unnamed, first-time conference attendee said "I am appalled by this film ... it takes a delicate issue and muddles it ... what was the goal?" Avery Williams, the chair of the Black Caucus, was outraged over the indignities the film leveled at black people, and called for a meeting of caucus members immediately after the session; Bob Wright, a professor of library science at the University of Pittsburgh, said he'd "remove the name of ALA" from the film (*ibid.*).

After the membership meeting finished, at least two groups headed off for a late night of continued conversation over what to do about the film, and at the second membership meeting two resolutions—one from SRRT and another from the Black Caucus—were presented. The SRRT resolution, presented by former coordinator Nancy Kellum-Rose, resolved that ALA remove its name from the film on the ground that

> the subject matter of the film is, at most, peripheral to the experience of libraries and librarians in intellectual freedom ... it fails to address relevant intellectual freedom issues ... in favor of a hypothetical issue set outside of a library ... and does not well represent the concerns of either librarians or ALA [1578].

Avery Williams made a motion to substitute SRRT's resolution with one from the Black Caucus, which objected similarly to the poor treatment of intellectual freedom issues, and went a step further to address racial aspects of the film.

> In the portrayal of the races, the characterization of the blacks is negative and stereotyped.... *The Speaker* is condescending, simplistic, and insulting to blacks ... the development of the theme utilizes the black characters as victims and scapegoats [*ibid.*].

E. J. Josey, who would become president of ALA in 1984, reminded members of the tumultuous period ALA had gone through in the early 1960s when he and others had to convince Council that librarianship could no longer tolerate the existence of Jim Crow library associations in the South. In 1964, Josey led the effort to pressure the library associations of Georgia, Alabama, Mississippi, and Louisiana to put an end to racial segregation within their own ranks. Although ALA policy had long forbidden racial segregation, the practice was tolerated in the South. Josey recalls the 1964 conference,

> Much to my chagrin, the Mississippi Library Association was honored there [at the 1964 ALA conference] for its National Library Week Activities. I exploded! I was seething with anger, for I remembered that three civil rights workers—Andrew Goodman, James Chaney, and Micheal Schwerner had been murdered and lay dead and buried somewhere in Mississippi, their bodies not yet discovered. I also remembered that the Mississippi Library Association had withdrawn from ALA rather than give membership to Negro Librarians [Josey 314].

Here Josey was, thirteen years later, confronted again with racism in the heart of the profession to which he dedicated his life. "I'm asking you," he said, speaking in support of the Black Caucus resolution, "to support the humanity of black people" (Berry 1579).

The resolution was defeated, by a margin of 2 to 1, with 385 against and 197 in favor (*ibid.*). Later, a white Columbia University librarian, Pamela Darling, said that she was "heartsick" that the debate had utilized "the red herring of race" (*ibid.*).

With the failure of the resolution to substitute the Black Caucus resolution for SRRT's, debate then returned to the simple question of whether or not ALA's name should be removed from the film. After some initial confusion over the vote count, and then a second vote, the resolution was defeated—334 against, 318 in favor. Why a second vote was taken is unclear, but four additional members voted, and several changed their votes. The first vote had defeated the resolution, but by a much narrower margin—326 against, 322 in favor.

When the Black Caucus and SRRT resolutions reached Council, debate was limited to 30 minutes and both were defeated by a margin of 2 to 1, which caused E. J. Josey to question the humanity of those who voted the defeat. Although debate was then closed, "in a tricky double waiver of its rules," Council permitted Ella Yates, the sole African-American who spoke out in favor of the film, to propose that the film's discussion guide include a statement from the Black Caucus outlining their objections, and that a new introduction be made to the film itself. Yates' proposal was duly approved. However, the Black Caucus refused to participate on the grounds that a statement in the guide would have "little or no effect" (Berry 1579). Needless to say, no new introduction to the film was ever made. *The Speaker* on YouTube today is exactly the same as seen by ALA members on 19 June 1977.

From denial to acknowledgment and reparation?

The membership and Council votes against the Black Caucus resolution were nothing other than a denial of the experience and knowledge black librarians had of racism. By majority vote, a majority of white librarians essentially said to a majority of black librarians "We know what racism is, and this film isn't that." In 2014, OIF's revival of the film conveyed the exact same message. The only difference is that the leadership of the Black Caucus now shares Yates' perspective on the film. The Black Caucus in the 21st century appears to be able to tolerate detestable ideas better than its predecessors.

The question is: What do white librarians know of the countless degradations to which our black colleagues have been subjected over the course of their lifetimes? Where along the spectrum—from lynch mob to Ivy League eugenicists to mass incarceration of African-American men—does racism begin to register on white consciences? How far do the blinders of white privilege allow a librarian to see, to *acknowledge* the multitudinous manifestations of white supremacy—the talking over, the patronizing comment, the cab that won't stop, the off-limits real estate and inner-city gentrification, the stereotypes and the type-casting, the achievement gaps, the shut doors, jail cells, compromises, "hands up, don't shoot," blood on the sidewalk, blood in the park, blood on the streets?

In the book *States of Denial: Knowing About Atrocities and Suffering* (2001), sociologist Stanley Cohen investigates the many ways in which acts of denial, in a variety of forms, are used by individuals, families, governments, and other groups to cover-up the causes and mechanisms of violence against others. Cohen describes how both victims and perpetrators of violence—from domestic violence to massacres—engage in a process of normalization in order to ignore or explain away suffering that is allowed to continue in personal and public spheres alike. One form of denial Cohen identifies is tolerance. In an example from domestic violence, Cohen writes

> ... tolerance is a form of social control, discouraging or even forbidding any acknowledgement of the problem.... Not only is the wife blamed for her husband's violence, but her tolerance is a mirage, hiding the fact that passivity ("Why doesn't she tell," "Why doesn't she leave?") results not from free choice but lack of choice [Cohen 52].

Perpetrators of suffering engage in several forms of denial to avoid social condemnation. Cohen cites five: denial of responsibility, denial of injury, denial of the victim, condemnation of the condemners, and appeal to higher loyalties (61).

In the context of all the debates regarding *The Speaker*, we see the last two forms of denial at play. Those who objected to the racist and misleading aspects of the film were condemned as censors. The hurt felt by those who objected was explained away as the necessary "collateral damage" to serve loftier loyalty to the First Amendment.

Not only were black librarians blamed for their own suffering, being "overly sensitive" to *The Speaker*'s racist content, but were forced to tolerate this treatment or be labeled a censor.

The truth of both their emotional hurt and analysis of the film denied, trust betrayed, friendships strained, appeals to human decency fallen on closed ears, members of the Black Caucus left Detroit, returned home, back to families and patrons, reference desks, budgets, collection development, and library outreach programs. Anger and hurt simmering, a decision was made to compose a statement to be delivered at the next midwinter meeting. In January 1978, Clara Stanton Jones read on the floor of Council,

> We, the undersigned members of the American Library Association, have requested this opportunity to make a statement because we believe that neither the Executive Board, the

Council, nor the membership feels or subscribes to what we perceive "The Speaker" to be representing in the name of the Association. In the heat of discussion immediately after viewing the film at the annual conference last summer, there was not enough time to gain proper perspective, especially on a film that is as subtle as this one. It is important to us and to the ongoing welfare of the Association for you to know how we feel about "The Speaker." It would be easier for us to remain silent, but that would mean acting as if the issue were either resolved or dead, or that it does not matter. It is no insignificant charge that we make: first, that the central thesis of "The Speaker" is counterfeit and falsely identifies as a First Amendment issue; and second, that the example chosen to illustrate the principle of free speech is presented in a highly unsuitable and irresponsible fashion, insensitive, in poor taste and skillfully racist [Black 1].

After summarizing the film, the statement explains Caucus members' objections,

We maintain that "The Speaker" is fraudulent in nature because it rests upon a misrepresentation of the First Amendment; that the interpretation set forth is a manipulation of the First Amendment to deftly force the ordinary program-planning function of choosing a speaker to conform to imaginary First Amendment strictures. This distortion completely discredits and invalidates "The Speaker." This fundamental error, established at the beginning of the film, is never corrected. The twist of the truth is so subtle that it glides by easily and is woven into a sequence of superficially logical arguments and actions to support the deception....

A great many librarians viewing "The Speaker" at the 1977 Detroit Conference sensed that there was something fundamentally wrong about the film, even if they could not immediately identify all the reasons. It takes a while to sort out the half-truths and untruths, amidst the web of subtle nuances. Dr. Boyd's thesis presumes the superiority of the white members of the audience and their in-born right and authority to judge the mental fitness of other races. The black students would become invisible men and women in such an audience, while their erstwhile peers are being instructed in the cardinal principles of white supremacy. The school's consent to these terms would result in the students being categorized and addressed as "superior" or "inferior" [Black].

While the majority votes that denied the legitimacy of objections raised by the Black Caucus and SRRT in 1977 is not surprising, insult was added to injury 37 years later when not only the OIF, but the new generation Black Caucus also refused to address their founding members' objections either in general or specifically. In May and June 2014, many librarians who knew of the original debate were bewildered, some outraged, by the Black Caucus' co-sponsorship of *The Speaker*'s revival.

Caucus president Jerome Offord, Jr., issued an open letter on 11 June, offering an explanation,

Times have changed and the BCALA Executive Board felt it was time for us to discuss this political hot button. We felt it was time to speak truth about our past and to allow our colleagues, whom many fight for the freedom of speech, to share their thoughts and feelings about this film without banning, blocking, or attempting to halt this educational moment [Offord 1].

Offord never explains what "truth about our past" was ever left undiscussed, but an indication of just how much times have *not* changed comes at the end of his letter when he suggests that members of the Black Caucus in 1977–78 shied from discussing this "hot button." Concluding his letter, Offord wrote that BCALA chose to collaborate on OIF's

"Speaking About *The Speaker*" program so that a new generation of librarians would not be afraid to engage in difficult conversations.

> It is time to talk! We invite you to join us and discuss the issue. Let's work together to make a positive change so the next generation isn't afraid to look at historical moments/ challenges such as this and shy away from discussing something their grandparents couldn't [2].

To tell today's new generation of librarians that the generation of the '60s and '70s "couldn't" discuss *The Speaker*, that their response was to "shy away" from it, is absurd and a complete denial of the historic record—it was the *supporters* of the film who "couldn't" discuss any of the objections raised. They couldn't, and wouldn't, because engagement in a serious conversation would have meant accepting the legitimacy of their black colleagues' concerns. Instead of conversation, the film's supporters immediately went on the offensive, accusing opponents of "censorship" which, combined with rote appeal to their clever slogan We—Must—Tolerate, had a chilling effect on the debate. Yet, despite this chilling effect, members of the Black Caucus *insisted* on discussion. They did not "shy away." There would have been no discussion had not the Black Caucus and allies insisted on speaking their minds.

Furthermore, in 2014 the level of denial was ratcheted up to the max when OIF, BCALA, and LHRT all decided that *no one* who had objected to the film would be speaking about *The Speaker*. A suggestion made that John Berry of *Library Journal* be added as a panelist to "Speaking About *The Speaker*" to share the perspective of those who opposed the film, fell on closed ears.

What Offord's letter represents, more than anything else, is a measure of the OIF's current hegemony over any discussion of intellectual freedom. Today, even the Black Caucus seems unwilling to engage in a critical discussion of the film. That the Library History Round Table too engages in superficial rather than critical analysis turns the entire invitation of "It is time to talk!" into a charade.

No wonder, despite the intolerable and persistent racism that continues to saturate American society, and no wonder, despite the crying need for conversations about racism, that *The Speaker*'s interpretation of intellectual freedom has so ossified librarianship's thinking that we cannot stand back and actually address objections raised nearly 40 years ago.

Former director of ALA's Office of Literacy and Outreach Services Satia Orange, in an email to me, shared her thoughts that "Speaking About *The Speaker*" would give ALA members a much needed opportunity to discuss racism and other issues raised by the film. In her message, she repeated two points made in the 1978 statement from the Black Caucus, which could have been a starting point for a real discussion in Las Vegas:

> —Why in the film does no one talk about the denial of the students' rights to invite whomever they wanted to speak?
> —Why in the film is there no discussion of options other than Dr. Boyd as sole speaker?

To which could be added other questions raised by signers of the 1978 statement (Satia Orange's father A. P. Marshall among them) and allies like Miriam Braverman and Zoia Horn:

—Is the humanity of black people a legitimate topic of debate?
—Does the First Amendment's guarantee freedom of speech *also* guarantee a public platform?
—Are accusations of censorship ever used as a bullying tactic?
—Why must we tolerate ideas we detest? What purpose is served by such tolerance? And, whose interests are served?
—In what ways is the racism of the early 21st century different from that of the late 20th and what does that difference mean for librarianship?

In some communities "hate speech" is not only not tolerated, but has been made criminal. Cohen describes how several European countries have outlawed Holocaust denial in the belief that such thinking is morally reprehensible, and should not be tolerated for fear that anti–Semitism could take hold as it did in the 1930s.

Toleration of ideas we detest allows those ideas to stay alive, sometimes to thrive. The objection will be raised that the white supremacist detests the idea of racial equality, and for this reason alone we must accept *The Speaker*'s interpretation of intellectual freedom. Otherwise, what happens when the tables are reversed, and it is the antiracist's speech that gets censored?

Indeed, one of the questions suggested in the discussion guide for *The Speaker* is: "If the majority in a community has the right to 'protect' itself from minority opinions, would, for example, Dr. Martin Luther King Jr. have been permitted to express views that were clearly unpopular in many communities?" (McMullin 10). Recall that in the film Dr. Boyd (the character representing William Shockley) is not allowed to speak at the high school when the school board cancels the current events committee's program. The school board is the "majority" that is "protecting" itself from a "minority view."

The problem here, and at the heart of the entire episode, is that this parallel places Dr. King and his ideas on equal standing as those of Dr. Shockley. The civil rights leader is on par with the eugenicist. The aspirations of an antiracist community are argued to be equivalent to those of a racist community. A demand for human rights for all citizens is presented as equivalent to a demand for the sterilization of black citizens. An appeal to the fundamental equality of all people is ultimately the moral equivalent of an appeal to the fundamental superiority of whites. The world becomes a place where morality has no role, where the scales of justice have no tipping point, justice and injustice must balance.

This is the level of complexity *The Speaker* presents. The film says we must tolerate the intolerable, give the stage to proponents of ideas that divide, humiliate, oppress, in order to honor their First Amendment rights.

The problem with this perspective is that there is no *moral* equivalency between the ideas of Dr. King and Dr. Shockley/Dr. Boyd. This was the point made by the Black Law Student Association at Harvard in 1973, a point that the dean of Harvard Law School considered persuasive and legitimate grounds for canceling the Innis-Shockley debate. The fact that there is no moral equivalency between Dr. King and Dr. Shockley/Boyd, however, seems to have carried no weight in the thinking of Professor Archibald Cox, Vision Associates filmmakers, and IFC subcommittee members.

If we in the United States truly believe that all humans are created equal, each deserving "life, liberty, and the pursuit of happiness," and if we truly want a country with "freedom and justice for all," then each one of us must, individually, answer the question "Whose side am I on?" Dr. King's or Dr. Shockley's? As long as librarianship continues to insist on neutrality in the face of moral choices like this one, the profession will, in fact, side with those willing to wield big sticks.

The silencing power of the billy-club and the bully pulpit, the taser and the lockdown, is swift and certain, efficient and effective. On the other hand, dialogue, debate, and democracy among equally empowered human beings is time-consuming, cumbersome, messy, and sometimes demands the acknowledgement of having been in the wrong, of having made a mistake, of changing one's views. Silence and neutrality in the face of ideas that promote violence and oppression is always complicity, while open debate between opposing perspectives and the persuasive power of intellectual engagement are expressions of hope in the possibility of non-violent change.

Imagine, for a moment, Judith Krug in 1977 saying, "We made a mistake in excluding others from the process. It never occurred to us that the film might be construed as promoting racist ideas. Please forgive us. Let's spend a little more money and fix this film." What would such an admission have cost her? Imagine Robert Wedgeworth in 2014 saying, "ALA made a mistake in 1977. Let us not compound it. Let's spend a little more money and fix this film. Let's edit it to include the debate that for 40 years has surrounded it. Let the healing begin."

As Cohen writes, only when acknowledgment is made of injury done can healing begin—for both victim and perpetrator. Krug is gone, but the OIF is not: neither is ALA. A few of those who engaged in the 1977 debates are still alive. A new generation is curious. Perhaps it is time for a truth-and-reconciliation type process regarding *The Speaker*. Perhaps it is time for some sort of reparation.

Unfortunately, the road ALA and OIF seem to be headed on in terms of *The Speaker* and the controversy surrounding it is one of continued denial. And, the only purpose served—even if unintentionally—by giving *The Speaker* to the YouTube generation is to legitimatize the notion that the First Amendment means that we must continue to tolerate the intolerable, and to legitimize racist rants cloaked in academic robes by insisting that they have a "right" to public platforms.

And, just what does it mean anyway that harm is, or might be done "unintentionally"? How can intelligent, generally caring people be unintentionally racist? Do we not have the reflective capacity to intentionally, in full consciousness free ourselves of the racist social stew in which we swim? As Todd Honma writes in his article "Trippin' Over the Color Line: The Invisibility of Race in Library and Information Studies," we must pay attention to this notion of unintentionality,

> … we need to figure out how this seemingly innocuous term really translates into complicity with dominant oppressive social structures and the failure to recognize the material effects of histories of racism and white supremacy [Honma 14].

The Speaker is an expression of unexamined, deep-rooted, epistemological white privilege. The film's proponents were in charge of all definitions: the First Amendment means this; racism is that; *you* are a censor; *we* have no obligation to consider anything *you* have to say because you are wrong and we are right.

The Speaker is an unintentionally racist film. It is also a film that misinforms its audience about the rights granted by the First Amendment. Whether the latter was also unintentional is an open question, but it was certainly a choice of interpretation based in a specific (and highly questionable) ideological position. Intention, however, does not justify interpreting *The Speaker* as either nonracist or accurate in its representation of First Amendment rights.

If one were to ask, at the most basic level and in the real world, whose interests are best served by the ideas conveyed and the stereotypes presented in this film, the answer would be unacceptable to any librarian who values social justice and accuracy of information. The portrayal of black students as mostly emotional, potentially violent, plays to racist stereotypes, and the film's defense of an advocate of a racist theory is an argumentative construct that, intentionally or not, serves the maintenance of white privilege in a racist society. In the United States, white people have become so used to determining who is good, who is not, who matters, who doesn't, that when their definitions are challenged they just claim the challenger to be wrong. No, slavery is not bad. No, there is nothing wrong with children of the poor working in mines and mills. No, this film is not racist. No, that character is not a stereotype. No, your argument is not worth my time, much less a response. In fact, you are being a censor!

As for the film's insistence that detestable ideas must be given public platforms in order not to violate constitutional rights, this is simply inaccurate, and serves to whitewash the real reason that such ideas are given access to mass audiences, namely, that detestable ideologies serve the interests of certain sectors of society. Slavery and child labor served the interests of economic elites. Racists given mass audiences serve the economic and political interests of today's elites.

This is not to say that the Dr. Boyds of the world are to be "shut up." The First Amendment rightly prevents the silencing of any individual no matter how detestable their views. Additionally, platforms can be given to any individual regardless of the ideas they communicate. That right is also protected, it is what freedom of the press is all about. But to insist, as *The Speaker* does, that a platform *must* be given, is simply inaccurate as several well-informed people noted during the actual incident at Harvard Law School that provided the basis of the fictionalized *Speaker* film. There is a difference here that librarianship must acknowledge if we are to be true proponents of First Amendment rights. If we as a profession do not have an accurate understanding of these rights, how can we consider ourselves responsible advocates of those rights in our communities?

A *mea culpa*, an apology, was in order from IFC subcommittee members, but neither was forthcoming. Instead the accusation they and their supporters leveled against black colleagues echoed throughout the Association, and reverberates to this day—Censor!

To this accusation of censorship, the Black Caucus responded,

> We have <u>never</u> asked that the film be censored. The Association has had experience with handling a finished study, which was considered unsatisfactory and never published by the American Library Association. We feel that there are solutions to the crisis created by "The Speaker" which have not been utilized.... Disturbance over "The Speaker" is deepening, not subsiding. Its lingering, troubled presence has cast a pall over the Association that will

not just go away. The American Library Association's integrity is at stake. It will not be easy to resolve this dilemma, but we have confronted other difficult problems before with wisdom and courage [7].

This statement is as relevant in 2015 as it was in 1978. Racism is not gone from the United States. The fact that the OIF would not permit an opponent of *The Speaker* to speak at its Las Vegas program is symptomatic of racism today. Voices are simply excluded so that prevailing ideology appears to be the only one that exists, the only one worthy of notice. Of course, the OIF can invite whomever it wants to its stage. The First Amendment protects that right. (Do note that no one, in 2014, accused the OIF of censorship because it refused to invite John N. Berry III to speak.)

Unfortunately, the consequences of allowing *The Speaker* to stand—as is—as a representation of our profession's understanding of First Amendment rights are the perpetuation of muddled thinking and unintentional (but very real) advocacy of racism.

Notes: 1. *Many thanks to colleagues in critlib-Seattle for bringing Honma's work to my attention.* **2.** *Many thanks to Mark McCallon for information on the survey categories.*

2. Singing (and Silencing) Solidarity—Interrupting Legacies of Racism and the Anti-Apartheid "Book Boycott"

> ... *history's psychosis will be cured*
> *once soft shack-born melodies explode*
> *in love-loving hollers*
> *in the womb of the future*
> *exposing the shallow trenches*
> *of make-believe history to the fury*
> *of the midday sun ...*
> —Keorapetse W. Kgositsile, 1969

This one's for Soloman Linda then, a Zulu who wrote a melody that earned untold millions for white men but died so poor that his widow couldn't afford a stone for his grave.
—Rian Malan, 2012

On November 16, 1989, the first librarian ever to be elected to the U.S. Congress, the Honorable Major R. Owens of Brooklyn, N.Y., rose to speak on the floor of the U.S. House of Representatives. "Mr. Speaker," he began, "I rise to commend the American Library Association for its recent passage of its 'Guidelines for Librarians Interacting with South Africa.'" After briefly describing ALA's involvement in the anti-apartheid solidarity movement, and noting the role librarians must play in keeping abreast of political and social developments "such as the freedom movement in South Africa, 'glasnost,' 'perestroika,' continued growth for African-American political power," Representative Owens concluded by stating,

> I applaud the American Library Association and its member librarians for making their voices heard on the most important issue of liberation for the 23 million Africans oppressed under the racist minority regime of South Africa, and for seizing the opportunity to educate Americans as to the true nature of the horrific policy of apartheid [Owens 29628].

By sheer coincidence, five days earlier in a room in the old McGraw-Hill building on West 42nd Street in New York City, over a dozen librarians from up and down the eastern seaboard (and one from Minnesota) met to discuss establishing an organization that would shortly become the Progressive Librarians Guild. Before the year was out PLG became involved in the thick of a debate within ALA regarding the very Guidelines of which Rep. Owens spoke, and would dedicate the first issue of its journal, *Progressive Librarian*, to the matter of apartheid (*Progressive*).

Congressman Owens, short in stature, mighty in activism, was elected to Congress in 1982 following a long career as a librarian. As an African-American he was well tuned-in to matters regarding civil rights struggles, both in the U.S. and abroad. As a left-leaning progressive, he was attentive to issues of class and had a keen interest in international affairs. As the only librarian in Congress, Owens kept abreast of the world of librarianship via longtime friends and colleagues from his years at Brooklyn Public Library—he worked as a community librarian "placing BPL collections in public places such as laundromats, stores, bars, and anywhere people gathered" (Berry 10). He was involved in ALA and active in the New York Social Responsibilities Round Table. Prompted perhaps by communications with an old library friend, Owens' words on November 16th resulted either from a bout of wishful thinking or a miscommunication, or as a political maneuver, for he was in error—ALA as a whole had not at that time endorsed the Guidelines, and, as it turns out, never would. The Guidelines had, however, been endorsed by the Social Responsibilities Round Table of ALA, and would be under consideration for ALA's endorsement at its upcoming 1990 midwinter meeting in Chicago.

What might not have been a coincidence, indeed, what might actually have prompted Owens' remarks to the House of Representatives on the 16th, was the release on that very same day of a report entitled "The Starvation of Young Black Minds: The Effect of Book Boycotts in South Africa." The report, produced following a visit to South Africa by Robert Wedgeworth, then dean of the School of Library Service at Columbia University and former executive director of ALA, and Lisa Drew, vice-president and senior editor of William Morrow and Company, was issued under the auspices of the Association of American Publishers, and claimed that the cultural boycott initiated by the anti-apartheid movement, and officially endorsed by ALA, was depriving South Africans of information—of books—and, therefore, constituted nothing short of censorship.

The political perspectives embodied in these two documents, the SRRT Guidelines and the AAP report, were at variance and polarized subsequent debate within ALA regarding its support of the anti-apartheid movement. Pitted against one another were two old foes, sometimes allies—advocates of librarianship's social responsibilities versus intellectual freedom "purists." Tensions between these two camps has been extensively addressed in the library and information literature—the Berninghausen exchanges and Swan/Peattie debate, and so many other conversations/discussions/arguments aired in journals, on the floor of Council, riding the Gale bus at conferences. The debate concerning anti-apartheid sanctions and boycotts is used in what follows as an example of the rhetorical use made of "intellectual freedom" for political and economic purposes.

The purpose of this chapter is to recount the "book boycott" debate and tensions arising between advocates of human rights and those intellectual freedom "purists"; to introduce the concept of the political responsibilities of those who benefit from extreme violence; to tease-out threads from history that informed actions by librarians that have interrupted legacies of racism in both South Africa and the United States; and to present a brief overview of the development of the anti-apartheid sanctions movement.

For consideration first is the concept of the responsibilities of beneficiaries of extreme violence, for it is from among people who acknowledge these responsibilities that movements for social change arise. Reference will be made to the work of Stephen

Esquith and his book *The Political Responsibilities of Everyday Bystanders* (2010). The next section presents strands of the threads woven through the history of antiracist solidarity movements. For many librarians, especially those coming of age after the fall of South Africa's apartheid regime, the story of antiracist activism within librarianship, an activism fully informed by struggles for civil rights for black Americans, is a distant, if not unknown, one. In presenting this abbreviated history, my guiding question concerned how librarians of my own and the preceding generation might have first become aware of apartheid. What I discovered in pursuing this question was that the threads of antiracist movements in both the U.S. and in South Africa intertwined in such a way that the stories became nearly inseparable. Although the civil rights movement in the U.S. and the freedom struggle in South Africa have their own unique and rich histories, in the period following World War II the parallels between racism in both countries were clearly revealed, and antiracist activism became informed by anticolonial movements around the globe. Following this description of consciousness-raising within librarianship around Jim Crow and apartheid is a brief account of the history of the anti-apartheid sanctions movement. All this then leads to the final part of the chapter, which is the "book boycott" debate itself. This debate will be used as an example of the longstanding social responsibilities "versus" intellectual freedom tensions often found within dialogue and debates in ALA.

Acknowledging responsibility for the extreme violence of racism

The American Library Association's relationship with South Africa is longstanding, and the profession's relationship with apartheid is closely, complexly entwined with and informed by racism in the United States.

Apartheid and Jim Crow grew from European colonialism and its brutal exploitation of the labor of indigenous and enslaved human beings, and the theft of natural resources from their homelands. The ruthless violence of this economic system was given moral force through the invention of various ideological forms of superiority—Christianity, whiteness, Western civilization. Ideologies of racism and systems of exploitation passed from one generation to the next, with adjustments made from time to time to accommodate threats to white supremacy.[1] Religious authorities claimed the white man's superiority to be the will of the Christian God. Political authorities claimed civilization to be the special province of "Western" traditions. Economic structures rewarded whites with land, wealth, and leisure when they participated in the maintenance of racist beliefs and practices. And anyone who questioned white supremacy was punished, some more than others.

Peoples subjected to racism had plenty of reasons to doubt the fundamental fairness of these forms of supremacy—they recognized that strength, intelligence, beauty, and creativity were not exclusive provinces of whites; they were wise to the contradictions between the teachings of the white man's religion and his behavior; and the abhorrent violence and constant humiliation under which they lived was never alleviated, no matter how hard one worked or attempted to please. People of color knew that white superiority was a myth, but whites were slower to that realization. Slower, because they reaped the system's rewards either materially or psychically, sometimes both. However, questioning attitudes developed among small numbers of whites, and the notion that race was a justification for violence and oppression began to crack.

No sector of society within either South Africa or the United States, including librarianship, was free of entanglement with racist attitudes and practices. For centuries, racist ideas, images, and stereotypes had so thoroughly saturated the culture, individual psyches, social relations, language, and built infrastructures that racism became part of the background, the "way things are." If the U.S. were a "melting pot," racism was the stock, and librarianship, evolving in this social soup, was not free of its influence.

ALA's relationship with librarianship in South Africa developed initially via correspondence, then face-to-face at meetings and conferences, and through exchanges of various sorts. One finds in the first volume of *American Library Journal* mention of South Africa in the March 31, 1877, issue (Announcements). An announcement that the Grey Collection in Cape Town was changing curators was tucked between notices on the updated catalogs of the Bodleian Library, Biblioteca Mexicana, the British Museum, and a new Chinese Bibliography.

ALA's ties to Jim Crow are equally longstanding, and the profession cannot separate itself from this history. We have our own shameful stories of exclusion, of denying basic literacy and education, of silently abiding by or loudly promoting measures that disenfranchised immigrants, blacks, and the working class. Carnegie's millions, for example, came from the labor of human beings who worked in his steel mills and who mined the minerals that fed those mills. Every librarian who walks through the portal of a Carnegie library benefits, in some small part, from the misery and exploitation of those workers even though they lived and labored long ago.

In thinking about the ramifications of this dynamic, of the benefits that accrue from violence for which one has no direct responsibility, the work of philosopher Stephen L. Esquith is helpful. Consideration of this dynamic is essential in understanding how a bystander, how a beneficiary of violence half way around the world, might come to decide that time has come to actually take responsibility for ending that violence. Librarians in the United States, after all, were not the perpetrators of pass laws, arrests, imprisonments, state-condoned murder in South Africa, but the diamond in one's engagement ring might well have come from there. Such an intimate connection to the brutal reality of a black man toiling in a diamond field, separated from wife and children, exploited for labor, robbed of comfort. The emotional charge and meaning of an engagement ring, inextricably linked to a form of extreme violence from which any glowing bride-to-be would recoil *if she were aware and acknowledged* the blood behind the glitter. Where awareness begins, acknowledgment can follow, sometimes leading to activism against the violence. Awareness and acknowledgment of this sort motivated ALA's support of the anti-apartheid movement's call for sanctions. And, as we shall see, economic interests pushed publishers and library allies to pressure ALA into dropping support of sanctions via an appeal that prioritized intellectual freedom values over those of human rights.

In his book *The Political Responsibilities of Everyday Bystanders* (2010), Esquith explores violence as a political tool and examines the role and responsibilities not so much of perpetrators and their collaborators in acts of violence, but rather of the indirect beneficiaries of violence, the bystanders, those individuals who have varying degrees of awareness of the violence, and do little or nothing (at least initially) to oppose it.

Esquith defines violence as "unwanted and harmful suffering" (5) and is concerned with what he calls "severe violence—the hunger, poverty, famine,[2] civil war, wars of conquest and invasion, epidemics and pandemics, and genocide" (1). Jim Crow segregation and apartheid are both forms of severe violence used by political actors to maintain power. Esquith describes the political nature of this violence:

> There are ... two senses in which severe violence is political: what we might call its material and its semantic senses. First, severe violence is materially political because of the decisions and actions, sometimes proximate, and sometimes remote, that create it. Second, it is semantically political because of the way in which responsibilities for the benefits and burdens that flow from such violence are shirked, shouldered, or shared [5–6].

In other words, people make decisions and engage in actions that result in violence, and people make use of language that justifies, glosses-over, hides, or challenges that violence. The purpose of both political tools—the material and the semantic—is to disenfranchise the victims of violence, to drive them from their homes, render them powerless in strange places or situations, to silence their voices. What unites all victims of severe violence is

> ... the cruel way they have lost their political voice and have no legitimate political way to regain it.... They have been geographically displaced, legally dispossessed, politically disenfranchised, or militarily "disappeared." Those individuals and institutions that have *caused and contributed* to this radical depoliticalization certainly bear a wide range of moral duties and legal and political responsibilities. They are the perpetrators of severe violence and their collaborators. Those bystanders who have *benefited* from severe violence bear a different kind of responsibility, which I describe as shared and institutional political responsibility [9–10, emphasis in the original].

In both the U.S. and in South Africa, members of the library profession participated in Jim Crow or apartheid in their personal and professional lives. In terms of Esquith's framework, librarians in their work places are not so much perpetrators in severe violence (although we shall see some who were). Librarians are among the collaborators of severe violence, and the bystanders who benefit from an unjust system through apathy, indifference, fear, inaction. Librarians, after all, enforced the humiliations of segregation in libraries in both the U.S. and in South Africa. Librarians burned the banned books. Our libraries are filled with objects originating in one or another type of violence—the gold on the gilt edges of books; the rubber of the library property stamp and in the wheels of the bookmobile; the mahogany of chairs and tables; the fruits and vegetables on the table at the opening reception. Miners and rubber-tappers, lumbermen and farmworkers, all those who grow, mine, manufacture, and transport these items to us, keep them in good working order, what do these human beings experience of political and economic violence in their daily lives? What is our responsibility toward these people? Do we in our relative comfort shirk, shoulder, or share responsibility for the alleviation of their hardships, miseries, or unbearable burdens?

Varying levels and intensities of violence—material and semantic—create conditions of economic and political power. Consider, for instance, a speech on September 20, 1963, in which President Kennedy spoke of apartheid in an address to the General Assembly of the United Nations.

> The United States of America is opposed to discrimination and persecution on grounds of race and religion anywhere in the world.... We are unalterably opposed to apartheid and all forms of human oppression.... Our concern is the right of all men to equal protection and opportunity—and since human rights are indivisible, this body cannot stand aside when those rights are abused or neglected by any member state [Mezerik 39].

Fine words, but, in the mid–1960s, eight countries (the U.S., Britain, West Germany, France, Italy, the Netherlands, Belgium and Japan) accounted for more than 75 percent of South Africa's foreign trade and investment (Mezerik 1964, 43). In 1963, when Kennedy made his speech, 33 percent of all U.S. exports to Africa went to South Africa (*ibid.*, 161); the U.S. exported $60.2 million in goods to the country, and U.S. investors earned a profit of 27 percent on investments, which, according to Mezerik was "the highest in the world for equivalent investments." Apartheid was nothing if not profitable. Very profitable. And this trend continued.

Research done a decade following Kennedy's speech by Ann and Neva Seidman indicate why apartheid was so profitable. In their book *South Africa and U.S. Multinational Corporations* (1978) the Siedmans write,

> In 1974, the profits of the gold mining companies soared to $2,340 million, almost two thirds of the companies' total income. The total wages bill, on the other had, was only about 18 percent of total mining company income. More than half of these wages were paid to whites, only slightly more than 10 percent of the labor force. Non-whites, who constituted 88 percent of the labor force, received only $302 million, less than eight percent of the total company income. Their wages, in other words, were equal to only 12 percent of total profits that year [Seidman 47–8].

Eighty-eight percent of the work force in South African gold mines received in wages a mere 12 percent of the profits of their labor. In other words, 12 percent of the work force (whites plus owners and investors) received some share of 88 percent of the rest of the profits, and certainly not equal shares at that.

The strength of racism as a tool wielded by power elites has always resided in its use as a lever to divide people who might otherwise unite given mutual interests and shared subjugation. This dynamic is as present today as it was in the decades leading up to ALA's involvement in the anti-apartheid movement, and the levels of violence and ideological control now available to power elites are orders of magnitude greater than ever before. However, growing recognition of race as a social construct and the inherent equality of all human beings, and the determination of individuals to express their solidarity and to act in alliance with others have their own power.

Two months following Kennedy's speech, *Library Journal* arrived in the mailboxes of librarians and libraries across the country, a mere week, plus a few days, before the assassination of the President, an event that certainly overshadowed for U.S. librarians one news item from South Africa. The November 1, 1963, issue of *LJ* reported that,

> While the American Library Association in recent years has made several pronouncements and moves to bring down the color barrier in library service and in the library profession,

the South African Library Association, at its conference last November, passed a resolution affirming its support of complete apartheid in the profession [S. African 4180].

The article goes on to note that while membership in the South African Library Association (SALA) had originally been open to librarians of all races, since 1948 the Association had not allowed black and colored librarians to attend its conferences. Also reported by *Library Journal* was the presence of South Africa's Minister of the Interior, J. de Klerk, at the passage of this resolution. A future president of South Africa, de Klerk informed SALA conference attendees that apartheid laws would be enforced within all professional associations. Interestingly, it was under de Klerk's presidency more than 30 years later that apartheid finally ended.

Although U.S. librarianship took little note of this event in SALA, our British colleagues were extremely concerned, and in January 1964, *ALA Bulletin* carried a letter from H.D. Barry, secretary of the Library Association, conveying the news that the organization had passed a resolution deploring the decision by SALA to maintain apartheid within its ranks. The British resolution "strongly urges the Association to reconsider its decision" (9).

Librarians act to interrupt legacies of Jim Crow and apartheid

In the U.S. librarians had given attention to racism long before the 1960s, and some had used their positions and skills in the service of educating colleagues, ALA, library users, and readers in general about the injustices of racism and of the task of ridding society of racism's influence and practices. The history of race and librarianship in the U.S. is, by turns, fascinating, disheartening, inspiring. In 1902, the library board in Atlanta refused a request from a delegation headed by none other than W.E.B. DuBois that the city provide library services to *all* Atlanta residents. "Gentlemen," said DuBois to the library board members,

> we are a committee come to ask you to do justice to the black people of Atlanta by giving them the same free library privileges that you propose giving to whites. Every argument which can be adduced to show the need of libraries for whites applies with redoubled force to the negroes. More than any other part of our population they need instruction, inspiration and proper diversion; they need to be lured from temptation of the streets and saved from evil influences, and they need a growing acquaintance with what the best of the world's souls have thought and done and said. It seems hardly necessary in the twentieth century to argue before men like you the necessity and propriety of placing the best means of human uplifting into the hands of the poorest and lowest and blackest [Yust 164].

Later, when Carnegie offered funds for a black library in Atlanta, the African-American community refused because the library board would not allow a black to serve on the board, leaving administration of a library for the black community fully in the hands of an all white board. Although black Atlantans did eventually get a library, the racist attitudes of the board were slow in changing. In 1959, faced with demands that the central library be desegregated, the board called in the police chief for advice on how to keep the library segregated (Atlanta-Fulton).

In the 1920s, New York Public Library's Ernestine Rose (a white woman) was assigned as head of the 135th Street branch library in Harlem. In that capacity she broke the color bar by hiring the first black staff members at NYPL, sponsoring the first black student at NYPL's Library School, and establishing the Division of Negro History and Literature, which became the world renowned Schomberg Center for Research in Black Culture (Sink).

The first, *literal* outpouring of condemnation of racism amongst librarians came in 1936 when the annual conference of ALA met in Richmond, Virginia. Black members of ALA who attended the Richmond conference were subjected to the city's Jim Crow practices—prohibited from dining with white colleagues, "graciously" allow to use the same entrances to meeting venues, but forced to be seated separately. Conference organizers knew black members would be subjected to these humiliations and sent out a letter to inform them, which simply added fuel to the fire. Why would ALA agree to such conditions? The outpouring of letters to *Library Journal* and *ALA Bulletin*, and the subsequent policy enacted by ALA against holding meetings at segregated venues, stand as an important measure of both ALA's disregard of indignities suffered by black members and the profession's growing awareness of the challenge segregation posed to its professed values. In a letter to the *Bulletin*, Edith N. Snow, librarian at Providence Public Library, wrote,

> Better than an apology for unequal treatment of members at an annual conference would be the announcement that the A.L.A. has joined with the growing number of organizations that insist upon equality for all its members [571].

Statements such as Snow's were no small matter. A letter to the editor might have cost an ALA member her or his job. It might have threatened the prospects of future employment. Each writer knew the risks.

In the 1940s, librarians at New York Public Library's Schomberg Collection raised awareness of the struggle against racism via an "Honor Roll of Race Relations." This was a survey conducted annually, asking for nominations of 12 black and 6 white individuals, organizations, or institutions that contributed to the cause of racial equality and justice. The list was an educational tool enlightening fellow librarians of the work being done by blacks and whites to combat racism. To provide an example (and introduce an early and important actor in the anti-apartheid movement), in 1942 the honor roll included anthropologist Franz Boas and world renowned actor, singer, and political activist Paul Robeson. Boas, who had died that year, was recognized as one "whose scientific studies have done much to shatter the myth of race." Robeson, once referred to as "the living refutation of racist myths" (*Dimensions* 9), was recognized by the Schomberg librarians "for symbolizing and promoting the folk art of many lands and peoples and for his performance last summer in the leading role of Shakespeare's immortal play *Othello*" (Race 215).

Two years later, in 1944 a similar educational push, the Librarians Section of the City Wide Citizens' Committee on Harlem, compiled a reading list of books recommended by "outstanding Americans" which was published in *Library Journal* under the title "Understanding America's Race Problem." The outstanding recommenders included Ruth Benedict, Thomas Dewey, W.E.B. du Bois, Langston Hughes, Eleanor Roosevelt, and Arthur Hayes Sultzberger. Among the 24 books on the list were: Herbert Aptheker's *Negro Slave Revolts in the United States, 1526–1860*; Herbert R. Northrop's *Organized Labor and the Negro*; Lillian Smith's novel *Strange Fruit*; and Richard Wright's *Native Son* (Marquess 694–5).

Also in 1944, ALA announced the first of what came to be known as the Notable Books list. This was a list of fifty books, fiction and nonfiction, selected by librarians for the adult reading public. Books were to be aimed at a general audience, i.e., not requiring specialized knowledge of the field covered by the book. Selection criteria were as follows:

> A book may be selected as notable for at least one, and preferably more than one, of the following reasons: it possesses exceptional literary merit; it expands the horizons of human knowledge; it makes a specialized body of knowledge accessible to the non-specialist; it promises to contribute significantly to the solution of a contemporary problem [Blackston 299].

From the very start, racism appears to have been one "contemporary problem" of which selectors were cognizant, and between 1944 and 1963 at least one book written by either an African or African American author was selected in each of all but six years. There were books, of course, written by nonblack authors that addressed racial issues, one of the first being Lillian Smith's *Strange Fruit* which (along with John Steinbeck's *Grapes of Wrath*), "evoked serious censorship problems" for ALA resulting in the passage of an addition to the Library Bill of Rights that "books believed to be factually correct should not be banned or removed from the library simply because they are disapproved by some people" (Thomison 145).

Smith's bestselling novel, with a title borrowed from Abel Meeropol's 1937 song, popularized by blues and jazz singer Billie Holiday, tells the story of the black and white communities in a small town in Georgia in the years following the First World War, and of the relationships, social attitudes and psychological underpinnings that lead to the lynching of an innocent black man when his lifelong white friend is murdered. In addition to its selection by the Librarians Section of the City Wide Citizens' Committee on Harlem, Smith's book was named an ALA Notable Book for 1944.

Two years later, the nation was horrified by the brutal lynching of two African American couples in Walton County, Georgia. Demands for federal antilynching laws were immediately forthcoming. Paul Robeson led one delegation to speak with President Truman, urging him to use the power of the federal government to outlaw lynching. The NAACP also sent a delegation to Truman with the same demand (Goodman, p. 173). Truman, well aware of the powerhouses represented by Southerners in the Senate and House, was reluctant to do anything about lynching, so in order to appease those demanding the outlawing of lynching he established a committee to look into the state of civil rights in the country.

ALA issued no statements on the murders, but in 1947 its Notable Books Council selected the report of Truman's Committee on Civil Rights entitled *To Secure These Rights*. In a possibly unprecedented editorial review of a Notable Book, Mrs. Mona Harrop McElfresh, of the Cincinnati Public Library, described some of the report's contents—lynchings, employment discrimination, restrictive housing covenants, poll taxes and denial of voting rights, unequal educational opportunities and facilities, discrimination in medical care and judicial processes, denial of pensions and unemployment compensation to agricultural and domestic workers, and segregation in theaters, restaurants, shops and in transportation (McElfresh 74). Action was slow to follow sentiments condemning racism, and the profession continued to tolerate segregation within the library world.

The first reference to the word "apartheid" in the Association's monthly publication *ALA Bulletin* (today's *American Libraries*) is in a publisher's advertisement for a book selected as a Notable Book for the year. A close look at this book is worthwhile in what it reveals of the sort of contradictions that can be uncovered in the attitudes expressed by people who might express opposition to racism but find subtle, semantic ways to justify it. As we shall see, lip service given in sympathy to victims of racism, is—over and over again—belied by inaction and semantic spin on the part of some within librarianship.

In 1953, ALA's Notable Books Council selected a book entitled *Struggle for Africa*, by Vernon Bartlett, as one of the best 50 books published that year, calling it, "A clear, authoritative survey of today's Africa, giving a constructive, impartial picture of that country's [sic] problems as a whole" (Notable 155). The fact that the annotation written for Bartlett's book describing the Council's reason for including it on their list, refers to the *continent* of Africa as a "country" reveals something of the problem.

Bartlett, a British journalist and, in 1953, a recently retired Member of Parliament, devoted nearly one-third of his book to South Africa, a country in which he'd traveled. Members of the Notable Books selection committee probably considered it "impartial" because Bartlett does describe the horrid conditions and humiliations South African blacks were subjected to by the apartheid regime. But the book is far from impartial: the frontispiece map is titled "Africa—Europe's Hinterland"; the first chapter is "Continent Without History"; in the four chapters dealing expressly with South Africa, no mention is made of the African National Congress (ANC), any of its leaders, or actions. The overall attitude conveyed by Bartlett is patronizing in the utmost toward black South Africans as can be seen in the following passage,

> The crime of the Nationalists [the ruling political party responsible for legislating and enforcing apartheid] is less that they want to maintain the dominance of the white man than that they are doing so by destroying the hope and faith of the black man. But to put the black man immediately on the same electoral footing as the white man, because the fundamental ideas of democracy include universal suffrage, would be a reprehensible act of folly; the torch of civilization cannot be handed on to other races until they are more or less prepared to carry it [Bartlett 28].

In the book's conclusion, while Bartlett calls for racial harmony and partnership, he gives the reader a wholly patronizing picture of the "backward Native" whose ambition "for the moment may not soar much above the empty gin bottle," but who will probably have a son with greater ambitions. The problem, as Bartlett see it is that Africans "cannot acquire even the gin bottle without European help" and that Europeans can't get access to the mineral and agricultural resources of their "hinterlands" without the "co-operation of Native labor" (234).

Bartlett's silence in regard to the ANC is especially suspect as it is quite unlikely that he, a seasoned journalist and politician, was unaware of the African National Congress's Defiance Campaign in 1952. The ANC (founded in 1912) decided in 1951 to demonstrate against celebrations planned by whites to mark the 300th anniversary of Dutch colonist arrival at the Cape of Good Hope on April 6, 1652. Co-sponsored by the South African Indian Congress (SAIC), the April 6th demonstrations were the first multiracial protests against apartheid, and launched a series of civil disobedience actions in the summer and fall of 1952 resulting in the arrest of 8,057 people. Among those arrested was Nelson Mandela on charges of violating the Suppression of Communism Act (Defiance Campaign n.d.). The violent suppression of these multiracial acts of civil disobedience led to calls for sanctions. In 1954, a white, British anti-apartheid organizer, Father Trevor Huddleston, an Anglican priest stationed in Sophiatown, called for a cultural boycott of South Africa.

> I am asking those who believe racialism to be sinful or wrong ... to refuse to encourage it by accepting any engagement to act, to perform as a musical artist or as a ballet dancer—in short, to engage in any contacts which would provide entertainment for any one section of the community [Nixon 157].

The fact the Huddleston called on *entertainers* to engage in a *cultural* boycott is a reflection of the extent to which musicians, actors, artists, dancers, writers, and athletes were culturally and politically engaged with South Africa. We will look at examples of such relationships more closely shortly, but for the moment, it is important to note that, while Bartlett's book is the first to be tied to the word apartheid in the library literature, it is not the first to have dealt with the realities of that system of extreme violence.

Six years earlier, in 1948, ALA's Notable Book Council had brought the horrors of South Africa's racist practices to the attention of the reading public with the selection of Alan Paton's *Cry the Beloved Country*. While librarians and readers in the U.S. learned about apartheid second hand, others, like actors and musicians and athletes, often experienced it firsthand. For instance, in 1951, Paton's book was made into a British film, starring two prominent U.S. actors, Canada Lee and Sidney Poitier, playing the characters of the Reverend Kumalo and the Reverend Msimangu, respectively. Lee and Poitier had to be smuggled into South Africa *as indentured servants* for the filming (Canada). Lee died the following year of a heart attack, but Poitier went on to become not only a very famous actor, but an activist in the civil rights movement, and an outspoken critic of apartheid as well.

Another example from the world of art and culture of a person who, very early on, spoke out against apartheid and Jim Crow was Paul Robeson. In 1936, Paul Robeson co-founded the Council on African Affairs (initially called the International Committee on African Affairs). The purpose of the Council was to keep people in the U.S. informed of developments, political and cultural, on the African continent. In 1946, after the brutal suppression of striking South African miners, the Council sponsored a rally on June 9th at Madison Square Garden, attended by 15,000 people, featuring Robeson speaking and singing (*Dimensions* 11). He was then at the height of international fame for both his artistry and political activism against racism and on behalf of the struggles of the working class. In March of 1949, shortly before the U.S. Department of State banned him from international travel, Robeson made a speech in London in which he succinctly identified the ties between Jim Crow and apartheid. "We are often reminded," he said,

> of the "cold war" said to exist between the two great sections of the world, the capitalist section led by the United States, and the socialist section at the head of which stands the Soviet Union. But little is said of the cold war of racial hatred, malice and intolerance, which is being waged with an intensified fury in an attempt to hold millions of people of non–European race in permanent subjection. At the head of the aggressive forces in this cold war, too, stands the United States. But occupying a prominent place by its side is the Union of South Africa. They are at once agreed in their policies of racial discrimination, but they differ in their practical approach....
>
> We in America have good reason to be alert to the danger that South Africa represents. We know that it is impossible to compromise with Jim Crowism and Anti-Semitism.
>
> We cannot afford to tolerate the advocates of White Supremacy in South Africa, any more than we can agree to the activities of the Ku Klux Klan in Georgia or Mississippi.
>
> We know that racialism of this kind must either be stamped out or it will spread [Tribute 65–67].

This is the political milieu in which members of the Notable Books Council in 1954 selected Bartlett's book. The "impartiality" they read into his descriptions of South African blacks stemmed in all likelihood from their own unexamined and widely held stereotypes regarding blacks. Unless selectors of Notable Books were paying attention to the ways in which Africans, African history, and culture were described in comparison to descriptions of Europeans, they would miss (or dismiss) the belittling treatment of the former and the excuses for the unjust, but somehow "understandable" laws and behaviors of the latter. Such was the paternalistic and denigrating perspective of a book recommended from ALA, not only during a time when African peoples throughout the African *continent* were engaged in struggles for independence from colonial powers, quite serious and sober Africans at that, but also at the very time when calls for the civil rights of African-*Americans* were increasing in volume and had, in fact, already been heard clearly within the profession for nearly two decades.

South Africa, the United Nations, and the origins of anti-apartheid sanctions

While a minority of U.S. librarians were working to educate their colleagues and fellow citizens on race relations in the late 1940s, during this same period the United Nations was being established. The spirit of internationalism in the quest for peace following World War II also found expression in librarianship. To further develop the story, however, one must pick up the thread of apartheid as it wove itself into the United Nations for this was the stage on which the South African apartheid regime's intransigence and the aspirations for independence among the world's colonized peoples faced off, and demands for sanctions began to take hold.

Strangely enough, it was none other than Jan Smuts, a future prime minister of South Africa, who drafted the preamble to the U.N. Charter taking special care to include *recognition of human rights*. During debates regarding the U.N. Charter, Smuts spoke eloquently for the inclusion of human rights in the document,

> I would suggest that the Charter contain at its very outset and in its preamble, a declaration of human rights and of the common faith which has sustained the Allied people in their bitter and prolonged struggle for the vindication of those rights and that faith.... Let us, in this new Charter of humanity, give expression to this faith in us, and thus proclaim to the world and to posterity ... that for us, behind the mortal struggle, was the vision of the ideal, the faith in justice and the resolve to vindicate the fundamental rights of man, and on that basis to found a better, freer world for the future [Shearar 13–14].

The fact that the source of this appeal for the recognition of human rights on an international level came from a proponent of white supremacy in his own country is simply one example of the schizophrenic mindset of proponents of apartheid—the Charter included recognition of the fundamental equality of all people, *of all races*. Jeremy Shearer, author of the book *Against the World: South Africa and Human Rights at the United Nations, 1945–1961*, notes, "It is hard to reconcile Smut's international persona with his domestic policy. His proposal for the Preamble was grounded in an appreciation of global politics rather than the situation at home" (18).

When Smuts delivered the Charter to the South African Parliament for ratification on February 6, 1946, he received little thanks for all his diplomatic work. Smuts, a member of the ruling Liberal Party, was confronted with outrage from the leader of the Nationalist Party, Dr. D. F. Malan:

> Before [white South Africa] is swept away by the non–European in this country, before its future is destroyed, there will be a fight to the death here in South Africa. There will be a blood bath. This [the U.N. Charter] is a rupture of world peace, not the other thing [14].

The next item on the U.N. agenda fared no better among white South Africans. This was the drawing up of what became the Universal Declaration of Human Rights, which was voted on and approved on December 10, 1948, by which time Dr. Malan was prime minister of South Africa and the National Party in power. Although involved in the debates initially, South Africa withdrew from the discussions and abstained from the final vote. What follows is an example of the mindset of the South African delegates. The first article of the draft declaration read,

> All human beings are born free and equal in dignity and rights. They are endowed by nature with reason and conscience, and should act towards one another in a spirit of brotherhood.

To which the South African delegation replied,

> This article is not a statement of fact. All men are not born free and equal, nor are they all endowed with reason and conscience. The article as a whole might well be deleted [64].

Another of the articles in the UN's Universal Declaration of Human Rights that the South African delegation had rejected was Article 11: *Freedom of movement; right to leave any country and to return to one's own*. South Africa was not about to release control of the movement of workers within the country (Shearar p.68). Pass laws, in existence since 1809, rigidly controlled, upon threat of arrest and imprisonment, the ability of black and colored South Africans to travel anywhere, and were much hated. Indeed, the intolerable pass laws were what generated decades of civil disobedience among South Africans leading to the international movement against apartheid.

In his autobiography *Let My People Go*, Albert Luthuli, president of the ANC from 1952 to 1967, described the history of antipass demonstrations that would flare up then subside in one geographic location, only to flare up and subside in another: 1913 in the Free State; 1919 in Johannesburg; 1930 in Durban; in 1952 the Defiance Campaign spread to many parts of the country; in 1956 in Pretoria women gathered in a massive all-races antipass demonstration, some traveling more than a thousand miles to attend (106–7).

Then came March 21, 1960, in Sharpeville where the Pan-African Congress (a breakaway group from the ANC) had organized an antipass demonstration. Residents of the community, a township outside Johannesburg in the mineral rich Transvaal, were instructed to leave their passes at home and walk to the police station to turn themselves in, having broken the law regulating blacks' mobility by not carrying their passes, the idea being to incapacitate police forces by overwhelming them and their jails with "criminals." The crowds were peaceful, the PAC had insisted that this was to be a nonviolent demonstration. At some point, police and military forces, who had been quietly amassing around the police station simply opened fire on the gathered crowds. The military brought in armored personnel carriers and airplanes. No one in the crowd was armed, except with rocks, which were lying on the ground. In the aftermath of the shooting, 69 people were dead, 180 injured—the dead and injured included women and children. Many were shot in the back as they turned to flee the armed police and soldiers.

The Sharpeville Massacre led to huge demonstrations throughout South Africa and prompted international condemnation of apartheid and the South African government. In the days that followed blacks refused to work, riots erupted, and Luthuli publicly burned his own passbook, and called on blacks to stay at home. The protests forced the police to suspend the pass system, but the government retaliated by banning the ANC and PAC, forcing both organizations underground. By the end of March, the government had declared a state of emergency and outlawed all anti-apartheid organizations. On April 1, 1960, the United Nations Security Council adopted Resolution 134 condemning the actions of the South African authorities, offering sympathy to the families of the victims, calling upon the South African government to abandon apartheid, and requesting that the U.N. Secretary-General Dag-Hammarskjöld meet with South African officials for discussions on how the country could be brought into alignment with the U.N. Charter of which it was a signatory. France and Great Britain abstained from the vote.

Luthuli called on the world to impose economic sanctions against South Africa. In Britain, the Trade Unions Council (TUC) and 20 municipalities supported the boycott, and in the aftermath of Sharpeville, the British Labour Party, Liberal Party, and the TUC called for a consumer boycott. Reaction in the U.S. was similar. The U.S. State Department issued a statement deploring the massacre, and in June 1960 the American Committee on Africa, along with trade unions and the NAACP urged the U.S. government to cease buying gold and other minerals from South Africa, called for a consumer boycott of South African goods, encouraged dockworkers to refuse to unload these goods, and tried to dissuade U.S. businesses from investing in South African concerns.

In the wake of Sharpeville, the U.N. delegation from Ghana proposed sanctions at the 15th General Assembly which was approved by a simply majority of votes, but fell short of the two-thirds required for adoption by the body, despite the fact that Ghana's motion was made in light of the massacre at Sharpeville in March. The following year a vote was made to expel South Africa from the U.N., which met the same fate as the previous year's vote on sanctions, but another urging member nations to persuade South Africa to abandon apartheid was adopted by a vote of 72 to 2, with 27 abstentions.

Sharpeville triggered another call for boycotts and sanctions—at the 1960 summer Olympic Games.

In 1960, the use of boycotts in the service of civil rights and the fight against racism was far from unknown. In the U.S., memories were still fresh of a boycott that led to significant changes in our own brand of racism—the Montgomery bus boycott of 1957–8. Those memories, combined with feelings of racial solidarity inspired by black athletes at the Olympic games, ensured that calls for economic sanctions and boycotts against apartheid would find sympathetic listeners. That summer, sports fans around the world watched on television, listened on radios, and read newspaper reports of Cassius Clay winning the gold medal in light-heavyweight boxing; of Wilma Rudolph, who as a child had suffered from polio, being acclaimed "the fastest woman in the world"; and of Ethiopian Abebe Bikila running the marathon barefoot to become the first black African to win a gold medal. No surprise then that when South Africa's representatives, all white athletes, arrived at the Olympics their presence generated global protest and condemnation. Outrage at this flagrant show of racist exclusion in an arena devoted to contests between the best athletes of all nations, led to the banning of South Africa from participation in Olympic games until the abolition of apartheid. From 1960 until 1992, white South African sports teams were isolated from all levels of competition in countries around the world.

The issue of segregation in South African sports, however, did not spring from the Olympic Games of 1960. In 1955, the year of the Freedom Charter, the cultural magazine *Drum* (based in Sophiatown, the heart of black culture until razed to the ground in the late '50s by police) published a special issue on sports, focusing on the question of interracial sports teams. Anti-apartheid militants considered sports, and the isolation of white South African teams in international contests, a potentially powerful pressure point against apartheid. As Rob Nixon describes the sports boycotts in his book *Homelands, Harlem and Hollywood: South African Culture and the World Beyond* (1994),

> From its first organized beginnings in the late 1950s, the sports ban registered some of the earliest and most sustained successes in popularizing the anti-apartheid cause abroad. In countries where the premier sports overlapped with those of South Africa—Britain, most of Africa, India, New Zealand, Pakistan, the Anglophone Caribbean, France, Ireland, Australia, Sri Lanka, Italy, and Argentina—outrage over competition against white South African teams gave vital impetus to local anti-apartheid movements [Nixon 132].

Author Nixon explains the absence of the United States from this list as being due to the fact that South Africa and the U.S. at that time had no common sports to compete within. However, even the eyes of American sports fans fastened on South Africa when, in the wake of the Sharpeville massacre, the 1960 summer Olympic games opened in Rome and the only South African athletes were white.

At the end of 1960, the World Council of Churches, meeting in Johannesburg, condemned apartheid, and the Nobel Peace Prize was given to Albert Luthuli. In his acceptance speech Luthuli called for sanctions.

> I shall not argue that the economic ostracism of South Africa is desirable from every point of view. But I have little doubt that it represents our only chance of a relatively peaceful transition from the present unacceptable type of rule to a system of government which gives us all our rightful voice. The alternative ... [is that] violence, rioting, and counter-rioting will become the order of the day. It can only deteriorate into disorder and ultimate disaster.
>
> The economic boycott of South Africa will entail undoubted hardship for Africans. We do not doubt that. But if it is a method which shortens the day of bloodshed, the suffering to us will be a price we are willing to pay. In any case, we suffer already, our children are undernourished, and on a small scale (so far) we die at the whim of a policeman [Hanlon 191].

On November 6, 1962, a UN resolution for the very first time called for diplomatic and economic sanctions against a member state—South Africa. The expulsion of the South Africa from the United Nations was considered for violating the UN Charter. The vote is telling of national attitudes toward racism: voting in favor of expulsion were 67 countries (African, Asian, and socialist countries); 16 against (Western states, members of the British Commonwealth, the U.S. and Japan); and 23 abstentions (Latin American countries and Nordic states). The resolution stated that the UN General Assembly,

> Requests Member States to take the following measures, separately or collectively, in conformity with the Charter, to bring about the abandonment of those policies [apartheid]:
> (a) Breaking off diplomatic relations with the Government of the Republic of South Africa or refraining from establishing such relations;
> (b) Closing their ports to all vessels flying the South African flag;
> (c) Enacting legislation prohibiting their ships from entering South African ports;
> (d) Boycotting all South African goods and refraining from exporting goods, including all arms and ammunition, to South Africa;
> (e) Refusing landing and passage facilities to all aircraft belonging to the Government and companies registered under the laws of South Africa [Mezerik 42].

Despite worldwide awareness and increasing condemnation of apartheid, white South Africa continued to resist change and used increasingly violent means to enforce apartheid. In 1964, a special committee of the United Nations charged to investigate apartheid policies and practices, released a report documenting, among other things, the use of torture against political prisoners. Here is one excerpt from the report:

> They put a wet sack round his head and tied the cords at this neck till he blacked out. After reviving him, they made him stand on one leg, holding a stone above his head while they stuck pins into his raised leg. The soles of his feet were then beaten with batons, and electrodes were placed on the toes with the current flowing. Finally they held him by the ankles out of a window 40 feet above the street in trying to get a confession [*Africa* 224–5].

With reports of such atrocities raising the consciousness of people around the globe, including the U.S. public, demands for sanctions increased. In 1964 the U.S. State Department threatened to revoke Ford Motor Company's export license should it export four-wheel-drive vehicles to South Africa for military and police use. And in 1965, from the worlds of music, literature, film, theater and education, came more support for the anti-apartheid movement. The American Committee on Africa released a statement entitled "we say NO to apartheid—a Declaration of American Artists" which read, in part,

> Let it be known that we the following, do pledge ourselves to do all within our power—
> ARTISTS AND SCULPTORS...
> *not to allow our work to be displayed in any South African exhibition;*
> NOVELISTS, POETS, AND ESSAYISTS...not to permit our books to be published in South Africa;
> PLAYWRIGHTS...not to permit performances of our plays in South Africa;
> COMPOSERS, CONDUCTORS, AND MUSICIANS...not to conduct or perform music in South Africa, or to allow performances of our works there;
> FILM PRODUCERS...to prevent the showing of our films in the Republic of South Africa [American].

The pledge was signed by luminaries from all those fields. Among signers were Joan Baez, Harry Belafonte, Leonard Bernstein, Dave Brubeck, Dianne Carroll, Sammy Davis, Jr., Henry Fonda, Julie Harris, Arthur Miller, Ashley Montagu, Odetta, Sidney Poitier, Jerome Robbins, Paul Robeson, Pete Seeger, Nina Simone, Ed Sullivan, Eli Wallach, and more.

An interesting side story, brought to mind because of the presence on the list of television show host Ed Sullivan, is the following. In Rob Nixon's book about sanctions is a chapter entitled "The Devil in the Black Box." The "devil" being ... television! Television was basically outlawed in South Africa until 1976, by which date the country "had become TV's final frontier in the industrialized world." Nixon writes that in a speech on March 9, 1960, "Apartheid's chief architect Prime Minister Hendrik Verwoerd, urged that TV be regarded with the same circumspection as poison gas and the atom bomb" (Nixon 45). Such was the state of the "free flow of information" in South Africa.

Ostracizing apartheid—IFLA and ALA become involved

Writing candidly in the journal *Libri* in 1954, the great librarian S. R. Ranganathan, then professor of library science at the University of Delhi, shared his thoughts on the International Federation of Library Associations (IFLA). The Federation was founded in 1929 at a meeting in Rome, attended by 1,400 librarians who, according to an editorial in the December 15 issue of *Library Journal*, "were received by the Pope, the King and the Duce [Mussolini]" (Editorial 1929, 1028). IFLA's warm welcome from authoritarian dignitaries suggests a potential alliance between some librarians and fasicism. But that was long before Ranganathan's involvement in IFLA. And in 1954 one aspect of this international organization especially claimed his attention—its Eurocentrism.

> Since 1948, I have attended several meetings of the IFLA. They have been all courtesy. But in their proposals and action, the old view that "international" in IFLA is exhausted by Western Europe and Northern America persists. It may be unconscious and even unmeant on their part. But to us outsiders, it is as clear as daylight in the tropics [Ranganathan 1954, 183].

A generation later, IFLA evidenced a similar narrowness of perspective with regard to the word "integration" when the matter of apartheid showed up at its doorstep as it had to the word "international" in Ranganathan's day.

It was through IFLA that anti-apartheid activism entered into ALA, which is not to say that IFLA acted in solidarity with the movement, just that it was the first stage on which apartheid appeared within librarianship. It is fitting that this section opens with the words of Ranganathan, because of the immeasurable role his countryman, Mahatma Gandhi, played in developing the nonviolent tactics used by both the anti-apartheid and civil rights movements. In this case, the tactic of ostracism was used to powerful effect in galvanizing the anti-apartheid movement within librarianship.

Ostracism is the informal or formal exclusion or banishment of an individual or group from society or social entity. We have already seen one early use of ostracism by ALA when in 1936 it excluded from its list of potential conference sites any venue practicing Jim Crow segregation. Several state library associations, however, insisted on maintaining segregated status. Indeed, in several states black librarians established their own associations in the 1930s and '40s because that was their only option for engaging with colleagues professionally (*Handbook* 51–82). In 1954, civil rights activists within the Association were successful in getting ALA to go on record as stating that there should be only a *single* library association in each state in an effort to *force* integration. The tactic worked in a few states, and in 1956 ALA held the first completely desegregated conference in Florida in Miami Beach. However, several whites-only state associations—Alabama, Georgia, Louisiana, and Mississippi—refused to integrate, and ALA did nothing more to pressure change. Throughout the late '50s and early '60s, individual librarians persisted in bringing racism to the attention of the Association, and civil rights activists began to use libraries as sites of nonviolent protest against Jim Crow practices.

The *Handbook of Black Librarianship*, 2nd edition, includes a timeline from which can be culled a sketch of activism in ALA around segregation. In 1960, Rice Estes questioned ALA on its position regarding race and libraries. In 1961, Annette Hoage Phinazee demanded an accounting from ALA on racism and American libraries, resulting in a report published in 1963 entitled *Access to Public Libraries*. The report documented patterns of discrimination throughout the nation's libraries. Exasperated with the Association's foot-dragging complacency in the face of such clearly documented discrimination, in 1964 E. J. Josey proposed a resolution to the ALA membership meeting that prohibited ALA staff and officers from attending the meetings of segregated state associations. This action finally brought an end to segregation in ALA's state affiliates. Segregation in libraries themselves was dealt a legal blow when in 1966 the U.S. Supreme Court ruled in *Brown v Louisiana* that "persons could not be punished for using a library peacefully to protest the illegal segregation of the library itself" (*Handbook* 9).

Over the course of this history of librarians coming to terms with the injustices and violence of racism, there have been those who argue that ostracism, boycotts, sanctions of this sort were not an appropriate activity for ALA. During the 1936 debates, one librarian (most likely a white librarian) put forward a when-in-Rome-do-as-the-Romans-do argument,

> Librarians are supposed to be adaptable. It is my feeling that the customs of any country, community, or home should be honored and respected by a guest of that country, community or home. It is extremely unfortunate and very bad politics to propose a boycott of Southern cities for A.L.A. conferences. The South may need the A.L.A. but not more than the A.L.A. needs the South [Cunningham 515].

A 1961 editorial entitled "ALA and the Segregation Issue" appearing in *ALA Bulletin* argued, "The Association exists to further the development of libraries, not to regulate the manner in which they are operated" (Editorial 1961, 485).

Still later, in 1975, Herman Liebaers, transitioning from presidency of IFLA to chief advisor to the Belgian king, gave an interview to Shirley Elder, reporter for *American Libraries*. Asked about UNESCO sanctions against IFLA for refusing to expel South African institutional members engaged in apartheid, Liebaers said,

> I can assure you that 99 percent of the members of IFLA are against apartheid ... but I was opposed to the UNESCO resolution [requiring the expulsion of apartheid institutions] ... for the very simple reason that if there is some liberal literature still coming into that country, if there is still literature antagonizing to the official government, it is through us [Elder 76].

Liebaers' perspective, that IFLA was doing a good deed in sending "liberal literature" to apartheid South Africa, a nation where librarians directly engaged in enforcing censorship laws, turns up again in the "book boycott" debate.

Such was the spectrum of arguments opposed to acts of solidarity on behalf of civil rights in the U.S. and in South Africa. Each foreshadows the claim that would be made in 1989 by the AAP Report that sanctions calling for the prohibition of shipments of books to South Africa were short-sighted, counter-productive, and harmful to the very people the sanctions were intended to help. We turn now to the path via which librarianship entered into the anti-apartheid movement.

Robert Doyle, director of ALA's Library/Book Fellows Program and staff liaison to the International Relations Committee, compiled a fact sheet on South Africa, which consisted of two timelines describing actions taken by ALA and IFLA on matters regarding apartheid. The timeline begins in 1970 with UNESCO's adoption of a resolution regarding apartheid and colonialism in which the United Nations Educational, Scientific and Cultural Organization (UNESCO) began investigations into which of its members maintained relations with racist organizations and government agencies, especially those in southern Africa.

At its meetings in Paris in the fall of 1971, UNESCO's Executive Board reviewed the investigations and decided to suspend relations with any organization that had not responded to its questions and requests for information. The International Federation of Library Associations (IFLA) was in this category, not having responded satisfactorily with assurances that no IFLA members engaged in racial discrimination. The IFLA was one of 41 other international UNESCO members receiving notices that, until assurances were made, membership from UNESCO was suspended (267 members had responded satisfactorily to UNESCO's requests and so there was no disruption of relations between them).

The International Federation valued membership in UNESCO for several reasons, including a financial one: IFLA enjoyed consultative status in UNESCO, which meant that anytime UNESCO discussed library matters, IFLA was invited to participate. The UNESCO was also the source of millions of dollars for various IFLA projects and operational expenses.

President Herman Liebaers reported in the February 1972 issue of "IFLA News" that IFLA's board believed that UNESCO's investigating committee had been "unfair to IFLA" but it was reviewing its relations with the South African Library Association (Liebaers 1972a, 1). The next issue of "IFLA News" contained the text of Liebaers' letter on the matter informing UNESCO Director-General that,

> On the grounds of the information which we were able to collect, we have decided to break off relations with the South African Library Association.
> As to our associate members: the State Library in Pretoria, the University Library in Cape Town and the South African Library in Cape Town ... information which they have given us ... as well as information gathered from other sources have convinced us that each of these institutions "in spite of complying with the law on apartheid, continues its previous work among all races without any significant and harmful change in that work"....
> Consequently we have not deemed it necessary to take measures to break off relations with one or other of these institutions [Liebaers 1972b, 1].

As it turned out, information gathered regarding these three institutional IFLA members' involvement in racial discrimination was inadequate, and in 1973 UNESCO asked once more for assurances regarding member cooperation with apartheid laws (International 1973, 3). The following year voting rights for the three South African institutional members were removed, only to be reinstated in 1977 (Doyle 6). For *eighteen years* following UNESCO's first request to IFLA regarding these matters, IFLA continued to admit institutional members from South Africa, only to be requested to investigate those members' participation in apartheid, at which IFLA would engage in yet another study. In a 2008 article in *IFLA Journal*, Al Kagan describes how a group of mainly African, European, and U.S. IFLA members "continued the struggle to get the IFLA officers and staff to implement the 1985 resolution," which called for the expulsion of South African apartheid institutions from the organization.

> The group would assemble every year; make an appointment with the IFLA President and/or Vice-President, and demand implementation. Instead, the official officers would avoid implementation by commissioning various surveys and studies. In the end, apartheid was overthrown without any implementation of the resolution [Kagan 2008, 231].

Interesting to note that during this period, the Secretary-General of IFLA from 1971 to 1987 was Margreet Wijnstroom of the Netherlands, the country from which descended the white Afrikaner population of South Africa, and which from the days of the Dutch East India Company had substantial, vital, economic relations with South Africa. The headquarters of IFLA is also in the Netherlands, in The Hague.

To their credit both Ms. Wijnstroom and Herman Liebaers (IFLA president from 1969 to 1974) both refused, while on visits to South Africa in 1967 and 1968, respectively, to meet with Herman De Vleeschauwer who was director-general of libraries in Pretoria. Vleeschauwer, a Nazi collaborator during World War II, was tried for war crimes in 1945 and condemned to death *in abstentia* as he was in hiding. When the Nationalist Party came to power in 1948, Vleeschauwer sought entry and employment under a false identity, and was welcomed into South African academia with an appointment at the University of Pretoria's Merensky Library. Within the climate of the National Party, ideologically allied with Nazism, it became unnecessary for Vleeschauwer to maintain his false identity, and he managed to control complaints regarding his background by accusing anyone who might raise the matter of being a communist. Such accusations could land a person in prison, if not worse, in South Africa (Dick).

Liebaers had been a student of Vleeschauwer's and wanted nothing to do with the war criminal. Wijnstroom refused to meet him on similar grounds, and for her refusal was taken to a police station and questioned about the matter. Liebaers writes, "she declared that she had Belgian friends, who suffered under the German occupation and she was immediately released" (Liebaers 2002, 8). Despite these leaders' personal knowledge that *librarianship in South Africa harbored a Nazi war criminal*, IFLA continued to stall when it came to severing ties with South African institutional members. Excuses to refrain from doing so included the notion that IFLA was a professional group, not a political one, and that isolating its South African members would not achieve the intended purpose of ending apartheid. Of course, UNESCO and anti-apartheid activists had a different opinion of the matter.

The suspension of IFLA from membership in UNESCO prompted ALA in 1972 to adopt a new policy regarding affiliations with organizations "which violate its [ALA's] principles and commitment to human rights and social justice, as set forth in ALA's policies, procedures and positions statements and the Universal Declaration of Human Rights" (Doyle 1).

In the "Intellectual Freedom" column of *American Libraries*' September 1975 issue, is a report on new measures taken by the South African government in censoring books, journals, magazines, newspapers, films and music produced within the country and coming from abroad. Merrill Proudfoot, professor of philosophy at Park College in Kansas City, had been in South Africa teaching and was keeping abreast of developments there regarding censorship. "*Jacobsen's Index of Objectionable Literature*," writes Proudfoot,

> ... which has kept South African librarians out of trouble by its careful reporting of the 15,000 titles banned by the South African government over the past 12 years, seems likely to accrue entries at an even faster rate under new censorship legislation that went into effect recently [Proudfoot 497].

He goes on to note that 190 censors had been appointed to both *initiate* and process complaints against publications. He ends the article by describing the "law most irksome to librarians," which required them, every time the government issued a ban on a person, to purge all mention of that person from library collections.

Opposition to apartheid among ALA members developed along with the rest of the public, as violence in South Africa rose in the late 1970s: the Soweto uprising and its brutal suppression by police; the arrest, torture and death in prison of Steve Biko a popular leader of the South African Student Organization; the expulsion from South Africa of journalist Donald Woods whose photographs of Biko's battered body enraged anti-apartheid activist worldwide, to mention just a few. All these incidents, and more, added fuel to the determination of the anti-apartheid movement, and in 1978 Council passed a resolution stating that ALA

> ... condemns the abridgement of free expression and urges President Carter and the Congress to impose sanctions against South Africa and instructs the ALA delegation to the International Federation of Library Associations and Institutions (IFLA) to introduce to that body a resolution censuring South Africa for violation of human rights [Doyle 1].

In 1979, the South African Library Association, succumbing to these pressures, announced its dissolution, to be followed on January 1, 1980, by the establishment of the South African Institute for Librarianship and Information Science, which was to have "membership open to library and information workers regardless of their colour, race, or creed" (South 1980, 183).

Over the course of the next decade, ALA's activity on apartheid grew to the point where, in 1985, the Association divested its endowment funds of all holdings of companies that operated in South Africa. ALA had arrived as a full-fledged member of the anti-apartheid movement—or, more accurately, some *sectors* of ALA were 100 percent on board the anti-apartheid train. Not only were resolutions forthcoming from ALA, but, like their predecessors in the 1940s, librarians recommended books about apartheid and compiled bibliographies and film guides; Sandy Berman informed readers of *American Libraries* that the Library of Congress did not recognize "apartheid" as a subject heading; and libraries abided by new municipal regulations that required businesses to certify that they had no holdings in South Africa. And, it is here, in discussions about what companies libraries could or couldn't do business with that one finds the genesis of the "book boycott" debate.

The "book boycott"—solidarity or censorship?

Although it should go without saying, librarianship does not exist outside the context of the economy, the politics, the social mores, and the times of the nation within which it functions. Librarians in South Africa tolerated a Nazi war criminal among their leadership, tossed banned books onto the flames, maintained segregated library facilities and services, and followed the rules of a system of white supremacy. Librarians in the cataloging department of the Library of Congress did not establish "apartheid" as a subject heading, for the same reason that they maintained as a subject heading "the patently offensive MAMMIES deriv[ing] from slave-*owners* parlance" (Berman 77). The LC catalogers were simply doing their jobs, following established rules, not looking out at the world around them to see if any changes might be needed, any additions or corrections made.

A librarian in the U.S. could be wholeheartedly supportive of anti-apartheid boycotts and sanctions, but what happened if her job necessitated a trip to the National Library in Pretoria? What if new municipal ordinances required that the Baker & Taylor contract had to be cancelled because its parent company had operations in South Africa? How should one deal with an interlibrary loan request from the library of the De Beers Corporation? These were the sorts of questions confronting librarians in the 1980s, and how one answered placed that person in one of three general "camps" regarding the anti-apartheid movement: supporters of full sanctions, advocates of partial sanctions, opponents of sanctions. Sanctions and boycotts took a variety of forms: consumer boycotts, trade embargoes, stock divestment, and sports, academic and cultural boycotts. Additionally, in the late '80s, the ANC and mass democratic movement (MDM, a coalition of anti-apartheid organization) began to call for modifications of the cultural boycotts then in place. This call ended up dividing anti-apartheid activists within librarianship, and it is to this debate we now turn.

In 1987, Penguin published *The Sanctions Handbook*. Written by Joseph Hanlon and Roger Omond, the book provided readers the opportunity to grapple with arguments for and against sanctions from multiple perspectives. The book includes chapters such as "Blacks Against Sanctions" and "Whites Against Sanctions." Arguments of those in favor and opposed in Britain, and those in favor and opposed in the United States. Information was provided on the types of sanctions and their possible impacts on jobs, trade, education. The *Handbook* included a "Directory of Sanctions" 65-pages long, with detailed information regarding South Africa's imports, exports, and the quantity of materials exchanged with all their trading partners.

The initial impetus behind the need for such extensive information came in 1984 when Archbishop Desmond Tutu was given the Nobel Peace Prize, and when Jesse Jackson raised the issue of South Africa during the presidential debates. In Tutu's acceptance speech of the Nobel Prize, he gave the South African government a timeline by which it had to take steps toward ending apartheid. If the timeline was not met, Tutu would call for worldwide sanctions against the apartheid regime. He gave the government one year to meet this demand, and when December 1985 passed without any change, in April 1986 Tutu called on the people of the world to exert sanctions and boycotts as nonviolent pressure on the intransigent government. That year, the U.S. Congress overrode a presidential veto of sanctions legislation, and communities across the country passed municipal codes prohibiting any public agency from engaging in business relations with any entity connected to South Africa. Within ALA, steps to divest of South African holdings began in 1985, and by 1986 growing support of sanctions and municipal prohibitions were met with both enthusiastic support and outraged condemnation.

San Francisco Public Library was faced with severing its contracts with Baker & Taylor whose parent company W. R. Grace had South African operations. Baker & Taylor failed to send SFPL the affidavit verifying its compliance with the sanctions law, and so SFPL prepared to switch purchases over to Brodart and Yankee Book Peddler. At the same time, Baker & Taylor announced that it *did* comply with a similar ordinance in Chicago. These libraries together did $2.5 million in book purchases and periodical subscriptions with Baker & Taylor (Grace 741).

Just as library vendors were beginning to feel pressure from libraries working to comply with economic sanctions, an op-ed piece in the *New York Times* revealed that it was the CIA who tipped off South African authorities to where Nelson Mandela could be found, resulting in his capture on August 5, 1962, and subsequent 28-year imprisonment. In "A Loophole in U.S. Sanctions Against Pretoria," Andrew Cockburn informed readers that the sanctions legislation passed by Congress, overriding President Reagan's veto, contained a serious loophole—it allowed U.S. intelligence agencies to continue long-standing collaboration with apartheid agencies, specifically with South African armed forces. Regarding Mandela's capture, Cockburn wrote "…Mr. Mandela was traveling to meet a C.I.A. officer who was working out of the United States Consulate in Durban, the capital of Natal. Instead of attending the meeting, the C.I.A. man told the police exactly where and when the most hunted man in South Africa would be found." Cockburn ends his op-ed piece noting revelations during the summer of 1986 of the "assistance being rendered in the cause of white supremacy by the National Security Agency"—the NSA was monitoring communications of the ANC and supplying information to South African authorities whenever requested (Cockburn A19). For many librarians, this story of long-standing and ongoing U.S. complicity with apartheid added to their determination to support the sanctions movement.

Again, there were those in librarianship who did not wish to participate in anti-apartheid movement sanctions. In 1987, the public library director in Houston, Texas, requested an exemption from that city's code on the grounds that compliance with the ordinance would deprive the library of essential goods and services. The library had joined its request to another by the Houston zoo claiming that it could only purchase an antivenin needed at the zoo from South Africa (Houston 889).

The controversy over whether or not libraries should comply with municipal anti-apartheid laws came to ALA at its 1987 annual conference in New Orleans when a resolution seeking to put ALA on record as opposing such ordinances was presented at a membership meeting. The resolution, entitled Access/South Africa, was endorsed by the Intellectual Freedom Round Table Executive Board and stated that

> … such laws and ordinances result in the inability of libraries to purchase a diversity of materials … depriving citizens of their right to a full range of viewpoints and information … and also puts libraries in conflict with the ALA resolution "Abridgement of Human Rights in South Africa," which urges American libraries "…to develop collections on South Africa that reflect the full diversity of viewpoints and experience in the at country,"
>
> THEREFORE, BE IT RESOLVED, That the ALA and its members reaffirm that free access to information is pivotal in the individual's freedom of choice, and that access to materials, information and ideas must not be abridged because of the social or political ideologies of the creators of such materials or the geographic origin of their source … [Resolution].

The resolution also called on ALA and its members to reaffirm commitments to "the free flow of information among countries" and to "work with the vendor community and other interested parties to oppose and challenge any restrictions." The resolution claimed that such "restrictions violate the First Amendment to the U.S. Constitution," recommended that "the imposition of penalties upon vendors exercising their First Amendment rights to disseminate information is to be challenged whenever and wherever it occurs," and ended by resolving "that the ALA request the Freedom to Read Foundation to be alert to the appropriate opportunities to challenge the constitutionality of such laws and ordinances as affect access to information" (*ibid.*).

Despite coming from the Executive Board of the Intellectual Freedom Round Table, the resolution was not passed at the membership meeting following several statements in opposition. Herbert Biblo argued that the resolution went "around the back door …

to undermine the struggle for human rights in South Africa." And former ALA President E.J. Josey called it "a racist resolution" on the grounds that it was "more of a pro–South Africa resolution" than one concerning the First Amendment and access to information (Members 550).

The Access/South Africa resolution voiced two basic objections to municipal ordinances. First, sanctions interfered with the "free flow of information," depriving library users in both the U.S. and in South Africa of a "full range of information and perspectives." Second, ordinances that interfered with business-customer relationships were claimed to violate the First Amendment on the grounds that *choice* of what to buy and who to buy it from would be constrained.

Concerning the first objection, the entire *purpose* of sanctions is to interfere with the free flow of business-as-usual, whether flows be of diamonds or data, books or bombs. Members of the anti-apartheid movement were willing to forego the benefits of any such flows in exchange for the resulting pressure on the entire apartheid infrastructure. Similarly, supporters of anti-apartheid sanctions outside South Africa, were equally ready to sacrifice any benefits accruing from the severe violence of apartheid—brides-to-be willing to boycott South African diamonds in their engagement rings and wedding bands; database vendors willing to stop the flow of data to South Africa's security forces.

The situation of Baker & Taylor offers an excellent lens through which to analyze the second objection, that the ordinances violated vendors' First Amendment rights.

If W.R. Grace's holdings in South Africa prohibited continued relations with Baker & Taylor, clearly a library could partner with a different vendor, one without any ties to apartheid. Such a change in vendors might be onerous, might not be *convenient*, but moral decisions generally are made *without regard to convenience*. Additionally, the First Amendment concerns freedom of expression and of the press, *not* the "freedom to choose" where to shop. The First Amendment arose at a time and within a society concerned with the protection of thinking citizens, *not* of consumers. Although countless people today might believe and behave as if choosing between brands of toilet paper, breakfast cereal, running shoes, and automobiles constitutes an act of freedom on par with the freedom of speech, it is simply not true. The ideology of consumption thus generates arguments like the one we find in the Access/South Africa resolution. In the midst of a political movement struggling on behalf of the *entire range* of human rights, it is certainly odd/callous/hypocritical/self-serving to argue that a business relationship with elements of an oppressor regime trumps solidarity with the oppressed. Nothing short of arrogant disregard for the suffering of others can explain the insistence of librarians in the U.S. that Baker & Taylor's right to do business in South Africa outweighs the rights of *all* South Africans to vote, to travel, to express their thoughts freely. Advocacy for the rights of businesses over those of human beings is surely what moved Josey to characterize outright the Access/South Africa resolution as racist.

With the defeat of Access/South Africa, ALA remained committed to anti-apartheid sanctions. Of course, opponents to sanctions also remained steadfast. The argument that sanctions abridged the First Amendment rights of library vendors would not be used again, however, as shall be seen when we finally look at the AAP's report.

At this time an important change was occurring: the anti-apartheid movement was growing, gaining strength and influence, and the economic impacts of sanctions were being felt by the apartheid regime. In this atmosphere of expansion and increasing power, the African National Congress and the Mass Democratic Movement (the multiracial coalition of anti-apartheid organizations) decided that cultural and academic sanctions should be modified. Modifications were necessary to strengthen relationships between anti-apartheid groups within South Africa and their supporters worldwide.

On May 28, 1989, the ANC released a statement explaining the reasons behind modifications in sanctions:

> In the process of struggle, the people of South Africa have evolved a democratic culture of liberation, which expresses their social and political aspirations. This culture, though distinctly South African, is infused with an internationalist, humanist spirit that draws upon the best of the cultural heritage of all the population groups of our country and that of the rest of humanity. It encompasses the artistic, intellectual and material aspects of culture.
>
> In order to grow and develop this emergent culture of liberation needs to interact with, and be exposed to, the progressive intellectual and cultural currents in the rest of the world [African].

Economic sanctions were to remain in place, but recognizing that a new, democratic South Africa would need support and inspiration from already existing democracies, the cultural boycott was revised to allow for exchanges between anti-apartheid individuals and groups, while maintaining prohibitions on all relations with apartheid supporters, both individuals and institutions. Academic and library communities in the U.S. responded to the ANC's call for modified sanctions with guidelines to assist their members' continued support of the movement.

In June 1989, SRRT discussed and adopted a document entitled "Guidelines for Librarians Interacting with South Africa." The Guidelines, based on a similar document originating in the Archives-Libraries Committee of the African Studies Association in the U.S., were shared widely with other units of ALA for discussion. In January 1990, at the midwinter meeting, the Guidelines were formally approved by the Association of College and Research Libraries, the Black Caucus, the International Relations Committee, and International Relations Round Table.

The Guidelines consisted of six sections. The first section on Guiding Principles reiterated opposition to apartheid; expressed dedication to the highest levels of library service and values; recognized social responsibilities; restated commitment to the library's community; re-emphasized the necessity of free and full access to information; and ended with the statement that "Libraries do not exist in isolation from the dominant trends and conflicts in the world arena" (Guidelines 7–9). The second section with the heading "The Issue" provided (1) a context for the need of the Guidelines, namely the international sanctions movement to isolate apartheid; (2) the ANC's modifications of the boycott and sanctions; (3) recognition that the emerging nonracial democracy in South Africa required a two-way free flow of information for continued development; (4) an emphasis on the fact that the apartheid regime continued to impair the free flow of information via censorship and propaganda; and (5) a statement that librarians "must strive to balance our methods to promote the free flow of information with work activities that are morally and politically responsible" (*ibid.*).

The next four sections contained recommendations: General Recommendations; Recommendations for Collection Development, Reference Service and Outreach; Recommendations Regarding Professional Travel to South Africa; and Recommendations for Action. The following are a sampling of the recommendations:

3.1 Librarians should encourage discussion and debate on the South African situation.
3.3 Librarians are encouraged to work within the political process to isolate the South African Government and all apartheid institutions.
3.4 Librarians are encouraged to be of service to the South African mass democratic movement in the context of their professional work.
4.1 We recognize the need to build balanced collections relating to South Africa. Because the South African Government maintains a large worldwide program to distribute free pro-apartheid materials to libraries and other institutions, librarians are especially encouraged to aggressively acquire and publicize counter materials, especially those published by the mass democratic and liberation movements.
5.1 Librarians should only travel to South Africa at the invitation of anti-apartheid groups and institutions.
5.2 Talks and seminars at, or contractual relationships with apartheid institutions should not be undertaken.
6.1 Librarians and library associations are encouraged to promote legal and other humanitarian assistance to South African librarians and library workers who suffer the consequences of their actions in opposing apartheid [Guidelines 1–2].

Simultaneously with developments within the ANC and MDM that led to the Guidelines, the Board of Directors of the Association of American Publishers was holding discussions of its own. In January 1988, AAP directors passed a resolution opposing "boycotts of books and other informational and educational materials to any country" and "pressures being applied by some cities, school boards and educational institutions to force book publishers to boycott South Africa" (*AAP*). In the spring of 1989, publishers joined forces with librarians, in the persons of Lisa Drew and Robert Wedgeworth, respectively, on a mission to see firsthand the impact of the "book boycott" in South Africa. Drew, vice-president and senior editor at William Morrow and Company, and Wedgeworth, dean of the School of Library Service at Columbia University and former executive director of ALA, returned from their visit in late–May and issued a report entitled "The Starvation of Young Black Minds: The Effect of Book Boycotts in South Africa." AAP released its report on the same day that Congressman Owens stood on the floor of Congress to offer premature congratulations to ALA on the passage of the Guidelines.

The fundamental difference between the recommendations of the Guidelines and those of the AAP report was that the former adhered to the ANC's call for continued isolation of apartheid and modifications to sanctions impacting members of the anti-apartheid movement, while the AAP recommended the dropping of all sanctions regarding books, journals, databases, and other information *regardless* of the allegiance of the recipient to apartheid laws and practices. The AAP report, in fact, cherry-picked from the ANC's May 1989 statement on the cultural and academic boycott one paragraph in support of their position, while the Guidelines reflected the entirety of both the spirit and letter of the statement. The paragraph from the ANC statement used by the AAP to support their call for a complete cessation to sanctions on book and information reads as follows:

> 2.6. The suppression and circumscription of the inflow of information, cultural products and artifacts from outside South Africa is an important weapon in the arsenal of the oppressor regime, which it wields to consolidate its power vis-à-vis the oppressed and exploited majority. The NLM [National Liberation Movement] and the MDM support the inflow of progressive cultural products, artifacts and ideas into our country so that these become readily accessible to the widest sections of our people. We support and encourage the dissemination of all cultural products, artifacts and ideas that enhance the struggle for democracy and promote democratic, humanist values as opposed to the oppressive, retrograde values and misanthropic ideas. This applies to books, newspapers, journals, magazines, video, film and sound recordings manufactured and produced outside South Africa [Position].

What the AAP report failed to note was an important preceding paragraph that *qualified* 2.6, namely,

> 2.1 The Cultural and Academic Boycott of *Apartheid* South Africa (i.e. those bodies, institutions, cultural workers and their product that promote, defend and give aid and comfort to the system of White minority domination) *must consistently and continuously be strengthened* as part of our overall strategy for the isolation of the Apartheid regime [emphasis added].
>
> No cultural workers, artists, sportspersons or academics should be permitted to travel to South Africa to perform or to impart their services and expertise, save and except in those instances where such travel is clearly in furtherance of the national democratic struggle or any of its objectives [*ibid.*].

Anyone familiar with the Lusaka statement in its entirety would know the AAP had taken paragraph 2.6 out of context to support its recommendations. Later on when it became clear that Wedgeworth and Drew were claiming ANC support for their mission and report recommendations, members of the Progressive Librarians Guild contacted the ANC directly for a statement clarifying their position.

Drew had cited a June 4, 1990, letter from the Congress of South African Writers (COSAW), a member of the Mass Democratic Movement, as evidence that the AAP recommendations were in alignment with the modifications made in Lusaka in 1989. After expressing endorsement of the ANC's position, and calling for donations of books to "our libraries" (meaning those within the anti-apartheid movement), the COSAW letter states,

> There is also the general misconception that the cultural boycott encompasses sanctions on books. The position of the Department of Arts and Culture (ANC), which is supported by a range of progressive organizations in South Africa, is that books must be made available to *progressive* organizations in order to enrich and strengthen democratic culture [Congress; emphasis added].

"Progressive organizations" was another way to reference, in a positive manner, *antiapartheid* organizations. However, the AAP report's recommendation was to "urge its members and other publishers to discontinue the boycott of books and other educational materials for South Africa" (*Starvation* 10). The unqualified reference to "South Africa" encompassed *all* of that country—apartheid and anti-apartheid—certainly not in keeping with either COSAW's position or the ANC's.

In a letter responding to the Progressive Librarians Guild's request for clarification, Juniad Ahmed, general secretary of COSAW, wrote on June 20, 1990, "we firmly uphold the [ANC's] culture boycott policy.... [W]hen appealing for support to strengthen the progressive democratic culture in South Africa, we are in no way advancing the breakdown of this policy." After stating that any actions to lift sanctions could only be done in consultation with the MDM, Ahmed concluded, "We would also like to state that COSAW is in no way aware of the AAP mission, report or recommendations, or of the sponsors thereof" (Congress).

If we look at what the differing recommendations would mean in the case of Baker & Taylor, as far as the Guidelines were concerned the company would continue to be boycotted as long as W. R. Grace did business with the apartheid regime. The AAP, however, would exclude Baker & Taylor from sanctions because it bought and sold *books*. In addition to its call for normalization of publishers' business dealings with all of South Africa, the AAP report encouraged "charitable donations" to the victims of apartheid. This later suggestion led one South African librarian, Vincent Kolbe, in a letter dated early June 1990 to Al Kagan and John Bruce Howell, to express his anger,

> Sections of the Wedgeworth/Drew report read like a Department of Foreign Affairs publication, soft peddling apartheid for foreign investors. The sham concern for young black minds is obnoxious. Black youth in South Africa are some of the most clued up people in the country. They are not thirsting for AAP publications. They want freedom and the power to determine their own future; AND THEY are close to achieving it [Kolbe 2].

Within ALA both the Guidelines and the AAP report generated considerable discussion—in public, in private, at committee meetings and in an open hearing sponsored by the International Relations Committee. SRRT sent the Guidelines to Council for consideration, and Council decided to refer them to the Intellectual Freedom Committee and the International Relations Committee with the expectation that both committees would make recommendations for further action at the 1990 annual conference.

Possibly the most detailed documentation of the debate between the advocates of the two positions is to be found in the Minutes of the Intellectual Freedom Committee held during the 1990 midwinter meeting (8–10, 17–18, 22–26). Corinne Nyquist, representing SRRT, was invited to speak with the IFC members regarding a possible IFC endorsement of the Guidelines. Some members of the IFC had issues with one particular point in the Guidelines: "2.3 We note that the free flow of information to and from the mass democratic organizations and anti-apartheid institutions in South Africa is of benefit to the evolution of South African democracy."

Gordon Conable, IFC chair, wanted clarification on the point as to whether or not "SRRT is recommending a blanket retraction of sanctions on the free flow of information or a partial one" (*Intellectual* 9). Nyquist agreed the section supported a partial retraction and noted that SRRT was seeking IFC endorsement of the entire set of Guidelines, not sections of it. Pointing out past precedent for SRRT's position, Zoia Horn, another guest at the meeting and former IRC member and chair, noted that ALA policy still had language dating to the civil rights movement era that prohibited the provision of materials to racist organizations.

Robert Croneberger, IFC member, summed up the main sticking point which made IFC endorsement problematic by noting that "human rights issues seem to be lined up on one side while the intellectual freedom issues are lined up on the other side." He concluded that "If the segment [2.3] on free flow of information is intended to express limitations, then the Committee simply is not able to accept the document" (*ibid.*).

In a follow-up discussion, at which Nyquist was not present, the committee members recognized that an impasse had been reached. Citing previous discussions, including that of the Access/South Africa resolution in 1988, Croneberger expressed the dilemma succinctly,

> ...one of the main reasons the discussion has not moved forward in the last four years is that the people who have been rejecting the IFC proposals have done so not because they believe intellectual freedom principles are diminished in this debate, but rather because the IFC is asking them to accept that intellectual freedom is higher morally than the other principles involved in the discussion [22].

Pamela Klipsch shared her opinion that SRRT was asking the IFC "to adopt some of the same tactics used by the repressive and discriminatory government of South Africa.... [N]o matter how great the evils we see in South Africa, we cannot use the same tactics—we cannot use evil to respond to evil." Klipsch was expressing a sincere and ardent support of intellectual freedom, but sincerity seems to have clouded her thinking. An economic boycott is not, after all, evil. She then said that whites in South Africa are as much the victims of apartheid as blacks, and that,

> Unless the [white South Africans] have access to information available from this democratic society [the U.S.] on democratic ideas, they will continue to victimize and to be victims.... The only way to fight bigotry and racism in South Africa is to bring education and to force the people of South Africa to come to terms with what bigotry represents [25].

Conable noted during the meeting that throughout all discussions in previous years, "the intellectual freedom 'purist' label had been applied in a manner synonymous with calling someone a racist." This observation deserves a close look. Is a person who places intellectual freedom rights before all other human rights a racist? Not necessarily. However, in demanding that information flow freely to apartheid's supporters in South Africa, intellectual freedom advocates certainly put themselves in a position of aiding and abetting a racist regime. The question then becomes, is a person who supports a racist regime a racist him- or herself? Perhaps not, but his or her actions place that person in the position of *collaborating* with racism, and collaborators stand closer to victimizers than they do in solidarity with victims. Were all Nazi collaborators, in the deepest reaches of their hearts, anti–Semites? It is impossible to know. However, it is one's *actions* that count when determining an individual's allegiance with regimes responsible for atrocities.

What was being asked for by the Guidelines, in keeping with the ANC's modifications to sanctions, was that librarianship continue to refrain from collaboration with apartheid and begin to establish stronger collaborative ties with the mass democratic movement. This request was not acceptable to the majority of members on the Intellectual Freedom Committee, which insisted that books and information flow freely to *both* apartheid and anti-apartheid supporters. Therefore, in their resolute refusal to recognize this as a collaborative relationship with apartheid, IFC members invited upon themselves the appellation of "racist." Furthermore, in all honesty the IFC should have been willing to openly acknowledge their collaborationist position, accepting their share of responsibility for all that relationship entailed in terms of morality, continued oppression, and violence. Given the depth at which "white privilege" resides in the psyches of some, it is highly unlikely that any member of the IFC ever even considered that the benefits they were demanding (the free flow of information) were inextricably tied to the severe violence of apartheid and would assist one party in maintaining that violence. Instead, the IFC simply claimed the moral "high ground" and insisted that intellectual freedom had no meaning unless the victimizer was granted equal status with the victim.

Another striking feature of this position was that, while the IFC was certainly well aware of the apartheid regime's use of censorship, they seemed to find nothing odd in arguing for a free flow of information *to a censor*.

Apartheid South Africa maintained one of the most extensive systems of censorship the world has ever known, and the library profession in South Africa was thoroughly implicated in that censorship. Librarians maintained and abided by lists of "banned books." Librarians removed references to "banned" people from their collections, quite an onerous task. Librarians dutifully locked books in closets. Librarians *burned* books. There was no "free flow of information" to or from or within South Africa. That flow was *highly* regulated by a system that would *imprison* people who possessed any publication deemed against the interests of the apartheid regime. The IFC's position made no sense. If one is sending books to a censor who will lock them up or burn them if they contain information deemed unacceptable, how does that "educate" or "force" bigots to change? It doesn't. Sending books on democracy to South African censors could assuage the conscience of the sender who could say "Well, at least I *tried* to get ideas on democracy into South Africa." And it also, more tellingly, allows the *seller* of the material to pocket the cash whether or not the books reach their intended destination or are locked-up or burned along the way.

Apparently, the intellectual freedom purists in ALA and their colleagues in the AAP were willing to play this game with South African censors. The anti-apartheid movement was not. The impasse had nothing to do with prioritizing human rights, of valuing intellectual freedom as a lesser or greater right. Intellectual freedom *is* a human right, one that was systematically denied to black South Africans for decades by every person, including librarians, who enforced the laws and practices of apartheid. The impasse between SRRT and the IFC had everything to do with conjuring up the *appearance* of standing high above the political fray, keeping one's hands clean, while doing business with *both* sides of the apartheid struggle. Klipsch had suggested that through education (think textbook publishers here), the supporters of apartheid could be forced to face their bigotry. The truth of the matter is that the apartheid system did not lack for education (or shiny new textbooks). Three centuries of education had done little but to more firmly and more violently entrench apartheid. What apartheid lacked was not education, but a human heart.

It should be noted here, that while many South African librarians dutifully complied with censorship, there were others who used their positions to support the anti-apartheid movement. Archie L. Dick's book *The Hidden History of South Africa's Book and Reading Cultures* gives an excellent picture of the role librarians and libraries played in the liberation struggle, as well as an arm of apartheid. In his chapter "Politics and the Libraries: The 1980s Townships" Dick describes the work of Vincent Kolbe (whose letter to Al

Kagan and John Bruce Howell is quoted above), which serves as an example of the "other" face of librarianship in South Africa.

> Kolbe ... became a source of such banned literature, as well as trade union material, books by Antonio Gramsci and others that dealt with the Nicaraguan, Chilean, and Cuban revolutions. He collected African American political activist Angela Davis's books, and British Broadcasting Corporation (BBC) audio recordings and video cassettes. He kept these in a sporting equipment bag under the lending desk, and activists secretly used them [Dick 108].

The Guidelines would have had U.S. librarians working in solidarity with South African colleagues like Kolbe, and all those like him who used the library, its space, services, and collections on behalf of the anti-apartheid movement. The ANC's modifications to the cultural and academic boycotts were designed expressly for this purpose. The AAP report encouraged "charitable contributions to worthy and progressive recipients" and a return to business-as-usual with *paying* customers. One might note that charitable contributions are often tax deductible. Morality versus profitability.

As noted above, ALA Council also requested that the IRC review the Guidelines and the AAP report. Chaired by E. J. Josey at this time, the IRC's approach to review was quite different from the IFC's. An open hearing was called where any member who wished to explain their support of the Guidelines would be heard by committee members. Al Kagan, in his book *Progressive Library Organizations: A Worldwide History* (2015), recalls the hearing,

> Many SRRT members testified, and all called for rejecting the [AAP] report except for Mr. Wedgeworth, who spoke last and then walked off in a huff. As a result, ALA reaffirmed its policy [supporting sanctions] by rejecting the AAP report [188].

Not long after ALA's midwinter meeting, on February 11, 1990, Nelson Mandela was released from prison, following the unbanning of the ANC and other anti-apartheid organizations. Although apartheid would not end for another four years, the U.S. dropped sanctions when South Africa's Prime Minister F. W. de Klerk announced multiracial, democratic elections. ALA never adopted the Guidelines Congressman Owens credited it with, and members of the AAP resumed business-as-usual with customers in South Africa, only now there was indeed a change. Apartheid was dying. Some argue that it would have died without sanctions and boycotts, without demonstrations and protests, without struggles in solidarity with the dispossessed of South Africa. The U.S. Department of State credits the collapse of the Soviet Union and the end of the Cold War as a critical factor—the U.S. no longer needed an anticommunist ally in Africa (United States n.d.). Others argue that rugby played a central role in turning white fans against segregated sports leading to apartheid's collapse. Whatever the mix and weight of causes in apartheid's demise, librarianship can surely claim some small part through acts of solidarity and alliance with the anti-apartheid movement, just as it played a role in the end of Jim Crow here at home. In the end, Congressman Owens was ultimately correct in commending solidarity, especially in light of concerted efforts by the IFC and AAP to silence it.

Notes: 1. *For readers interested in how racism has evolved in the United States via slavery and Jim Crow segregation to the 21st century's school-to-prison-pipeline, see Michelle Alexander's* The New Jim Crow: Mass Incarceration in the Age of Colorblindness *(New York: New Press, 2010).* **2.** Three Famines: Starvation and Politics *(New York: Random House, 2010).* **3.** *Statement by Leslie O. Harriman of Nigeria, chairing a Special Meeting of the Special Committee Against Apartheid on the 80th Anniversary of the Birth of Paul Robeson on 10 April 1978, p. 9.*

B.6.1 The American Library Association establishes these objectives and responsibilities for its international relations programs...To promote and support human rights and intellectual freedom worldwide.

3. Censuring a Censor—
The Debate on Censorship in Israel and the Occupied Territories

And who will remember that there was once here that other [Arab] Hirbet Hizah, from which we evicted and inherited? We came, we shot, we burned, we blew up, we repulsed and shoved off, and we drove into exile. What the hell are we doing in this place!?
—S. Yizhar, 1949

Book banning may seem like a minor inconvenience compared to home demolitions and mass deportations, to name just two of the better-publicized tactics employed by Israel in its war against the Palestinians. Yet while censorship does not maim like a rubber bullet or a soldier's club, it is meant to obliterate the national consciousness—the very soul of a people.
—Robert I. Friedman, 1993

Convention center exhibit halls are cavernous, as capable of displaying fighter jets and RVs as they are books and glass beads. During the 1993 midwinter meeting in Denver, one section of the hall was given over to a field of roundtables. Clustered around the tables were small groups of librarians meeting to discuss … whatever—cataloging and outreach, hypertext and bibliographic instruction, storytime and bookmobiles—whichever of the multitude of topics librarians gather to discuss.

Looking across the expanse of tables and people, I caught sight of my colleagues on SRRT's International Human Rights Task Force (IHRTF) and hurried to join them. We were meeting to discuss next steps on a project to support libraries in the Occupied Territories. As I approached the table, one of two unfamiliar men standing nearby rushed up to me, demanded my name, grabbed my conference badge, scrutinized it, then pulled a small notebook and pen from his pocket, and wrote down my name and affiliation. All happened in less than a minute, caught me off-guard, left me dumbfounded, a bit frightened, and quite angry. When I asked him who *he* was, he said something to the effect that he was "a friend of Israel's."

The SRRT coordinator, Stephen Stillwell, described his experience that winter morning in an article for the *Washington Report on Middle East Affairs*,

> An ALA member, who identified himself as a member of the Anti-Defamation League, took hold of my convention badge, pinned to my sport coat, so that he might copy my name and affiliation down correctly, an action which I found rather threatening [Chandler].

Why this act of intimidation at an ALA conference? ALA members might disagree on any number of issues, but few rarely, if ever, resort to intimidation. My ancient (copyright 1971) *American Heritage Dictionary* defines intimidate as (1) to make timid, to frighten, (2) to discourage or inhibit by or as if by threats. If these two ALA members had a bone to pick with the IHRTF, why not do it in a civilized manner? However, on that day in Denver these men's actions were dictated, not by norms of behavior generally practiced within the library profession, but by a sense of entitlement to bullying tactics that are accepted, if not actively promoted, in some organizations. These lapel-grabbing men were wearing, not their ALA hats that day, but ADL's.

Founded in 1913, the purpose of the Anti-Defamation League (ADL) was "to stop the defamation of the Jewish people and to secure justice and fair treatment to all" (Anti-Defamation). As the organization's efforts to combat anti–Semitism grew, it established an undercover, intelligence-gathering unit to infiltrate hate groups like the Nazis and Ku Klux Klan in order to counter their activities and propaganda. Subsequently, the ADL broadened spying activities to include leftists, civil rights leaders, and anti-apartheid activists, supplying information about individuals and organizations to local police, the FBI, the CIA, and both Israeli and South African police forces (Friedman 1993). As opposition to Israel's treatment of Palestinians grew, the ADL began labeling anti–Zionist activism as anti–Semitic. Much easier to simply label an opponent anti–Semitic, than to actually address the multifaceted oppression of Palestinians by Israeli government policy, Israeli Defense Forces, and settler populations.

In relation to librarianship, in 1989 the ADL had launched a campaign against a bibliography published by the Chicago Public Library (CPL). *The Palestinian/Israeli Conflict: A Select Bibliography* was compiled by David Williams, CPL Social Science and History Division reference librarian in charge of Middle East acquisitions. Somehow, the bibliography came to the attention of ADL officials. In August 1989, a prominent Jewish patron of CPL contacted the chief librarian, Samuel F. Morrison, charging that CPL had published a biased bibliography. After investigating the charges, Morrison wrote to the patron saying that the bibliography was determined to have a balanced array of perspectives on the conflict. Morrison's response was not to the liking of the ADL, which took a number of additional steps to discredit the bibliography, the library itself, and Williams personally, "bombarding" Chicago aldermen in Jewish neighborhoods with complaints; they in turn contacted the library and Chicago's mayor. According to Friedman,

> In January 1990, a shell-shocked Morrison offered the ADL a compromise. He would update the bibliography, adding many more pro–Zionist books. Not satisfied, the ADL demanded that Morrison place 38 books it chose [in addition to the original 147 titles] in a new bibliography and forbid Williams from working on this and future reading lists [Friedman 35].

The CPL administration caved in to ADL demands the following week. However, the *Chicago Sun Times* picked up the story and, after alluding to Chicago's longstanding history of strong-arm persuasion tactics to "fix anything," asked its readers, "But have you ever heard of people using their clout to get a library reading list changed?" Advocates of intellectual freedom then joined the fray, denouncing both CPL's capitulation to the ADL's demands, and the ADL's campaign to censor a highly regarded bibliography. The chair of the University of Chicago's history department, John Coatsworth wrote,

> For the general reader, Williams has put together an extremely useful and carefully balanced list of important works on this important topic. As usual, Mr. Williams's work conforms to the highest standards of professionalism. Criticisms by groups with strongly partisan sympathies in respect to the Palestinian-Israeli conflict should, in my judgment, be dismissed out of hand [36].

Williams was instructed to revise the bibliography by adding some of the ADL-approved titles, including Claire Sterling's *The Terror Network*, for which Williams provided some balance with the inclusion of Edward Herman's *The Real Terror Network*.

In January 1990, the ADL had lost round one with the Chicago Public Library. In July 1992, it lost round two when ALA passed a resolution condemning censorship in Israel and the Occupied Territories. And in January 1993, when the two ADL members showed up at our meeting in Denver, the *San Francisco Examiner* reported that the San Francisco district attorney had just initiated an investigation into charges that ADL information-gathering activities violated the constitutional rights to freedom of speech, assembly, and privacy, of thousands of individual U.S. citizens and more than 900 political groups (39).

Such is the milieu within which the debate regarding censorship in Israel and the Occupied Territories took place in ALA Council in the early 1990s. On one side, the library profession with its practice of reasoned, informed debate, and a predilection to listen, and weigh various perspectives. On the other side, a partisan community dedicated to maintaining popular images within the U.S. of the Israeli state as a full-fledged democracy; ready to denounce as anti–Semitic the slightest challenge to that image regardless of its veracity or moral strength; and using without hesitation its political clout to denounce bibliographies and overturn resolutions.

Censorship—image control and cultural genocide

Despite the ebb-and-flow of violence and peace negotiations over the course of the past nearly seven decades, the conflict in Palestine and Israel, and throughout the international community, has continued unabated since 1948. Outbreaks of extreme violence, the lull of ceasefires, demolitions of Palestinian homes and orchards, the throwing of stones, launching of missiles, and unrelenting levels of physical and emotional tensions throughout all the region's communities have given rise, in each of the past seven decades, to calls for the recognition of Palestinian rights to live in peaceful coexistence with the Israeli state. In order to understand the position taken by members of the progressive and socially responsible library community on censorship in Israel and what were then known as the Occupied Territories, it will be helpful to look at the ideological and historical framework informing that position.

Fundamental to the position sympathetic to both Palestinians and Israelis who oppose censorship is a commitment to the ideals of democracy, the role of citizens in governance, the rights of individuals to freedom of expression, association, and privacy, and the freedom of the press. This perspective is also informed by a preference for nonviolent social change, coupled with an understanding that violence tends to provoke violent responses, and a critical assessment of the varying levels of responsibility for violent provocations. Additionally, there is a commitment to the notion of self-determination as a right of groups of people who identify *as a people*. Lastly, the position is informed by the historical record which reveals patterns of behavior that have become habitual, routinized over the course of the last seven decades of the Zionist project of turning the territory that was, prior to 1948, home to the Palestinian people, into an exclusively Jewish nation.

Censorship has been used from the founding of the state of Israel for two basic purposes: to establish and control Israel's image as a benevolent and beleaguered democracy surrounded by hostile Arabs, and as a means of cultural genocide against the Palestinians through the removal and denial of any evidence documenting or supporting Palestinian claims to nationhood (Benvenisti 1983; Masalha 2012; Selfa 2002). Image control via censorship determines who has access to what information in order to maintain sympathy toward Israel, sympathy essential for maintaining financial and military support from its allies. Censorship as a means of denying Palestinian rights as an indigenous people to the lands coveted by Zionists has been used to erase all trace of the Palestinians from the landscape, history, and present-day of the region.

Support for Israel is often based on the notion that Israel is the "only democracy" in the Middle East. Before making any comparisons to other nations, however, one might ask just what sort of democracy Israel actually practices. In general, the assumption is made that Israel is a democracy like the United States—an assumption actively *fostered* by Israel and its supporters. However, this image is both unwarranted and false. For example, Israel has nothing like the U.S. Bill of Rights. There are no laws guaranteeing citizens and the press with freedom of expression. Indeed, Israeli laws governing the press would come as a shock to most in the U.S.

An early example of image control via censorship comes in a *Washington Post* report on February 6, 1949, "The story of the foreign volunteers who helped the fledgling army of Israel win the battle of Palestine is one of the hardest here to tell. It's a problem of censorship" (Long). James M. Long, Associated Press correspondent in Tel Aviv, informed readers that, "it was not permitted to write about foreigners in the fighting forces. As recently as two months ago, censors wanted to cut out all references to Gentiles in the Jewish army." He ends his report noting that most of the pilots in the Israeli air force were either from the U.S., Britain, or South Africa. Long speculates that the reason for the censorship might be that "the Israeli state does not want to be accused of importing mercenaries" and that foreign fighters endangered citizenship in their own nations by fighting in another country's armed forces. Probably of even more importance, the popular image of Jews fighting for a Jewish state could be undermined if it were known that "well up into the thousands" of non-Jews were behind Israel's military victory. Nation building, after all, requires a considerable amount of rallying support via appeals to patriotism, the mythologizing of people and events, fine-tuning public support and sentiment through media control, image management, and the demonization of the enemy. And, to be fair, Israel inherited censorship practices from the British, who knew a thing or two of not mere nation building but of empire building.

Immediately after World War II, the British, who were given charge of Palestine at the time, imposed an "emergency" Defense Regulation in 1945 to continue their pre-war censorship practices, which had prohibited, for instance, reports in the Hebrew press on what was happening to the Jews under Nazi occupation. The British Press Ordinance of 1933 required licensing of newspapers, review of content prior to publication, and criminal sanctions for editors and publishers who violated the Ordinance. The postwar 1945 regulation established a Military Censor who was "authorized to prohibit the publication of any material that in his opinion, would be, or be likely to be, or become prejudicial to the defense of the State or to the public safety or to public order" (Benvenisti 19).

After Israel was given statehood in 1948, the law remained in effect despite opposition from the new Israeli Ministry of Justice, a fact that is essential to any full understanding of the dynamics of censorship within Israel and the Occupied Territories. There has *always* been opposition to censorship throughout some portion of Israel's citizens, Jewish and Arab.

In the early years of Israel's statehood, for instance, the Military Censor's powers were voluntarily curtailed somewhat when an Editors Committee (an official body of military personnel, editors, and publishers) agreed to abide by lists of permissible and prohibited topics in exchange for the Censor's leniency in enforcing the law. A little *quid pro quo* through which the press allowed the military to determine content, then engaged in self-censorship, in return for a little leeway in pushing the boundaries of the law. Of course, there were (and are) in Israel advocates of freedom of the press, who refuse to limit news reported to what the military censor permits. In such instances reporters, editors, or publishers can be, and have been, penalized by having press credentials revoked, fines imposed, jail sentences administered, and publications destroyed. Relations between censors and the press have long been described as a cat-and-mouse routine, with the cat pacing smaller and smaller circles around the press.

In 1976, for instance, *Washington Post* reporter Yuval Elizur in Jerusalem described proposed legislation to "expand censorship regulations" allowing for the criminal prosecution of journalists if

> [newspapers] publish messages exchanged between Israeli and foreign officials or if they report on meetings between Israeli officials and those countries with which Israel has no diplomatic relations…. The new regulation … provides for a jail sentence of up to 15 years for those who reveal information and up to seven years for those who publish it… [Elizur A12].

One leak prompting this proposed legislation occurred in a report stating that Israeli Prime Minister Yitzhak Rabin had visited King Hussein of Jordan. While such a visit might embarrass a prime minister who publicly vilified the King as among Israel's worst enemies, to put a publisher in prison for seven years for sharing this information with the public is not the sort of thing one expects of a democracy.

In another example, in 1980 Israel revoked the press credentials of a CBS reporter, Dan Raviv, who had gone to Rome in order to broadcast a report on the testing of a nuclear bomb by Israel off the coast of South Africa. Raviv went to Rome to report because Israeli censors were known to "pull the plug" on electronic transmission of news reports. Raviv was punished, not because his report was inaccurate, but because it revealed both that Israel was developing nuclear weapons (a fact that Israel and the U.S. State

Department had long denied), and stood as evidence of Israel's ongoing, close relations with the apartheid government of South Africa at a time when the Israeli Foreign Ministry was "attempting to renew diplomatic ties with a number of black African states who are opposed to South Africa's policies" (Claiborne A7).

We will return to the relationship between Israel and South Africa, and the matter of cultural genocide later on in this chapter, but first let's turn to the first instance in which censorship in Israel was brought to ALA's attention.

ALA investigates Israeli censorship—Part I: 1983–1987

At ALA's 1990 midwinter meeting in Chicago, the compiler of the controversial Chicago Public Library bibliography, David Williams, attended one of SRRT Action Council's meetings seeking assistance in bringing censorship in Israel and the Occupied Territories for Association action. This was not his first attempt.

Several years earlier in December 1983, Williams had approached ALA's Intellectual Freedom Committee and its International Relations Committee with a request that Israeli censorship be investigated, following Israel's invasion of Lebanon. Williams provided both committees with the documentation then available of Israeli censorship practices.

The previous month, November 1983, the Fund for Free Expression issued a report entitled *Israeli Censorship of Arab Publications: A Survey*. The study was directed by the Israeli scholar Meron Benvenisti, a former deputy mayor of Jerusalem (1971–1978) and descendent of a long line of rabbis, who in the introduction of the report thanks U.S. columnist Anthony Lewis for suggesting the study. In March 1982, Lewis had written in his op-ed column At Home Abroad a piece entitled "Looking the Other Way" in which he castigates Israeli government officials for maintaining a list of banned books, which included George Orwell's *1984*. Lewis's revelation of blatant censorship was a source of considerable embarrassment to Israelis.

In its 167 pages, *Israeli Censorship of Arab Publications* provides background on the practice of censorship predating the establishment of Israel in 1948. An inheritance, as noted earlier, of the British empire, laws that established censorship for political and military purposes were incorporated into Israel's own legal codes and have been in regular use throughout the entire history of the nation. Benvenisti's report goes on to detail survey researchers' close examinations of the censorship of four Arab publications over a one-year period, from May 1982 to April 1983. The report includes photocopies of galleys with censors' marks and rubber stamps of either approval or rejection. Articles excised range from reports on PLO activities, coercive actions against Palestinians, sports club news, and poetry, to obituaries. Here are three examples of material axed by Israeli censors:

> Jerusalem—The Israeli authorities arrested the day before yesterday the parents of three girls from the Dheshieh refugee camp on the pretext that the girls had not paid fines imposed on them by the Israeli military court, for demonstrating. In their news, the Ramallah court fined Jamal Hamash from Dheshieh camp with a fine of IS 20,000 [US $5,000] and imprisonment for two years [57].

> Gaza—The athletic clubs in Gaza have taken a decision to stop participation in the annual tournament because of the situation in Lebanon. The clubs asked for a postponement of the tournament till a later date [66].
>
> Gaza—The Israeli forces attacked the Palestinian Women's Club early in the week and confiscated the map of Palestine which had been there since 7/2/64. Many Israeli personalities had visited the union several times in the past and no one had ever objected to the map. The authorities also took 64 books, amongst them "The Palestine Rules and Laws" and another book with the word Palestine in the title. When the director objected to their actions, the responsible personnel told her the books would be examined and returned, but so far no books have been returned [64].

One wonders how any of these passages, excised from Palestinian newspapers by Israeli censors, could be construed as endangering the security of the Israeli state.

While the Benvenisti report surely had a limited readership, at the time of its release Israeli censorship of *U.S. media* was not only widely known, but had been personally experienced by millions of TV nightly news viewers. During the period Benvenisti's survey investigators were hard at work, U.S. television viewers got a picture of Israeli censorship up close. In all likelihood some of these TV news viewers were librarians, perhaps even those IFC and IRC members who ended-up serving on the joint subcommittee to investigate Israeli censorship. Here is the story.

The July 12, 1982, issue of *Time* magazine carried a report by William Henry III and Leroy Aarons entitled "A Double Standard for Israel?" describing TV viewers' experience of nightly news censorship in the U.S. by Israeli military censors. Their article is well worth taking a close look at, not only for the factual information it provides on the topic of Israeli censorship, but even more importantly as an example of the manner in which citizens of Israel's closest ally, the United States, find ways to excuse practices that violate basic principles of democracy and human rights.

> Suddenly, during a TV news report on the Israeli conflict in Lebanon, the screen goes blank. White lettering appears on a stark black background: "22 seconds deleted by Israeli censors." Or footage is left intact, but a legend is superimposed: "Cleared by Israeli censors." Night after night during the past couple of weeks, such unfamiliar signs of censors' instructions have punctuated newscasts on ABC, NBC, and CBS, usually in stories about suffering by Lebanese civilians in bombed-out Beirut.
>
> Almost all nations censor reports during war, and many do so in peacetime, either overtly or through surveillance and obstruction of journalistic enterprise. Israel, in fact, has claimed the right to censor stories on security grounds, whether for domestic or foreign audiences, ever since the nation was founded in 1948. But the sudden visibility of Israeli censorship has spurred concern that a generally free nation for the foreign press is becoming a more restrictive one [Henry].

The last sentence in the above quotation contains a first example of giving a positive spin to a long tradition of Israeli censorship. The authors' contention that Israel has been a "generally free nation for the foreign press" and is now "becoming a more restrictive one" belies previous reports in the mainstream U.S. press regarding censorship. Henry and Aarons were either ignorant of that past or, more likely, were obligingly sticking with the popular characterization of Israel as a democracy in the sense that most of *Time* magazine's readers know of the U.S. as a democracy—a place where freedom of speech and the press is constitutionally guaranteed. Here are three *Washington Post* headlines from the past regarding this "generally free nation for the foreign press":

> Israel Will Censor All UPI News Copy (October 15, 1974, A18)
> Foreign Press Hits Israeli Censorship (October 29, 1976, A13)
> Israel Penalizes [CBS] Reporter for Violating Censorship (February 25, 1980, A7)

Indeed, Henry and Aarons then interview the presidents of all three TV news networks regarding the censorship witnessed several weeks running by viewers, and they too appear either ignorant of the history between Israeli censors and the U.S. press or unwilling to maintain a critical stance toward the censorship, opting instead to promote the myth of Israeli democracy:

> ABC News President Roone Arledge: "This is a massive change from what Israel has always stood for."
> NBC News President Reuven Frank: "I think we are picking on them [the Israelis]. Not that anything we have said [about the Israeli censorship] is factually wrong, but we have left the impression that these are bad people doing bad things to journalists when, in fact, they are pretty good."

Arledge claims the censorship "is a massive change" and Frank seems contrite that NBC made the "pretty good" military censors look bad. Both news presidents are attempting to polish Israel's image, tarnished among the TV news viewing public after witnessing its censorship up front and in person. In keeping with this salvage effort, the title of Henry and Aarons' article, "A Double Standard for Israel?" produces for the reader an element of ambiguity. The question mark in the title followed immediately by the description of the nightly news broadcasts coming from Beirut via Israeli censors, does indeed place Israel's image as the "only democracy in the Middle East" in a questionable light. Israeli military censors took it upon themselves to decide what U.S. viewers should and shouldn't know. However, two-thirds of the way through the article, the reader encounters a second accusation of double standards at play when the director of Israel's Press Office Ze'ev Chafets is quoted as saying, "We let the networks use our facilities for sending material from an entity in a state of war with Israel. We did them [ABC, CBS, NBC] a favor. And they attacked us."

Never mind that Chafets makes it sound like the Lebanese invaded Israel, not the other way round, but how do the presidents of ABC, CBS, and NBC news respond to his complaint? Each one admits that maybe U.S. journalists are holding Israel to a higher standard than any other nation.

ABC's Arledge, "It is true, there is a double standard. We criticize the Israelis for not allowing us to get some footage of Beirut, whereas we do not criticize people who do not allow us to get stuff out at all. That is because Israel has always proclaimed itself a model of democracy and has been one."

The accusation of holding a double standard now has shifted in the direction of U.S. journalists who really have no grounds to complain about Israeli censorship because they don't complain about being the targets of censorship by unnamed others. Who occupies the moral high ground now? The good Israeli censors "doing bad things" to U.S. journalists, or U.S. journalists holding Israel to a higher standard than other unidentified democracies? *Time* allows its readers to answer that question for themselves, and a case might be made that the article is actually a "balanced" bit of reporting except for the fact that the only people interviewed are among the most prominent members of the mainstream media. Not one expert on Israeli censorship was interviewed, nor anyone known to be a critic of Israel generally.

Lastly, this article ends with a rather astounding bit of information.

News anchor Dan Rather had apparently said that Israel could have avoided the entire public relations fiasco caused by censored news broadcasts simply by not giving journalists access to its TV transmission facilities. Whether or not Rather's comment/ advice was responsible for what followed, Henry and Aarons report that "last week Israel realized it had stumbled into a no-win situation and withdrew its transmission service for all foreign bureaus in Beirut." A complete news blackout, after all, is invisible to nightly news audiences. If no one actually sees the censorship, then there is no cause for complaint. Such advice coming from a mainstream journalist like Dan Rather certainly puts into question his trustworthiness as a source of reliable news.

Censorship by Israel, then, was not an esoteric topic when David Williams contacted ALA in late 1983, but was well documented and even directly experienced by millions of television news viewers in the U.S. In a letter to ALA which included documentation on the matter of censorship in Israel and the Occupied Territories, Williams wrote:

> Not being familiar with ALA structure and procedures, I can't suggest a particular action that you might take on this issue, but have brought it to your attention in at least the faint hope that ALA could be prevailed upon to study the matter and make some pronouncement (e.g., a resolution?) [Doyle 1].

Although Williams apparently did not know at the time, ALA was well prepared to handle his concern. In a policy adopted by ALA Council on July 12, 1974, a process was spelled-out for addressing threats to or denials of freedom of expression and the press anywhere in the world. In light of subsequent events surrounding Williams' request that ALA address Israel's practice of censorship, the policy follows in its entirety.

POLICY ON ABRIDGEMENT OF THE RIGHT OF FREEDOM OF EXPRESSION OF FOREIGN NATIONALS

Freedom of thought and freedom of expression are rights basic to all. This concept is now expressed in the Universal Declaration of Human Rights, which was adopted and proclaimed by the General Assembly of the United Nations. Article 19 of this Declaration reads as follows: "Everyone has the right to freedom of opinion and expression; this right included freedom to hold opinions without interference and to seek, receive, and impart information and ideas through any media and regardless of frontiers."

Aware that this priceless right is still being threatened, the Association affirms its stance that threats to the freedom of expression of any person become threats to the freedom of all and therefore adopts as its policy of governance the principles of Article 19 of the Universal Declaration. The Association will address the grievances of foreign nationals where the infringement of their rights of free expression is clearly a matter in which all free people should show concern. Resolutions or other documents attesting to such grievances will be brought to the attention of the Executive Board and council by both of the Council's committees involved in the area: Intellectual Freedom Committee and International Relations Committee and will be subject to the joint endorsement of both.

Upon adoption, the resolutions will be sent to the U.S. Department of State, the United

Nations, international library associations, the national library association or associations of the nation involved, the nation's embassy, and such other bodies as may be deemed appropriate by the resolution's drafters [Council 1974].

As he did with ALA's involvement in anti-apartheid boycott and sanctions, ALA staffer Robert Doyle compiled a fact sheet on the Israeli censorship controversy within the association. The first part of the timeline documents the work of the joint subcommittees established by IFC and IRC beginning in January 1984 and culminating in June 1987, when the IFC decided to withdraw as an official consultative body in matters regarding intellectual freedom countries outside the U.S. and as established by the resolution above. The abdication of responsibility in this area is a strange step for the ALA committee whose sole purpose, expertise, activity, realm of concern, and advocacy focuses on intellectual freedom and opposition to censorship. Let us look at what led up to this seemingly unjustified withdrawal.

In adherence to the above Policy, the IFC and IRC promptly established a joint subcommittee to investigate Williams' concerns. According to Doyle's timeline, the subcommittee sent requests for information to Freedom House, the Israel Library Association, and the American-Arab Anti-Discrimination Committee (AAADC). Apparently, the later organization was the only entity to respond with information, which Doyle characterizes as "documentation and reports concerning Israeli censorship and curtailment of academic freedom in the occupied territories" (Doyle 1).

In his initial approach to ALA, Williams had provided a copy of an AAADC 1983 publication *The Bitter Year: Arabs Under Israeli Occupation in 1982*, of which over 50 of its 276 pages focus exclusively on restrictions of the press, book censorship, and threats to and denial of academic freedom by the Israelis in the Occupied Territories. Three examples from the report echo the Benvenisti investigators' findings. The first comes from an editorial published in an English-language weekly summary of the Arabic daily newspaper *Al-Fajr*:

> Almost fifty percent of the original material prepared for our pages in the year 1982 was totally wiped out [by Israeli censors]; some 25 percent was passed through a sensitive filter that resulted in [each news report's] being either mutilated—rendered meaningless or contrary to the original idea—or without the most important parts ... [*Bitter* 38].

From a May 7, 1982, editorial in the paper *Ha'Aretz* by Israeli writer Amos Elon:

> In the last two weeks, it has been at last possible to study a thick file in the offices of the IDF [Israeli Defense Forces] spokesman in Jerusalem containing, as far as this can be ascertained, an up-to-date collection of all the military orders which forbid the distribution and the possession of 1,100 books in the West Bank and in the Gaza Strip. This is the first time that such a collection—the Catholic Church called it "Index"—has been revealed to the public. The revelation was forced upon the IDF by the continuing international scandal around the censorship imposed by the "People of the Book" on books in the Administered Territories. The revelation will, most probably, put an end to the confusion and the mystery which has surrounded this subject hitherto, whether by intent or due to bureaucratic inertia or a simple foul-up. But the scandal will go on [185].

The third example comes from a news article published on November 30, 1982, in *Al-Fajr*:

The military authorities in the occupied territories continue their conspiracy against the [Palestinian school] curriculum in a number of ways, including the banning of a large number of textbooks and changes in essential sections of other textbooks. It is clear that the purpose of such arbitrary steps is to attempt to prevent students from developing a national consciousness. We have to keep in mind that after the 1967 war, the occupation authorities outlawed the distribution of many history and geography books and that all maps labeled "Palestine" were confiscated and replaced by maps bearing the name "Israel." The military authority removed from textbooks all UN Resolutions concerning the legitimate national rights of the Palestinian people, especially the right for self determination on their own land. The authorities also removed everything which may develop a feeling of belonging to the homeland or working the land [202].

Having reviewed evidence such as this, Doyle notes that the joint committee "concluded that the case appears to have broadened from simply a list of banned books and one question of censorship, to concerns of larger issues, which deal with freedom of the press, academic freedom and the general adverse effects of a 'military occupancy'" (Doyle 1). The subcommittee's work accomplished, the IRC then took the next step and recommended at its June 1984 meeting in Dallas that the ALA Council reaffirm Policy 58.3 in a resolution that stated in part,

...WHEREAS, During the past year, the Association has been asked to take a stand on the matter of constraints of individual rights and intellectual freedom in the occupied area of the West Bank of the Jordan, and its Intellectual Freedom and International Relations Committees have been unable to ascertain the details of such constraints, but are convinced that there must be some inequity that has provided the basis for statements of concern ...

RESOLVED, That one of the best exports the American Library Association can provide is intellectual freedom and a dedication to it throughout the world [American 1984].

One wonders, in light of the documentation provided in this chapter's brief overview of the matter, documentation which was readily available to the subcommittee, how it was that the IFC and IRC could claim in good conscience to "have been *unable* to ascertain the details of such constraints." Be that as it may, Council approved the resolution, Reaffirmation of Freedom of Expression of Foreign Nationals, on June 27, 1984.

However, opposition to the reaffirmed resolution must have begun to smolder among members of the IFC because at the following midwinter meeting in January 1985, the IFC requested that Council rescind the reaffirmation resolution on the ground that, "the fourth 'whereas' clause was inadvisable in a public statement since it can be interpreted as contrary to the concept of justice that one is innocent until proven guilty" and that in putting forward its recommendation to Council the IRC had acted without getting the IFC's official endorsement first. The IFC noted that it had concluded its business in June 1984 while the IRC was drafting its recommendation. Doyle notes in his Fact Sheet that the timing of deliberation and decision making were such that the IRC decided simply that IFC could address any outstanding concerns from the floor of Council. They did not.

At the time, in January 1985, the IFC's position and arguments were persuasive enough to cause a majority of Council members to rescind the reaffirmation, In retrospect (and perhaps to some at the time) the grounds of the IFC's complaints seem quite flimsy. While an appeal to the notion of "innocent until proven guilty" certainly is essential in courts of law, and in circumstances where an innocent might be subjected to false accusations, and suffer fine, imprisonment, or even execution, there is nothing in the whereas clause quoted above that condemns an innocent. The implied equation made by the IFC that a "statement of concern" is tantamount to a verdict of guilty is disingenuous at best, as was the subcommittee's claim that it had been unable to ascertain details of Israeli censorship. As for the IFC's objection that the IRC recommendation (which was fully informed by the work of members of a *joint* IFC/IRC subcommittee) violated the policy on foreign nationals, that seems more of a grasping at straws than substantial ground for rescinding the resolution. Surely the IFC could have made a request at the June Council meeting for the matter to be tabled for further consideration with a report back by midwinter. Such a step would have been normal, a fully understandable position for IFC to have taken.

No further action on the matter of censorship in Israel and the Occupied Territories seems to have occurred for the next two-and-a-half years, but something must have been brewing within the IFC, because in June 1987 it officially withdrew from official involvement as a consultative body in ALA on matters regarding intellectual freedom in countries outside the U.S. A joint recommendation from the IFC and IRC resulted in the revision of the policy on foreign nationals to simply exclude the name of the Intellectual Freedom Committee, an action that raises serious questions and appears to be a rejection of professional responsibility as the arm of ALA charged with advocacy of intellectual freedom. Perhaps the IFC wished to have only an informal relationship with the IRC when concerns on the status of intellectual freedom arose in other countries. Perhaps it did not want to be drawn into prickly political positions, wishing to be free to pick-and-choose the international grievances with which to become involved. Perhaps members of the IFC realized that censorship in Israel and the Occupied Territories would surely be revisited within ALA and did not want to be forced into involvement by ALA policy. Whatever the reason, perhaps further research in this area of ALA's history might one day shed more light on IFC's move.

For the next three years, silence reigned within ALA on the matter, until David Williams reappeared, this time with a more fully informed sense of how ALA works. Before launching into the second Council debate on censorship in Israel, it will be helpful to consider why librarians in ALA were willing to support Williams' efforts to get the association to take a stand on this matter. Why "single out" Israel for censure? How, in the U.S. where nearly anything Israel does is met with unconditional support, does one distance oneself enough from mainstream opinion to gain a critical perspective on Israeli actions?

The web of ideology—born stuck and breaking free

In a letter dated December 27, 1989, to E. J. Josey, former ALA president and then-chair of the International Relations Committee, David Williams requested that the Committee place an item on its agenda for the upcoming midwinter meeting regarding a matter of concern to him as a librarian—censorship by the Israeli authorities both within Palestinian areas where its military was an occupying force and within Israel itself. "Under the 20-year occupation," Williams wrote,

> there has accumulated a list of hundreds of banned publications, allegedly for Israeli "security" but actually aimed at stifling any independent expression of Palestinian scholarship

and culture, within the context of a general suppression of Palestinian national and human rights [Williams 1989].

He went on to state that while Israel was not the only country in the region to engage in censorship, given (1) the Israelis' claim to being the only democracy in the Middle East, and (2) the $3 billion U.S. taxpayers annually provided for the maintenance of the Israeli state and military, the country should be held accountable to standards of democratic governance and international law. Williams recognized that "there is little that ALA can do about the broader dimensions of the Israeli-Palestinian conflict, but we can and should speak out on censorship and intellectual freedom issues" (*ibid.*).

Offering to present documentation on the issue at the IRC's January meeting, Williams also expressed his willingness to assist the IRC in drafting a resolution.

At the IRC meeting, Williams shared three documents—the bibliography he had compiled for Chicago Public Library users that had generated so much controversy; a chapter from *World Report 1988: Article 19 Information, Freedom, and Censorship* edited by Kevin Boyle; and *Israeli Censorship in the Occupied Territories (Preliminary Report)* by Karima Bennoune (1990). (Bennoune is currently a professor of law at UC–Davis and author of the prize-winning *Your Fatwa Does Not Apply Here*; Boyle, now deceased, was a lawyer in the U.K. and the first director of the NGO Article 19 headquartered in London.) The IRC responded to Williams, establishing a subcommittee to investigate.

Williams also spoke at a meeting of the SRRT Action Council, where most members either immediately recognized the legitimacy of Williams' request or were open-minded enough to support his efforts to bring the issue to the attention of ALA members via programming and other activities. During the January 1990 midwinter conference, SRRT proved its ready support and passed a "Resolution on Israeli Censorship."

> WHEREAS there is ample documentation from Article 19 and other organizations showing massive and stringent Israeli censorship in the Occupied Territories of the West Bank and Gaza and within pre–1967 Israel itself, and
> WHEREAS this censorship, administered by the Israeli military and justified on grounds of Israel's alleged security needs is in reality aimed at suppressing information about and criticism of Israeli treatment of the Palestinians under occupation, and
> WHEREAS this censorship is also aimed at suppressing awareness of Palestinian national and cultural identity and serves to undermine Palestinian academic freedom and education, and
> WHEREAS this sweeping and arbitrary censorship is in violation of universally accepted principles of intellectual freedom and human rights, including Article 19 of the United Nations Declaration on Human Rights, and
> WHEREAS the United States has maintained a special relationship with the State of Israel, which receives upwards of $3 billion annually in American military and financial assistance, while claiming to be the most democratic country in the Middle East,
> BE IT THEREFORE RESOLVED that the Social Responsibilities Round Table Action Council of the American Library Association condemn this massive and stringent Israeli censorship and call upon the State of Israel to abide by universally recognized norms of intellectual freedom and human rights [SRRT 1990, 2–3].

Those SRRT members who volunteered to work with Williams had a more-or-less shared understanding of the history and political dynamics of Israel; others knew enough about the dynamics of political and social power to question and examine mainstream assumptions regarding the righteousness of Israel's treatment of the Palestinian people. For instance, Stephen Stillwell, SRRT Action Council coordinator quoted at the beginning of this chapter, was a gay rights activist, and so had a very personal experience of political and social oppression. Stillwell also had studied diplomatic history with a special interest in the Middle East. He had visited Israel. Other SRRT members arrived at individual understandings of Israel via a variety of routes.

One's critical perspective on Israel in the early 1990s might arise from personal experiences via relationships with Israelis or Palestinians, or via reading works such as Maxime Rodinson's *Israel and the Arabs* (1967), Fawaz Turki's *The Disinherited: Journal of a Palestinian Exile* (1972), Livia Rokach's *Israel's Sacred Terrorism* (1980), Jacobo Timerman's *The Longest War: Israel in Lebanon* (1982), Lenni Brenner's *Zionism in the Age of the Dictators* (1983), Noam Chomsky's *The Fateful Triangle: The United States, Israel, and the Palestinians* (1983), Edward Said's *After the Last Sky: Palestinian Lives* (1986), and the journal *Middle East Report* from MERIP, the Middle East Research and Information Project. Being a critical consumer of the mainstream media, seeking alternative media sources, and becoming adept in reading and viewing "between the lines" reportage of the conflict, was common practice for librarians involved in SRRT, part of our information literacy "toolkit."

Another experience many of us had in common, in terms of personal political education, was the jarring discovery of the brutal underside of the land of the kibbutzim, with their folksongs and dancing through the star-studded desert nights. Like an abused child grown to adulthood, the victims of centuries of pogroms, ghettos, and Nazi concentration camps had not all matured free of the cycle of abuse. Victims often become victimizers. The romance of Israel as portrayed, for instance, in *Exodus*, the bestselling book by Leon Uris (and the resulting blockbuster film directed by Otto Preminger, staring Paul Newman and Eva Marie Saint), when contrasted to reports of the disinheritance and repression of Palestinians, prompted unavoidable questioning of the carefully constructed and widely accepted image of Israel as a simple defender of the Jewish people. Were Palestinians evil incarnate, or the victim of the victims of anti–Semitism?

In my own case, which is probably fairly typical at the time of those librarian colleagues who believed that Palestinians and Israelis could coexist peacefully either as separate nations or as one, my activism in solidarity with the Palestinians was spurred by Israel's invasion of Lebanon in 1982. I was a senior at the University of Utah, and had several friends from the Middle East, many of whom I came to know via another friend, Mark Rosenzweig, a leftist of Jewish descent. A few years later both Mark and I were students at Columbia University's School of Library Service, and after graduating eventually helped found the Progressive Librarians Guild.

Until the late 1970s, my views on Israel were constructed during childhood via *Weekly Reader* at school, the morning newspaper (*Stars and Stripes, Eugene Register-Guard, Clarion-Ledger*), and the nightly television news with Chet Huntley and David Brinkley at NBC, and sometimes Walter Cronkite at CBS. Through these media, my vision of Israelis was that of a peace-loving people, more than deserving of their own country. In junior high, I used the sound track of Preminger's film for a solo dance piece I choreographed and performed for PE class. As one whose life had been uprooted every three years by the Air Force, used to being treated poorly as a new kid at school, for me the idea of Israel and the kibbutz seemed a Shangri-La. Everyone was new in Israel. Israelis worked and played and sang together in these communities, children were cared for by all, they didn't even have to live at home. As a high school student reading James Michener's *The Source* (1965), the idea of Israel really caught hold. I imagined myself, *goy* that I was, living on a kibbutz. Never did it occur to me that something was wrong with this romantic image until I met people whose knowledge and experience were informed by the greater reality of the Jewish state, whereupon I began reading the works of historians who told stories of Israel from different perspectives.

Turns out, I'd been born, like most in the U.S., into a pre-existing web of ideology, an unconscious, unquestioned acceptance of a particular storyline in which Israel was always the peaceful David fighting the murderous Arab Goliath. But who, really, was the giant here? The Palestinians had no army, no air force, no continuously replenished stockpiles of weapons made in the USA, no atom bomb. Most of them lived hand-to-mouth existences in refugee camps and had lost their homes—to Israeli settlers, dynamite, bulldozers.

I wondered, how could a people who over the *centuries* had experienced so much suffering and repression as the Jews turn around and subject another people to the same? Did it simply boil down to a difference in philosophy—an eye for an eye versus do unto others as you would have them do unto you? The "hawks" against the "doves"? What about all the money the U.S. gave every year to Israel? Tax-payers' money? As a worker whose taxes contributed to Israel's military, what was *my* responsibility in the bombing of refugee camps, the bulldozing of houses, uprooting olive tree groves?

As a college student, all I could think of in answer to that question was to inform myself and fellow University of Utah students about perspectives on Israel and Palestine that were either outright excluded from or obscured by the nightly news, and mainstream magazines and newspapers. I joined the November 29th Coalition, a solidarity group organized in 1981 by Palestinian activists in the U.S. (Abdulhadi 2004, p. 240). Over the summer and fall of 1982, my friends and I set up weekly a literature table in the student union building, organized a film showing, an author's presentation, and a public forum.

In my own education, Livia Rokach's 1980 book, *Israel's Sacred Terrorism: A Study Based on Moshe Sharett's Personal Diary and Other Documents*, gave me a glimpse into the struggle amongst Israelis over the treatment of Palestinians. Just as there are dissenters within the U.S. public toward government policies and military actions, so too within Israel.

Moshe Sharett began keeping a diary in October 1953 when he became Israel's second prime minister. In the diary he records personal and political events, conversations, and reflections. As a political leader, he prioritized diplomacy over military action, and believed Israelis and Palestinians could coexist on peaceful terms, a belief rooted in his own experience, having come to Palestine from Russia as a 12-year-old boy with his family in 1906. In the book, Rokach weaves passages of Sharett's diary with her own commentary illuminating several events in Israel's past, revealing Sharett at odds with hardliners in the government who were intent on forcing Palestinians into exile using whatever force they deemed necessary.

For our purposes, of note is the fact that Rokach's book was itself subjected to an attempt at censorship. In its Appendix V are excerpts from an article written by Uri Avneri, a member of Israel's Knesset, which opens like a potboiler:

The son of the Prime-Minister of Israel is fighting the daughter of the Israeli Minister of Interior because of a book produced by an Arab organization.

This is no myth; it is happening in reality.

The story of this fight started a few months ago. At the time, it became known that the Association of Arab-American University Graduates was planning to publish a booklet based on the personal diary of Moshe Sharett, who was Israel's first Foreign Minister, and her second Prime Minister. The booklet was written by Livia Rokach, the daughter of Israel Rokach who served as Minister of the Interior in Sharett's government....

Sharett's personal diary was edited by his son, Yaqov ("Kova"). Upon the publication of such a blatant document, which revealed many of the most hidden secrets of the Ben-Gurion–Sharett era, he realized that it was impossible to limit that information to the country's borders. Such an explosive material, that explodes many of the most sacred myths of Israeli propaganda, was bound to have echoes in other countries. But Sharett the son resented the fact that the publication was done by an Arab organization [Rokach 71].

Yakov Sharett hired an attorney in the U.S. to pressure the Association of Arab-American University Graduates to cease publication of Rokach's book. When the publisher refused, and issued *Israel's Sacred Terrorism*, Sharett attempted to sue the Association, but was dissuaded from doing so by the Israeli Foreign Office. According to Avneri, "The Jerusalem politicians decided that pursuing a legal course ... would be a mistake of the first order, since this would give [the book] much more publicity" (72).

The last paragraph quoted from Avneri's lengthy article, indeed the last paragraph in the book, reveals how well attuned Israelis are to the U.S. media,

> The Israeli reader who reads the excerpts from Sharett's diary ... cannot be shocked by these revelations, in spite of their severity. However, the impact of such a publication abroad is bound to be sharper. Indeed, the lack of legal intervention by the Israeli Foreign Office prevented a widespread dissemination of the booklet. The Arab-American organization that published the booklet does not have the required means to disseminate it widely, especially when faced with the conspiracy of silence imposed by the pro–Israel American media [73].

Tucked inside my copy of Rokach's book (its glued binding long-dried to that brittle state where individual pages begin to liberate themselves of the spines' restraint) is a December 20, 1982, *Newsweek* review of another book from that era—Jacobo Timerman's *The Longest War: Israel in Lebanon*. Timerman, a journalist and lifelong Zionist, whose release from prison in Argentina in 1979 had been assisted by the Israeli government, was granted citizenship immediately upon his arrival in Israel and given a hero's welcome. The honeymoon between this politically astute new Israeli and his beloved Jewish homeland was short-lived, the relationship seriously imperiled by the invasion of Lebanon.

The Longest War was widely denounced in Israel and throughout the Zionist diaspora for its criticism of the invasion, its portrayal of Prime Minister Menachim Begin as mentally unbalanced, and its description of the collapse of moral direction for the Zionist project. In the last chapter, struggling to comprehend the massacre of nearly 500 Palestinian men, women and children in the Sabra and Shatila refugee camps in southern Lebanon in mid–September, Timerman asks,

> What is it that has turned us [Israelis] into such efficient criminals? I fear that in our collective subconscious, we may not be wholly repelled by the possibility of a Palestinian genocide. I don't believe we Israelis can be cured without the help of others [Timerman 167].

In my own wondering about the roots of what I too perceived to be the criminality of the invasion of Lebanon, I turned to Maxime Rodinson's *Israel and the Arabs* (1970), written in the immediate aftermath of another Israeli invasion—that of Egypt and Jordan in 1967.

Rodinson, a French scholar and Marxist, son of a founder of the Jewish Workers Trade Unions in Paris, presents the history of Zionism, the relationship of what became Israel with its Arab neighbors, the development of anticolonial and nationalist movements throughout the Middle East during the first six decades of the 20th century, and the post–World War II power plays—economic, military, diplomatic—between the Zionists, the Arabs, Great Britain, France, the Soviet Union, and the United States. Rodinson describes Zionism as "unlucky" because it was a colonial enterprise arising at a time in history when colonized people decided they'd had enough of imperial domination (217). The Arabs had also been promised varying levels of independence by colonial powers in the aftermath of both the world wars as rewards for fighting Turks in World War I and Germans in World War II. In the context of a trail of promises broken by Western powers, Arab hostility toward the awarding of Palestinian land to the Zionists takes on a dimension generally ignored in discussions concerning the founding of Israel.

Concluding his history of the relationship between Israel and its Arab neighbors, Rodinson predicts that "it will be difficult for Israel to digest" Gaza, the West Bank, and the Golan Heights, and that, unless Israel includes Arabs as full citizens in a democracy, "the Arabs will be treated as second-class citizens, discrimination will become institutional, a kind of South African policy [apartheid] will be introduced" leading to "increasingly savage repression" which Rodinson suggests "will lose Israel the support of world public opinion" (236).

Three books, countless conversations with friends, nightly news reports, exchanges—sympathetic and hostile—over the November 29th Coalition literature table in the University of Utah's student union, all coalesced to establish for me a new, more fully informed picture of Israel. Free of the web of ideology that was my birthright as a U.S. citizen, I now had a more realistic picture of the conflict in the Middle East. And, eight years later, when David Williams came to SRRT Action Council in January 1990, at which I was in attendance, there was not the slightest doubt in my mind that ALA should take a position on censorship in Israel, and I was willing to help.

ALA investigates Israeli censorship—Part II: 1990–1993

Over the course of the next two and a half years, the issue of Israeli censorship was addressed within ALA in several arenas and manners. IRC subcommittee members quietly collected documentation, issued a report, and made a recommendation for IRC action. IRC subsequently made a recommendation to ALA Council. SRRT, through the International Human Rights Task Force, soon chaired by Williams, organized several conference programs at which a wide variety of individuals with either direct experience with Israeli censorship, or scholarly or journalistic expertise in the matter, spoke on panels and addressed questions posed by their librarian audiences.

ALA conferences can be overwhelming for their shear size, array and diversity of activities, and geographic area to navigate. The number of conference attendees averages 10,000 for midwinter meetings and 20,000 for annual conferences. While most conference goers are from the U.S., there are always librarians, exhibitors, and authors from countries around the world. The conference handbooks easily run to 300 pages. At any given time of the day, dozens of official meetings, programs, events, activities are scheduled simultaneously. While conference venues are clustered in the downtown area of the host city and Gale Publishing Company sponsors shuttle bus services between conference hotels and the convention center, there are always events that take one off the beaten path to libraries, museums, schools, and restaurants that call for walking shoes, taxicabs, rental cars, public transportation, and sometimes even bicycles. The variety of events is far-flung as well: ALA governance meetings and book-truck races, poster sessions and blockbuster author presentations, exhibit hall raffle drawings and the presidential inaugural ball. Add to the variety the levels of involvement and experience of attendees: the librarian attending for the first, and possibly only, time alongside the librarian who has served 30 years on one ALA committee after another and seems to know everybody. Then there is the array of libraries represented: librarians from the Library of Congress and the tiniest rural libraries in every state from Wyoming to Alabama. Librarians from K–12 public schools rub shoulders with librarians from Harvard, Yale, Stanford. Library directors stand in the Starbucks line next to library clerks, a wildly equalizing mix that both belies and challenges long established hierarchies within the profession. ALA conferences are a veritable candy shop array of dilemmas over what to do, who to see, where to go, in a largely celebratory environment—celebrating the virtues of libraries, the wonder of books, the wow of new technologies, the in-gathering of the tribe.

In their sensible (or far-from-sensible) shoes, conference goers climb aboard buses, step onto escalators, roll into elevators, threading their way, some deliberately, others aimlessly, toward a meeting, a panel discussion, an autograph session, a corner armchair, a serendipitous encounter.

On the evening of June 23, 1990, an auditorium at DePaul University, just inside the southeast "corner" of Chicago's loop, was one choice of destination for ALA attendees and members of the general public.

While not on the official ALA program because the program's organizers hadn't either known or been able to meet ALA's deadline for inclusion in the conference schedule, the event was announced at various ALA venues and via Chicago-area media by cosponsoring groups, which included the Committee on Israeli Censorship (CIC), the National Lawyers Guild, the Palestine Solidarity Committee, the Palestine Human Rights Campaign, and the Progressive Librarians Guild (PLG). Featured speakers were Dr. N. Aruri, author of *Occupation: Israel Over Palestine* and board member of both Amnesty International and Middle East Watch; Francis Boyle, a professor of international law at the University of Illinois, Champaign-Urbana; Dennis Brutus, South African poet and anti-apartheid activist; and Mark Rosenzweig, a librarian at the New York Public Library and PLG cofounder. Panelists presented information about the occupation, the role censorship plays in the occupation, parallels between the struggles of black South Africans against apartheid and of Palestinians against Israeli repression, and on the responsibilities of U.S. citizens whose tax dollars were subsidizing Israeli-style apartheid. Also discussed was the role librarians could take in providing our users with alternative sources of information about the conflict, and in opposing the censorship practices of the Israelis.

In his report on annual conference activities, Williams noted that "many sympathetic contacts were made" and that future work would include documenting the attitudes of the Israel Library Association toward censorship, the differences in library services within Israel to Jewish and Arab communities, and reviews of collection development policies in both Israel and the U.S. on the subject of the Israel and Palestine conflict (Williams 1990, 6).

The report-back to the IRC from its succinctly named Subcommittee on the Alleged Banning of Palestinian and Arab Books in the Israeli Occupied Territories as It Related to Article 19 as Adopted by the American Library Association Council in 1989, painted an altogether different picture of the matter. In her report of May 17, 1990, subcommittee chair Sara Fine wrote,

> The Subcommittee found that it was impossible to gather sufficient unbiased and impartial documentation that takes into account the various points of view and interpretations in these matters.

However, she writes in the very next sentence,

> The Subcommittee also was concerned about a role for ALA in censuring one country when there are other countries about whom there is equivalent documentation from Article 19 and elsewhere concerning censorship activities [Fine 1].

The later clearly contradicts Fine's statement on the impossibility of gathering reliable information. If the subcommittee had found documentation that could support an ALA condemnation of other countries for censorship, and that information was "equivalent" to documentation describing censorship in Israel, then the subcommittee had certainly *not* found it "impossible to gather sufficient unbiased and impartial documentation." The problem was not that the subcommittee could not find reliable evidence of Israel's censorship practice, but that it apparently did not want ALA to go on record as objecting to Israel's ongoing violations of intellectual freedom rights, freedom of the press, and academic freedom.

Instead of accepting its subcommittee's recommendation that the IRC should claim it was unable to collect reliable evidence and reluctant to censure a specific country, the IRC instead appointed a new subcommittee to investigate the matter further.

During the 1991 midwinter meeting, members of the IHRTF continued to visit various units of ALA seeking support and cosponsorship of informational programs. Williams reports in the March 1991 *SRRT Newsletter* that the Intellectual Freedom Round Table (IFRT) and the International Relations Round Table (IRRT) agreed to cosponsor a "formal debate between critics and defenders of Israeli government [censorship] policies … if reasonable efforts are made to organize a balanced panel." He also reported that both the Jewish Librarians Caucus of ALA and the Ethnic Materials and Information Exchange Round Table (EMIERT) voted "to take no position critical of Israel," although the latter agreed to cosponsor a program "on condition that [IHRTF] obtain from the Israeli government—by January 24, 1991—the name of an official spokesperson to be on the panel" (Williams 1991, 3). This deadline, following on the heels of the midwinter meeting at which it was proposed was unlikely to be met. For its part, the IRC expected its new subcommittee to have a recommendation for action by the time of the annual conference in Atlanta.

As it turned out, the IHRTF's proposed debate did occur, and at the last minute found a defender of Israeli censorship willing to participate. The evening event took place on June 30th in Atlanta and featured as speakers Noha Ismail, a Palestinian-American librarian; Nubar Hovsepian, an expert on Middle East affairs; Josepha Pick, law librarian at Tel Aviv University; and Israeli publisher Dror Greenfield, an exhibitor at the conference who agreed on the very day that it occurred to participate in the debate. Williams reported that the program "went well overtime as the panelists and audience debated Greenfield's justifications for Israel's censorship policies and closings of Palestinian institutions" (Williams 1991b, 3). An interesting side note is that Bob Doyle's "Fact Sheet" does not mention Greenfield's participation on the panel, but does note that invitations to the Anti-Defamation League and the Israeli consulate requesting their participation were declined.

Council actions at the Atlanta conference took a decidedly bureaucratic course on the controversial topic. Despite the IRC subcommittee's examination of documents attesting to well- and long-established censorship practices, and Williams' suggestion that the IRC utilize language from SRRT's January 1990 resolution, the recommendation forthcoming from IRC to Council focused not on censorship within Israel at all, but on censorship generally in the Middle East. The resulting resolution sent from the IRC to Council under the title "Censorship in the Middle East Including Library Closures in the Occupied Territories," did not mention Israel by name, only by inference—the Occupied Territories were occupied by Israel. No specific country was named, and no specific instance of censorship was mentioned. The resolution was passed by Council, but only after all references (three of them) to the Occupied Territories were excised.

In a lengthy "Letter to the Editor" of the *SRRT Newsletter* in the December 1991 issue, Williams detailed the IRC's handling of the resolution's evolution. After noting that part of the documentation establishing Israeli censorship practices, which the IRC subcommittee had reviewed, was copublished by none other than ALA itself, and should certainly have been considered a reliable, objective source of accurate information, Williams wrote,

> While "objecting" to Israeli censorship and library closings in the Occupied Territories, the draft resolution also contained the ambiguity of calling for respect for human rights to be "balanced" against the "security needs of all inhabitants" of the Territories. By the time the IRC resolution reached ALA Council, any direct mention of Israel had been dropped in favor of a general objection to censorship in the Middle East as a whole, but it did retain a reference to library closings in the Occupied Territories. Council, however, removed this on the grounds that use of the phrase "Occupied Territories" amounted to "Israel-bashing." Clearly the ALA leadership was dead-set against even mild public criticism of the Shamir government, even though the censorship and human rights violations are clearly documented by reports published by ALA itself! [Williams 1991b, 5].

The publication to which Williams referred was *Information Freedom and Censorship: World Report 1991* (London: Library Association Publishing Ltd. and Chicago: American Library Association). The chapter on censorship in Israel and the Occupied Territories is nine pages long. In an "On My Mind" opinion piece published in the January 1992 issue of *American Libraries*, Zoia Horn, former chair of the Intellectual Freedom Committee, asks "Why doesn't ALA act on Israeli censorship?" After describing the failure of the IRC to present a resolution that censured Israel for its censorship practices, Horn writes,

> Since the "Middle East" is not a political entity, but a convenient name for a geographical area, it can hardly be held accountable for censorship or anything else. The resolution had become nothing but a farce [Horn 92].

At about the time that Horn's article appeared, the implementation report of Council's 1991 actions provided information on the distribution of the resolution and a response received by ALA from one of the recipients. When passed, Council directed that the resolution be sent to the Secretary General of the United Nations, the U.S. Secretary of State, the Director of Article 19, and the ambassadors from all Middle Eastern countries with which the U.S. had diplomatic relations.

The implementation report notes that the ambassadors of Saudi Arabia, Egypt, Syria, Jordan, Israel, and Lebanon were sent copies, along with Frances D'Souza of Article 19. Neither Javier Perez de Cuellar, U.N. secretary general at the time, nor James A. Baker III, U.S. secretary of state, were listed as recipients. Was their absence a simple oversight? A lapse in the attention of the person typing the report? A politically motivated decision? Regardless, at least one of the recipients was moved enough by the resolution to send ALA a reply.

Maddoud Maalouf, chargé d'affaires from the Lebanese embassy sent a letter, a brief excerpt of which is quoted in the implementation report:

> ...Article 13 of the Lebanese Constitution affirms Lebanon's commitment to the freedom of speech, education, printing and publishing, and religion. Lebanon also upholds and respects the tenants of human rights. In fact, Lebanon has not only endorsed Article 19 of the Universal Declaration of Human Rights, but was also involved in its drafting. Please be assured that Lebanon will always be committed to the principles of human rights and democracy ... [Council 1991, 5].

The *World Report 1991* copublished by ALA appears to confirm this claim from the Lebanese embassy. In the section on the Middle East, indeed throughout the entire book, there is not one mention of violations of freedom of expression or censorship in Lebanon. Either censorship in Lebanon is so complete that no information regarding violations of freedom of expression ever leaks out, or Article 19 was not paying any attention to this Middle East country, or the Lebanese government actually is "committed to the principles of human rights and democracy" as claimed in Maalouf's letter to ALA. As Horn pointed out, the Council's decision to issue a blanket condemnation of censorship in an entire region ended up holding no national government accountable. It also seems to have accused Lebanon unfairly, simply by reason of its geographic location!

Apparently, ALA received no reply to the resolution from Israel, although it is not unheard of for Israeli officials to respond to censorship concerns from organizations. The *World Report 1991*, for instance, notes several such responses to Article 19 communications regarding Israeli censorship. One example mentioned was a response to an Article 19 letter sent on October 5, 1989, protesting the six-month prison sentence of

Abie Nathan, an Israeli citizen and peace activist, who interviewed a PLO representative on his radio station, an act of civil disobedience against an Israeli law prohibiting Israeli citizens from communicating with Palestinian organizations. In its letter, Article 19 also urged the repeal of this 1986 law. Israeli officials replied to Article 19, justifying the imprisonment of a peace activist by stating that, "Nathan was a citizen of Israel, tried by an Israeli court, and sentenced in accordance with Israeli law" (Article 377).

The gulf between the evidence of Israeli censorship and Council's response to it, was a source of frustration and renewed determination by those who wanted to see ALA issue a principled statement.

During the 1992 midwinter meetings, SRRT Action Council decided to forge ahead with an unambivalent resolution to be presented at the annual ALA membership meeting in San Francisco. Discouraged that the IRC as a body was unwilling to take to task the Middle East's "only democracy," SRRT activists drafted a new resolution which was approved "in spirit" pending final word-smithing for the ALA membership meeting. The IHRTF had made concerted and supportive efforts to take the controversial matter through proper ALA channels and processes in a respectful manner, only to be treated, as Horn put it, to a "farce." Now was the time to bypass the bureaucracy with a direct appeal to rank-and-file ALA members.

Between the January meeting and June, members of IHRTF debated whether the resolution should include reference to the military occupation. Perhaps it would receive greater broad base support if focused more narrowly on censorship and library closings. The draft resolution, for instance, contained the following,

> ... violations of the freedom of information and expression are part of a military occupation which for 25 years has also been depriving the Palestinian people of basic human rights along with their land and water resources; and
>
> ... large amounts of U.S. aid provided to Israel help to offset the costs of this indefinitely-prolonged occupation, [make] the U.S. and its citizens a party to this tragedy ...
>
> ... on this 25-year anniversary of the Israeli military occupation, the SRRT calls for an end to the Israeli occupation of the West Bank and Gaza through a negotiated agreement respecting both the right of the Palestinians in those Territories to self-determination and the right of Israel to peaceful and secure borders [Action 1992a, 3–4].

Concerns were also raised that exclusive activity around Israel was precluding action on other human rights concerns of interest to IHRTF members. A decision was made to initiate a new SRRT Task Force on Israeli Censorship and Palestinian Libraries, in order to free-up IHRTF. There was also some disgruntlement over Williams' chairmanship of the task force. He could be difficult to work with, sometimes making decisions and publicizing them without consulting others, creating unnecessary friction, confusion, and hard feelings.

The resolution that resulted from SRRT deliberations and which was presented at the ALA membership meeting in June 1992 was as follows:

RESOLUTION ON ISRAELI CENSORSHIP

WHEREAS ALA in its Policy #57.3 states that "threats to the freedom of expression of any person become threats to the freedom of all; therefore ALA adopts as policy the principles of Article 19 of the Universal Declaration of Human Rights by the United Nations General Assembly. The association will address the grievances of foreign nationals where the infringement of their rights of free expression is clearly a matter in which all free people should show concern"; and

WHEREAS ALA has over many years voiced its criticism of various countries for practicing censorship and other endangerments to intellectual freedom, in the hope that these countries would stop these practices in response to international concern; and

WHEREAS ALA reaffirmed its commitment to Article 19 in 1991 by quoting it in Policy #57.4: "Everyone has the right to freedom of opinion and expression; this right included freedom to hold opinions without interference and to seek, receive and impart information and ideas through any media regardless of frontiers"; and

WHEREAS the Article 19 International Center on Censorship's 1991 *World Report on Information, Freedom and Censorship* (co-published by ALA) documents the following forms of censorship by the Israeli government in the Occupied Territories of the West Bank and Gaza: banning publications and books; harassing, imprisoning, and deporting journalists; closing university, research institutions (and libraries); censoring telecommunications, etc.; and

WHEREAS Israel considers itself to be a democracy established with the express purpose of creating a safe haven for the Jewish people; and

WHEREAS Israel has enjoyed a special relationship with the United States as the recipient of the largest amounts of annual U.S. aid per capita; and

WHEREAS the special relationship and annual aid helps offset the costs of the 25-year Israeli military occupation, making the U.S. a party to these censorship practices and other violations of human rights; and

WHEREAS the tight censorship in the Occupied Territories serves to stifle dialogue and nonviolent expression which are preconditions for a just and peaceful solution to the Palestine/Israel conflict, and has led to serious forms of censorship in Israel itself;

THEREFORE BE IT RESOLVED that the Social Responsibilities Round Table of the American Library Association calls upon the Government of Israel to end all censorship and human rights violations in the Occupied West Bank, Gaza, and in Israel itself; and

BE IT FURTHER RESOLVED that the Social Responsibilities Round Table of the American Library Association encourages representatives of the Israeli and Palestinian peoples in the quest for a peaceful and just solution of their conflict, including an end to the prolonged military occupation of the West Bank and Gaza; and

BE IT FURTHER RESOLVED that the Social Responsibilities Round Table of the American Library Association encourages its members to develop ways to support Palestinian and Israeli librarians, journalists, educators, and others working for peace, human rights, and freedom of information and expression, and that ALA establish a Task Force toward these ends; and

BE IT FURTHER RESOLVED that copies of this resolution be sent to the Israeli Government, the U.S. Department of State, the United Nations, the Article 19 Organization, the International Federation of Library Associations, and the Palestinian Liberation Organization [Action 1992b, 2–3].

Before moving on to the ultimate fate of this resolution, note must be made of two victims of Israeli censorship whose cases played a role in the debates at the ALA membership meeting and at Council—Michel Schwartz and Omar al-Safi.

In Article 19's *World Report 1991*, mention is made of a case in 1988 in which Israeli authorities cancelled the license of a bi-weekly newspaper, *Derech Hanitzotz/Tariq al-Sharara*, a joint Hebrew and Arabic publication. In addition, five of the paper's editors, all Israeli Jews, were arrested. Four of them were charged and convicted of belonging to the organization Democratic Front for the Liberation of Palestine, which the authorities treated as a terrorist group. The editors received prison sentences of between 9 and 30 months. One of the editors, Michel Schwartz was imprisoned for nearly a year, three months of which was in solitary confinement. Ms. Schwartz, as one of the speakers at the IHRTF program on June 28, described her experience as a victim of her country's system of censorship. The following day, at the ALA membership meeting during the discussion of the Resolution on Israeli Censorship, Ms. Schwartz asked if she could speak.

Omar al-Safi, a librarian at Bir Zeit University located in the occupied West Bank, was being subjected to an "administrative deportation," which under Israeli law requires no evidence of wrongdoing and offers no hearing or right to a trial. SRRT had prepared a resolution condemning the treatment of al-Safi, and calling on the Israeli Attorney-General to stop the deportation or provide him with a trial at which evidence against him would be presented (Action 1992c, 4).

The July/August 1992 issue of *American Libraries* reported that the first ALA membership meeting, the evening of June 29, drew a large crowd, with some 900 people attending. On Membership's agenda were a wide variety of matters ranging from fallout of the sudden and rumor-ridden resignation of ALA Director Linda Crismond; antigay legislation in Oregon which would prohibit libraries from making information about homosexuality available; calls for a boycott of H. W. Wilson Company for the firing of columnist Will Manley which led to the resignation of *Wilson Library Bulletin* editor Mary Jo Godwin; a proposal for direct election of the Executive Board; and the bestowing of a special award—"Library Hero"—to U.S. Representative Major Owens.

The resolution concerning Omar al-Safi generated heated debate. One member complained of an "obsession and single-minded fixation on Israel" while others argued that ALA had a professional and moral responsibility to advocate on behalf of a fellow librarian criminalized without charge or trial. *American Libraries* reported fireworks between two members,

> Shmuel Sever, librarian at the University of Haifa in Israel, spoke against the resolution, outraging Sandy Berman, who called Sever's suggestion that David Williams (a staunch supporter of the resolution) was an instrument of the Palestine Liberation Organization "rank slander" [Kniffel 1992a, 564].

A vote was taken, and the Resolution on the Deportation of Bir Zeit University Librarian Omar al-Safi, was passed, laying the ground for the Resolution on Israeli Censorship, and duly placed on the agenda for Membership II on July 1.

Sandwiched between an "emotional farewell" report by outgoing ALA Treasurer Carla Stoffle, and a resolution opposing antigay legislation in Oregon, was the Resolution on Israeli Censorship. *American Libraries* reported that, as at Membership I, some dozen people rose to debate the second Israel-related resolution on the agenda.

> James Chapin, Ruth Gordon, Joel Rosenfeld, and others opposed to the resolution argued again that singling out Israel was useless in such a complicated political situation. Proponents, including E. J. Josey, Herb Biblo, Al Kagan, and Mark Rosenzweig, pointed out that the resolution was in keeping with established ALA principles [Kniffel 1992a, 564].

In his *SRRT Newsletter* report, Williams wrote,

A highly dramatic moment in the debate came when Schwartz, not an ALA member, asked to address the meeting. She made an impassioned plea for the membership to pass the resolution and put pressure on her government to end these censorship practices [Williams 1992, 8].

Two years of informational programming, Horn's "On My Mind" column, the personal plea from a victim of Israel's draconian censorship laws, memories of nightly news broadcasts cut by Israeli censors, growing recognition of the contradiction between Israel's claims to vulnerability and its actual standing as a military powerhouse in the Middle East, images of Palestinians standing helpless as Caterpillar bulldozers razed homes and crops, pictures of boys throwing rocks at armed Israeli soldiers.... Who knows what reasons or impulses lay behind individual decisions of ALA members that day who voted their conscience in support of the Resolution on Israeli Censorship. Whatever the motivation, the majority of those present at the ALA membership meeting did, by a show of hands in accordance with ALA by-laws, vote in favor and thereby automatically placed the resolution on Council's agenda.

Lest one get the erroneous impression that debate on censorship in Israel occupied most of Council's time and energy at the 1992 annual conference, here is a list of some of the other items on Council's agenda:

- approved an ALA self-study proposal
- approved a resolution concerning the dismissal of Will Manley
- approved a resolution opposing antigay legislation in Oregon
- approved a resolution calling on libraries to refrain from the use of loyalty oaths as a condition for employment
- debated for a "great deal" of time "rehashing" recommendations from a special committee looking into ALA's election process (outcome not clear from the report)
- approved a resolution on reauthorization of the Elementary and Secondary Education Act
- approved a resolution concerning copyright and royalties for material in the ERIC database
- approved a resolution on public access to the papers of former government officials
- approved a resolution opposing royalty charges for government information

Within ALA governance, it has long been considered a rule-of-thumb that any resolution passed at a Membership meeting gets support from Council. The idea being that the majority of Councilors, elected at-large in an association-wide election by ALA members, take into consideration the "will of membership." The spirit of representative governance is alive in ALA, and Council members are often inclined to consider, on any given issue, the positions that might be held by the electorate. Whatever reason for Councilors' votes, on the first occasion at which they were presented with an opportunity to take an unambivalent stand condemning censorship in Israel and the Occupied Territories, the majority voted in favor.

The debate on the Resolution on Israeli Censorship was brief, and the resolution passed by a vote of 97 in favor (57 percent); 38 opposed (22 percent); 10 abstentions (6 percent); and 26 (15 percent) not voting, having been excused because of meeting conflicts or inability to attend the conference (ALA 1992, 857–8). There were no councilors who simply did not cast a vote. An attempt was made during debate by Councilor Beverly Lynch, also a member of IRC, to substitute the resolution with a reiteration of the 1991 resolution on censorship in the Middle East. Lynch's motion to substitute, however, failed by a vote of 89 opposed; 45 in favor; 9 abstentions; 26 excused from voting; and 2 present but casting no vote.

Votes on the Resolution on the Deportation of Bir Zeit University Librarian Omar al–Safi were similar to the censorship votes, with 91 votes in favor (53 percent); 24 opposing (14 percent); 27 abstentions (17 percent); 1 not voting; and 26 excused from the vote (15 percent) (ALA 1992, 857–8).

While neither of the resolutions passed by anything near an overwhelming majority, even if all persons abstaining, excused, or not voting had joined the opposition, both resolutions would have passed with slight margins. Clearly not a mandate for action, but in keeping with ALA's by-laws, both votes gave the Israeli Censorship and Omar al–Safi resolutions ALA's official imprimatur, and were duly sent to all parties concerned. Later, one pro–Israeli letter-writer would chastise ALA for abetting terrorism by virtue of having mailed the PLO a copy.

Never had the State of Israel been taken to task for censorship by a mainstream U.S. organization with the international stature of ALA.

Fallout from the resolutions' passage swiftly followed, with opposition developing both externally to ALA and internally. Internally, at least some, if not all, members of the IRC, given its longstanding prevarication over the issue, must have been appalled that the Resolution on Israeli Censorship committed the IRC to developing strategies to implement the resolved clause

> That ALA encourages its members to develop ways to support librarians, journalists, educators and others working for peace, human rights and freedom of information and expression in the Middle East and that the International Relations Committee (IRC) be asked to develop strategies towards these ends ... [Council 1992a, 2].

An additional source of internal opposition came from within ALA's Executive Board and took two forms: an investigation into SRRT's role in the resolution and into David Williams' actions as chair of the IHRTF; and compliance with IRC recommendations.

External opposition came from supporters of Israel, some librarians, many not.

> We were astounded to note that the American Library Association saw fit to support the cause of terrorism in the Middle East during your Membership Meetings of June 29 and July 1, 1992. The two resolutions passed at that time condemning Israel's legitimate self-protective measures against incitement to murder of Jewish civilians were truly shocking [Rogoff].
>
> Your resolutions are a propaganda victory for Jew haters and Israel bashers [Greenburg].
>
> If our profession has a "Hippocratic oath," it is an assumed pledge to guard against censorship. Inability or unwillingness to think critically about exactly what this pledge means is, however, becoming our professional Achilles heel. Just say the word "censorship" to today's librarian and sadly he/she can no longer think straight. Powers of independent reasoning are not called upon to examine the correctness of any claim of censorship. Knee jerk reaction sets in. Anyone accused of censorship is automatically assumed guilty; no one

even bothers to consider the possibility that they might be innocent. In the case of "ALA vs. Israel," it has been nothing short of a witch hunt [Zyroff].

The American Library Association represents people of many different political and social opinions. This is now the fourth year in a row that the Social Responsibilities Round Table and more recently its Task Force on Israeli Censorship and Palestinian Libraries, has sponsored a program in which they sing their one note, Israeli censorship. Has it not become clear by now that this is a group with its own agenda that it couches in a library issue of censorship? How is such a task force formed? Where do they get their mandate? How do they justify inclusion in the official ALA program? Are these groups monitored or are they simply self-appointed judges with no jury? [Wackerman].

According to a report by Stephen Stillwell, SRRT Coordinator, published in the March 1994 *SRRT Newsletter*, he had been told that ALA received 156 such letters. He'd also been told that he would receive copies of all the letters, a promise, Stillwell notes, that "[m]ysteriously ... was omitted from the minutes of the Executive Board meeting, although it was made before a room full of witnesses" (Stillwell 6).

> To date, I have been allowed to see sixty-eight of these letters.... One was an inquiry and stated no opinion on the issue. Nine were duplicates.... One was actually an internal SRRT memo on the issue. Of the remaining fifty-seven, six endorsed the position taken and fifty-one were against it. Nearly 41 percent (21 of 51) charged ALA, SRRT, and individuals within these groups with anti–Semitism.... No letters that I have been allowed to see level charges of misconduct or violent behavior against any member of the ICPL Task Force or SRRT. This is contrary to what we had been told was in these letters [*ibid.*].

Although such pressure from outside the Association was to be expected, instead of preparing to defend the position taken by a clear majority of ALA's policy-making body (i.e. Council), ALA leaders chose instead to distance themselves from the documentation of Israeli censorship. The methods they chose were, first, to find fault with the *process* of the resolution's adoption, and, second, to question SRRT's advocacy of the resolution, and to charge David Williams of using ALA to pursue his own personal agenda.

"Oh my, did we goof!"

Paula Goedert was an attorney on retainer to ALA, and in late October 1992, she had stronger words than Betty Turock's "Oh my, did we goof!" to characterize the passage of the Resolution on Israeli Censorship. Goedert is quoted in the December 1992 issue of *American Libraries*, as having said at an Executive Board meeting, "I don't want to say sedition, but...." *AL*'s report further states that Goedert "advised that the resolution, in going directly to a foreign government, 'could be viewed as a hostile act'" (Kniffel 1992b, 963).

Goedert's comments echoed those raised by the IRC in a report, written for the Executive Board by Nancy John, summarizing discussions at an IRC meeting just twelve days earlier. By this time, John had taken over as chair of the IRC following the end of E. J. Josey's term.

> IRC is deeply concerned that Council has in the past several [years] passed a number of resolutions, speaking to foreign governments <u>directly</u>, thereby setting a precedent that may put the Association at risk [John 3].

What potential risks might ensue, the report does not say. Goedert's characterization of ALA's condemnation of Israel's censorship as short-of-seditious and possibly hostile, suggest that in the opinion of legal counsel, ALA needed to back-peddle on the resolution—and fast!

Why would John and Goedert engage in fear-mongering tactics? Nothing in the resolution smacks of an attempt to overthrow the U.S. government much less to launch an aggressive attack on Israel. If Israel's hold on political power was so tenuous that censorship was indispensable, perhaps ALA's position might be viewed as hostile. A pinprick of sorts, busting the bubble of the only-democracy-in-the-Middle-East myth. And if that myth is so easily challenged, then perhaps ALA's public revelation of Israeli censorship and U.S. financial support of it was enough to irritate ALA's friends at the State Department.

And, yes, ALA has long had friends in the U.S. Department of State. In fact, ALA staffer Bob Doyle, liaison from ALA headquarters to the IRC, was in charge of the ALA/USIA Library Fellows program, which received its own financial (and political) support from the State Department.

Although in the early 1990s, the United States Information Agency (USIA) was not formally a unit of the State Department, it had been from its inception in 1953 until the mid–1970s, at which time its reputation as a propaganda agency for U.S. foreign policy had become such a huge liability to international relations that it was placed outside the State Department in an attempt to establish a new image of independence. In 1999, USIA was dissolved with parts being incorporated back into the State Department. Libraries had always played a central role in USIA's mission, which was in part "to understand, inform and influence foreign publics in promotion of [U.S.] national interest" (United).

In his book *USIA: Public Diplomacy in the Computer Age* (1989), Allen C. Hansen writes of one way in which USIA libraries were used to demonstrate computer technologies around the globe. Quoting from a report by the Overseas Development Council, Hansen describes the push in the late '80s for markets for the growing computer industry,

> It is in the fundamental economic interest of the United States and its leading economic sectors to foster a process of technological development in the Third World that stimulates demand for microelectronic products [Hansen 219].

He goes on to describe USIA's decision to put computers into its overseas libraries with access to databases like Dialog, Nexis, Legi-Slate, and Wilsonline. Acting as precursors to CompUSA, the USIA libraries served to showcase hardware, software, and databases to potential computer industry customers and database suppliers.

In 1990, as members of ALA were gearing up for the annual conference, the State Department announced that the U.S. would not be rejoining UNESCO (a matter of standing concern to ALA) in part because of what it considered UNESCO's "political bias against Israel" (Oberdorfer). A Lexis Nexis printout of the article was among papers found in the ALA archives, labeled 1989–90 EBD#107, testament to the fact that as ALA leaders prepared for the second time to deal with Israeli censorship, they had also been freshly reminded that any statement construed to be evidence of "political bias against

Israel" could be used by the U.S. government to deny funding not only to worthy organizations like UNESCO, but ALA too.

The minutes of IRC's 1992 midwinter meeting mention a State Department grant to the National Commission on Libraries and Information Science of $182,000 for use to "assist international conventions, scientific organizations, in lieu of U.S. participation in UNESCO." NCLIS would serve as clearinghouse for grants made from this fund. Two months later, the March issue of *American Libraries* contained a glossy 20-page insert advertisement—Information Ambassadors, USA 1990–91—describing the Library/Book Fellows Program, directed by Robert Doyle. The insert contains profiles of eight U.S. librarians who served in libraries around the globe.

ALA's relationship with USIA did not go unnoticed. The Library/Book Fellows insert generated one objection and another defense of the program in letters to the editor of *American Libraries*.

In the May 1992 issue, Sanford Berman questioned the ethics and wisdom of ALA's collaboration with USIA on the grounds asking why ALA would work with an agency whose purpose and activities were in opposition to ALA's own values. Citing his experience with USIA as a librarian working in Germany and Africa he said the agency "functioned more like a Ministry of Propaganda than a model of openness and diversity" (Berman 363). In the July/August, issue a former participant in the Library/Book Fellow Program described her experience in Hyderabad, India, and concluded that, "At no time were my professional ethics or commitment to the free flow of information compromised" (Powell 552).

Given that any position ALA might take on Israel, no matter how well documented, would not go unnoticed by someone in the State Department, it would be naïve to think that concerns regarding this relationship did not play an ongoing role, even if never voiced, in IRC deliberations, and Council actions on Israeli censorship in both the 1980s and '90s.

On October 17, 1992, seven of the IRC's members and Robert Doyle gathered for a fall planning and orientation meeting. After first noting in her "Summary for the ALA Executive Board" concern that Doyle's continuation as ALA staff liaison to the IRC was in question given an expected increase in his workload as ALA/USIA Fellows Program director due to an expansion of the program, Nancy John described in detail the committee's discussion on the Israeli censorship resolution.

As an example of how people can use bureaucratic processes and semantics to give an appearance of impartiality, John's report is a fascinating document.

First, she reports that the Resolution on Israeli Censorship was discussed "as a case study of ALA practice, policy and politics." In treating the resolution as a "case study," the IRC was sidestepping the mandate given it by Council to develop strategies in *implementing* the resolution. John writes that, "the motion has not yet been transmitted to the IRC." Two members of the IRC, both present at the Oct. 17 meeting, were members of Council and had voted on the resolution—Lynch against, Sherman in favor. John seems to be taking a particularly narrow approach to what it means for the motion to have been "transmitted." Additionally, she writes that "because the IRC did not review the motion for Council" committee members decided to discuss the process, the resolution itself, its implementation, and possible actions/outcome—clearly *not* what the IRC was directed to do by the resolution. In other words, the IRC simply announced that it had not received any "transmission" from Council and, therefore, did not need to treat the resolution as an official ALA position.

Additionally, John seems to be playing a game of semantics. In referring to "the motion" she ignores the fact that the *resolution* was no longer a motion to be referred for anybody's review. When the *motion* was made at Council to accept, or not, the resolution presented, it was voted on and became official policy. Also disingenuous of John was to use the fact that the IRC had not reviewed the motion as an (unstated) excuse for sidestepping the will of Council. While technically true, the IRC had *not* reviewed the motion because *motions* are a parliamentary procedure and do not get reviewed by committees, the IRC certainly had—for the previous two years—been reviewing the *issue*. The Resolution on Censorship in Israel did not appear from nowhere, or unbeknownst to IRC, on July 1, 1992.

In any event, committee members discussed the resolution as if had not been passed, choosing instead to basically ignore the charge given it. John outlined what did get discussed:

    a. Should ALA have a process for political resolutions?
    b. What is the relationship of membership initiatives to Council action?
    c. Who reviews the "whereas" clauses…? What is IRC's role for international resolutions?
    d. Should ALA speak directly to foreign governments?
    e. What is the relationship between units of ALA for developing, presenting, and reviewing resolutions?
    f. How can ALA avoid "always reacting to member initiatives/opportunities…. Is there a model/framework which can be developed to handle one-issue individuals and problem areas so that ALA has a balanced view?"
    g. Is diplomacy ALA's international mission?
    h. How does IRC have a greater presence with Council and in ALA, and why doesn't it have more ALA staff support? [John 3].

Regarding (a), some members of IRC were experienced enough at ALA governance to know that any attempt to officially characterize resolutions as "political" or not would open a huge can of unwanted worms. Who, for instance, would have that responsibility? What scale would be used to measure any given resolution's political content? In asking (b), (c), and (e) the committee appears to have suffered from collective amnesia. For an answer to (b) the committee only needed to refer to ALA's bylaws, and for (c) they need have looked no further than Policy 57.4 the Policy on Abridgment of the Right of Freedom of Expression of Foreign Nationals, which would have answered (e). The problem with this particular issue was *not* that the IRC didn't know the process or who was responsible for resolutions of international concern, but that the IRC *preferred not to take a position* on censorship in Israel and the Occupied Territories. As for (f) ALA is a *membership organization*. Asking how ALA can avoid addressing issues raised by members goes against the very spirit of democracy—the right of the citizen (member) to petition the government (ALA) for a redress of grievances (action on a matter of concern). As for how to handle "one-issue individuals," David Williams came to the Association twice with a legitimate concern and request for review and possible action. SRRT agreed that this one-issue individual's "problem area" was, indeed, cause for serious study and, ultimately, action. John seems to be requesting the power to pick and choose which member concerns are worthy of IRC's attention. SRRT took the Resolution on Israeli Censorship to the ALA Membership meeting, because it was frustrated with IRC's refusal to take action on that very specific issue. The "goof" was in IRC's court.

As for (d) and (g), given that ALA housed the ALA/USIA Library/Book Fellows Program the answer to the latter was, yes, international diplomacy is indeed part of ALA's mission. The USIA described its programs as cultural and educational aspects of "public diplomacy." Others have called its activities "political propaganda." Regardless, sitting at the meeting on October 17 was an ALA staffer who could easily have answered this question. As for whether or not ALA should speak to foreign governments, until a decision is made otherwise, nothing prevents such communication. ALA can muzzle its ability to communicate however it sees fit. Better, of course, to leave all channels of communication available for a "free flow of information."

Next in her summary to the Executive Board, John describes concerns raised at the meeting regarding both the resolution and its implementation. Again she notes that the IRC had "not received" the resolution. The committee assumed, John writes,

> that no action had been taken by the ALA [on the resolution] and that ALA had more options than it has. The IRC Chair was informed on Oct. 20, 1992 that ALA has in fact acted on clauses 1, 2, 4 so our advice is no longer useful in terms of shaping that action, but some of our advice is repeated here as an example of what consultation, through ALA's resolution-review process, might have yielded [John 2].

(*Note*: The Resolution on Israeli Censorship passed by Council was exactly the same as the one passed by SRRT, which appears earlier in this chapter, with the exception of the 2nd and 3rd resolved clauses. Council removed from SRRT's 2nd resolved clause references to the military occupation, Gaza, and the West Bank. In the 3rd resolved clause, the charge for action was given by Council to the International Relations Committee.)

Why the IRC thought it had a role to play in "shaping" ALA action on the 1st, 2nd, and 4th resolved clauses is anyone's guess. The resolution clearly stated a role for IRC only in the 3rd clause. Neither advice nor action from IRC is referred to anywhere else in the resolution. Nonetheless, IRC members took the initiative to arrogate to itself the power to interpret how a resolution passed by Council should be implemented. Presumably, IRC's advice might have yielded a decision not to mail copies of the resolution to the Israeli government, the State Department, United Nations, Article 19, IFLA, and the PLO. What follows are the IRC's suggestions for dealing with the resolution:

- accept the resolution, do what it says, and take our lumps
- bring back to Council and ask them to rescind
- accept resolution and do nothing
- bring back resolution to revise it to correct whereas/resolves
- reaffirm DC91–43.3
- improve stance to position ourselves better for when we revisit the issue (as we surely will)
- put forth a replacement resolution [*ibid.*].

Ultimately, IRC's recommendation to the Executive Board was that

> a new resolution be offered to counter the irregularities in this one. However, it is unlikely that a group of volunteers can prepare the quality resolution the Association needs; we need someone to research and draft such a resolution for us. We are prepared to advise on the structure and content, but we can not undertake the work needed to research the facts [3].

Finally, John's summary recognized the possibility that the IRC could be forced to "take its lumps" were Council to finally transmit the resolution to IRC with instructions to implement the 3rd resolved clause. In that event, the IRC drew up a list of possible responses, which included "ignore" the mandate or to "do something, but very slowly" (*ibid.*).

In the end, IRC chose to go to Council to have the already-passed resolution sent officially to IRC for review on the grounds that: the process followed in June/July 1992 was faulty; the resolution itself was "fundamentally flawed" and included "inflammatory language"; the mailing of copies to foreign countries was "possibly a dangerous practice" (*ibid.*).

At the 1993 midwinter meeting, this is exactly the tack taken by IRC, and Council, roundly chastised for not following protocol and passing an inflammatory and potentially dangerous resolution, complied. At the very conference where Anti-Defamation League members hovered over the Israeli Censorship and Palestinian Libraries Task Force table in an act of intimidation, Council passed the following by a vote of 156 in favor, zero opposed, zero abstentions, 2 not voting, and 13 excused from the vote.

> Resolved, That the Resolution on Israeli Censorship be referred to the ALA International Relations Committee for study and recommendations; that the parties previously informed of the resolution be told that ALA has referred the matter to its International Relations Committee for study and recommendation; and that the Council and membership receive a report back from the International Relations Committee at the New Orleans Conference" [ALA 1993, 850].

The IRC reported back in New Orleans with the recommendation that the Resolution on Israeli Censorship be revoked. Voting in favor were 110 councilors, opposed 15, abstaining 14, casting no vote 13, and excused from voting 20—the first time in ALA's history that Council had revoked a resolution it had seen fit previously to approve.

What is to be concluded concerning the debates surrounding censorship in Israel and the Occupied Territories in the 1980s and '90s? The Intellectual Freedom Committee withdrew as a formal consultative body from matters regarding intellectual freedom in countries outside the U.S. The International Relations Committee twice claimed it could not substantiate claims regarding Israeli censorship, despite considerable documentation. A resolution denouncing Israeli censorship was passed at a membership meeting and by Council, only to be rescinded later. SRRT, of course, stood firm. Overwhelming evidence existed for anyone to see, except those wearing blinders, and those who didn't want to see it. As for the argument that ALA should not "single out" Israel for condemnation, as long as the U.S. government continues to "single out" Israel for special treatment in terms of financial and military support, there will always be U.S. citizens who object to any and all manifestations of support for a nation engaged in genocide. Growing activism these days in the Boycott, Divestment and Sanctions movement ensures that Israel's long history of censorship will come to ALA's attention again.

Postscript

The story of the Resolution on Israeli Censorship cannot be concluded without mention of ALA leadership's "witchhunt" against SRRT and David Williams, and SRRT's subsequent removal of Williams from his position as chair of the Israeli Censorship and Palestinian Libraries Task Force. The former was inexcusable, the later was a sad ending to a worthy cause.

With the passage of the Resolution on Israeli Censorship, opponents unwilling to challenge the actual charges leveled against the Israeli state, chose instead to vilify Williams, and critics external to ALA chose to charge him with anti–Semitism.

At the annual conference in 1993, President Marilyn L. Miller announced that she had established a Presidential Special Task Force on the Conduct of Meetings and ALA Values. Task force members were three past-presidents—Patricia Berger, Edward G. Holley, and Regina Minudri—and its purpose was to:

- evaluate the purpose, goals, and activities of the SRRT Task Force on Israeli Censorship and Palestinian Libraries and how they related to the goals of the ALA and the ALA organizational structure and values;
- to review allegations of censorship, personal harassment, and suppression of freedom of expression in the conduct of task force meetings and programs;
- and to respond with recommendations on the resolution of concerns that have arisen from these allegations [Presidential 1993].

Both Stephen Stillwell, SRRT Action Council Coordinator, and David Williams were asked to meet with the Executive Board to answer questions regarding concerns outlined above. Stillwell was asked what oversight SRRT exercised over its constituent task forces, and about the Resolution on Israeli Censorship. The report on this meeting in *American Libraries* (July/August 1993), states that Stillwell responded that SRRT had just voted to reaffirm the resolution. When asked why such a vote was deemed necessary, Stillwell replied, "I felt that the resolution had been passed by the will of ALA's membership and that will was being threatened." Conversation moved to the "singling out" of Israel for censure and how Jewish people might feel about that. Stillwell noted that Jewish members of SRRT had found no problems with the resolution, and noted that the object of the resolution was the Israeli government, not Jewish people. Later at the ALA membership meeting, attended by some 600 members, Stillwell also noted that despite all the controversy over the resolution no one had "disputed the truth of the allegations contained within it" (Flagg).

Williams had words of his own for the Executive Board in a prepared five-minute statement, which he read, at one point calling Miller's proposal for a special task force a "McCarthyite witch-hunt." Williams was questioned nonetheless, and Judith Sessions asked, "Do you think you're speaking for 56,000 [ALA] members?" To which Williams replied that it was ALA's own governing Council that passed the resolution, not him, pointing out to Sessions that he was not even a member of Council.

Williams wasn't alone in thinking Miller's task force was heavy-handed. During debate at the first Council meeting over Miller's proposed task force, Councilor Herb Biblo urged that ALA "not slip into a witch-hunt mentality"; Bernard Margolis called the proposal "ill advised"; Norman Horrocks, ever ready with citations to ALA by-laws, noted that "any parent body may establish a task force, determine its duration, monitor its progress and terminate its function." "With all due respect," Horrocks is reported to have said, "is our president a parent body?" (Flagg 1993). A motion was made to disband the fledgling special task force, whereupon someone moved to table the motion to disband.

Miller's proposal was revisited at the third Council meeting, coming to the floor in the report of the Committee on Organization (COO). According to *American Libraries*, COO chair Karen Whitney claimed that, "when a unit of the Association is functioning in violation of policy, it is COO's job to investigate." Whitney's report generated heated discussion, with Norman Horrocks expressing concern that efforts might have been afoot to dissolve SRRT, to which Regina Minudri replied, "There is absolutely no move to disband, dissolve, or do anything else to a unit of this Association!" Al Kagan, a member of SRRT's Action Council, asked permission to address Council, and expressed SRRT's distress over the Executive Boards' task force, and requested that SRRT simply be allowed to deal internally with any concerns regarding its task forces.

How SRRT chose to address concerns was to direct that the Israeli Censorship and Palestinian Libraries Task Force select a new chair, and until that happened "all correspondence from the current [chair] ... be funneled through the SRRT Action Council Coordinator" (*SRRT* 1993, 7).

In a statement published in the same issue of *SRRT Newsletter*, Williams wrote,

> This censorship edict is aimed at hampering the Task Force until such time that it can be buried more discreetly. Upset with the Israeli censorship controversy and the obstacle it poses to harmonious relations with the ALA leadership, they have heaped a disproportionate amount of blame on me for the virulence of the debate and our defeat at the hands of the combined forces of the Israel lobby and the ALA leadership. In taking this unprecedented action, they have betrayed the best traditions of SRRT, whose role in the ALA has often been to advance controversial and initially unpopular positions. And so—ironically and tragically—the failure of the ALA to stand by its criticism of Israeli censorship is now leading to the censoring of such criticism within a professional association professing dedication to the principles of freedom of information and expression [Williams 1993, 8–9].

Problems continued, and at the 1994 annual conference in Miami, the SRRT Action Council, in an unprecedented closed meeting, passed the following resolution,

> WHEREAS the behavior of David L. Williams has shown and continues to show a continued disregard for the spirits and ideals which the Social Responsibilities Round Table hopes to exemplify:
>
> WHEREAS this behavior has been manifested in both oral presentations at various fora at American Library Association meetings and in written works distributed at and between these sessions;
>
> THEREFORE BE IT RESOLVED that David L. Williams is:

1) removed from his appointed position as Co-ordinator of the Task Force on Israeli Censorship and Palestinian Libraries;
2) prohibited from assuming the position of At-Large Member of Action Council to which he was elected; and
3) banned from any elected or appointed office with the Social Responsibilities Round Table or any of its several Task Forces, now existent or which may be created, until the close of the 1997 Annual Conference, scheduled for San Francisco [*SRRT* 1994, 4].

This chapter in SRRT's history was brought to a conclusion the following summer when the SRRT membership meeting voted to ratify the above resolution (*SRRT* 1995, 1).

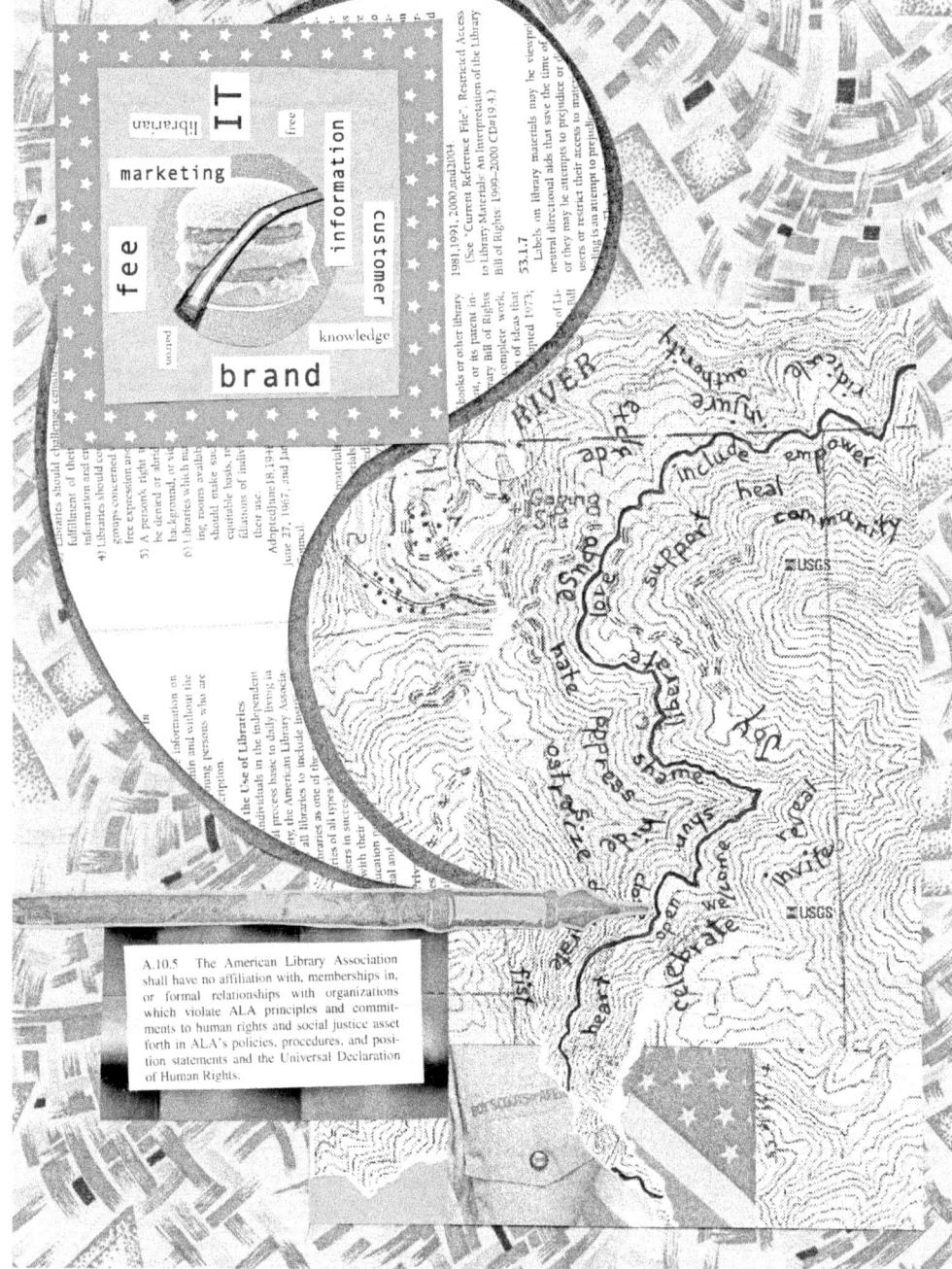

4. Speaking with One Voice, Strangling Others?—McDonald's and the Boy Scouts of America

Health food is socially responsible.
—Chris Sokol, 1991

Words have been used to hurt: faggot, dyke, fairy, queer, pansy—we've heard them all. But words can also define and clarify and heal and empower.
—Christine Jenkins, 1986

... criticism is disloyal and might break up the team.
—Worsley (quoted in Rosenthal)

The front cover of the July/August 1992 issue of *American Libraries* featured, in living color, the smiling faces of ALA members participating in San Francisco's annual Gay Pride parade. Decorated with the familiar, blue library icon, their banner read "Gay and Lesbian Task Force, American Library Association." Marchers held cardboard signs reading "Check it out—Lesbian & Gay Materials," "San Francisco Public Library," and "Coming Soon! Gay & Lesbian Center at the New Main." Juxtaposed to the spirit of pride, was that of prejudice. Just days earlier, SRRT's Gay and Lesbian Task Force (GLTF) had sponsored a preconference program called "When Sex Is the Question: Who Asks, Who Answers?" One speaker, Sherry Thomas, the owner and publisher of Spinsters and Aunt Lute book companies, reported that she had "noticed more overt homophobia on the exhibits floor at recent ALA conferences." She also noted that she experienced less homophobia at the American Booksellers Association meetings because booksellers knew her books were quite marketable (When 9).

Homophobia in Libraryland reared its ugly head as the gay cover of *American Libraries* appeared in mailboxes across the country. Tom Gaughan, *American Libraries* editor, used his editorial space in the September issue to describe the fury:

> ... just 24 hours after the advance copies of the July/August issue of *AL* reached our office, I began to get educated by readers who were irate over the cover photo of ALA's Gay and Lesbian Task Force. Now I know that the word homophobia isn't histrionic [Gaughan 612].

He described taking a telephone call from a man so angry that he had a difficult time speaking, but managed to tell Gaughan that he lived in a good neighborhood and "didn't want anyone to see something like *AL*'s cover in his mailbox." A school librarian didn't want her students to see the cover either, while another caller asked if *AL* would next be putting photos of murderers on the front cover. When Gaughan shared his shock at these calls with co-workers, one black colleague responded that "no amount of fear and loathing surprised her," and a gay colleague informed Gaughan that homophobia was the "last socially acceptable prejudice" (*ibid.*).

Events during the 1992 conference in San Francisco raised the ire not only of homophobes and Zionists (see Chapter 3), but soon to join in a raucous mix of complaints against ALA were proponents of healthy food and opponents of ALA's ties with the Boy Scouts of America.

Today it seems unbelievable that there once were times when blood boiled at ALA meetings during debates over whether or not children and teens should be encouraged to use the library, or foreign language materials collected, or Jim Crow libraries desegregated, or Library of Congress subject headings for GLBTQ resources changed to something other than "SEE sexual perversion." In the mid-1990s, however, a combination of issues—the Resolution on Israeli Censorship, plus a statement issued by SRRT protesting a reading campaign that amounted to free advertising for McDonald's fast food restaurants, and topped off with questions raised regarding ALA's relationship with the homophobic Boy Scouts of America—spurred ALA leaders to consider taking measures to prevent future outbreaks of controversial issues likely to produce public and member relations "trouble." These efforts coalesced into: the idea that ALA should "speak with one voice"; an investigation of "ALA units that violate policy"; and a decision to increase quorum for membership meetings, which effectively eliminated that arena as a source of controversial resolutions going to Council until several years later.

Private conversations regarding the establishment of some sort of control over problematic resolutions led to proposals for special task forces, then into a full-blown organizational self-study, and a by-laws change. Motivation among some within ALA leadership circles to control statements issued by its various units was strong. Proponents of these efforts claimed ALA could only be effective if it spoke with "one voice" on matters related to its purpose and mission. Opponents considered "speaking with one voice" to be the muzzling of many, and antithetical to the Association's claims to be a cornerstone of democracy.

In subsequent years, from time to time on the floor of Council someone would make reference to the "one voice policy," usually in an attempt to derail discussion of a controversial topic. Whenever this appeal was made it would be countered with a demand that the policy be identified, that the number of the so-called policy be shared, its secret page number in the *Handbook of Organization* revealed. Such moments began to take on an element of farce when no "one voice policy" could be produced, and the demand that the policy be adhered to would just fizzle out. While there never was a resolution or committee recommendation that produced any such policy, there certainly were a series of recommendations and resolutions, each containing an element of the "one voice" formulation. This was enough to create among Council members who had served during those years, a collective, historical memory of fragments congealed into a *myth* of a policy. "Speaking with one voice" became a code phrase used in debate to caution members of Council that they were treading into danger zones, that one should proceed with care.

Impetus behind efforts to ensure that ALA speak with one voice arose largely from negative reactions to three SRRT initiatives: the Resolution on Israeli Censorship (see Chapter 3), and two SRRT resolutions on which this chapter focuses: "On corporate sponsorship issues" and "Resolution on the ALSC/Boy Scouts Relationship."

"Together is Better"—under the golden arches

In the fall of 1992, some 16,000 public libraries across the United States received (unsolicited) a package filled with posters, bookmarks, stickers, reading logs and a program guide announcing ALA's national reading program for 1993. In the program guide's introduction, Mollie Bynum, chair of the National Reading Program Committee (NRPC) of the Association of Library Services to Children (ALSC), wrote that the program, entitled Together is Better…Let's Read!, "reaches out to young and old alike with an exciting, intergenerational approach that brings children and adults together to promote reading" (*Together* 2).

The colorful materials featured artwork by the popular children's book author and illustrator James Stephenson—a watercolor of a dapper, elderly gentleman who sits between the roots of a mighty old tree, reading to a group of smiling children, a cow, a dog, and a turtle. A second audience quietly gathers behind (and above) the mustachioed man—a bear, rabbit, two ducks, a frog, and a squirrel—all as attentive as the children. Clearly an intergenerational (as well as interspecies) sharing of a good story! The elderly gent's speech bubble declares, "I can't believe what happens next!"

Members of ALSC and the program committee surely identified with the old man's astonished disbelief at developments following the national distribution of the cheerful materials. As it turned out, not all 16,000 recipients of the surprise packages were quite as happy as Stephenson's storytime audience. The problem was that the NRPC had invited the McDonald's Corporation to be its primary funding partner, and the corporation had taken full advantage of the opportunity to use the posters, bookmarks, stickers, reading logs and program guide for advertising purposes—every item prominently featured the fast food restaurant's iconic golden arches logo.

Furthermore, immediately following Bynum's introduction, the program guide contained a full page of information about McDonald's sponsorship: background on the corporation, instructions to librarians seeking partnerships with local franchises, plus an injunction regarding the use (misuse, abuse) of their logo.

> The McDonald's logo is wholly owned by the McDonald's Corporation. As McDonald's is the exclusive national quick service restaurant (QSR) sponsor, at no time may the McDonald's logo be covered or removed from the "Together Is Better" collateral materials or artwork. The artwork provided must be reproduced as is, with no alternations to the size, color, or style [3].

The background information in the guide suggests a powerful incentive for McDonald's willingness to foot the bill for the printing and distribution of 16,000 packages. Worldwide, at that time, McDonald's had 12,400 restaurants with 8,900 in the U.S. In 1992, therefore, nearly twice as many libraries as McDonald's had restaurants were required—if they wanted to use ALA's national reading program materials—to advertise exclusively for this QSR, even in communities that had no local McDonald's franchise.

Members of ALSC's National Reading Program Committee were well aware of potential concerns, if not outright objections, to the "commercialization" of library programs and services. The minutes of ALSC's board of directors 1992 meetings at both midwinter and annual contain specific mention of such concerns. At ALSC's past presidents' breakfast meeting, Immediate Past President Barbara Barstow reported on "discussion of commercialism at ALA, because it presents a 'catch 22' situation. ALA needs and wants visibility, but when it's done, it gets labeled commercialism" (Association 1992a, 6). At the time, no mention was made of specific concerns regarding potential commercial sponsorship of the national reading program, or any other ALSC activities.

At the annual meeting, however, commercialization was raised directly within the context of the national reading program. Committee chair, Mollie Bynum, reported that the committee "needs some input from the Board about commercial sponsorship of this reading program" (Association 1992b, 51). One member noted that a number of commercial sponsors were prepared to help fund the summer reading program, but that "it would be the sponsor's program" with Bynum adding "we must walk the thin line between profitability and literary integrity" (*ibid.*).

Some ALA members opposed commercialization of library services, programs, and resources on several levels: the use of corporate names and logos could imply library support for the products and services of those corporations; advertisements in the library turned public and noncommercial space into a P.R. bonanza for those businesses so favored; the ubiquity of advertising made commercial-free places ever more rare and desirable. Despite concerns about what corporate sponsorships might involve, ALA Graphics insisted that if it were to continue the production of reading program materials the project must be profitable. The NRPC requested that the matter of commercialization be discussed and advice provided by ALSC directors at the 1993 midwinter meeting. By that time, however, McDonald's had been brought on board, materials produced and distributed, and questions raised regarding commercialization at ALA in a manner which ruffled feathers not only within ALSC but on Council.

At that 1993 midwinter meeting in Denver, Sandy Berman, whose library had received one of the famous QSR's packages, proposed at a SRRT Action Council meeting that SRRT issue a statement condemning the marketing of fast foods under the guise of reading advocacy. Of concern was the fact that in highlighting McDonald's as the source of the posters, bookmarks, and reading logs, libraries would essentially be *advertising* for the fast food restaurant, encouraging library users to patronize their local franchise, not a particularly responsible act if one considered the healthfulness of McDonald's fast food. Berman's suggestion was discussed and promptly acted on.

ON CORPORATE SPONSORSHIP ISSUES

WHEREAS there can be little quarrel with the American Library Association seeking funds from private sources to support worthwhile projects; but

WHEREAS the recent collaboration between ALA and McDonald's Family Restaurants on the "Together is Better" national reading program has resulted in an advertising windfall for McDonald's, libraries clearly and deliberately being used as a promotional and marketing medium for fast foods;

THEREFORE BE IT RESOLVED that the Social Responsibilities Round Table urges ALA to avoid collaboration or funding arrangements in the future that in effect equate books, reading, and libraries with hamburgers or other commodities;

AND BE IT FURTHER RESOLVED that copies of this resolution be sent to Marilyn Miller, ALA President; Ed Resni, McDonald's President/CEO; *American Libraries*; *Library Journal*; and *School Library Journal* [On 3].

Action Council had no plans to take the resolution any further, content with simply having expressed concern to all parties involved. However, word of the statement quickly spread during the conference, and ALSC's executive board, outraged at SRRT's denunciation of the partnership, endorsed a resolution brought to Council by Councilor Mary Jane Anderson and ALSC's own Division Councilor Frances V. Sedney. The resolved read,

> ... the Council of the ALA joins the Association of Library Services to Children in expressing to McDonald's its sincere appreciation of their support (past, present, and anticipated future), our assurance that the Social Responsibilities Round Table (SRRT) speaks for itself in this matter and not for the Association, and our hope that libraries that voluntarily decide to use the materials that have been sent to 16,000 of them and order others through ALA Graphics, will find that the materials do indeed achieve their purpose: to encourage more and more "reading together" [Voting 1993, 851].

This resolution on McDonald's, also officially endorsed by the directors of the Young Adult Library Services Association (YALSA), passed Council overwhelmingly in a vote of 137 in favor, 3 opposed, 1 abstention, 24 excused from voting, and 6 casting no vote.

Council minutes report that Anderson, in speaking to her resolution, said SRRT "impugned the motives" of McDonald's, and she argued for passage of the resolution on the grounds that McDonald's "might not understand that ALA units such as round tables speak only for their members and not for the Association." Anderson believed her resolution "might counteract some of the embarrassing damage that could be done to a positive relationship with the McDonald's Corporation" (Council Minutes 1993, 38).

During Council debate, SRRT Action Council Coordinator Stephen Stillwell was permitted to speak and meeting minutes report him to have said that SRRT's resolution

> ... was not targeted at McDonald's but at ALA procedures, particularly, the deluging of overworked library staff with unsolicited, and in some cases, unwanted materials. The intention of the SRRT resolution was never to speak for ALA, but only for SRRT [*ibid.*].

In his post-midwinter editorial, John N. Berry III, editor-in-chief of *Library Journal*, questioned how many libraries would be using the materials and suggested that many might have "doubts about equating reading and libraries with fast food and McDonald's" (Berry 1993,104). Lillian Gerhardt, editor of *School Library Journal* reported,

> It seems that SRRT decided that ALSC should not be cooperating with the purveyors of cholesterol-laden hamburgers that SRRT believes are only using ALSC for their own advertising and image purposes [Gerhardt 129].

The incorporation of the golden arches logo onto Stephenson's artwork, and the detailed, legally enforceable guidelines regarding the logo both strongly suggest that McDonald's partnership with ALSC was, indeed, contingent on using the reading program materials to advertise. A fleeting glance at one of the stickers, bookmarks, reading logs or posters would immediately connect the viewer's mind to McDonald's first, and to reading, books, sharing of stories, or being out-of-doors secondarily. And nothing of immediate notice makes a connection to libraries. Only when one actually scrutinizes one of these items, reading the tiny font used for copyright and illustration credits does one learn of the connection to copyright holder—the American Library Association.

As if a mental first connection to McDonald's were not enough, adjacent to the golden arches on every printed piece and on the program guide's cover, in readily legible font, was the not-quite-accurate statement: "This program is brought to you by your neighborhood McDonald's™ family restaurants." The statement is misleading on several counts.

First, the program was designed with minimal input from McDonald's. Rather, it was the work of members of the National Reading Program Committee. Secondly, it is unlikely that "neighborhood McDonald's™ family restaurants" had any idea the reading program was taking place unless contacted directly by a participating neighborhood library. All outreach suggestions for the program were addressed to libraries contacting restaurants, not the reverse. Thirdly, the pronounced contrast between Stephenson's pastoral watercolor and McDonald's ubiquitous, bold, yellow-and-red logo under the words "Together is Better" convey the implied, and immediate, message that "together" means *with McDonald's*. That is how advertising works. In response to Stephenson's elderly reader's exclamation, "I can't believe what happens next!" one expects any of his listeners to jump up and shout "They all go to McDonald's for burgers and shakes, sodas and fries!" Well, maybe not the cow.

Not only does McDonald's claim full credit in its "brought to you by" statement, but the prominence of both logo and statement overshadow any credit due to ALSC. SRRT was taken to task by Council, *Library Journal*, and *School Library Journal* editors for not communicating its concerns to ALSC before issuing the resolution "On corporate sponsorship." In all fairness, however, there was little reason to connect the materials to ALSC. None of the materials, except the program guide, gave any credit to ALSC. The guide's introduction did identify author Mollie Bynum as the chair of the National Reading Program Committee of the Association of Library Services to Children, but all copyright credit was held by ALA. Anyone seeing only the materials designed for public consumption would never know they were produced by a division of ALA.

School Library Journal's coverage of the controversy is worth taking a moment to review, as it seems to have been written by a reporter who was not present at the conference. The report states that McDonald's assisted in printing and distributing "recommended reading lists." Although the program guide did contain 150 recommended titles, to describe the varied materials, activities, guidelines, reproducibles as a "reading list" greatly diminishes the work, creativity, and extent of the program. Next, *School Library Journal*'s reporter chastises SRRT for not consulting with ALSC's directors "who were meeting down the hall from SRRT Action Council" as if SRRT actually knew the materials originated from ALSC, or that ALSC directors were immediately available for consultation and would welcome a new agenda item. More pointedly, however, was the erroneous assertion at the end of the report that SRRT had assumed "ALA's authority to speak for the organization" (Gerhard 129). One need only read "On corporate sponsorship issues" to know that SRRT was urging ALA to consider the matter of commercializing library programs. "SRRT urges ALA" are words that unambiguously convey a request *from* SRRT *to* ALA. To characterize the resolution as an assumption of authority is either the result of misinformation or inattention, or a determination to simply characterize SRRT as acting in violation of ALA policy.

Both *Library Journal* and *School Library Journal* might instead have pointed fingers at ALSC for failing to have addressed concerns raised the previous summer by the NRPC regarding the commercialization of the reading program. Mollie Bynum directly requested guidance from ALSC's Board of Directors on the issue of commercialism during its 1992 annual meeting. Her request must have arisen from questions raised by NPRC members or from other colleagues or constituencies, although the impetus behind these concerns was never reported in meeting minutes. As an ALSC agenda item at midwinter 1993, the commercialization of the national reading program leaped in status from back-burner to hot-button.

In her report as NPRC chair, Bynum "advised that her committee has been discussing both the pros and cons of the issue of corporate sponsorship, particularly in light of the McDonald's controversy generated by the Social Responsibilities Round Table" (Association 1993, 11). Interestingly, SRRT is charged with generating the controversy, despite the fact that Bynum's request for guidance from the ALSC Board of Directors certainly indicates that she had anticipated that controversy might well arise from the commercialization of the reading program. From another point-of-view, responsibility for the controversy could be placed in ALSC's court as the party responsible in the first place for permitting McDonald's to use national reading program materials for advertising.

Bynum also mentioned telephone calls received by committee members that were "negative about corporate sponsorship," but countered this opposition by noting that ALA Graphics had "received over 600 reply cards ... and all, but one or two ... were overwhelmingly positive" (*ibid.*). Of course, 600 positive responses out of a possible 16,000 can hardly be taken as a reliable measure of enthusiastic utilization of the materials.

SRRT had certainly ruffled the feathers of ALSC, and stood accused of assuming ALA's authority. The McDonald's controversy, however, was a minor kerfluffle compared to what came next: a direct SRRT challenge to another ALSC partnership—with the Boy Scouts of America.

Best books for Boy Scouts

A mature man attending a meeting of the governing body of his professional association dressed in his Boy Scout uniform is not a common sight. Yet that is exactly how Michael Golrick chose to dress for a session of Council at ALA's 1998 annual conference. The caption of a photo of Golrick standing at the microphone in the August 1998 issue of *American Libraries*, notes that he "stands uniformed and ready to debate the ALA–Boy Scouts connection" (Kniffel 97).

To capture the full spirit of Councilor Golrick's readiness, a better caption would have read "uniformed and *prepared*" in keeping with that universally known Boy Scout motto "Be Prepared." The motto, coined by Scouting's founder Robert Baden-Powell, was deliberately chosen to immortalize his nickname B-P (Rosenthal 163). Unfortunately for Golrick, his preparedness that day was all for naught. Council refrained that year from debating the ALA–Boy Scout relationship, opting to postpone consideration of the longstanding partnership to the following midwinter meeting. Golrick had, however, made his point—on Council was at least one member prepared to defend ALA's relationship with an organization that openly excluded certain people: atheists, homosexuals, and women (accepted as den mothers, but not as scoutleaders).

The matter of the relationship between ALA and the Scouts had arisen at least twice previously, first in 1988, then again in 1993, and by 1998, ALA's waxing-and-waning affiliation with the Boy Scouts of America (BSA) was more than eight decades old. In 1915, ALA Council approved a resolution supporting a Boy Scout initiative, which had already received the endorsement and active involvement of the American Booksellers Association (ABA).

Franklin K. Mathiews, chief Scout librarian for the BSA and a Baptist minister, attended the ABA's annual meeting in 1915 seeking to bring its members' attention "to the menace of the moment that threatens the youth of our country" (Mathiews 1915, 1487). The menace of which Mathiews spoke was the "thriller," sensational stories—with improbable plots and impossible boy heroes—voraciously consumed by real boys, and which "by over stimulation, debauch and vitiate, as brain and body are debauched and vitiated by strong drink." Mathiews described the imagination as one of a boy's "most valuable assets" and declared that the thrilling book lures a boy's imagination "into an expectation that is hopeless" (1489). "In my judgment," he declared,

> all such books should be classed with explosives, and there should be a law compelling publishers to label them "Dynamite! Guaranteed to Blow Your Boy's Brains Out".... Through the reading of these cheap books, ideals are lowered, high aspirations are throttled, tastes of every sort are vitiated, language is vulgarized, good manners coarsened, amusement standards lowered. In a word, the nobler mind, the finer emotions, are seared as with a red-hot iron. *This is the danger of which as parents we need to be afraid* [*ibid.*; emphasis in original].

His appeal to the booksellers was that they actively promote good books for boys.

> Give him ... a storybook about a man that's genuine and strong and grave. Let it be a book vivid in events, rich in incident, sound in principle. If the hero is too utterly utter in his virtue, your boys won't care much for your gift. But if he is just as boys ought to be, without any agony about it, your boy will be charmed, and in his imitative, imperfect way, will make that history repeat itself [*ibid.*].

To the purpose of promoting books with sound characters and principles, Mathiews revealed that the Boy Scouts of America had arrived at the idea of "Juvenile Book Week," a week in late November or early December when booksellers, libraries, women's groups, churches, and others, could encourage parents to purchase the "best books" for their boys as Christmas gifts. "Best," of course, to be determined by the Boy Scouts, and publicized through published lists, displays, and advertisements. Mathiews ended his presentation with an appeal that "ABA endorse our plan for a Juvenile Book Week, naming, if they will, the time best suited for such an observance" (1491).

Charles Scribner, chairing the ABA meeting responded in a rather curious manner,

> If this had been a real Methodist meeting, I believe we would have had "Amens" coming from all over the room as Mr. Mathiews read that paper.... I thought as I sat here this morning and heard him talk that probably the boys of the day had gotten hold of some of those wonderful books that he tells us about, and that that is the reason that they are coming to us and asking us for men's salaries [Laughter.] [*ibid.*].

Little did Scribner (apparently) know, but a central tenet of the Scouts was unquestioning obedience and loyalty to God, king/country, and employer, so he needn't have worried that books endorsed by the Boy Scouts would encourage demands for better pay from child laborers. And it is to here, in this placid, early 20th century setting, in a room filled with the captains of the publishing industry, that one can begin to follow a thread of ideology running through subsequent decades, weaving together an outlook shared by Scouting, industry, and some circles within librarianship about the values to be inculcated into boys via books and the great "game" of scouting.

Of all the "best books for boys" selected by scouting officials, booksellers, and librarians, the one topping the list year-after-year would undoubtedly, if unofficially, be the *Boy Scout Handbook* in all its evolving editions. For a young boy, the information contained in the *Handbook* represented the voice of a trusted authority on everything from building campfires to tying knots to repressing "worries." Not surprising then, that librarians working with the Boy Scouts, presumably sharing scouting's commitment to unquestioned loyalty, clean living, and manliness, were prepared to defend the relationship between the Scouts and ALA which began in 1915.

A foray into Baden-Powell's notions of how to build a boy's character in order for him to become a man, is worthwhile, and a brief account of Scouting's ideological and historical underpinnings sets the stage, and begins with the writings of the founder. The first edition of *Scouting for Boys*, written by Robert Baden-Powell and published in 1908 in Great Britain, contained the Scout Law, later adapted for use in the United States when scouting was imported here in 1910. The second of the "laws" reads as follows,

> A SCOUT IS LOYAL to the King, and to his officers, and to his country, and to his employers. He must stick to them through thick and thin against anyone who is their enemy, or who even talks badly of them [Rosenthal 109].

Concerning a boy's duty to stick to authority "through thick and thin," Baden-Powell (widely regarded as a war hero for his exploits during the Boer War) had extreme views on the lengths one must go in one's loyalty. For example, he was a great admirer of the Japanese sense of honor and loyalty. In *Boy Scouts Beyond the Seas* (1913), Baden-Powell describes Japanese soldiers who committed suicide rather than surrender to the Russians:

> They did not kill themselves by the easy method of shooting themselves, but by the painful way of disemboweling themselves with their swords. They did this because it was the more honourable way in which the *Samurai* or knights of Japan did it [127].

In *Yarns for Boy Scouts*, he tells another story of a Japanese boy who kills himself rather than reveal to bandits that his father was alive,

> Well, he was a plucky boy, wasn't he? He is one example for every boy, and especially every Scout, to follow in Being Prepared to give up all, even his own life if necessary, for the sake of another. That is what is meant by "Bushido," or self-sacrifice [*ibid.*].

At the time of the ABA meeting, the spirit of scouting would not have tolerated complaints about wages or working conditions. Indeed, a true Scout would face any amount of adversity or deprivation with a cheerful attitude and a smile on his face. If unemployed he might even commit *bushido*—Baden-Powell himself wrote that in the animal kingdom bees had the best policy on busy-less worker bees: "They are quite a model community, for they respect their queen and kill their unemployed" (183).

In relation to Scribner's comment in 1915, which so amused his colleagues, it is interesting to note that the second law of Scouting caused considerable consternation in Britain, so that in 1930 the Scout Executive Committee, under pressure from trade unionists and socialists (who had good reason not to want their sons indoctrinated into blind loyalty to employers) began to debate whether loyalty to employers should be removed from the law. The Executive Committee arrived at four possible solutions to the problem,

  1. To use the word "employment" instead of "employers."
  2. To cut down the definition and leave the law as—"A Scout is loyal to King and country"—this being what is done by the Girl Guides Association.
  3. That the Law should read after the words "King and country," "and to those over and under him."
  4. To read "A Scout is loyal to his King and country and to others to whom loyalty is due" [114].

However, Baden-Powell insisted on allegiance to employer,

> Re the proposal to omit from Scout Law "Loyalty to Employer"—The main objection has been raised by socialists to this. They maintain that the boy should be loyal rather to his Trades Union than to his employer. But boys don't as a rule, I believe, belong to Trades Unions, so there is no harm in their being loyal to their employers. It is their duty and they should be reminded of it. The fact that we do put it to them is the reason why so many employers prefer to give employment to Scouts [115].

On the other side of the Atlantic, in the anthology *The Boy Scouts Yearbook* (1932), edited by none other than Mathiews himself, one of the contributors was industrialist, banker, real estate magnate, and philanthropist John D. Rockefeller, Jr. First published in 1928 on the verge of the Great Depression, and reprinted every subsequent year as unemployment, breadlines, and tent encampments grew, Rockefeller writes in his essay "Character and Business" that the traits of integrity, obedience, clean living, and loyalty are the highest attainment to which a man should aspire. From his own position of wealth and privilege, Rockefeller tells his young readers that, "…in this money mad age we do well to remind ourselves that after all the real purpose of our existence is not to make a living, but to make a life—a worthy, well-rounded, and useful life" (Rockefeller 71).

These traits, in and of themselves worthy in any child or adult, become problematic when defined solely in terms of service to authority, business, empire, flag, male dominance, heterosexuality, and white privilege, and frozen into unquestioning reflexive action on behalf of other manifestations of injustice, ignorance, inhumanity. The definitions assigned to these characteristics and the behavioral expectations of boys benefited the status quo of the times, and were the ones accepted and promoted by the Boy Scouts, the booksellers, and the librarians.

One other aspect of Scouting's ideology was its relationship to militarism. In the wake of Britain's colonial wars and World War I, many parents did not want their sons' being trained for military service, and Boy Scouts activities and values seemed militaristic. In his response to accusations that the Boy Scouts was a platform for military training, Baden-Powell speaks out both sides of his mouth. On the one hand he claims his critics have not read what he has written very carefully, or (self-deprecatingly) that he has "expressed himself very badly" (Baden-Powell 300). But then he immediately goes on to say that, "Even if I had advocated training the lads in a military way (which I have not done), I am impenitent enough to see no harm in it" (*ibid.*). He then goes on to describe all the ways in which the training of boys to serve their country in preparation for war is the only sensible thing to do. War is inevitable, and "peace-scouts" for the Empire are necessary.

> Those who preach shutting our eyes to what is quite patent to all who dare to look out will themselves be guilty of tempting the enemy on, of bringing war upon our country, and of the blood and ruin which will assuredly follow.... With our rising generation brought up as good citizens, sensible of their responsibilities and duties in return for the benefits which they enjoy in a free country, there would be no danger for the State; but without manliness and good citizenship we are bound to fall.
>
> Manliness can only be taught by men, and not by those who are half men, half old women [301].

The last seems a dig at any who would refrain from preparations for war, and while Baden-Powell wanted parents to entrust their sons to his Scouting regimes and so had to appease their concerns, he also made it clear that the boy whose character was formed as a Boy Scout would become a MAN, ready to loyally and unquestioningly serve country, employer, God, and superior officers when necessary.

Returning to the ABA's (and ALA's) response to Mathiews' proposed Juvenile Book Week, it is worthwhile to briefly unravel what Mathiews' might have meant when he cautioned against books with heroes "too utterly utter" in virtuousness. In this unraveling, we see a psychological mechanism by which the characters of boys were molded via the teachings conveyed via "best books for boys."

In his capacity as chief Scout librarian, Mathiews' wording places him in accord with Baden-Powell's insistence that Boy Scouts *act*, they don't think. In Rosenthal's description of Baden-Powell's attempt to model character development of boys after practices used in the "public" schools of the British ruling class, he writes,

> Effeminate, incompetent, and doomed to failure, the man who is tempted to criticize had better think twice about it. The successful scout (or adult) must never traduce his ideals by wondering about them [Rosenthal 93].

Question, reflection, doubt, debate were not among the ideals of scouting. Indeed, they were anathema to loyalty, action, duty, obedience. The boy who doubted or questioned could never become a *real* man—a man of action. This was the mindset to be promoted during Juvenile Book Week, and both the ABA and the ALA signed on wholeheartedly.

The ABA's 1915 resolution was written and presented by none other than Frederic G. Melcher, future president of R. R. Bowker, founder of both the Newbery and Caldecott book awards, and in 1999 named by ALA as one of the 100 most important people of the 20th century. The resolution read,

> RESOLVED, That the Association approve the suggestion of the Boy Scouts of America for a country-wide canvass for better books for children, both by the co-operation of a special week in November, and by an offer on our part to raise the standard of children's reading, as offered by our stores and by the publishers [Good 1273].

The same report in *Publishers Weekly* for October 14, 1916, also contained the resolved clause of ALA's statement,

> RESOLVED, That the Council of the American Library Association welcomes the aid of the Library Commission of the Boy Scouts of America in its efforts to improve the reading taste of the boys of the country; that the Council of this Association approves the plans of the Library Commission of the Boy Scouts for a week, when by vote of the American Booksellers' Association, the retail book-trade shall place special emphasis on juvenile books, and that the Council of this Association commends this plan, as announced by the Boy Scouts of America to the favorable consideration of the public librarians of the country [*ibid*.].

Thus, in the midst of World War I, publishers, booksellers, and librarians joined forces with the Boy Scouts of America to promote an ideology of unquestioned loyalty, action, and a highly constrained definition of manliness, all purposefully designed to sow within a boy's conscience and character seeds that would mature into an adulthood of service to authority, be it the waning British or waxing U.S. empire of the early 20th century. The ideology of Scouting was antithetical to another ideal: that of the informed citizen, capable and ready to participate in democratic governance with its myriad questions, dissensions, uncertainties, and challenges to both authority and self—the spirit of Democracy, utterly utter in its virtues.

The event signed on to by ABA and ALA was slated for December 4–9, 1916, and was called "Good Book Week" with accompanying slogan "Buy the Best Books for Your Children." In announcing the campaign, *Publishers Weekly* included a list of advice for how booksellers, libraries, public schools, women's groups, churches, YMCAs and the Boy Scouts itself could best participate.

"Authoritative book lists" and a poster were available for distribution, and *PW*'s advice included displays of good books, sermons on the importance of children's reading, and the drafting of library assistants by bookstores that week in order to use their expertise to recommend to customers good books for Christmas gift purchases. Churches were encouraged to "See that Sunday School teachers, giving books as Christmas gifts to their classes, make the right selections" (*ibid*.). Among the list of promotional materials available for "Good Book Week" was a 4-page pamphlet with the horribly graphic title— "Blowing Out the Boy's Brains." A reprint from the magazine *Outlook*, the article "Tells of the modern menace of the book bound thriller, the nickel novel in disguise," and included a bibliography of the "very best books for boys" selected by the Library Commission of the Boy Scouts of America (1274). The BSA Library Commission included Mathiews, librarians from the Washington, D.C., and Pittsburgh PA public libraries, the superintendent of libraries for the New York City Board of Education, the librarian from Pratt Institute in Brooklyn, and three editors of the Boy Scouts.

This collaborative effort between scouting and publishing in the U.S. echoed that of Baden-Powell's own close relationship with C. Arthur Pearson and his publishing empire in the U.K. That partnership had been essential in the first years of scouting, as Pearson's promotional genius was single-handedly responsible for the launch and immediate popularity of Baden-Powell's ideas (Rosenthal 81–87).

Collaboration between scouts, publishers, and librarians continued at a steady pace for the next several decades.

In a 1939 article in the October issue of *ALA Bulletin*, Huber William Hurt, national director of the BSA's Reading Program, encouraged librarians to assist in the Scouts' "aggressive advance" along the reading front by establishing spaces in libraries for teens. "In certain libraries," he wrote,

> the children's section is exactly that and the adult section is adult. The young scout (and even more so the 300,000 over fifteen) is between juvenile and adult and is sensitively aware that he is neither! [Hurt 688].

To promote good books for boys, Hurt reported that many libraries had established a "Scout Nook" or "Scout Shelves" as spaces to attract adolescent boys.

> Progressive libraries are making subject lists of their available books so that troop reading advisors can readily refer scouts to what the library has on aviation, mountain climbing, submarines, radio and the like. This practical "magic," which summons a subject list out of the dim fastnesses of the impersonal mysteries of the card index, is an application of salesmanship to books. Department stores have no card index of wares for customers—they show their wares. An attractive book may win a reader even as in a book shop it lures a prospective buyer [*ibid.*].

Hurt goes on to describe libraries assisting scouts with merit badge information, handbooks, and reading lists, and the services scouts might in turn provide the library, "scouts watch for chances to serve and help ... taking books to shut-ins, helping the library on special exhibits and special occasions, assisting in book repair" (*ibid.*).

In 1960, the Boy Scouts honored ALA with a Fiftieth Anniversary Certificate of Appreciation in a ceremony held at the Donnell Library in New York City, to recognize the longstanding assistance librarianship had provided to Scouts over the years (Boy 1961, 197). And, as late as 1986 (by which time the BSA was becoming embroiled in lawsuits regarding discrimination against gay Scouts) librarians were being encouraged to assist with merit badges and reading lists, and at national jamborees. In an *American Libraries* article entitled "Library Outreach to the Boy Scouts," Paul E. Garrison credits ALA members with helping the 1,290,000th scout earn his reading merit badge, and lauds the Association for Library Service to Children and its Advisory Committee to the Boy Scouts of America for 25 years of cooperation and support (Garrison 140). He cites ALSC's work at the 1973 quadrennial Boy Scout National Jamboree where librarians participated in setting up a booth on the Merit Badge Midway to promote and support reading merit badge activities. Over 50,000 boys visited the booth where books donated by publishing companies were given away for free, and where help and advice on earning the badge was available from librarians.

Statistically, if estimates that 1 of every 11 people are homosexual hold true, ALSC librarians at the 1973 Jamboree received visits from 5,500 gay Boy Scouts, each of whom were, surely, warmly welcomed at the ALSC booth where free books and friendly advise were distributed indiscriminately to gay, straight, bisexual, and questioning boys.

Fair and equal treatment at the 1973 Jamboree, of course, was far from a reflection of acceptance of homosexuality within either the Boy Scouts or ALSC. Rather, it was a measure of the extent to which gay Scouts hid their homosexuality from others—often from themselves as well.

Not every reader of *American Libraries* was as enthusiastic a promoter of the Boy Scout/ALA relationship as Garrison. Not every gay Scout remained silent. And ALA's Gay and Lesbian Task Force had been around since 1970.

In January 1988, just months after a decision by the Connecticut Supreme Court that the Boy Scouts of America was within its rights to exclude women as troop leaders, questions were raised regarding ALSC's Boy Scouts of America Advisory Committee, and a suggestion was made that this stand-alone committee (one with a sometimes substantial budget) be placed under ALSC's umbrella group, the Liaison with National Organizations Serving the Child Committee (LNOSC). In February, ALSC member Ruth I. Gordon wrote a letter to Anitra R. Steele, chair of the committee charged with investigating the matter.

Gordon expressed her strong objection "to ALSC's intimate relationship with the Boy Scouts" on the grounds that gay and handicapped boys were not allowed to become Eagle Scouts, and that women were not allowed to serve as scoutmasters, although women had long served as den mothers for Cub Scouts. She wrote to Steele,

> Too many people have chaired the BSA Committee and hold it to themselves with a loving tenderness. However, others mentioned that they would like to see BSA removed from its special place [in ALSC]. I, for one, only see that ALSC cooperates with BSA but receives little or nothing in return. Above all, my concern is for the exclusivity of BSA when it considers the "different" unfit for Life and Eagle ranks [Gordon 2].

Having opened her letter expressing reluctance to have "this particular bunch of dirty laundry go to ALA's Social Responsibility Round Table or the Gay Caucus," Gordon ends by saying that if no action was forthcoming from ALSC she would "take it to SRRT or Gay Caucus."

A mere three days after Gordon wrote, a decision was made by the Scouts' national executive board to allow women as scoutmasters. Having fought a 12-year legal battle to exclude women, BSA officials realized time had come to change. In a letter to ALSC Executive Director Susan Roman, the BSA's national Director of Education/Community Relationships John W. Larson wrote,

> It is time to recognize that in a changing society the unique strength of our organization lies in the dedicated efforts of both men and women. Our efforts must be focused on obtaining the best possible leadership—male or female—to carry forward the work of the Scouting movement [Larson].

He also wrote that accommodations for Scouts with handicaps were made so they could earn merit badges. Regarding the matter of homosexuals, Larson informed Roman that "The courts have determined that the Boy Scouts of America is a private membership organization and homosexuals will not be allowed to participate" (*ibid.*).

Although Scouting proved amenable to some change, Steele wasn't, and shared her "gut reaction" to committee members in May that "NO WAY" should the Boy Scouts of America be relegated to LNOSC like just another organization served by ALSC. She then averred that the decision would be made by the committee, not by herself alone (Steele 1988a). As it turned out, however, Steele's personal opinion on the matter seems to have been shared by all others consulted. In a memo dated June 28, 1988, she writes that those queried do not "feel a change in status for the Boy Scout Advisory Committee is in the best interest of ALSC" (Steele 1988b).

And there the matter hibernated, until the summer of 1993, which saw SRRT Coordinator Stephen Stillwell not only facing a hostile ALA Executive Board on the matter of SRRT's role in the Resolution on Israeli Censorship *and* defending SRRT's McDonald's statement before Council, but also, on a quiet afternoon, perusing ALA's *Handbook of Organization* looking for potential SRRT allies.

Stillwell, a librarian at Harvard University with a master's degree in the history of diplomacy, knew well the value of alliances, and was determined to help SRRT develop positive relationships with units throughout the Association. Before becoming Action Council coordinator, he had been active in SRRT's Peace Information Exchange Task Force and, along with his longtime partner Tom Wilding, in the Gay and Lesbian Task Force of SRRT. Therefore, when he noticed among the list of ALA affiliate organizations the Boy Scouts of America, he knew he'd run up against another issue on which SRRT had to act. With the McDonald's brou-ha-ha fresh in mind, and his considerable understanding of international diplomacy from which to draw, Stillwell knew how to proceed and "made preliminary contacts with the powers-that-be at the ALSC vis-à-vis the BSA issue" (Stillwell 1), thus launching what would become a five year debate regarding what amounted to a nearly 80-year-old relationship between ALA and the Boy Scouts of America.

Before moving on: while little is known about Baden-Powell's views on homosexuality, there does exist one telling bit of documentation.

In the late 1930s, Baden-Powell, desirous that the Boy Scouts establish ties with the youth organizations of both Hitler and Mussolini, revealed his disdain for homosexuals in a letter dated October 8, 1937. In the letter, Baden-Powell urges the director of Scouting's International Bureau to consider that "the British movement at any rate, ought to do something to be friendly with the Hitler Youth." Responding to one of the Bureau director's objections to such a move on the grounds that a German man working to establish an alternative to the Hitler Jugend was sent to a concentration camp for his efforts, the founder of Scouting replies that the man was imprisoned "not for international tendencies, but for homosexual tendencies!"—the suggestion being that homosexuals (more so than communists or antifascists) might deserve to be put in concentration camps (Rosenthal 277).

Reading and s-e-x

Long before children began to question, identify, and openly claim their sexuality, lesbian and gay adults emerged from the confines of closeted lives in order to celebrate the fullness of selfhood, companionship, and community, and to challenge constraints imposed upon them by the heterosexual majority and by the hypocrisy of priests, teachers, uncles and even Scoutmasters who hid their own homosexuality behind walls of silence and intimidation. Within librarianship, gay and lesbian librarians came out in a big way at ALA's annual "jamboree" in Dallas, Texas. The year was 1970. With an eye toward normalizing homosexuality within the profession, the Task Force on Gay Liberation in SRRT came up with a creative, daring, even fun promotional booth on the exhibit hall "midway." For $1 a pop, any conference-goer could.... Hug-a-Homosexual! (Wiegand 104).

In the next 20 years, the Gay and Lesbian Task Force would evolve into the Gay, Lesbian, and Bisexual Task Force, eventually deciding on independence from the Social Responsibilities Round Table, to become the GLBT Round Table of ALA. During these early years, the GLTF established book awards, organized programs at conferences, and worked to spread throughout the profession a recognition of the information needs of library users of all gender identifications, and the acceptance of members of this library user population as human beings deserving respect and services equal to those of the heterosexual majority. As Tom Gaughan learned in 1992 homophobia was then, and is still today although decreasingly so, one of the last socially acceptable forms of prejudice.

Within the Boy Scouts of America, however, official recognition of homosexuality was slower in arriving. Not until 2013, after over three decades of lawsuits, did the BSA officially declare that openly gay boys could be accepted as Scouts, and in 2015 the BSA finally allowed openly gay men to become scoutmasters. At the time of our story, however, prohibitions against gay scoutmasters was rooted not only in BSA's homophobia, but also in a long history of officially covered-up sexual abuse of boys by scoutmasters. In 1991, the *Washington Times* had published a state-by-state list of reported cases of sexual abuse of boys by scoutmasters. The list included 416 cases in all fifty states reported over the course of the 20 previous years (Abusers).

While homosexuality, regardless of the nature of actual relationships, whether loving or abusive, was shrouded in silence by the Boy Scouts, the organization did not altogether ignore the sexuality of boys. From the very beginning of scouting, Boy Scout manuals included information, if indirectly, on sex. Baden-Powell himself wanted the manuals to treat boys' developing sexual drives openly, but the prudishness of Edwardian England would not permit even the word "sex" in a book for good boys. Not that Baden-Powell celebrated sexual drives, far from it. He wanted sexual energies channeled and controlled. In the first edition of *Scouting for Boys*, information regarding sex is contained in the chapter Notes for Instructors under the heading "Continence."

Baden-Powell wrote that omitting the subject of "continence" would be a "crime" arguing that silence on the matter would leave a boy to his own imagination and devices in dealing with his emerging sexuality, something to be avoided at all costs (Rosenthal 186–90). Instructors were responsible for helping boys develop methods of dealing with the temptations of masturbation which, according to Baden-Powell is more harmful than smoking, drinking, and gambling, because the temptations of "'indulgence' or 'self-abuse'" are more powerful than these other vices, and if indulged in bring about "weakness of heart and head, and, if persisted in, to idiocy and lunacy" (Baden-Powell 316). He also strongly warned Scout instructors against any "prudish sentimentality" that might prevent adult leaders from talking with boys about "continence" frankly and openly.

In the 1948 edition of the *Scout Field Book*, information on sexuality is offered in the section headed "Taboo" under the subheading "Conserve Your Power." A description of how the sex glands produce natural changes in a boy that "make a MAN of you," is followed by a passage on wet dreams, which "are perfectly natural and healthy ... a sign that nature has been permitted to take care of the situation in its own correct manner" (*Scout* 464). However, the passage goes on to say that some boys "do not permit nature to have its own way with them but cause unnatural emissions—masturbation." A habit that makes a boy "feel cheap" or "cause him to worry." "Any real boy knows that a habit that lessens his self-esteem should be mastered and discarded. To any *real* boy such a habit is TABOO!" (*ibid.*, emphasis in original). Suggestions to readers on how "to keep your manly self-respect" include "perfect cleanliness," "vigorous games and hikes," "hobbies," and "last, but not least, your own high ideals and hopes for your great future as a man."

By the mid–60s, the tone of information on a boy's budding sexuality had softened considerably. For example, masturbation "may do no physical harm" but is still a source of worry, and any "real boy" avoids or overcomes such worries. Fortunately, the 7th edition of the *Handbook* informs the reader that he is not alone, "just about all boys have the same problem," i.e., mastering sexual urges, and readers are recommended to discuss "any question which bothers you about your development from boy to man: with parents, physician, spiritual advisor (*Boy* 1966, p. 425).

Over the course of the next 30 years, the *Handbook*'s coverage of sexuality changed considerably. By the 1998, 11th edition, "Taboo" had given way to "Sexual Responsibility." Sexual maturity is equated with "the ability to father a child," and sex "is never a test of manliness." Gone are any mention of wet dreams and masturbation. Instead, a boy reads of his sexual responsibilities: first, toward a young woman, with advice against "unplanned pregnancy"; second, toward his future fatherhood, with advice on "waiting until you are prepared"; third, toward his beliefs, as "Abstinence until marriage is a very wise course of action"; and, lastly, toward himself—"wholesome sexual behavior can bring lifelong happiness"—with a warning that the first consequence to oneself of irresponsible or uninformed sexual conduct is AIDS, followed by "other diseases" and "unplanned pregnancy" (*Boy* 1998, 376–7). Following these two pages is an entirely new section on physical, emotional, and sexual abuse.

Outside of Scouting circles, information and activism regarding expressions of all forms of sexual orientation began to spread beginning with the publication of *The Homosexual in America* in 1951, moving on to Stonewall in 1968, the rise of gay pride in the '70s, and on through the '80s and '90s. While an excursion into the history of sexual liberation, whether gay or straight, is well beyond the scope of this chapter, a brief review of developing attention to the information needs of children and teens on homosexuality will be helpful in establishing the evolving context of adult commitment as advocates for boys and young men struggling for acceptance in Scouting.

A 1974 book entitled *Love Is for All*, written by a nurse raising her children in a lesbian household, argued for the open acceptance of homosexual relationships in order for children to be raised in homes filled with love rather than inhibited by secrecy.

The parents cannot be secretive about their relationship in terms of their caring and concern for each other. They cannot be ashamed of the kind of love they share whether it is homosexual or heterosexual. Obviously, sexual activity that goes beyond affection is not for the eyes of children but open caring and signs of affection such as holding hands, helping with chores and giving of love gifts are affirmations of stability to a child [Schuster 50].

Noting that in 1973 the American Psychiatric Association had debated whether or not "homosexuality should be dropped from the catalog of mental illnesses," Schuster recommended that educational efforts be continued in all spheres of life to continue movement toward acceptance of gay and lesbian relationships as normal and as healthy as those of heterosexuals. She also recognized that not all relationships are healthy, quoting from a 1961 study by UCLA researchers,

> Some homosexuals, like some heterosexuals, are ill; some homosexuals, like some heterosexuals, are preoccupied with sex as a way of life. But probably for a majority of adults, their sexual orientation constitutes only one component of a much more complicated lifestyle [Hooker quoted in Schuster 50].

This recognition is what the Boy Scouts, and a homophobic society in general, long failed to make—abuse exists across the entire spectrum of sexual orientations, but so do loving, supportive, healthy relationships between individual adults and their children. Schuster urged readers to share her book, to show films, write letters, give information to doctors, schools, counselors.

Pamphlets, books, and films made expressly for young readers and viewers were slow in coming and being made accessible, but they did begin to appear.

In 1980, Alyson Publications in Boston, published a U.S. edition of *Young, Gay & Proud!* originally published by the Gay Teachers and Students Group of Melbourne, Australia. Geared to high school students, the book covered in an approachable, matter-of-fact manner everything from how one knows one is gay or lesbian, to the fears and joys of coming out, to "doing it," paying close attention to health issues. *Young, Gay & Proud!* had, in addition to recommended reading lists of fiction and nonfiction, a final chapter entitled "Put this book where it belongs," which included advice about how to get the book into both the public and school libraries. Recognizing that *Young, Gay & Proud!* would, at least initially, be read by adults, Alyson encouraged readers to get the book into the hands of teens,

- [A]sk your local library to order this book, and give them the address below. Many libraries have a policy for ordering virtually any book that is requested.
- If you're a teacher, ask your school library to also order it....
- If your library won't order a copy, donate one to them. We'll help—send us the name and address of your school, city, or other library, and $3 per address. We'll send them a copy of *Young, Gay & Proud!* with a letter explaining how important it is for them to make it available to young people [*Young* 94].

The last point recognized the possibility (in 1980, the *probability*) of library resistance to acquisition of a book openly acknowledging, informing, and encouraging homosexual teens. Indeed, as late as 1993, the governing boards of both the Young Adult Library Services Association (Young 129) and ALSC (Association 1) refused to support a resolution going to ALA Council which called for an amendment to the Library Bill of Rights on the inclusion of the terms "gay," "lesbian," and "bisexual" as categories of people to be protected from discrimination in library services.

In 1989 and 1991, respectively, two picture books were published, *Heather Has Two Mommies*, by Lesléa Newman, and *Daddy's Roommate*, by Michael Willhoite. The time had come for adults to advocate, not only on behalf of themselves as individuals, but for children and youth too. These two books received both accolades and denunciation. Schuster would have been delighted at their publication, for both normalized lesbian and gay family life.

Twenty years after the publication of *Heather Has Two Mommies*, Lesléa Newman provides a glimpse of the controversy stirred by her book of love and family, writing

> I had no idea [the book] would become part of the congressional record and be debated on the Senate floor. I had no idea it would be defecated upon by a library patron in Ohio, stolen by a minister from a library in Texas and the cause of a New York City school superintendent's downfall. Not to mention being parodied on Jon Stewart's *The Daily Show* on a regular basis [Newman 58].

She describes the inspiration behind the book—a friend raising her daughter with her lesbian lover wishing out loud one day for a book within which her young child could see reflected her own family's life. The lack of familiar family experiences in books resonated strongly with Newman whose own Jewish culture, traditions, and names never found a place in books when she was a child. Nancy Drew celebrated Christmas, as did the Bobbsey Twins. Where was Hanukkah in children's literature? Similar experiences had motivated black authors and illustrators to create books for and about the lives and families of African-American children and teens, with librarians joining in the promotion of these books via the Coretta Scott King Award established in 1970. The time had come for books about and for kids in gay and lesbian families, and for books about and for gay and lesbian children and teens.

In her article, Newman concludes that, even with the passage of 20 years, she remains baffled by the controversy. The essential message of *Heather Has Two Mommies* is that "The most important thing about a family is that all the people in it love each other" (*ibid.*).

Scratch the surface of Newman's bafflement, however, and revealed is the time-layered and tectonically-folded strata of attitudes toward sexuality now brought into the light of the present, coexisting, with the most recently laid soil alive, nourishing, while substrata burp up the fossilized remains of once unchallenged homophobia, misogyny, and white male dominance. In today's social strata, gay pride exists alongside vitriolic intolerance toward sexual orientations of any sort, an intolerance nurtured by eugenicists, religious, political and military leaders, doctors and psychologists, parents, teachers, children. The Boy Scouts were only one conduit of such attitudes into society at large.

"ALA speaks with one voice"

Midwinter 1993 met in Denver, capital of Colorado, whose voters three months earlier had approved an amendment to the state constitution denying the civil rights of its lesbian, gay, and bisexual citizens. Amendment 2 read, in part

> Neither the State of Colorado, through any of its branches or departments, nor any of its agencies, political subdivisions, municipalities or school districts, shall enact, adopt or enforce any statute, regulation, ordinance or policy whereby homosexual, lesbian or bisexual orientation, conduct, practices or relationships shall constitute or otherwise be the basis of, or entitle any persons or class of persons to have or claim any minority status quota preferences, protected status or claim of discrimination [Council Voting 1993, 849].

Opposition to Amendment 2 caused some ALA members to cancel plans to attend midwinter. Others seized the opportunity to protest, and SRRT's Gay and Lesbian Task Force organized a rally, attended by some 200 conference-goers who listened to a speech by ALA President Marilyn Miller, and then marched from the convention center to the state capitol building. In her remarks, Miller recognized that ALA was a guest in Colorado, that most conference goers would leave the state at the conclusion of meetings, but would be leaving behind colleagues, friends, family members whose livelihoods and physical well-being could be endangered by the implementation of Amendment 2. Citing ALA's long-standing support for the protection of human rights, commitment to diversity, and concerns that Amendment 2 could negatively impact library collections, services, and access, Miller went on to say,

> We know how the line can blur between access to information and denial of our human rights. We learned this during the book burnings in NAZI Germany. Any erosion of human liberty can lead to an erosion of intellectual freedom [Remarks 3].

The rally and speeches were only the beginning of expressions of the Association's opposition to Amendment 2. Council took opposition to the next level and passed two resolutions—the first moving ALA's 1998 midwinter meeting *out* of Colorado, the second establishing a policy whereby ALA would not contract conference services in *any* city or state that actively denied the rights of lesbians, gays, bisexuals.

Other Council resolutions positively supporting the rights of GLBT community members were in the works, to be presented at the 1993 annual conference. One would add the words "gay," "lesbian," and "bisexual" to the Library Bill of Rights. The other was a directive to the Intellectual Freedom Committee to write an interpretation of the Library Bill of Rights with explicit focus on the rights of people of differing sexual orientation. As noted previously, both YALSA and ALSC boards refused to endorse the former, but they did endorse the latter. When the resolution that would have revised the Library Bill of Rights came to a vote at the annual meeting, the body voted overwhelmingly to table the issue indefinitely. To this day sexual orientation is not included in the fifth section of the Library Bill of Rights, which reads, "A person's right to use a library should not be denied or abridged because of origin, age, background, or views" (*Library*).

However, Council unanimously approved the IFC's interpretation:

> The American Library Association stringently and unequivocally maintains that libraries and librarians have an obligation to resist efforts that systematically exclude materials dealing with any subject matter, including sex, gender identity, or sexual orientation.... The Association also encourages librarians to proactively support the First Amendment rights of all library users, regardless of sex, gender identity, or sexual orientation [Interpretations].

Important to note regarding these two resolutions is that supporters of the failed revision to the Library Bill of Rights wanted ALA's support of gays, lesbians, and bisexuals to be *explicit*, i.e., to be incorporated into the body of the statement that is most known to all librarians regardless of their familiarity with the ALA Policy Manual. The Library Bill of Rights is often printed, framed, and placed in a public location for all the world to read. IFC's interpretation, however, lies hidden in the Policy Manual to be found only if one knows or suspects the existence of such a statement. In this manner, Council straddled the fence, so to speak, with a public document that is silent on sexual orientation and sex-related information, while having an internal statement positively supporting both. Perhaps a future Council will finally add "sexual orientation" and "gender identity" to the Library Bill of Rights—they belong there.

Returning to 1993: At the same time that ALA decided to boycott conference sites governed by antihomosexual legislation, and incorporated GLBT rights into policy, efforts were launched to constrain the venues, processes, and rights through which ALA members could raise concerns and potentially impact policy. Members concerned with matters such as advocacy of GLBT rights, the commercialization of ALA programs, relationships like the one ALSC had with the BSA, and issues like censorship in Israel and the Occupied Territories, had made use of various aspects of ALA policy to effect change. ALA membership meetings, the meetings of the various units of ALA, and Council were all places where concerns could be raised, discussed, and acted upon.

Member activism in the 1960s and '70s had brought an end to an "old boys" power structure within ALA, enacting policy and governance changes that opened the Association up to greater involvement of rank-and-file members. A spirit of democracy infused ALA Membership meetings with hundreds of members attending to deliberate, debate, and impact policy. Beginning in 1993, a three-pronged approach to tightening the reins of access to ALA policy-making began. The first, during midwinter 1993, was a Council decision to increase the numbers required for a quorum for Membership meetings; the second was an Executive Board charge to the Committee on Organization (COO) to investigate the matter of "units which violate ALA policy"; the third was an organizational self-study of which one of five "guiding principles" was that "ALA speaks with one voice."

In a move that effectively shut down ALA Membership meetings, Council voted during midwinter 1993 to recommend a bylaws revision that would raise the quorum from 200 members to 1 percent of total personal members. The vote was 113 in favor, 43 opposed, zero abstentions, 3 not casting a vote, and 11 excused from voting (Council Voting 1994, 852, 859–60). The proposed bylaws amendment was put on the 1993 ballot, and a majority of the 20 percent of ALA members voting approved the revision, raising the quorum to (at that time) 500-some members. The fears of those opposed to the change were realized—the Membership meetings, which were not held during a no-conflict period in conference schedule and, therefore, competed with other activities for conference goers' interest, time and attention, became unable to conduct official business for lack of quorum.

In the case of SRRT's continuing concerns about ALSC's relationship with the Boy Scouts, the Membership meeting as a conduit to Council was lost, turned into a place for informal "chats" and organized "forums," a place where ice-cream bars and raffle tickets were offered to entice members in the hopes of corralling a quorum. As Stephen Stillwell put it in his "From the Coordinator" column in the September 1994 issue of *SRRT Newsletter*,

> ... the ALA bylaws change on membership quorum rules passed by a margin of nearly 8 to 1. This change virtually eliminates ALA general membership meetings. So much for democracy, even though it was done democratically. At this conference, because no quorum could be attained, we endured membership "chats." What a sham! Shame on ALA, its leaders and members for allowing such a travesty! [Stillwell 1994, 1].

Of course, members of Council sympathetic to SRRT could easily be found to take SRRT-initiated resolutions directly to Council, and did so. The matter of the Boy Scouts was picked up by Councilors Michael Malinconico and Frank Iacono, who brought to Council a resolution, "That the ALA Council and Executive Board enforce established ALA policy and instruct the ALSC to end a formal relationship with the Boy Scouts of America" (ALSC).

Speaking to the motion, Malinconico referred to ALA policy, which stated that ALA could establish relationships with organizations that "do not discriminate in membership on the basis of race, creed, color, sex, sexual orientation, age, disabilities, or national origin." Council minutes report Malinconico expressing concern that in recent years it "seemed that the Boy Scouts were teaching and promoting not only reading, but also intolerance and discrimination" (Council 1994b). He emphasized that the resolution did not prevent libraries from serving Boy Scouts nor did it prevent ALA, ALSC, or any other entity from producing and disseminating bibliographies to Scouts or participating in the quadrennial jamborees. The sole purpose of the resolution was to end an official affiliation with an organization that did not share ALA's commitment to inclusion, diversity, and universal human rights. The Boy Scouts of America was listed in the *Handbook* as one of many organizations with which ALA had affiliations, and ALSC's long-standing and budgeted Boy Scouts of America Advisory Committee represented an *official willingness* to publicly identify with an organization that discriminated against certain kinds of boys.

The resolution became a victim of parliamentary maneuvering when Councilors Mary Jane Anderson and Past President Marilyn Miller submitted a substitute motion that simply established an investigation into what did or did not constitute a relationship between ALA, or any of its units, and any outside organization, not naming the Boy Scouts of America.

> WHEREAS, for several years questions have been raised about external groups with which ALA and its units have engaged in short- or long-term relationships, liaisons, affiliations, alliances, coalitions, promotions, etc.; and
>
> WHEREAS, it has become apparent that ALA lacks clear policy, definitions and guidelines for these varying types of relationships; therefore be it
>
> RESOLVED, that the ALA Council direct its Executive Board to develop a mechanism for the full review of the Association's external relationships and the drafting of policy, definitions, guidelines, and review procedures for those relationships [Council 1994b].

Norman Horrocks requested the chair's ruling on whether or not the substitute was germane to the main motion. The chair ruled it was, and the substitute motion was voted on and approved. The vote was 94 in favor, 10 opposed, one abstention, 45 not casting a vote, and 20 excused from voting (Voting).

With this vote, action on ALSC's ties to the Scouts was derailed, substituted in favor of further bureaucratic delay, and, as the *SRRT Newsletter* put it, "action will not be deliberate or speedy" (SRRT 8).

Deliberate *and* speedy, however, certainly characterized COO's action between its midwinter and annual meetings in 1994 on the charges given it by the Executive Board. COO was to consider,

1) ways of dealing with ALA units taking positions contrary to ALA's official positions; and
2) ways units can monitor the use of ALA's name by their subunits [Council 1994a].

In its report to Council at the annual meeting, COO recommended a statement entitled "Units which Violate ALA Policy." Council approved the statement in a vote of 116 in favor, 14 opposed, 4 abstaining, 25 casting no vote, and 22 excused from voting (Voting 49–50). The statement read in part,

> If divisions, roundtables, other ALA membership units, or committees are thought to have violated the ALA Constitution, Bylaws, or Policies, the Council is empowered to take actions to ensure compliance with established ALA policy. The Council, ALA Executive Board, or other designated body may investigate the actions of the unit or committee and recommend a course of action. Actions which may be taken include, but are not limited to, internal sanction, limiting communication and/or spending by the unit or committee, or disestablishment of the unit or committee.
>
> If violations are found to be the result of an individual member presuming to act without the approval of the parent body, the ALA Executive Board may, under the authority of the Constitution (Article III, Section I), suspend that individual's membership in the American Library Association [Committee].

At first blush, this resolution simply makes sense. No doubt ALA should have a mechanism for dealing with units and members violating policy. Executive Board and Council members must have been relieved to learn that ALA's Constitution already did contain such provisions. The problem, however, was that the charge to COO addressed a problem that didn't exist. Perhaps Council simply wanted to be "proactive" in anticipating future violations, and up-to-date on its collective knowledge of ALA's constitution and bylaws. Or, as some suspected, the motivation behind the review was to "chill" future debate, to raise levels of caution in individual members, committees, roundtables, and divisions, and to express a lack of trust in Association members.

As we have seen in the case of the Resolution on Israeli Censorship, the Executive Board knew David Williams was speaking the truth. When accused of presuming to speak for the Association, he simply pointed out that *Council* had approved the resolution, not him. In the case of McDonald's, anyone who could follow a grammatically correct sentence would know that the words "SRRT urges ALA" clearly are not an indication of SRRT presuming to speak for ALA. The distribution of a statement clearly expressing the views of SRRT violates no ALA policies.

No, the problem behind the "Units which Violate ALA Policy" document, was that some members (and nonmembers) of ALA sometimes disapproved of positions taken both by units and by the Association's own policy-making body, Council—positions taken in accordance *with* ALA policy. Despite the fact that no violations had occurred, the cutting off of Membership meetings as a venue for member input, the broadcast threats of sanctions or dissolution of ALA units, and suspension of individual membership were deemed necessary in controlling expressions of professional concerns.

The last effort to constrain activism within ALA was an organizational self-study, of which one of five guiding principles was that ALA "speaks with one voice." The desire for control made abundantly clear.

> ALA's many units speak independently, sometimes in conflict with each other and/or ALA. A structure is needed that provides opportunities for internal disagreement and examination of different perspectives, avenues for building consensus, and procedures to ensure that ALA speaks with one voice in its external communications [ALA Organizational 4].

Advocates of "speaking with one voice" considered it a source of strength for ALA. In some situations this is true. However, the ability to issue association-wide messages does not require either the inhibition or prohibition of expression issuing from individual members or units. The outside world benefits from knowing that librarians have a variety of views on a variety of issues. If differences can be expressed only within the confines of the "family circle," then all that is seen from the outside is a façade of a united front. If librarians cannot model both agreement and dissension within the context of a democratic organization, then claims of being a "cornerstone of democracy" ring false.

In 1995, the Organizational Self-Study Committee (OSSC) was in the last of its three-year tenure, and had spent an estimated $100,000 reviewing ALA's structure, members' satisfaction with those structures, and possible alternatives (Kniffel 1995, 678). A draft proposal had been distributed, and conversations occurred throughout the annual meeting in Chicago.

The OSSC's draft proposal outlined a sweeping restructuring of ALA, and generated substantial and heated debate. Opposition arose from every sector of the Association (see Whitwell). Of interest here is that, in polling ALA members regarding dissatisfactions with the organization, the "sometimes contradictory and controversial" actions of round tables was cited as a reason for the committee's decision to take as a guiding principle the notion that "ALA speaks with one voice." Whitwell describes the OSSC as seeming

> to struggle with the current independence of the round tables. This independence was admired by the OSSC because it pushed ALA into new areas and exhibited dynamism and creativity. On the other hand, it was felt that this independence ... was one of the reasons members had complained about ALA speaking with many voices [Whitwell 691].

Many saw OSSC's proposal as an attempt to dissolve and silence the roundtables. Whitwell reports that during Council debate Maurice Freedman and others "argued that the idea of speaking with one voice was pernicious and stifling of debate." Others believed in the importance of ALA speaking with one voice to the outside world.

In the end, OSSC never formally presented their proposal, opting instead to establish a task force for the purpose of finishing the committee's work, the Structure Revision Task Force. One of the recommendations from this group was to create seats on Council for representatives of the round tables, a recommendation adopted by Council at the 1997 annual meeting.

One thing that never happened, however, was the establishment of a "speaking with one voice policy." Not even six years later when a rerun of "One Voice" prompted a critique from Mark Rosenzweig in the May 2001 *SRRT Newsletter*.

> We recognize the concerns of the Executive of the ALA about the necessity for presenting a strong, common front and public face in order to be effective on matters of Association-

wide concern. But we also have a need to project an image of an Association which practices what it preaches: there must be the highest degree of internal democracy and the rights of freedom of expression in ALA [Rosenzweig].

Although the ghost of this "policy" hovers in the air on Council floor to this day, it never had material substance. Of course, just like monsters under the beds of children, references to the "one voice policy" do have a powerful purpose—as an element of fear whenever authority is put into question.

History marches on

We return to Michael Golrick wearing his Boy Scout uniform in 1998. The library press had alerted readers that ALA's relationship with the Scouts was to be revisited at the annual conference in Washington, D.C.

"Debate Reignites Over Link to Boy Scouts," read the headline of *School Library Journal*'s May report. Describing the upcoming fireworks as yet another installment in "[t]hat 10-year-old on-again, off-again debate," reporter Reneé Olson informed readers that Councilors Mark Rosenzweig and Ruth Gordon would present a resolution to suspend ALSC's relationship with the BSA. Gordon, a longtime ALSC member, was quoted as saying about the Scouts' discriminatory policies, "I have worked too long with children to see them hurt." ALSC President Elizabeth Watson disagreed, saying "The only people you're hurting [by suspending ALSC/BSA relations] is the youngsters themselves," and also characterized the relationship at the national level as "so tenuous as to be gossamer" (Olson 18).

Olson also contacted the BSA for their perspective, only to learn from their official national-level spokesman, Gregg Shields, that he was "not aware of the relationship," and, in any event, did not understand, if one did exist, why it would be a problem. "While we may have standards for our members, we don't try to force our beliefs on others. We hope that the relationship [between the two groups] could continue" (*ibid.*). Of course, gay and atheist Scouts would probably disagree with Shields on the matter of forced beliefs.

In yet another, rather astounding development in May, ALA Associate Executive Director for Member Programs and Services Mary Ghikas requested from ALSC's Executive Director Susan Roman a definitive description of ALSC's relationship with the Scouts. In a memo dated June 5, 1998, Roman responded that the longstanding Boy Scouts of America Advisory Committee had been *dissolved* by the ALSC Board at its 1996 midwinter meeting. She further informed Ghikas that ALSC members continued to prepare reading lists for merit badge booklets, and to host the reading booth at Scout jamborees, but as could be seen, the Boy Scouts of America were no longer listed in the 1997–98 *ALA Handbook* as an affiliate (Roman). Services to BSA continued, but the committee which had existed for some four decades to design, coordinate, and implement that work was no more. ALSC had silently succumbed to pressure.

Also in May, the ALA Executive Board established a subcommittee to, once again, investigate ALA policy governing relationships with external organizations. Board members Sally Reed, Nancy Kranich, and Mary Somerville were charged to review the policy for possible revision. Recommendations from the subcommittee were expected to be presented at the annual conference (St. Lifer 13).

As Council convened for its 1998 annual meetings, many people besides Golrick were prepared to discuss the Boy Scouts of America, although only one other wore his uniform to do so. The debate was fed from two directions—from the camp advocating that ALA policy on external relationships needed clarification and revision, and from another that just wanted any ALA/BSA relationship to end, regardless of its nature (formal, informal, whatever).

The Reed/Kranich/Somerville subcommittee finished its work and the Executive Board had a recommendation for Council that the policy governing relationships with outside organizations "be revised to clearly define 'formal relationships' and 'informal relationship,' and that these two terms be used consistently" (Council 1998, 9).

By the time the BSA/External Relations items reached the floor of Council, the movers and supporters of the resolution to sever the ALSC/BSA relationship realized they'd been drawn into a morass of bureaucratic nitpicking. Semanticists, wordsmiths, the grammar patrol, policy wonks, i-dotters, and t-crossers could draw out action for another decade. A more direct approach was probably needed. So, when it became clear that Council did not have enough time for the anticipated debate, Rosenzweig, Gordon et al. breathed a collective sigh of relief, when both items were postponed to midwinter 1999. Perhaps the only councilors disappointed were the ones dressed for the occasion.

The intervening months saw the debate continue in the pages of *American Libraries*, *Library Journal*, and *School Library Journal*.

The June/July issue of *American Libraries* contained an interview with Michael Golrick and Tom Budlong, conducted by Gordon Flagg. Under the banner heading Social Responsibilities, the headline asked "A Dangerous Liaison?" The subheading instructed readers to "be prepared for the upcoming Council debate over ALA's ties to the Boy Scouts by reading this exchange...." The long and short of the 3-page interview was that Budlong supported a resolution for severing ties, while Golrick wasn't sure the relationship was formal enough to be considered official (Flagg 88).

In October, John N. Berry III of *Library Journal* chimed in with an editorial entitled "Boy Scout Values" in which he described his own experience as a Scout, wonders if as a father he did the right thing by his sons in keeping them out of the organizations, and expresses his outrage that instead of supporting SRRT's resolution, the Executive Board had reprimanded the round table for sending a copy of their resolution to the Scouts. "I am ashamed," wrote Berry, "that ALA would rather muzzle SRRT than end its relationship with the Boy Scouts of America" (Berry 1998, 6).

Then, on the eve of midwinter 1999, Carolyn Caywood, in her last *School Library Journal* column Teens & Libraries, injected a new element into the debate. Thinking (as all good school librarians do) from the perspective of a student, Caywood wondered "what a boy pursuing a merit badge learns if he tried to use the list of books provided by ALA and discovers that none are available" (Caywood 49). Unavailable, not because they are so popular that the waiting list is long, but rather because the lists are so old that many of the out-of-date materials are simply no longer on the shelves. As for whether

ALA should continue being friends with BSA, Caywood sides with Golrick, but for different reasons.

> Is it worth preserving any service to an organization that makes us look so out of date? When I see that ALA has no influence on keeping information credited to it current, I must agree with those who say that ALA really has no relationship with the Boy Scouts [*ibid.*].

And so, Michael Golrick donned his uniform once again for midwinter 1999, and Mark Rosenzweig and Ruth Gordon prepared to make a slight alteration to the 1998 resolution. At the microphone, Rosenzweig, the mover of the resolution, asked for Council consent in removing one of its main sticking points, the resolved that read "ALA suspend formal or official relations with the Boy Scouts...." Consent was granted, leaving only one resolved clause on which to vote:

> American Library Association urges the Boy Scouts of America to reconsider their policy of discrimination in the areas of sexual orientation and religious belief and demonstrate a commitment to human rights, inclusiveness, and mutual respect [Council 1999, 15].

As sometimes happens on Council, someone seeking perfection moves to amend, the chair makes a ruling, a councilor asks that the parliamentarian be consulted, the parliamentarian whispers something to chair and sometimes with the Executive Director, whereupon another councilor challenges the chair's ruling, which calls for an immediate vote of the body. Such was discussion over one of the resolution's whereas clauses. Participants were Mary Jane Anderson, Rita Auerback, President-Elect Sarah Long, Bernie Margolis, Executive Director William Gordon, Mitch Freedman, Gordon Conable, then back to Bernie, with more discussion, whereupon Mark Rosenzweig moved that the resolution be withdrawn, rewritten, and placed on the Council III agenda for consideration. The motion passed by consent. All in a day's work!

Armed with a rewritten resolution, minus the offending whereas clause, Rosenzweig rose once more to present Resolution on the Boy Scouts of America, Revised, CD#51-A. He briefly explained the revisions and debate got underway.

Councilor Golrick expressed his appreciation that the revision was much less inflammatory, but stated that the resolution was inaccurate in terms of the Scouts' requirements regarding religion. "The Boy Scouts do require that you believe in some Higher Being," he said, "and that is the only requirement in terms of religious beliefs" (Council 1999, 28). He then moved to table the motion indefinitely. The motion to table was defeated, and debate continued with Councilor Sally Gardner Reed speaking in favor of the main motion,

> I'm deeply proud to be part of a profession that not only celebrates diversity but supports it every single day in everything that we do. I don't think libraries can flourish in a society that's discriminatory and intolerant of differences. Libraries are a cornerstone of democracy, and I think we have not only the ability but the responsibility to speak out wherever discrimination flourishes [29].

Discussion continued, although the minutes do not record any further specifics. A vote was taken, and the resolution approved. Council moved on to the next item on its agenda, Resolution on S.22, the Government Secrecy Reform Act of 1999.

In 2011, ALSC and YALSA invited the Gay, Lesbian, Bisexual, and Transgender Round Table and its Stonewall Children's and Youth Literature Award to a place on the stage at the annual ALA youth media awards press conference—good books for ... gays, girls, and (who knows?) maybe even godless Boy Scouts!

In 2013, the Boy Scouts of America invited gay boys to join their ranks.

In late July 2015, a challenge from the New York City Boy Scouts Council in the spring (Barron) led the Boy Scouts of America to finally invite gay men to become Scout leaders.

Every silver-lining is surrounded by a cloud, and in this case the damper is that 71 percent of Scout troops chartered to religious organizations are allowed to maintain exclusionary practices in selecting leaders (Boy 2015). The still very homophobic Church of Latter Day Saints, for instance, holds the largest number of charters granted to religious groups. In some troops, therefore, the BSA will continue to be an unwelcoming environment, and pockets of the organization will continue to advocate against the rights of gay boys and men, against the rights of the entire GLBTQ community, for some time to come.

As Dr. Martin Luther King, Jr., once said, "The arc of the moral universe is long, but it bends towards justice."

One hundred years transpired between the Boy Scouts' invitation to the associations of American booksellers and American libraries to promote good books for boys, and their invitation to *all* boys grown into adulthood to serve as guides in the world of Scouting. When one thinks of all the lives made miserable, of beatings and suicides and murders grown from over a century of homophobia, the joys of change must be informed by still existing injustice. Just as racism has not disappeared in the aftermath of Jim Crow segregation, so anti–GLBTQ hostility will not disappear in the aftermath of decisions made by the BSA and the United States Supreme Court in the summer of 2015.

So, what is the lesson to be learned from this chapter in ALA's history? While ALA finally did the right thing and chastised the Boy Scouts of America for discrimination against gay boys who wanted to be Scouts and gay men who wanted to be Scout leaders, an action to be applauded and celebrated, there remains an uneasiness in these steps forward. The sense of unease comes from the elephant in the room that went largely unaddressed, unseen.

Strictures against gay boys and adults were only just one manifestation of the fundamental authoritarianism of Scouting. The Boy Scouts of America still refuse membership to atheist or agnostic boys and adults. Every Scout must sign a Declaration of Religious Principle that states in part, "The Boy Scouts of America maintains that no member can grow into the best kind of citizen without recognizing an obligation to God" (Manual). Loyalty to authority is paramount to Scouting. An atheist or agnostic *questions* the highest form of authority—God. If a person is allowed to question God, they might begin to question King or Country or the Mormon Church, they might begin to question the object of other loyalties—to flag, to church, to superior officer, to the National Security Agency, to ... whatever.

For our purposes here, it was those who questioned the authority of ALA and ALSC who were branded as troublemakers, who were taken to task for daring to take their questioning into the public arena. The chastisement of SRRT for its statement on McDonald's, for its letter to the Boy Scouts, for raising the issue of Israeli censorship, for its refusal to silence its voice and its questions, is simply another manifestation of an authoritarian mindset similar to that of BSA, but in ALA.

As I was finishing this book, an article by Henry Giroux, "The Plague of American Authoritarianism," came to my attention. Giroux explains how stereotypes of political fascism, that of Hitler's Germany and Mussolini's Italy, have rendered many in the U.S. incapable of seeing totalitarian tendencies developing right under our own noses. He refers to a metaphor used by Hannah Arendt to describe elements of totalitarianism in the U.S.—the "sand storm"—and he lists some:

> ... the culture of traditionalism, an every present culture of fear, the corporatization of civil society, the capture of state power by corporations, the destruction of public goods, the corporate control of the media, the rise of a survival-of-the-fittest ethos, the dismantling of civil and political rights, the ongoing militarization of society, the "religionization of politics," a rampant sexism, an attack on labor, an obsession with national security, human rights abuses, the emergence of a police state, a deeply rooted racism, and attempts by demagogues to undermine critical education as a foundation for producing critical citizenry ... [Giroux].

Swarms of little pieces, put into motion by powerful forces, gathering mob-like strength to penetrate into every nook-and-cranny of consciousness. Think Oklahoma dustbowl. Sand storms make vision impossible, but are always preceded by signs of erosion, drought, the approaching storm. Warnings are always present, if unheeded.

Giroux, writing shortly after the first nationally televised debate between candidates for the Republican Party's presidential nomination, described some of the characteristics long accepted as constituting the authoritarian personality: domineering, opposed to equality, desirous of personal power, and amoral. He notes that the mainstream media "treats this group of extremists who promote a culture of fear, racism, and hatred as eccentric, odd, crazies, colorful, or simply toxic" (*ibid.*). In other words, the media minimizes the political sand storm these people gather around them. And, that brings Giroux to the most important point of his article, such individuals are of little consequence unless they can gather a following, and in the fall of 2015 Donald Trump was ahead in popularity polls. In what ways does the culture of the U.S. breed and feed people's political attitudes in such a way that they find appealing a candidate like Trump?

Librarians must be attentive to the ways in which racism, sexism, xenophobia, and a culture of violence are laying waste to ideals of democracy and the public good. We must be attentive to the ways in which appeals to authority are made *within* our own professional circles, especially when the demand is made to "speak with one voice," because authoritarian mindsets belittle dialogue, debate, and democracy. Librarianship must work effortlessly to expand rights to ever-greater circles of humanity and life. ALA must continue, indeed intensify, working toward its mission to identify problems confronting society, and to engage in its social responsibility to help alleviate those problems. Voices that authority would squelch are often the ones democracy needs.

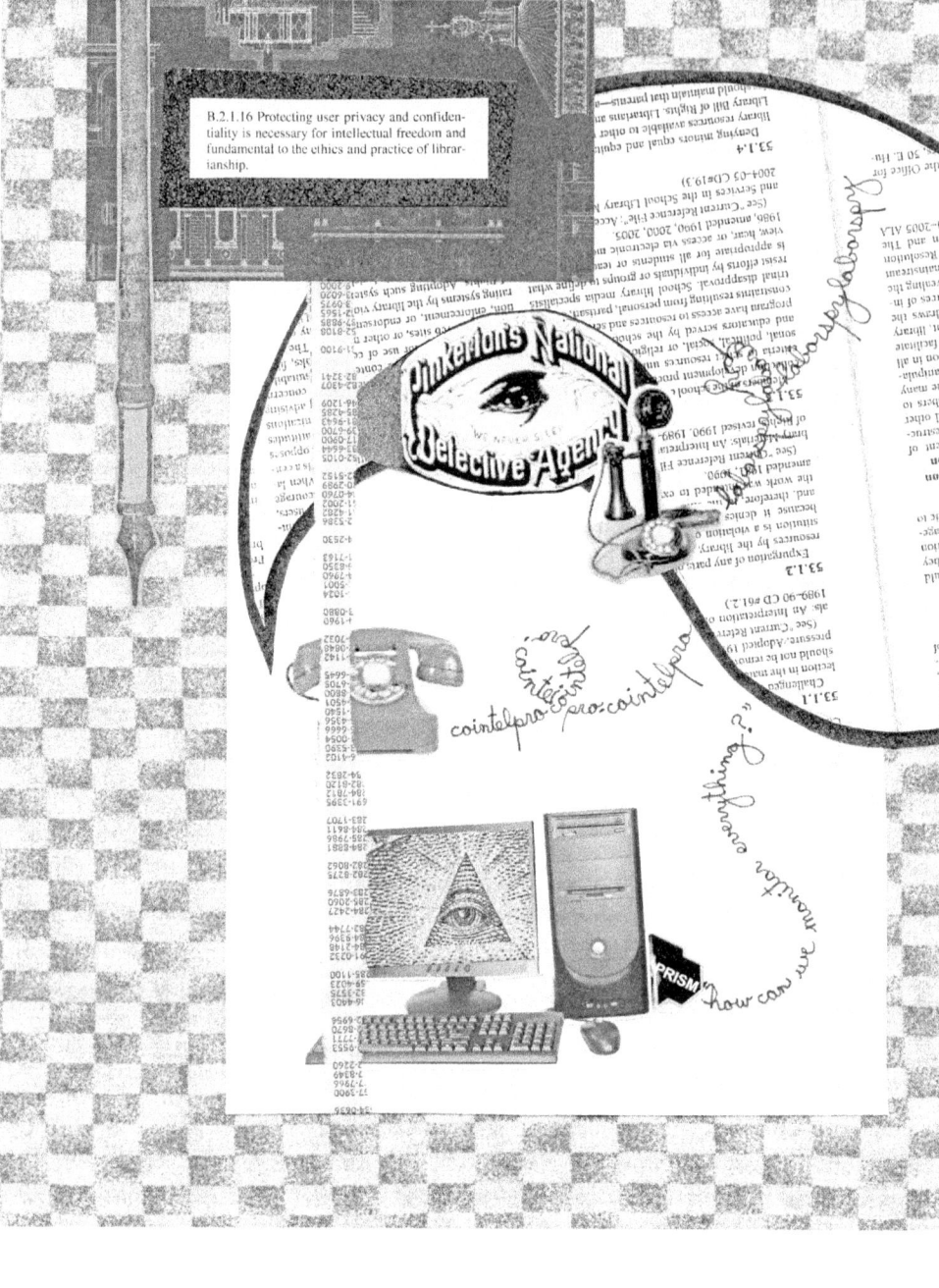

5. Abandoning Snowden...*and* Privacy?—Hegemony at Play in ALA

> *Decency, security, and liberty alike demand that government officials shall be subjected to the same rules of conduct that are commands to the citizen. In a government of laws, existence of the government will be imperiled if it fails to observe the law scrupulously. Our government is the potent, the omnipresent teacher. For good or for ill, it teaches the whole people by its example. Crime is contagious. If the Government becomes a lawbreaker, it breeds contempt for the law; it invites every man to become a law unto himself; it invites anarchy.*
> —Louis Brandeis, 1927[1]

> *Fear ... cannot be allowed to determine the policies and practices of the American Library Association, just as a practicing librarian should certainly never succumb to the censor for fear that his own salary or budget will suffer. If we believe in the importance of intellectual freedom, we must be willing to take risks in order to defend it.*
> —ACONDA Report, 1971[2]

Privacy, a state of being for which one closes a door, steps a short distance away, hangs out the "Do not disturb" sign, is required for any communication not yet ready for public consumption, whether conveyed via scribbled note, telephone call, text message, or scrawled across a diary "PRIVATE, do NOT read! Mom, that means y-o-u!" One utters the phrase "May I have a private word?" and communicates an implicit expectation of trust to both the invited and the excluded (hopefully without offense to the latter). Privacy, whether within the confines of one's own skull, between two or more individuals, is a requisite condition for grappling with personal troubles, for the tentative working through of new ideas, for arriving at a decision, for implementing a plan. Extended to another or others as the need arises, privacy is a human necessity. Children will choose to be mute, to keep their thoughts private rather than risk ridicule, correction, or rejection. Adolescents refuse to share the day's events with parents as being "none of their business." Adults expect private communications to actually *be* private—for phone and internet lines not to be monitored, for bedrooms and boardrooms not to be bugged. Not that what is said and done in private is wrong, crazy, illegal, immoral, or secret, only that it is simply not yet ready for public consumption.

While an individual's interest in and desire for privacy is largely a matter of personal predilection and situation, groups and societies have longstanding customs, traditions, and laws that define and protect individual and collective rights to privacy. The American Library Association, for instance, has a strong commitment regarding privacy rights, "In a library (physical or virtual), the right to privacy is the right to open inquiry without having the subject of one's interest examined or scrutinized by others" (*ALA*).

In the United States, commitments to privacy reach back into history and became legally codified in the Constitution, specifically in the Fourth Amendment of the Bill of Rights, which states,

> The right of the people to be secure in their persons, houses, papers, and effects, against unreasonable searches and seizures, shall not be violated, and no Warrant shall issue, but upon probable cause, supported by Oath or affirmation, and particularly describing the place to be searched, and person or things to be seized [Charters].

According to John Adams, second president of the United States, a speech delivered in the council chambers of Boston's Old Town Hall, in February 1761, by James Otis against "writs of assistance" was the fuse that lit the fire of the American Revolution. Adams, a newly-minted lawyer in 1761, heard Otis' speech along with his friend Samuel Quincy, and in 1817 wrote of the experience in a letter to another friend,

> The scene is the Council Chamber in the Old Town House in Boston.... Otis was a flame of fire! ... with a promptitude of classic allusions, a depth of research, a rapid summary of historical events and dates, a profusion of legal authorities, a prophetic glance of his eye into futurity, and a torrent of impetuous elegance. He hurried away everything before him. American independence was then and there born; the seeds of patriots and heroes were then and there sown, to defend vigorous youth. ... Every man of a crowded audience appeared to me to go away, as I did, ready to take arms against Writs of Assistance. Then and there was the first scene of the first act of opposition to the arbitrary claims of Great Britain. In fifteen years, namely in 1776, he grew up to manhood and declared himself free [Dash 39].

Writs of assistance, vague search warrants containing no information as to what was being searched for or toward whom the search was to be conducted, were the bane of colonial life, direct attacks on personal privacy. In the 6th century C.E., the Roman emperor Justinian coined the phrase "a man's home is his castle," giving expression to a sentiment carried down through the centuries that many consider natural, inviolable. The reality of home as castle has, of course, been an altogether different matter, given the predilections of authorities at any given point in history—including today.

Privacy of mind, body, and place turns out to be a social construct, differently expressed and enforced, of all human cultures. Every human possesses the privacy of her or his own thoughts, and usually enjoys the privacy of communications with at least one other human being. Privacy regarding the body, and bodily functions, varies widely, with some bodies completely hidden. Everywhere rules exist as to when, under what conditions, and to what extent one body may be seen or touched by another. Privacy regarding place also varies widely, and is likely rooted in our evolutionary past, in the lives and customs of mammalian ancestors who marked what they considered their territory and either invited, tolerated, or attacked trespassers. After all, if one can judge by the yaps and growls emitted from behind picket fences and closed apartment doors, a dog's home is as much his castle as a man's. It is not surprising then that the lived experience of American colonists in the second half of the 18th century had them fuming mad when King George's men would pop up at will with their writs of assistance, forcing entry into the homes of soon-to-be revolutionaries.

In the aftermath of the American Revolution and ratification of the Constitution, people realized that a statement establishing the rights of citizens was necessary as a counterbalance to any abuse of authority by the new democracy. Few were ready to place complete trust in those empowered by the U.S. Constitution, no matter how well-defined the checks-and-balances. Thus the Bill of Rights, the first ten amendments to the Constitution were debated, refined, and instituted.

Although an ardent belief in the sanctity of one's home and belongings is a political inheritance of every U.S. citizen, the application and interpretation of Fourth Amendment rights have been uneven over the course of the past nearly two-and-a-half centuries. Nonetheless, the profession of librarianship not only recognizes the value to individuals and to society of the right to privacy, but along with other professions—doctors, social workers, lawyers—declares a strong commitment to patron confidentiality. ALA's policy statement on confidentiality is as follows,

> Confidentiality exists when a library is in possession of personally identifiable information about users and keeps that information private on their behalf. Protecting user privacy and confidentiality is necessary for intellectual freedom and fundamental to the ethics and practice of librarianship [ALA B.2.3.16].

Librarians treat as confidential library users' reading, viewing, and listening to library resources. What a person uses of a library's collections is that person's business only. A teenager's reading of materials dealing with sexual identity, an entrepreneur's research into the feasibility of a new business, a pre–2013 Seattleite's curiosity on the cultivation of marijuana, all three trust the librarian not to share their reading and research queries with parents, competitors, police. Indeed, librarians have made headlines in recent years by insisting on proper search warrants on the occasions when local authorities or the FBI have demanded patron records. Some have gone to court. As a profession, privacy rights and the commitment to confidentiality are taken seriously.

Privacy, of course, is not the same as confidentiality, and neither are the same as secrecy, all three of which figure into the story of Edward Snowden and the ALA.

Confidentiality is an agreement, either formal or informal, between individuals or institutions. Confidentiality can be a personal promise or legal agreement between parties involved to keep something private (usually information). Doctors, journalists, lawyers, therapists, and librarians protect the privacy of patients, sources, clients, and users via practices and values establishing confidential relationships. Sometimes law overrides agreements of confidentiality as when a teacher breaks a promise to a student when keeping the confidentiality might endanger the student or others. Teachers are "mandatory reporters" in such instances, and can be held legally liable if they do not report an endangering situation communicated by a student regardless of any promise of confidentiality. Librarians treat information regarding patron borrowing and accessing records as confidential just as a doctor treats a patient's medical information. A person's reading and internet surfing habits are their private business, no one else's—unless, of course, "probable cause" warrants the breaking of confidentiality.

Privacy being a human need and confidentiality being an agreement or law, secrecy relies on both but is an entirely different matter. The philosopher Sissela Bok,[3] describes secrecy as follows,

> Secrecy is as indispensable to human beings as fire, and as greatly feared. Both enhance and protect life, yet both can stifle, lay waste, spread out of all control. Both may be used to guard intimacy or to invade it, to nurture or to consume. And each can be turned against

itself, barriers of secrecy are set up to guard against secret plots and surreptitious prying, just as fire is used to fight fire [18].

Bok defines secrecy as *intentional concealment*, and insists on its ethical neutrality—some secrecy is good, some is evil, while other secrets are neither. Secrecy generates high excitement in the minutes leading up to ALA's midwinter book award announcements; the secret identity of a donor to the Spectrum Scholarship or the Freedom to Read Foundation elicits deep appreciation but no high emotion; while other secrets, like the NSA's monitoring of telephone and internet communications, generate fury among some and approval among others. Privacy and confidentiality are essential in the entire process of secrecy, of intentional concealment, from generation, to development, to maintenance, to revelation (or not), but they are not the same. Not every private moment is confidential or secret, not every confidence is secret, it's just confidential. With these distinctions in mind, let us turn to the purpose of this chapter, and the conference at which Edward Snowden, privacy, secrecy, and ALA crossed paths. In presenting the case of the fate of a resolution dealing with Edward Snowden at ALA Council we have a quintessential example of hegemony at work within librarianship—hegemony being the establishment and maintenance of political power structures.

When the Commander-in-Chief speaks, people listen

In late June 2013, ALA members poured across the thresholds of Chicago's McCormick Place Convention Center, passing playful fountains squirting a Morse Code of watery arcs along the airy lobby. The main rush of members flowed eastward and upward toward the exhibit hall, conference programs, and coffee, while a small tributary briefly branched southward entering the cavernous room selected by ALA conference planners for the meetings of ALA Council. Over the course of the next four days, the issue of privacy played center stage in this room for a few hours—in public, and in private. Matters of secrecy lay everywhere, in the shadows, between whispers, on the front-page of the *Tribune*, tripping tantalizingly around exhibit hall surprises and out the doors of book prize committees.

Council is the governing body of ALA with 173 elected members representing either the membership at-large, one of ALA's divisions or round tables, or a state or territorial library association.[4] Meetings of Council, three at each midwinter meeting and annual conference, are chaired by the association's president with assistance from ALA's executive director, a parliamentarian, the Council secretariat, and, as need arises, by legal counsel, finance officer, the Washington Office, and other association staff and members. These individuals assist in the multifaceted work of Council that includes establishing ALA policy, budgetary matters, receipt of committee reports with action recommendations, establishing special task forces and committees, electing Council members to the Executive Board and other governance positions, and considering resolutions brought to the body either via ALA membership meetings or by members of Council itself.

On the morning of June 30, 2013, Council members, ALA staffers, members of the library press, and others interested in the work of Council filtered into the room. Councilors found seats at the long rows of tables, the curious and interested others took chairs in areas set aside for observers and special guests, while those presiding over the meeting found their places on the dais between two huge projection screens used for meeting identification, powerpoint presentations, the occasional video clip, and, primarily, for closed captioning for the hearing impaired.

Seats found, territories claimed with sweaters or jackets, iPads, the day's copy of *CogNotes*, councilors and visitors alike lined up at tables along the back wall to collect documents for the morning session. To assist in the organization of copious amounts of paperwork, agendas and documents are copied onto different colored paper for each session. Because this Chicago conference led up to the Fourth of July, session I, II, and III documents were printed on pink (in lieu of red), white, and blue paper respectively.

Latecomers to Council that morning arrived to see President Obama addressing the audience via video-clip on the two huge projection screens right and left of the dais where special guest Jackie Garner, acting director of Region 5 for the U.S. Department of Health and Human Services (HHS), stood.

Garner had just spoken, making a personal appeal to the governing body of the association before heading back to the exhibit hall to reach out to thousands of conference attendees. HHS was finally launching a national health care insurance program, following decades of failed attempts, rancorous national debate, and broad public demand. "Thank you all for everything you do to inform, advise, and assist everyone who walks through your doors," said Garner, then continued:

> As acclaimed author Neil Gaiman has said, "Google can bring you back 100,000 answers, but a librarian can bring you back the right one." ... Public libraries are unique local assets, not only a source for books and information, but a *trusted* community resource. Libraries are where people go to ask questions and find answers, and informing, educating and aiding patrons to discover and discern something new. That's what librarians do each and every day. That's why having you as our partners, helping ensure that everyone is better able to understand and enroll in the health insurance marketplace, is so invaluable [Council I].

Garner invited audience members to visit the booth for the launch of the new website healthcare.gov and call center—the public's portal to affordable health insurance—and to consider participation in HHS training to provide enrollment assistance. "You as the American Library Association are the first group we are coming to during our launch week, as we know that librarians are essential to the American public as they seek information about the marketplace and the Affordable Care Act." She then introduced the video of President Obama's appeal for assistance,

> I know that the President is also very grateful for your engagement, and I am now happy to be able to share with you a few words of appreciation from him for the work you, as librarians, are doing and will help us with your communities, as well as his challenge to do whatever it takes to make sure everyone knows what the new healthcare law and the new insurance marketplace means for them [*ibid.*].

What followed was a canned speech, directed at a generic audience, no mention of libraries or librarians, but nonetheless warm words of thanks from the President to all who would assist citizens to understand and avail themselves of the new health care insurance system. Within a matter of days, the HHS website and call centers collapsed, unprepared for the volume of site and phone traffic, leading to scandal for the Obama administration and website developers, but that is another story altogether.

The Affordable Care Act launch wasn't the only thing on President Obama's mind in June 2013. He was also caught up in another scandal. A whistleblower named Edward Snowden had collected and released documents indicating that the National Security Agency (NSA) was indiscriminately violating the privacy of U.S. citizens. On June 21st the Obama administration filed charges against Snowden under the Espionage Act of 1917 (Scott).

Birth of a Council resolution

On June 6, 2013, *The Guardian* began a series of articles revealing massive surveillance of internet and telephone communications by the NSA of the American public. On June 9, the paper revealed the identity of the NSA contract employee who leaked documentation of the programs. Edward Snowden, a 29-year-old U.S. citizen working for NSA contractor Booz-Allen Hamilton, had been employed by NSA, the CIA, and Dell and working in increasingly sensitive positions in Maryland, China, Switzerland, Japan, and Hawaii. Over the course of a nine-year period, he became disillusioned by the methods and activities of the CIA and NSA (Greenwald).

A young, white, patriotic, and intelligent U.S. citizen, Snowden found himself in a crisis of conscience, discovering that intelligence community operations were not conducted according to moral, ethical, or legal standards that he valued. Instead intelligence operatives and operations often ignored, even flouted, morality and law. In a state of disillusionment, Snowden took momentary refuge from the predicament in which he found himself in the hope offered by the 2008 election of Barack Obama, fully expecting the new administration to institute reforms to security agencies. When it became clear that reforms were not on President Obama's agenda, Snowden decided he needed to act on his own and took a job at Booz-Allen Hamilton with the express purpose of gathering evidence—and blowing-the-whistle—on NSA's criminal and unconstitutional actions. Among thousands of documents released by Snowden and published in *The Washington Post* on June 6 (Gellman and Poitras) was a timeline of agreements made between NSA and internet service providers to secretly funnel customer communications to the NSA—Yahoo, Google, and more.[5]

Shortly following revelations of NSA surveillance and Snowden's identity, Tom Twiss, government documents librarian at the University of Pittsburgh, posted an e-mail calling for interested volunteers to assist in the crafting of a resolution regarding Edward Snowden in time for the upcoming ALA conference in Chicago. For several years, Twiss had been active in the Social Responsibilities Round Table's International Responsibilities Task Force (SRRT and IRTF), and was an old hand at the resolution process. In 2004 he was both IRTF chair and SRRT's liaison to the Government Documents Round Table (GODORT), which at their meetings in Orlando considered and passed a "Resolution on Securing Government Accountability through Whistleblower Protection."

Initiated by the Government Information Subcommittee of ALA's Committee on Legislation (COL), and endorsed by the Federal and Armed Forces Libraries Round

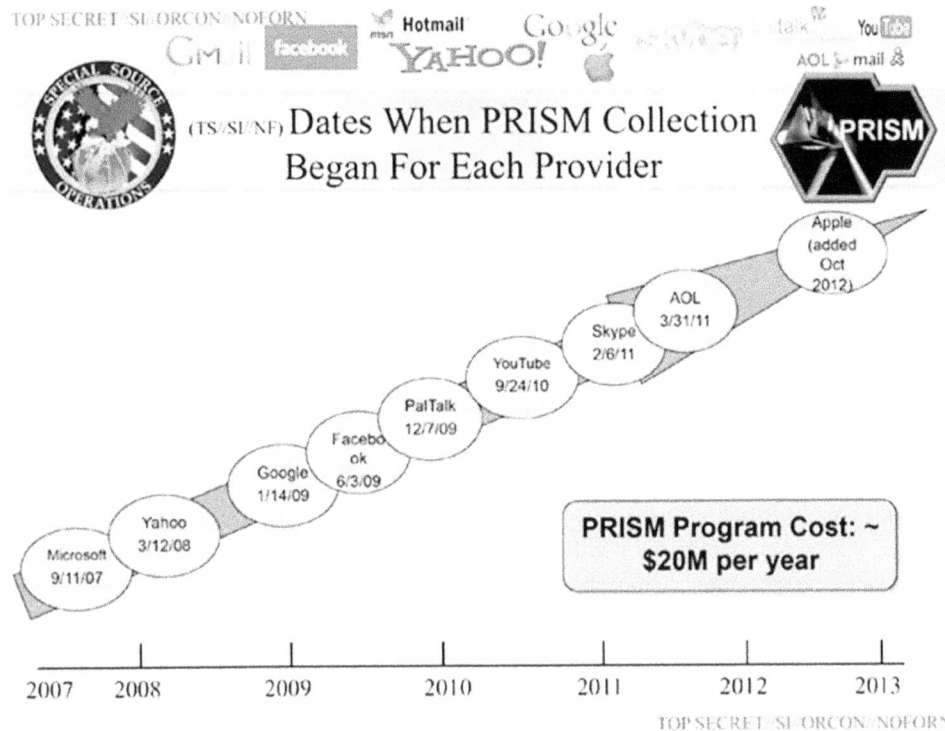

One of the documents released by Edward Snowden showing a timeline of data-mining agreements between NSA and the corporations listed.

Table, the Intellectual Freedom Committee, and GODORT, this whistleblower resolution was approved by ALA Council. Somehow, the Policy Monitoring Committee failed to include text from this resolution in the *ALA Policy Manual*, as sometimes happens. A search of the online manual turns up nothing with keywords "whistleblower" or variations. Given the absence of policy manual language, the full text of this resolution follows.

RESOLUTION ON SECURING GOVERNMENT ACCOUNTABILITY THROUGH WHISTLEBLOWER PROTECTION

WHEREAS, the American Library Association has a long standing policy of supporting free speech by all, including government employees; and

WHEREAS, open and unfettered access to information by and about government is a basic tenet of a democratic society and crucial to the public's ability to hold government accountable; and

WHEREAS, security concerns in today's environment have resulted in increased restrictions on access to public, unclassified government information, and actions of whistleblowers may be the only means of exposing problems in government; and

WHEREAS, whistleblowers often have alerted Congress, government officials, and the public to abuse, fraud, and waste in governmental activities; and

WHEREAS, libraries and librarians have a long tradition of assisting the public in learning about the activities of their government; and

WHEREAS, government employees who have uncovered abuse, fraud, and waste and become whistleblowers have suffered intimidation, loss of security clearance, reduced benefits, or loss of employment; and

WHEREAS, legislative efforts to strengthen governmental accountability through enhanced protection for whistleblowers, such as the "Paul Revere Whistleblower Act," are pending in Congress; therefore be it

RESOLVED, that the American Library Association affirms its support for accountable government and the role of whistleblowers in reporting abuse, fraud, and waste in governmental activities; and be it further

RESOLVED, that the American Library Association supports legislative efforts to provide increased support and protection for whistleblowers in the Federal government [Committee].

Concern within ALA regarding whistleblowers is not limited to this one document. Indeed, one of ALA's major divisions, United for Libraries, whose mission focuses on support and promotion of the work of library trustees, has on its website a "Sample Whistle Blower Policy." The sample policy puts the library that adopts such a policy on record as prohibiting "fraudulent practices by any of its board, members, officers, employees, or volunteers." Additionally, the library agrees to refrain from retaliation against any employee who reports conduct that she or he "believes in good faith to be a violation of the law." To reinforce support of whistleblowers, the sample policy suggests that the library "may take disciplinary action (up to and including termination) against an employee who in management's assessment has engaged in retaliatory conduct in violation of this policy" (United).

Given ALA's official policy regarding privacy, confidentiality, and whistleblowers, prompt action on the case of Edward Snowden was not surprising. ALA's *Code of Professional Ethics for Librarians* which states, "We protect each library user's right to privacy and confidentiality, with respect to information sought or received and resources consulted, borrowed, acquired, or transmitted" (American 1995, 45). The NSA had no probable cause to monitor communications of the entire population (including library users and librarians), and received no warrants to do so for the vast majority of the victims of their data-mining. Edward Snowden believed that NSA actions violated the Constitution. Had he been an employee or volunteer at a library that functioned according to a United for Libraries-style whistleblower policy, a prompt investigation of his concerns would have been required, without retaliation against him. However, despite federal laws protecting whistleblowers, Snowden had cause to act as though he most certainly would be retaliated against. For him to believe and behave otherwise would have strained credulity, and Twiss knew Snowden would be in need of a public expression of support and appreciation.

One week following the revelation of Snowden's identity, *USA Today* interviewed three former NSA whistleblowers—Thomas Drake, William Binney, and J. Kirk Wiebe. Drake came to the NSA from the CIA in 2001, serving as a senior executive until his resignation in 2008. Binney worked as a cryptologist for 40 years until he retired in 2001. Wiebe spent 30 years at NSA until he too retired in 2001. All three men tried through established channels to bring NSA wrongdoing to light, only to encounter resistance and retribution along the way. In 2002, Binney and Wiebe informed Congress of NSA surveillance and contractor corruption. In 2007, the FBI raided the homes of both men on the same day. Binney, held at gunpoint, was forced to watch with his wife and child as their home was ransacked by FBI agents. Neither men were ever charged with any crime. Drake was indicted for espionage in 2010, but the charges were ultimately dropped in a plea bargain. He pleaded guilty to a misdemeanor of "exceeding authorized use of a computer" and served one year of community service and probation. In the June 16th interview, *USA Today* asked these three men what treatment Snowden could expect from the federal government:

> BINNEY: Well, first of all, I think he should expect to be treated just like Bradley Manning (an Army private now being court-martialed for leaking documents to WikiLeaks). The U.S. government gets hold of him, that's exactly the way he will be treated.
>
> Q: He'll be prosecuted?
>
> BINNEY: First tortured, then maybe even rendered and tortured and then incarcerated and then tried and incarcerated or even executed [Eisler].

While the Obama administration demanded Snowden's extradition to face espionage charges, government watchdog groups and concerned citizens were demanding he be treated (and protected) as a whistleblower. On the same day as the *USA Today* interview, Mike Marlin member of Council and SRRT, posted to alacoun (the listserv of ALA's Council) a link to a statement issued by the Government Accountability Project (GAP) regarding Snowden, which made eight points regarding his actions, then elaborated on each:

I. Snowden is a Whistleblower
II. Snowden is the Subject of Classic Whistleblower Retaliation
III. The Issue is the Message and Not the Messenger
IV. Pervasive Surveillance Does Not Meet the Standard for Classified Information
V. The Public has a Constitutional Right to Know
VI. There is a Clear History of Reprisal Against NSA Whistleblowers
VII. We are Witnessing the Criminalization of Whistleblowing
VIII. In the Surveillance State, the Enemy is the Whistleblower

The GAP statement concluded, "…secrecy, retaliation and intimidation undermine our Constitutional rights and weaken our democratic processes more swiftly, more surely, and more corrosively than the acts of terror from which they purport to protect us" (Government).

On June 17th, councilor Ed Garcia, responding to Marlin's post, wrote on the ALA council listserv, "I hope there is a resolution being crafted on this topic." Shortly after, SRRT Councilor Al Kagan, knowing that Twiss was drafting a resolution, replied that one was "coming soon" thereby giving all councilors a heads-up that the matter would be on Council's upcoming agenda.

Twiss was joined in the writing of the Snowden resolution by Jim Kuhn, Fred Stoss, and Mike Marlin, and they drew on yet another longstanding ALA policy to support their resolution. In 1971, Council established a policy regarding government intimidation. The policy reads,

> The ALA opposes any use of governmental prerogatives that lead to the intimidation of individuals or groups and discourages them from exercising the right of free expression as guaranteed by the First Amendment to the U.S. Constitution. ALA encourages resistance to such abuse of governmental power and supports those against whom such governmental power has been employed [ALA B.2.4].

The policy on government intimidation has an interesting history. Initiated by Zoia Horn, head of reference at Bucknell University's library in Lewisburg, Pennsylvania, with assistance from colleagues Pat Rom and SRRT activist Jackie Eubanks, the resolution was prompted by Horn's own encounters with the FBI and intimidation via the grand jury process. Writing about the resolution in her memoir *Zoia! Memoirs of Zoia Horn, Battler for the People's Right to Know*, Horn recalls the resolution, quoting from it,

> The resolution asserted that the "freedoms to think, communicate, and discuss ... are essential elements of intellectual freedom, that these freedoms have been threatened by our federal government's use of informers, electronic surveillance, grand juries, and indictments...." And it asked that ALA recognize these dangers to intellectual freedom, go on record against the use of these grand jury procedures "to intimidate anti–Vietnam War activists and people seeking justice for minority communities," deplore and condemn the misuse of "the Conspiracy Act of 1968 as a weapon against the citizens of this country who are being indicted for such overt acts as meeting, telephoning, and discussing alternative methods of bringing about change and writing letters." It added two ethical provisos that ALA assert the confidentiality of the professional relationship of librarians to the people they serve and that "no librarian would lend himself to a role as informant, whether of revealing circulation records or identifying patrons and their reading habits" [Horn 166].

Although the resolution met with some resistance during discussion at Council, with some councilors attempting "to shunt it off to a committee" (*ibid.*), the Resolution on Government Intimidation passed and became ALA policy. Despite the association's official opposition to government intimidation, the following year the ALA Executive Board issued a statement that caused Horn deep distress.

> Policy notwithstanding, in the following year (1972), when I [Horn] had challenged the government's attempt to intimidate critics of the war in Vietnam, and was sent to jail as a consequence, the ALA Executive Board refused to support my stand. Moreover, they issued a public statement of their refusal without even asking me if I wanted their support or asking me to present my reasons for declining to testify [at grand jury hearings in the Harrisburg Seven case]. Their statement, which is actually a condemnation of my decision as well as a refusal to support, was published in *American Libraries*, which is sent to all 50,000 members [*ibid.*].

Although ALA policy *"encourages resistance to such abuse of government power"* one can see from Horn's experience that official policy does nothing to guarantee that actual support might be forthcoming from the Association. However, some ALA members, such as Horn and Twiss, dedicate themselves to holding the Association accountable in abiding by its policies.

Given appeals to ALA policy on government accountability, the right to privacy, the confidentiality of patron records, whistleblower protections, and opposition to the use of government intimidation, it should not have come as a surprise when the Snowden resolution was presented at the ALA Membership Meeting in Chicago, on June 29, and passed by a considerable majority—but it was.

Consider, for a moment, that although the Fourth Amendment has not disappeared from the Bill of Rights one sometimes wonders whether we have privacy rights or not, given the lack of commitment by police, lawyers, and judges to uphold those rights. Over the years, law enforcement practices and court rulings have weakened protections from unwarranted searches and seizures, in part because of the failure of citizens to hold authorities accountable for violations of the law. Similar fickleness is evidenced in ALA by Council and Executive Board prevarication over implementing its own stated values and commitments. Times change, so too the willingness of individuals and groups to question authority, to hold it accountable, and the passage of the Snowden resolution did, indeed, come as a surprise to its writers and movers. Within the context of a general climate of conservatism nationally, colored by budget cuts, heightened "security" concerns, a decade-long "war on terror," and continuing economic woes, activists within ALA expected little support for the Snowden resolution, especially in light of recent failures of similar resolutions regarding Army private Bradley Manning, who had released huge quantities of classified material documenting U.S. war crimes to Wikileaks.

But it did pass, and with passage by the membership meeting, the Snowden resolution was automatically placed on the Council I agenda for the following morning. On June 30, in its first session, Council *itself* passed the resolution. Discussion was brief, and there was *no* debate.

Jim Kuhn, mover of the resolution, spoke to it,

> We, for about the last decade, have been in this situation where access to the courts on issues related to domestic surveillance and privacy has been extremely limited. Over and over again, individuals and organizations and companies have been told they do not have standing to bring suit against domestic surveillance and broad attacks on privacy [because of lack of documentation]. Meanwhile our access to Congress has been extraordinarily limited. The oversight committees (we have learned) have been limited, lied to. We've had senators come out of closed-door hearings saying, "if only the American people knew what was happening in our name you would be outraged." Meanwhile those among us who are most affected by these laws, in particular Section 215 of the USAPATRIOT Act, are gagged from even speaking for good or ill about these pieces of legislation [impacting] our libraries and our library activities—even to our elected representatives. So we don't have access to the courts, we don't have access to Congress that is effective. Meanwhile the executive branch seems to have gotten religion about this issue in the past few weeks, but in fact if you compare the comments of President Obama when he was a candidate for Senate, when he was a candidate for president, and now when he is commander-in-chief, you'll see that his position on the issues of domestic surveillance and accountability for violations of privacy by government officials have been moving very much against us. Quite recently, the White House spokesperson said we should be engaging in a broad national debate about these issues, but, in fact, that national debate has not been brought forward by the executive branch. Under such circumstances, when the courts, the Congress, the executive branch, and the press are of no help—in fact, the press has been under an unprecedented level of attack by governmental intimidation—we need whistleblowers. Actions taken by Edward Snowden have given us an extraordinary opportunity to make important strides in public policy that relates fundamentally to [librarianship's] core values of privacy, open access to government information, over-classification, an informed electorate, and this [the Snowden resolution] is an opportunity to make it clear to folks who are taking great personal risk in revealing important details about what is going on in our name, that we *do* stand with them on the basis of our core values as a profession dedicated to an informed electorate and the role of an informed electorate in a democracy. Thank you very much [Council I].

Ann Crewdson spoke next, describing family conversations sparked by Snowden's revelations.

> Not only has this [incident] sparked dialogue nationally, but it has also allowed me to talk with my own family and my own teenagers about their privacy, their practices on Facebook and social media, and I think that's very good for a generation that seems to be more and more, being that they grew up in a ubiquitous surveillance society ... more complacent

than we'd like them to be, because it leads to many things in the future such as employment and their health insurance, and I've explained it to [my daughter] that every FB "like" she does, and everything she does online, it's a built-up datamine, and that's like a doppelganger, and when I pointed that out to her, I said, what if you knew there was a doppelganger out there and that's the thing that determines the rest of your life? She was absolutely floored by that [*ibid.*].

Nann Blain Hilyard then expressed appreciation and approval that during the previous evening's informal Council Forum, a 2nd resolved clause that would have put ALA on record as opposing "any attempts by the United States government to extradite or prosecute Edward Snowden," had been removed. After Forum conversations regarding the resolution, its movers decided to delete the original 2nd resolved clause, thinking approval might be possible without it. Hilyard said, "I appreciate the resolved clause that does not pass any judgment on Edward Snowden, it simply identifies him, and the bigger part is that we are opening up this dialogue, but aren't passing any judgment on him" (*ibid.*).

At this point, any Council member who objected to the resolution, or had questions, or needed clarification would have gone to an open microphone, identified him- or herself, and stated their mind. This did not happen. Perhaps anyone who opposed the resolution simply assumed it would fail. Perhaps, in the face of the resolution's supporting documentation, opponents could find no ethical way to argue against the resolution. Privacy rights, after all, have been a leading concern of ALA's since the 1930s. Between the resolution's passage at the membership meeting and the first session of Council, opponents had an entire afternoon and evening to formulate persuasive arguments, or even to decide to refer the matter to a committee, or to table it for a future meeting, but no opposing arguments or parliamentary maneuvers were forthcoming. Seeing no other members of Council at the microphones, the chair called for a vote and the resolution was approved with 105 in favor, 39 opposed, and 10 abstaining.

RESOLUTION IN SUPPORT OF WHISTLEBLOWER EDWARD SNOWDEN

WHEREAS, since 1939 the American Library Association (ALA) has affirmed the right to privacy in its Code of Ethics, which currently states, "We protect each library user's right to privacy and confidentiality with respect to information sought or received and resources consulted, borrowed, acquired or transmitted";

WHEREAS in "Principles for the Networked World" in 2002 ALA included among the "principles of privacy" the fact that "privacy is a right of all people and must be protected in the networked world" and the recognition that "the rights of anonymity and privacy while people retrieve and communicate information must be protected as an essential element of intellectual freedom";

WHEREAS in 2002 in "Privacy: An Interpretation of the Library Bill of Rights" ALA recognized that "privacy is essential to the exercise of free speech, free thought, and free association";

WHEREAS in 2003 in its "Resolution on the USA PATRIOT Act and Related Measures that Infringe on the Rights of Library Users" ALA criticized the "USA PATRIOT Act and other recently enacted laws, regulations, and guidelines" on the grounds that they "increase the likelihood that the activities of library users, including their use of computers to browse the Web or access e-mail, may be under government surveillance without their knowledge or consent" [CD#20.1, 2003];

WHEREAS in 2004 ALA passed a "Resolution on Securing Government Accountability through Whistleblower Protection" affirming its "support for accountable government and the role of whistleblowers in reporting abuse, fraud, and waste in governmental activities" [CD#20.7, 2004];

WHEREAS in 2005 in its "Resolution on Radio Frequency Identification (RFID) Technology and Privacy Principles" ALA insisted that "user privacy and confidentiality has long been an integral part of the mission of libraries" [CD#19.1, 2005];

WHEREAS in 2008 ALA passed a "Resolution Commending the FBI Whistleblower Who Exposed Abuses on the Use of Exigent National Security Letters" which called on Congress to "protect the rights of whistleblowers against retaliation" [CD#20.5, 2008];

WHEREAS since 2010 ALA has sponsored "Choose Privacy Week," an initiative "that invites library users into a national conversation about privacy rights in a digital age" and a campaign that "gives libraries the tools they need to educate and engage users, and gives citizens the resources to think critically and make more informed choices about their privacy";

WHEREAS Edward Snowden, a technical specialist for contractors employed by the National Security Agency, has admitted to providing classified information to reporters for *The Guardian* and *The Washington Post* newspapers;

WHEREAS this information revealed that, under a FISA court order issued in April 2013, the National Security Agency is collecting the telephone records of millions of U.S. customers of Verizon;

WHEREAS this information further revealed that since 2007 under its PRISM program the NSA has been collecting huge quantities of data on internet usage, including internet search histories, email, video and voice chat, videos, photos, voice-over-IP chats, file transfers, and social networking details, from internet service providers in the United States;

WHEREAS Edward Snowden has explained that his "sole motive" in revealing this information was "to inform the public as to that which was done in their name and that which is done against them"; and

WHEREAS Edward Snowden is now facing extradition and prosecution for releasing this information; now, therefore be it

RESOLVED, that the American Library Association (ALA) recognizes Edward Snowden as a whistleblower who, in releasing information that documents government attacks on privacy, free speech, and freedom of association, has performed a valuable service in launching a national dialogue about transparency, domestic surveillance, and overclassification [Resolution].

The vote on Council I was met with high-fives, smiles, and congratulations after the meeting by those who had worked on the resolution. The majority vote to recognize Snowden as a whistleblower was an informed and considered act. Council members who had attended the previous day's membership meeting or the Council Forum had ample opportunity to think about and discuss with others the position they would take on the resolution. Evidence of the previous day's discussions and resulting revisions to the resolution was described by Hilyard. Not one objection was voiced. Such vindication of an act of conscience was tremendously gratifying. ALA Council had done what the federal government refused to do—recognize Edward Snowden as a *whistleblower*. Not only that, but had commended him for his *service* to the nation.

Alas, some joys are short-lived, and such was to be the fate of the Snowden resolution.

Before moving on to the ultimate, and unprecedented, demise of the resolution, we should pause for a moment to consider the larger context of the Snowden resolution in order to see how an ostensibly democratic forum, a platform for free speech, can be easily swayed, so that a position challenging authority, is brought into alignment with authority. In other words, how an elite group ensures that the voice "says the right thing."

The bureaucratic maneuvering that followed on Council the very next morning, which overturned the Snowden resolution, is a prime example of an observation by Noam Chomsky,

> From a comparative perspective, the United States is unusual if not unique in its lack of restraints on freedom of expression. It is also unusual in the range and effectiveness of the methods employed to restrain freedom of thought. The two phenomena are related. Liberal democratic theorists have long observed that in a society where the voice of the people is heard, elite groups must ensure that that voice says the right things. The less the state is able to employ violence in defense of the interests of elite groups that effectively dominate it, the more it becomes necessary to devise techniques of "manufacture of consent" [Chomsky 19].

At the time of this debate, the federal government was calling Snowden a traitor, demanding his extradition for prosecution under the Espionage Act of 1917. The press largely echoed these characterizations. Whenever ALA Council passes a resolution, it gets distributed to the press, and to others concerned with the issue at hand. A copy of the Snowden resolution was destined for the White House. In these days of instant communication, word got out immediately that Council had taken the position that Snowden was a whistleblower and that he deserved appreciation for his actions, and just as instantaneously opposition to the resolution rallied, and found support from at least one Council member who voted against it. Why? Was it just sour grapes? Poor losers? As it turned out the challenger of Council's vote to support the Snowden resolution was a member of the ALA Executive Board, the elite of the elite. Not only that, but every member of Council serving on the Executive Board at the time, except Dara Ho, Sara Kelly Johns, and Jim Neal, voted against the resolution on June 30th. Why hadn't any of them spoken against it? And, what does it matter what ALA says about Edward Snowden.

Death of a resolution

Council's passage of the resolution would not have impacted Snowden's situation, although the resolution's message of recognition and solidarity might have slightly lightened the emotional burden of his exile and vilification. Nor would ALA's acknowledgment of Snowden's actions have tempered the government's pursuit of him, but the moral weight of this support would have been tremendous. ALA has influence with the public. Everyone loves librarians, and here was ALA, the professional association of favorite librarians across the nation not only recognizing Snowden as a whistleblower, but declaring that he'd performed a valuable service. Recall that not much more than an hour prior to Council's vote on this resolution, Jackie Garner of the U.S. Department of Health and Human Services had referred to libraries as a *"trusted* community resource"—emphasis being Garner's own. Libraries honor the trust of their communities by providing reliable information and protecting users' privacy.

There were, of course, 39 votes opposing the resolution, and following Council I, there must have been at least one private conversation, perhaps even some frantic politicking in Chicago the evening of June 30th, because the first action the following morning at Council II was a motion to reconsider the Snowden resolution and to refer it to the Intellectual Freedom Committee (IFC) and Committee on Legislation (COL). This motion to reconsider was unprecedented, coming only one day after the resolution's passage.

As the chair concluded reading Council II's agenda on the morning of June 31st, noting that under the 24-hour rule new resolutions on Bradley Manning, fossil fuel divestment, library services to communities in times of disaster, and prayer at ALA meetings had been placed on the day's agenda, John A. Moorman, member of ALA Executive Board, stood at microphone number four and was called on to speak.

Moorman stated his wish that another resolution be added to the agenda, that the Snowden resolution be "reconsidered and referred to the Intellectual Freedom Committee and the Committee on Legislation." Moorman, former director of the Williamsburg (VA) Regional Library and consultant with Dominion Library Associates, had voted against the resolution the previous day, although he did not reveal his opposition to the audience, merely explaining that

> I am very concerned that our action taken yesterday did not come with due deliberation and with the consideration of recommendations from two committees that are essential to the operation of our organization, and we should hear their input before we take action.
>
> CHAIR: Is there discussion? Oh [inaudible], so it's on the agenda? I've added it to the agenda. Thank you. Is there other new business? Hearing no further discussion, I declare the agenda adopted [Council II].

For Council consideration, resolutions are required to be submitted to the Council Resolution's Committee 24-hours in advance. Had Moorman's resolution met this requirement, it should have been printed on the agenda for Council II. It was not. At the time, the addition of Moorman's new resolution to the agenda was not questioned, probably in the belief that a rule of parliamentary procedure allowed for no advance period for a resolution to reconsider previously approved items. Council II proceeded, and eventually Moorman's resolution to reconsider and refer reached the floor.

Members of Council take seriously their responsibilities as elected representatives to the body that establishes policy for the association. Generally speaking, councilors arrive at meetings having done their homework. SRRT Councilor Kagan had posted the original version of the Snowden resolution on June 23rd to the Council listserv, a full week before it arrived on Council's agenda. Had any Council members felt uninformed regarding any element of the Snowden resolution, most would have spoken up. Those opposing the resolution also had ample time to frame their arguments against it. Asking a question, requesting a point of clarification, making an amendment, moving to refer, to table, to close debate—all these parliamentary procedures are second nature to many but the newest or shyest Council members, and are used with great regularity. As Hilyard's statement the previous day indicates, the original resolution had been changed following passage at Membership to accommodate objections, raised at Council Forum, to the call for the federal government to refrain from persecution of Snowden, a compromise the movers were willing to make in order to gain support from Council.

As a seasoned councilor, indeed a member of the Executive Board, Moorman himself, knowing he opposed the resolution, could have raised his objections during discussion on the 30th. One can only speculate as to why he did not. Perhaps he wasn't quite awake. Perhaps he assumed most councilors shared his opposition and therefore did not bother to speak, even to refer the resolution for committee review. Perhaps he was too embarrassed (or politically savvy) to openly acknowledge a wavering commitment to the privacy of American citizens—face-savingly easier after the fact to claim the resolution was passed without "due deliberation" than to stand on the floor of Council and explain his opposition to a resolution addressed directly to two ALA policies: privacy rights and support of whistleblowers. Ordinarily, Moorman would most likely have had the good grace to accept the will of the body and allow the resolution to stand as the official opinion of ALA regarding Edward Snowden. Win some, lose some—all in a day's work on ALA Council.

Moorman did not accept the will of the body, and when his resolution to reconsider and refer came to the floor, he offered the following explanation:

> Sometimes in Council we act in haste. As our procedures, as Bernie Margolis pointed out earlier, are in process in order to get us total information in situations and to get recommendations from committees within the organization that are assigned this responsibility. On Monday, neither the Intellectual Freedom Committee nor the Committee on Legislation had had the ability to review and make recommendations. I do know they are meeting this afternoon and that they will bring something back to Council tomorrow on this issue. I also feel it is very important that as we look at items that we discuss that we consider the implication of those items upon the ability of our Washington Office to work with legislators and the ability of librarians in their community to effectively discuss issues from a neutral stance. This is the reason for this resolution, and I urge its adoption [*ibid.*].

Moorman's position then was that (1) the vote the previous day was ill-informed, (2) the adoption of the Snowden resolution would negatively impact the Washington Office's ability to work on behalf of ALA, and (3) the adoption of the resolution would similarly impact librarians' ability to "discuss issues from a neutral stance." We will later return to the first two of Moorman's concerns, but the third can be dispensed with immediately. In regard to any of the issues raised by the Snowden resolution, none require a neutral stance. Librarianship is not neutral with respect to privacy rights, to laws protecting whistleblowers, or to government intimidation. Indeed, a neutral position with respect to any of these matters would implicitly condone invasions of privacy, the persecution of whistleblowers, and any amount of government intimidation, all in violation of ALA policies, values, and ethics. Librarians in their communities should be able and willing to advocate on behalf of privacy rights, whistleblower protections, and opposition to government intimidation. The fact that Moorman suggested librarians discuss such matters from a neutral standpoint called into question his own commitment to them.

Jim Kuhn then spoke:

> As the mover of CD 39 [the Snowden resolution] and a member of the Intellectual Freedom Committee, I stand here with some responsibility for which otherwise might appear as a procedural snafu or hiccup, but I have to say that responsibility is also shared by the calendar. It is extraordinarily hard, as we have seen this morning, to get full endorsement, to get full consideration. To get all the information we seek for these resolutions that come before this body with the 24-hour rule in place. That said, we did request that this be on the docket for Council II, it was in fact moved to Council I. Perhaps at that time I should have postponed deliberation. I did not, however, because in fact I was prepared to speak to it, and I did speak to it and I stand by what I said. The other thing I would like to say about that is, as an IFC member, I can report on extensive discussions about this resolution at some of our first meetings, discussion which influenced the version that came forward to Council yesterday. There was no vote by the IFC to endorse, and perhaps I should have

asked and actually moved as an IFC member that the committee vote on this, to endorse or not endorse. And I take responsibility for that. But I have to say, it is very important for this organization to be able to act on matters of grave concern to us in a manner that does not continually put off action until subsequent conferences, particularly on time-sensitive issues such as this one. We had lots of debate. We had lots of input. It was passed at membership meeting, it was passed by Council yesterday, so I will be voting against referring this to IFC and COL. Thank you [*ibid.*].

The debate that followed was not a hashing-out of whether or not Snowden was a whistleblower who'd rendered a valuable public service. Rather it boiled down to a debate centered around ALA bureaucracy and whether or not certain committees have a better understanding of the issues than members of Council. Statements that follow, taken from the sound recordings of the session (Council II), have been edited to provide the gist of the debate.

Mario Gonzalez, just elected ALA Treasurer, thereby becoming a member of the Executive Board, had voted against the Snowden resolution the previous day. Speaking to the resolution to refer Gonzalez said, "These committees have the intellect, the resources, and the ability to give us more information than, I believe, we had when we voted on the original motion."

Bobbie Newman, councilor-at-large, said, "I did vote in favor of this resolution yesterday, but in light of the information I've heard since then, I'm going to change my mind." She gave no indication as to what further information she'd received.

Brian Schottlander, ALCTS division councilor, had abstained from voting on the resolution "because I was deeply uncomfortable with it and I actually welcome the proposed reconsideration and referral to IFC and COL and strongly support councilor Moorman's recommendation."

Executive Board member Molly Raphael, who also voted against the resolution, commented,

> I speak in favor of this motion. I am actually kicking myself for not ... thinking of this [referral] when we were discussing the motion. We have committees that have taken issues from us, such as IFC and COL, and come back with resolutions that I think many of us have felt were much improved. I believe we will get reports back on this and I think the very fact that there are unintended consequences tells us that we should have been a little bit more deliberative, doesn't mean we wouldn't have passed it, but we should have been more deliberative.

Charles Kratz, councilor-at-large who had supported the resolution, said,

> I certainly have no problem with it being referred, but if it does get referred today, the geniis out of the bottle because *American Libraries*, right now on my iPad here, already has it announced that we've supported it. It was tweeted yesterday. We live in a social media world. It was tweeted and on Facebook yesterday.

Dianne Chen Kaley, who also had voted in favor of the resolution the day before, spoke next:

> I rise to second the motion because of three phrases important to council—prudent deliberation, thoughtful consideration, and unintended consequences. Yesterday during our deliberations the statement was made that the resolution did not pass judgment, but after more thorough discussion with the Washington Office and with councilors informally dur-

ing the forum and throughout the conference, I believe this is in fact not true. It jumps to a decision, it paralyzes our lobbyists, and our Washington Office from working effectively with legislators. William Binney, a whistleblower who also disclosed details of NSA's mass surveillance activities, stated in the press, after Snowden began leaking allegations that the U.S. was hacking into China "he was transitioning from a whistleblower to a traitor." Imagine, after events continue to evolve and we learn more, as Snowden continues to release these classified documents he has removed from our country, that his status is determined to be both whistleblower and espionage traitor. How would you like to consider supporting a resolution with a resolved clause that the ALA recognized Edward Snowden as a whistleblower and traitor who in releasing information that reveals government attacks on privacy, free speech and freedom of the press has performed a valuable service in launching a national dialogue about transparency, surveillance, and over-classification. Just the addition of those two words makes me uncomfortable enough to urge you, if you have any concern, to please move this for reconsideration.

Kaley's quote from Binney was accurate, although as Al Kagan stated immediately after she spoke, it was taken out of context. Kaley failed to note Binney's comment that he himself did not know at the time of the interview whether or not Snowden had access to documentation regarding NSA spying on foreign countries, specifically China. (Readers are referred to the full *USA Today* interview by Eisler.) Subsequent revelations showed that NSA was, indeed, monitoring the communications of even foreign heads of state. As for Kaley's hypothetical resolution that would have Council determine Snowden to be a "whistleblower and traitor," the absurdity of her suggestions speaks for itself.

Al Kagan, SRRT councilor:

> The Social Responsibilities Round Table brought William Binney to our conference. Many people heard him speak, he is a man of great integrity. I believe that the quote that was just made [by Kaley] must be taken out of context.... The whistleblowers in this case have shown that the NSA is monitoring all of our e-mail and all of our phone calls and more. William Binney told us about that.... Now that he has the documentation, this is now national news. Most Americans are offended by what the NSA is doing. ALA membership meeting was offended by what the NSA is doing, that's why they voted to support what we said about Ed Snowden. We overwhelmingly passed this resolution in the Council, and I think it's because the councilors are offended by the kind of Orwellian situation we have now in this country. To refer this back to committees that are not likely to even put Ed Snowden's name in their resolution tomorrow would be a travesty, and I hope we don't do it.

Diedre Conkling, councilor at large supported the Snowden resolution:

> I'm against reconsideration and referral [to IFC and COL] I voted with full knowledge of the resolutions and what they meant and I think I read it very clearly and I'm very satisfied with my vote. I know that when we get the information back from the Intellectual Freedom Committee and the Committee on Legislation they're going to send us something about we support open government, we support whistleblowers, we're going to work on educating our members about these issues, and we will no longer be supporting a whistleblower. I was pleased that we were actually supporting a whistleblower, and I do not want to refer this.

Mary Biblo councilor at large, another supporter:

> Here we go again, debating an issue that is pretty clear. We are on record that we support whistleblowers.... Now I've been here for as long as Molly Raphael, maybe longer, [and know] what referral like this to a committee means. We used to have a treasurer and if they didn't want this particular item to be brought to the floor, his main role was to get up to say let's refer this to BARC because it might have fiscal implications. I'm not saying you

might do this with the Intellectual Freedom Committee, it might come out in support, but I'm simply against referral. I learned my lesson sitting here in Council for a number of years, what referral meant. Thank you.

Lauren Comito councilor at large:

I'm against this motion. We voted yesterday to support this, and in my case, I voted in support because of the effect it has on my patrons. I deal everyday with people who have to worry that they need a password on their Smartphone because they get stopped and frisked. I deal with women of middle age who are just dipping into Facebook, who are very concerned with their privacy and so I really thought about this when I voted and I think most of us really did because privacy is a deeply held value that we have as librarians.

Jane Glasby, councilor at large and another supporter:

… we've been well-informed. I think we had a lot of documentation, the research that went in to the preparation of the resolution, all those whereas clauses referring back to all the legislation that we've passed, if you want to call it legislation, all the policy we've passed, so I think to say we don't have the intellect and we have to send it on to another body for their smaller body of minds, their intellect, I think it's a little insulting to ask, because I think we have thought about this issue and we are the policy making body, and we did think about it, and its timely and that to refer it back, we know what's going to happen.

People here have the history, and as Mary Biblo said, and Diedre Conkling said, we know it's going to come back as the same motion that we've had so many times. Same resolution, same content, same empty content, and we need to stand by our decision yesterday, and the membership meeting's strong endorsement also, and support an individual whistleblower as an instance of the whistleblowing we're all so keen on. And I'm also reminded about this thing, about unintended consequences, of when we were trying to move against segregation and some of the southern states, the library associations from southern states, were saying "Oh, please don't pass that because it will make it very difficult in our individual legislatures to negotiate in our individual states. Please don't make the national ALA force our hands."

Well, I think we have a responsibility to take a stand on some things and if there's going to be a problem, I'm sorry about that, it might make life more difficult for people going into negotiation in Congress, but I do think we need to take a stand on principle and not worry about those details.

So, what happened here? In a nutshell:

- On June 29, ALA members at the conference membership meeting considered and approved a resolution;
- that evening the resolution was revised to meet objections raised and to garner more supportive votes on Council;
- the revised resolution was passed on June 30 by the governing council with no debate, 105 approving, 39 opposed;
- on the morning of July 1, a member of the Executive Board, who had voted against the resolution the previous day, made a motion to reconsider and refer to two committees on the grounds that it hadn't been given "due deliberation";
- discussion ensued on this motion, concern was raised about "unintended consequences," and a vote was taken 96 approving, 42 opposed, 6 abstaining, and—unusual in council voting—15 councilors who were present at this meeting cast no vote;
- the resolution was sent to IFC and COL for "more information."

Moorman never publicly owned his opposition to the Snowden resolution. The same is true for Gonzalez and Raphael, neither admitting they'd voted against the Snowden resolution. (Although votes in Council are made public with a raising of hands, only the most attentive would know how any one councilor voted, as voting records are not made available until after each conference, and it is highly unlikely that for any given vote more than a handful of people would keep track of how a particular councilor voted.)

The motion to reconsider and refer "Resolution in support of whistleblower Edward Snowden" was, essentially, a slap on the wrists of all those council members whose "yes" vote was determined to be somehow wrong by the powers-that-be in ALA. Of the nine Executive Board members who voted on the resolution, six voted against it—an almost exact numeric reversal to the Council vote itself: of the 12 Executive Board members sitting and voting on Council those opposed to Snowden were the majority (67 percent), while the majority on Council (63 percent) favored the resolution. The Council vote to approve the resolution was deemed by an Executive Board member to be (a) uninformed, and (b) fraught with "unintended consequences." This might or might not have been a message officially backed by the Executive Board itself, but nonetheless was put forward by its members. Of interest is the fact that every Executive Board member who originally voted in favor of the Snowden resolution remained completely silent during the discussion to reconsider and refer. The unstated message of Moorman's motion was clear—Council screwed up, the Executive Board was opposed to this resolution, and now somebody more expert than Council had to fix the mess.

This tactical use of appeals to expertise in manufacturing consent, as a means of shaming "less expert" individuals or groups into compliance with the perspectives and agendas of superiors, is the modern day method of "whipping" others into alignment. Although members of ALA Council and the Executive Board largely consider one another as equals, as colleagues, and although Council is the constitutionally established policy-making body of ALA, the Executive Board largely steers the ship, and has the ability to redirect its course should a squall head ALA in the "wrong" direction. All of which is to say that, although members of Council are not "subordinates" to those of the Executive Board, the latter can act in the capacity of a superior if deemed necessary. This power dynamic at play is a common one, well delineated in the book *Authority* by Richard Sennett (1980).

Power once was exercised through brute force but with the rise of bureaucracies and the attendant "cult of expertise," power utilizes shame as a method of control. Sennett describes how violence gave way to shame over the course of the 20th century in the exercise of discipline in the workplace, in the school, in the home. Indeed, in my own lifetime use of corporal punishment in schools has gone from being not only an acceptable, but an expected, form of discipline to being literally outlawed. Students are no longer whipped or paddled for shortcomings or disciplinary infractions, but are shamed. Who has not written 100 times some version of "I will not talk back to the teacher." For example, I currently have a colleague who believes he is doing his middle school students a service anytime one ungrammatically asks a question regarding the math lesson. Whenever this happens the teacher silences the student and insists that the question be rephrased. The psychological impact of this instructional method on a child can be profound. The student doesn't understand a math concept or function, and gets a lesson in grammar. The student is doubly reduced by this authority who is expert both in mathematics and in grammar, and (generally) the student, being either an English language learner or an African-American, is shamed before his or her peers by their white, Euro-American male teacher. Here is how Sennett describes the phenomenon within the context not of student and teacher, but of worker and employer,

> Shame has taken the place of violence as a *routine* form of punishment in Western societies. The reason is simple and perverse. The shame an autonomous person can arouse in subordinates is an implicit control. Rather than the employer explicitly saying "You are dirt" or "Look how much better I am," all he needs to do is his job—exercise his skill or deploy his calm and indifference. His powers are fixed in his position, they are static, attributed qualities of what he is. It is not so much abrupt moments of humiliation as month after month of disregarding his employees, of not taking them seriously, which establishes his domination. The feeling he has about them, they about him, need never be stated. The grinding down of his employees' sense of self-worth is not part of his discourse with them; it is a silent erosion of their sense of self-worth which will wear them down. This, rather than open abuse, is how he bends them to his will. When shame is silent, implicit, it becomes a patent tool of bringing people to heel [Sennett 1993, 95].

In the case of the Snowden resolution discussion, we have a tiny subset (one member of the Executive Board) of an ostensibly democratic body of equals intervening to reverse a decision, not by presenting persuasive arguments or directly addressing the merits of claims that Snowden is a whistleblower, or even sharing his own personal objections to an action taken, but patronizingly through impersonally expressed chastisement via his use of "we" ("Sometimes on council we act in haste") and bureaucratic maneuver. With only a few exceptions, the chastised respond obligingly, not because any evidence was offered to show that their yes votes on Snowden-as-whistleblower were misinformed, but to agree with the superior that they voted "without due deliberation," or to prove they are team players. Three members of the Executive Board had spoken urging Council to reconsider and refer (all three had voted against the resolution). None of the Executive Board members who had voted in favor of the resolution spoke, all remained silent, handing the issue over to their Executive Board colleagues without a whisper of opposition, or even question. In a grand flip-flop, more than half of council members who the previous day had voiced their informed opinion that Edward Snowden was a whistleblower, backed off in apparent admission that they should have known better than to express an informed opinion on the matter.

The "substitute" resolution

The next morning, after what must have been an acceptable level of due deliberation, the Committee on Legislation and the Intellectual Freedom Committee offered the following as a "substitute" for the Snowden resolution,

> RESOLUTION ON THE NEED FOR REFORMS FOR THE INTELLIGENCE
> COMMUNITY TO SUPPORT PRIVACY, OPEN GOVERNMENT,
> GOVERNMENT TRANSPARENCY, AND ACCOUNTABILITY
>
> WHEREAS, Public access to information by and about the government is essential for the healthy functioning of a democratic society and a necessary predicate for an informed and engaged citizenry empowered to hold the government accountable for its actions; and

WHEREAS, "The guarding of military and diplomatic secrets at the expense of informed representative government provides no real security for our Republic"; and

WHEREAS, The ALA values access to the documents disclosing the extent of public surveillance and government secrecy as access to these documents now enables the critical public discourse and debate needed to address the balance between our civil liberties and national security; and

WHEREAS, These disclosures enable libraries to support such discourse and debate by providing information and resources and for deliberative dialogue and community engagement; and

WHEREAS, The American Library Association remains concerned about due process for the people who have led us to these revelations; and

WHEREAS, Libraries are essential to the free flow of ideas and to ensuring the public's right to know; and

WHEREAS, Since 1939 the American Library Association (ALA) has affirmed the right to privacy in its Code of Ethics, which currently states, "We protect each library user's right to privacy and confidentiality with respect to information sought or received and resources consulted, borrowed, acquired or transmitted"; and

WHEREAS, In "Principles for the Networked World" (2002) the ALA included among the "principles of privacy" the fact that "privacy is a right of all people and must be protected in the networked world" and the recognition that "the rights of anonymity and privacy while people retrieve and communicate information must be protected as an essential element of intellectual freedom"; and

WHEREAS, "Privacy: An Interpretation of the Library Bill of Rights" ALA recognized that "privacy is essential to the exercise of free speech, free thought, and free association"; and

WHEREAS, In 2003 ALA criticized the "USA PATRIOT Act and other recently enacted laws, regulations, and guidelines" on the grounds that they "increase the likelihood that the activities of library users, including their use of computers to browse the Web or access e-mail, may be under government surveillance without their knowledge or consent"; and

WHEREAS, Since 2010 ALA has sponsored "Choose Privacy Week," a campaign designed to raise public awareness about personal privacy rights by encouraging local libraries to provide programming, online education, and special events to help individuals to learn, think critically and make more informed choices about their privacy, especially in an era of pervasive surveillance; and ALA has created a website, www.ala.org/liberty, that provides substantive information about privacy, surveillance, open government, and overclassification as well as civic engagement tools to facilitate deliberative dialogues to help support libraries and librarians who create opportunities for public dialogues addressing these topics; and

WHEREAS, The public recently learned that the National Security Agency (NSA) is collecting the telephone call metadata of millions of U.S. customers of Verizon Business Services, AT&T, and Sprint pursuant to an order issued by the Foreign Intelligent Surveillance Court (FISC) under Section 215 of the USA PATRIOT Act; and

WHEREAS, Pursuant to a court order issued by the FISC under Section 702 of the FISA Amendments Act (FAA) the NSA is operating a program called PRISM that is collecting and retaining vast quantities of data on internet usage, including internet search histories, email, video and voice chat, videos, photos, voice-over-IP chats, file transfers, and social networking details, from internet service providers in the United States. Though intended to target communications of foreign persons, the NSA admits that it collects and stores Internet data from U.S. persons; now, therefore be it

RESOLVED, that the American Library Association (ALA):
- Reaffirms its unwavering support for the fundamental principles that are the foundation of our free and democratic society, including a system of public accountability, government transparency, and oversight that supports people's right to know about and participate in our government;
- In light of present revelations related to NSA's surveillance activities conducted pur-

suant to orders issued by the Foreign Intelligent Surveillance Court (FISC) under Sections 215 and 702 of the USA PATRIOT Act the American Library Association calls upon the U.S. Congress, President Obama, and the Courts to reform our nation's climate of secrecy, overclassification, and secret law regarding national security and surveillance, to align with these democratic principles;
- Urges the U.S. Congress and President Obama to provide authentic protections that prevent government intimidation and criminal prosecution of government employees and private contractors who make disclosures of wrong doing in the intelligence community;
- Calls upon the public to engage in and our members to lead public dialogues discussing the right to privacy, open government and balancing civil liberties and national security;
- Encourage the public to support bills and other proposals that both secure and protect our rights to privacy, free expression and free association and promote a more open, transparent government and be further resolved, that
- ALA expresses its thanks and appreciation to the members of Congress who work to protect our privacy and civil liberties [Office].

In their introduction of this resolution, the chairs of the IFC and COL explained that it was intended to cover the issues raised in the Snowden resolution and in another concerning Bradley Manning, which had come up at a previous conference. During discussion of this "substitute," accolades to IFC and COL, words of thanks for hard work in such little time, gushed from the microphones as councilor after councilor, most of whom two days prior had voted in favor of the Snowden resolution, now supported a resolution that said nothing about either Snowden or whistleblowers.

Following are highlights of discussion regarding the IFC/COL motion to substitute the Snowden resolution with the one above (Council III). The entire transcription appears in an earlier version of this chapter that appeared in *Progressive Librarian* (Harger). Provided in parentheses after each speaker's name is an indication of how s/he voted on (1) the original resolution, (2) the motion to reconsider and refer, and (3) the substitute motion. The way in which each councilor voted (Y = yes, N = no, A = abstain, E = absent and excused) is listed in order of the votes: first is the person's June 30 vote on the Snowden resolution; second is their July 1 vote on the motion to reconsider and refer; and third is their July 2 vote on the IFC/COL substitute resolution. Voting records are offered for whatever they might reveal of the speaker's comments. Finally, each speaker is a councilor-at-large unless otherwise noted.

> Al Kagan, SRRT Councilor (Y, N, N): Some of us, probably many of us, saw Alice Walker speak yesterday. She read a long peace titled "the case of Bradley Manning, what are we called to do?" Where she said, something transformative is happening here, when she talked about whistleblowers. And she focused on the inhuman treatment and torture of Bradley Manning. I would be happy to support this resolution as a separate resolution. I think a lot of what's in there we've already taken action on in the past, and if you looked at the Snowden resolution you'll see many ALA resolutions in our past that have led up to today, but I cannot, *cannot* support this resolution as a substitute resolution for what we passed on Edward Snowden. The Edward Snowden resolution was approved by a large majority at our membership meeting. It was approved by a large majority by this council meeting, and the will of this body should not be tampered with by ALA committees that are too worried about what might happen to our lobbying efforts in Washington on other issues. The library community has great legitimacy, and we need to be a little bit brave

once in a while when the country is going in the wrong direction, and our core issues are involved. Therefore I will vote against this substitution, but as I say, I'd be happy to vote for it as an *additional* resolution, not as a substitute. Thank you.

Eric Suess (Y, Y, Y): To me this speaks to exactly what I wanted to see. I wanted something that deals with not the symptoms, but the disease, and I think that's what we're looking at here. Everybody finds the things that we're talking about here abhorrent, but what we've done here is, I think, not come back with a watered-down version of what we're concerned about. I think this is strong, it goes straight to the heart of the problem and I feel that it, as a substitute for the three referrals, one from midwinter and two from this conference … serves that purpose well.

Larry Romans (Y, absent, N): I hope that this doesn't happen again. I've been a councilor for twenty-one years, and this is the first time that a resolution that has been passed by this body has ended up being referred to a committee. The Washington Office, the Committee on Legislation, the Committee on Intellectual Freedom work for us as council. We don't work for them, and the fact that the Washington Office and the committees on Legislation and on Intellectual Freedom didn't like the resolution that was passed is unfortunate, but they had many opportunities to deal with this before it got passed. Normally the Resolutions Committee would have referred this to them [COL and IFC], but since they didn't there are members of both of those committees who could have referred, asked that it be referred to the committee. The chairs could have asked to speak, and this is just a very bad way to go about doing this. As I said, I hope this doesn't happen again.…

Susan Roman (Y, Y, Y): I rise in very strong support of this substitute resolution. I'm impressed with how much stronger this document is, because it reaffirms our core values by striking a balance between the public's right to know, while protecting the individual's right to privacy, along with a balance between civil liberties and national security. I think this resolution is stronger because it doesn't tie this action to one individual or even two, but can be used for covering individuals now and in the future.…

Andrew Pace (Y, N, Y): I stand in support of this resolution. I also want to commend both the committees, I think there was some pretty strong language yesterday about what it means to refer something back to a committee, and though I tend to agree with Larry that things were a bit messy, sometimes democracy is messy.…

Karen Schneider (Y, Y, Y): I would like to commend the COL and the IFC for their swift and elegant work on this. It addresses the concerns I had yesterday. I believe very much that ALA should be addressing these issues, but I agreed in my heart that the previous resolution was not the document that did that. This shifts the point of view from the person to the crisis.…

Jane Glasby (Y, N, N): … I would not say this is about democracy being messy. I would say this was inside the beltway shenanigans that went on.… I, like councilor Kagan, support what is in this resolution. I think it's fine, it's good, and it's an accompanying resolution to the Snowden resolution.… I think this is a *parallel* resolution to the Snowden resolution, and I'd like to see the Snowden resolution stand, and to have this passed in addition.… I can't support this as a substitute motion. Thank you.

Mary Biblo (Y, N, N): ALA is on record in support of access to information, transparency, and whistleblowers. Yet, when it comes to supporting a whistleblower Council hesitates. It appears to me that we are talking out of both sides of our mouth. And I say it's a real, real sad day, and it's a hypocritical way of dealing with the issues. I'm ashamed of you.

Elizabeth Ridler (Y, Y, Y): I was at the forum meeting last night and I really do commend the two proposers of this resolution. There was some discussion about the shortness of the time, and not being informed and so on, but I think they gave a very clear explanation of the resolution at the time.…

Molly Raphael, Executive Board (N, Y, Y): I strongly support the substitute motion, I think it addresses all the issues that are so important to our association.… It proposes actual actions that we think the government should take, and I think this makes us the best we can be as a deliberative body. You know we make jokes all the time about Congress, and how they can't get anything done, but part of being a deliberative body is being able to really think through issues, and decide what is the best place for us to be and for us to stand. And I believe that this resolution provides that place for us to stand. I also want to say that I think the whistleblower law is a terrific law, but it is very complicated, and when we start making judgments about whether people are or are not whistleblowers based on what we read in the press, and we all know that the press has some biases and different directions, so when we make those judgments about individuals we're really stepping into an area where we do not have the facts and we do not have the expertise....

Let us pause for a moment here to unravel an essential problem arising from views like those expressed by Molly Raphael concerning expertise, the press, ordinary (i.e., nonexpert) citizens, and decision-making within a body ostensibly run utilizing instruments of democracy—information, deliberation, and consent. Raphael's concern here is with a "very complicated" law, a biased press, an absence of "the facts," and a lack of expertise. Hers is a question of confidence. What level of being informed is required in order for an individual, or group, to express an opinion or issue a statement on any given issue? This question gives way to another—who, exactly, sets the bar? Who decides what level of expertise is necessary in any given situation? The "elites" referred to by Chomsky perhaps? Is an "ordinary" person ever capable of taking a position regarding what they think about a matter of public concern? Who decides whether or not members of Council are qualified enough to use knowledge culled from a variety of press sources to express their combined views on a contentious topic of the day?

Consider the poster reproduced here from the U.S. Office of Special Counsel (OSC) describing whistleblowers. Presumably prepared, or at the very least approved, by experts in the complicated laws protecting whistleblowers from government intimidation, the poster was created to inform laypersons of the fundamentals of those laws and protections, be that person one considering becoming a whistleblower or one simply needing to be an informed citizen. Given this public information service, it does not appear that the OSC believes expertise is required to understand the laws protecting whistleblowers, and yet Raphael's statement suggests that OSC's confidence in the public's ability to grasp legal matters is misplaced.

On June 30th, the general public (including members of ALA) who followed the news knew that materials released by Snowden provided evidence documenting that the NSA had violated not just "any law" but the Fourth Amendment to the Constitution, a violation which, in and of itself, could reasonably be described "an abuse of authority" to use OSC's language. NSA's actions were not accidental or uninformed, they were deliberate, taken either in full knowledge of laws involved or in gross dereliction of duties and responsibilities. On that ground alone any statement declaring Snowden to be a whistleblower would have been considered an *informed* understanding of the law.

All of which leads to an even larger question concerning whether ordinary people, i.e., nonexperts, can be entrusted with decision-making at all in a democracy. Former ALA president Nancy Kranich wrote in 2000 stating that a free society "must ensure that citizens have the resources to develop the information literacy skills necessary to participate in the democratic process." Kranich's claim was that libraries (and librarians), being the institutions that provide the resources informing the public, are essential to a free society, a democracy. We also heard a government official state that "librarians are essential to the American public as they seek information...." If Raphael's yardstick of expertise sets the standard, then what are we to make of Kranich and Garner and the OSC's seeming confidence in the ability of informed albeit nonexpert people to understand complicated laws and to make decisions regarding them? Moorman, Raphael et al. appear to be taking advantage of their authority as an elite to get Council to "say the right thing."

With that in mind, let us return to the discussion.

> Mario Gonzalez, Executive Board member (N, Y, Y): ... I strongly support this resolution for two major reasons. One is the relevancy it provides to us and libraries and librarians, and also that it [is] a call to action from the highest level of government to the average citizen, to look at us and how we are protecting our privacy and civil liberties....
>
> John DeSantis (Y, absent, N): ... I want to go on record as strongly opposing the practice of reconsidering resolutions that have already been passed for the same reason councilor Romans outlined. I do not approve of approving this resolution as a substitute, I think as others have said, that it would be fine as an additional resolution....
>
> Mike Marlin (E, N, Y): I'd also like to echo the sentiments of councilor DeSantis, I think we really need to not indulge in this practice of trying to substitute for resolutions that have been passed by the membership as well as by council, and that this would be stronger if the names were in there. And I also feel it could be an additional resolution, but not a substitution....
>
> John Sandstrom (Y, N, Y): I do stand in support of this resolution. I thank you very much for your work. As an at-large councilor I talk to as many members as I can about the issues that are coming before us, and when I brought up the issue of Manning and Snowden I got very universal negative reaction. They are not considered whistleblowers by the majority of the members I was able to talk to. Therefore I could not support either of those resolutions. However, I can support this one. Thank you very much. [Note that the official voting record states that Sandstrom voted in favor of the Snowden resolution on June 30.]
>
> Valerie Feinman, Small Round Tables Councilor (Y, N, Y): I agree with everything that Molly Raphael said, and I support the motion.... I think this is a great beginning to lay out the positions that we have, and that sometime when we know a little more about the whistleblowers and how guilty or innocent they are, then we can add that....
>
> Brian Schottlander ALCTS Division Councilor (A, Y, Y): I also stand in support of the motion and its substitution for the previous motions.... [T]he beauty of this body, like any democratic body is that it reserves the right to change its mind. [*Applause.*]
>
> Maggie Farrell, ACRL Councilor (Y, Y, Y): [The Association of College and Research Libraries] did discuss this, and the substitute resolution is much more in line with what we believe is good for the association, and gives us the tools that we need to move forward. Again, like many others, [including] specific names and identifying them as whistleblowers is something that ACRL members, in general, were in opposition to. I'll also take a personal note as a vet who worked for Army intelligence for NSA, I can fully support this resolution on a personal note. It gives us the tools that we need in order to talk about privacy and security for our citizens, so I support it. Thank you.

Again, let us pause for a closer look at this quite astonishing statement. In the hierarchy of librarianship, academic librarians occupy loftier realms than public or school librarians, even though within the milieu of academia they are often relegated to the lower floors of the ivory towers. Here we have a librarian who is not only the councilor for the Association of College and Research Libraries, not only someone who worked in

Whistleblower Retaliation
5 U.S.C. § 2302(b)(8)

What Is Whistleblower Retaliation?

A federal employee authorized to take, direct others to take, recommend or approve any personnel action may not take, fail to take, or threaten to take any personnel action against an employee because of protected whistleblowing.

EXAMPLE: A supervisor directs the geographic reassignment of an employee because the employee reported safety violations to senior agency officials.

Protected whistleblowing is defined as disclosing information which the discloser reasonably believes evidences:

1. a violation of law, rule, or regulation,
2. gross mismanagement,
3. gross waste of funds,
4. an abuse of authority, or
5. a substantial and specific danger to public health or safety.

What Can You Do If You Believe Whistleblower Retaliation Has Occurred?

If you believe that you have been subject to retaliation for protected whistleblowing you can file a complaint with the Office of Special Counsel (OSC). OSC is an independent agency that investigates and prosecutes allegations of prohibited personnel practices (PPP) by federal employees. OSC has the authority to investigate PPPs, including allegations of whistleblower retaliation, and may seek corrective or disciplinary action when warranted.

For more information contact:

**U.S. OFFICE OF SPECIAL COUNSEL
1730 M STREET, N.W., SUITE 218
WASHINGTON, DC 20036-4505**

PHONE: (202) 254-3670*   TOLL FREE: 1-800-872-9855*
*Hearing and Speech Disabled: Federal Relay Service 1-800-877-8339

WWW.OSC.GOV

Rev. 12/03

Federal government's whistleblower awareness poster

military intelligence, who not only worked for the NSA, but who also *voted in favor* of the Snowden resolution. Surely Maggie Farrell cast her vote on June 30th with a reasonably well-informed level of certainty that Snowden-as-whistleblower was a correct position to take, and that it was important for ALA to issue a statement to that effect. Division councilors most often decide how to vote on any given issue not simply as private persons but as representatives of the divisions that elected them. One can only wonder what transpired in the two days between Farrell's approval of the Snowden resolution and her statement that "ACRL members, in general, were in opposition" to such resolutions. Farrell's change of opinion was quite a parade ground about-face. Perhaps she voted her own private conscience on June 30, disregarding what she knew of the opinions of "ACRL members, in general." Perhaps she voted her conscience without asking herself what ACRL members might think. Perhaps most ACRL members whose opinions on the matter she knew of actually agreed with her original opinion regarding Snowden. Perhaps, as a former Army intelligence and NSA worker, Farrell simply abandoned her conscience as soon as she realized that the "higher ups" did not approve. The Army, after all, trains soldiers to jump when superior officers say "Jump!"

> Paula Brehm-Hegger (E, did not vote on referral, Y): I rise in support of what's currently being considered. I do want to briefly speak to the discussion about the Manning resolutions. We have considered those repeatedly over the past couple of years. I think this body has expressed the will that that is not a direction we want to go in. I agree that is not the direction we want to go in. I do want to, as an outgoing councilor, I do, however, want everyone in the room to consider the fact that our friends who have been moving that resolution repeatedly, I think we owe them a debt, because they brought that forward before all of the rotten things going on were quite clear. And they alerted us rather early in the game that something probably was rotten and that we should be aware of it. And I don't know that everyone paid as much attention as we should, so even though the Manning resolution specifically did not get passed, and I think this is a better way to go, I want to say that I personally appreciate that. I think the group should appreciate that, and that is something that I think has gotten us in this direction. So thank them for doing that, even though that's not where we're at. It's been a significant thing and they were way ahead of that. [*Applause*.]

Brehm-Hegger's mention of the "Manning resolution" is a reference to the fact that the individuals who drafted and moved the Snowden resolution through ALA were also involved in earlier and very similar resolutions regarding Bradley (now Chelsea) Manning. Brehm-Hegger's note of appreciation raises an intriguing circumstance regarding the prescience of "our friends ... who alerted us rather early in the game that something probably was rotten and that we should be aware of it." Recognition is given here to a very small subset of Council members who, in Brehm-Hegger's estimation had (1) paid attention to (2) a situation and (3) had brought it to the attention of Council. "I don't know that everyone paid as much attention as we should…," she says, suggesting too that raising the case of Bradley Manning provided information and clarity on an important matter of public concern. Despite her own objection to an official ALA statement directly addressing whistleblowers, she is nonetheless moved to recognize movers of the Manning and Snowden resolutions for being "way ahead" of Council in being cognizant of situations relevant to the values of librarianship.

Discussion neared its conclusion, but not before generating a few sparks between the next speaker and the chair of the meeting.

> Tom Wilding (Y, N, N): I will support this resolution because I don't believe in throwing the water out with the baby, but I think this is the water. The Snowden resolution was the baby in this instance. And I have to express extreme disappointment with the process with which this was done because I'm not a suspicious person by nature, but I suspect strongly that the Executive Board made a decision that they needed to do something, and move parliamentarily to do something. And I think back to all the microphone speakers who put the resolution forward ... and it just adds up to a suspicious line to me. I would have liked this better if there had been transparency, had somebody come to the microphone and said "the Executive Board has reviewed this, and feels uncomfortable, and would like to put this on hold until after consideration by committees." I am increasingly of a mind that the Executive Board does not practice....
>
> Chair interrupts: Councilor Wilding, permit an interruption. I believe you are speculating and what you are speculating about is not true.
>
> Wilding: But I will continue to speculate that way. And suspect that way.
>
> Chair: And I have the responsibility of assuring this body of the facts, and that is not a factual statement.
>
> Wilding: That's fine, but I still think that the process by which this was done was unfortunate, and while I will vote for this I really have a very hard time seeing it as a substitute. It doesn't seem like a substitute at all to me.

In the end, Wilding voted against the substitute, perhaps from irritation at the chair's unusual interruption, or perhaps deciding that the resolution was not an adequate substitute swayed his vote.

Immediately following was a motion to amend the resolution slightly by David Hurley (Y, N, A). There was no discussion after Hurley presented his motion, and the vote to amend passed by 69–67. Discussion returned to the main motion, to substitute the Snowden resolution with that of the IFC and COL.

> Michael Porter, Executive Board member (N, E, Y): Speaking to this resolution, I find it impressive and effective in many ways, particularly considering the pressing time constraints that we were dealing with.... I do find, however, the politicking and maneuvering a bit unsettling.... There are hurt feelings here and suspicions around this process, and I find that very troubling. I have never written down a comment I was to make from the microphone, and I would also like to point out that I wrote that down before councilor Wilding stood and shared his suspicion. I would also like to commend him for sharing that suspicion because I think that people are feeling it, and it's important that it's addressed....
>
> Larry Romans (Y, absent, N): I also have great admiration for both of the committees. I know Vivian Winn personally, I think she's one of the most effective chairs of legislation there has been. At the same time this is not exactly a quick response. The Bradley resolution was referred to them six months ago. There is the ability to talk with each other, to e-mail each other and so forth, and I think it's important for committees to do their work between the conferences. And also, this kind of thing doesn't happen if people present their resolutions before the conference and people have a chance to discuss things. I think that these committees should have been working on this, and should have brought something forward, and that that would have precluded any of this problem with the Snowden resolution, and I hope they will do that in the future.
>
> Elizabeth Ridler (Y, Y, Y): Call the question.

Ridler's motion to close debate was approved, and followed immediately by a vote to substitute the Snowden resolution with the resolution proposed by the IFC and COL. The vote to substitute passed with a show of hands: 138 yes, 20 no, 3 abstentions. No one who was present failed to cast a vote.

A handful of members of an elite group, with the assistance of the Committee on Legislation and the Intellectual Freedom Committee, had taken an unprecedented step to silence the voice of Council. Moorman, either self-appointed and alone, or in collaboration with others, refused to accept the will of Council as expressed on June 30, 2013. Some hold that all is fair in love and war—intrigue, duplicity, abuse, violation—perhaps too on Council floor. What was most disturbing in this instance was the ease with which a body of well-informed adults so easily performed this political about-face. Council went from challenging the federal government's determination of Snowden as traitor to allowing this characterization to stand unchallenged. The original vote on Snowden had been 105 in favor, 39 opposed, 10 abstentions. The vote to substitute the COL/IFC resolution was 138 in favor, 20 opposed, 3 abstentions. The implications of the fact that four-fifths of those who voted for the Snowden resolution abandoned their position two days later are sobering. The voice of ALA fell silent before the federal government—from challenge to compliance within 48 hours, and ALA's leadership bodies proved themselves unwilling to jeopardize relations with the federal government. Are councilors so lacking in self-confidence as reasonably well-informed citizens to so easily abandon what they thought one day earlier was an informed position?

In his statement during the debate to substitute, Al Kagan said, "The library community has great legitimacy and we need to be a little bit brave once in a while when the country is going in the wrong direction and our core issues are involved."

Why does it matter that, with respect to Edward Snowden himself, ALA went from recognizing "Edward Snowden as a whistleblower who, in releasing information ... has performed a valuable service" to urging "the U.S. Congress and President Obama to provide authentic protections that prevent government intimidation and criminal prosecution of government employees and private contractors who make disclosures of wrongdoing in the intelligence community"?

Simply this: ALA abandoned a clear, unequivocal statement identifying Snowden as a whistleblower deserving of *already existing* "authentic protections," in favor of one appealing to two bodies, the legislative and executive, who ALA *knew* were actively, publicly, or otherwise *denying* Snowden such protection.

The Snowden resolution was a challenge to the federal government, while the IFC/COL substitute let the status quo go unchallenged and *simultaneously* allowed ALA to declare consistency with longstanding commitments to privacy rights. "Authentic protections" already exist in federal legislation regarding whistleblowers, but in this specific case the federal government refuses to recognize Snowden as a whistleblower, thereby declaring *prior to any investigation* that those "authentic protections" are *irrelevant* to his case.

Council's turnabout on Snowden is a perfect example of the phenomenon Chomsky referred to—freedom of speech is allowed, but an elite must ensure that the voice "says the right thing." And the "right thing" to say about Snowden was *nothing*, which is exactly what happened. The predictions of Conkling, Biblo, Kagan, and Glasby played out when the IFC and COL presented a "substitute" resolution, which did not mention Snowden, or the word whistleblower, or even any of ALA's own prior statements regarding whistleblowers.

The question, in analyzing this debate with an eye to the hegemonic role ALA plays within librarianship, is what would saying "the right thing" be in this instance? If saying Edward Snowden is a whistleblower who deserves ALA's thanks is the *wrong* thing, then were does that leave us? What does it mean that the "right thing" for ALA to say regarding the act and the actor which brought to light NSA's massive invasion of countless people's privacy can only be to say nothing, to be silent altogether, or to agree with the federal government that the person responsible for the revelations is a traitor?

When a book is banned from a library, the Office for Intellectual Freedom does not simply mail out a generic, blanket statement opposing the banning of books, rather OIF is specific, naming names—title, author, place of banning, public officials involved—along with a demand that the banning action be fully investigated toward returning the book to the shelves. When the next school of library and information science is threatened with closure, ALA will not simply decry the closing of LIS schools in general, but will identify the specifically threatened school in order to rally support.

In his report of the 2013 Annual Council meetings, Al Kagan wrote of the IFC/COL substitute resolution,

> In keeping with ALA's recent tradition, that resolution stripped out names of individual whistleblowers and just made broad policy statements. There is nothing wrong with the generalities in that document, but it will have little or no effect in supporting the people who are taking huge risks to bring out the misdeeds of our government.... I could not support this resolution as a substitute for the Snowden resolution, and a small number of Councilors agreed with this position and voted against the substitute resolution [Kagan].

Generic statements demand only generic responses. Calls for government transparency get met with we're-looking-into-the-matter responses. Specific statements demand specific responses. Recognition of Snowden as a whistleblower demands an investigation of his situation *as a whistleblower*. When the federal government is calling Snowden a traitor, *and* is spying on you, *and* controls federal funding to libraries, it requires a bit of courage to challenge that characterization. While researching this article, using the internet, I certainly wondered whether the NSA might be tracking people searching for information about Snowden. My name will certainly pop up from NSA's datamine if they want to know who's curious about "Edward Snowden." Guilt by association, no matter how tangential, is hardly unknown. In the words of a presidential review group of NSA spying released in December 2013,

> Knowing that the government has ready access to one's phone call records can seriously chill "associational and expressive freedoms," and knowing that the government is one flick of a switch away from such information can profoundly "alter the relationship between citizen and government in a way that is inimical to society" [Cole].

Even when six months later, at a time when more people were demanding that Snowden be recognized as a whistleblower, ALA Council failed at its January 2014 midwinter meeting to vote in favor of another resolution similar to the one of June 30th.

In a country where one is assumed to be innocent until proven guilty, government officials who decide off-the-bat that Snowden is a traitor before even investigating the possibility that he actually qualifies as a whistleblower are overstepping their sworn duty to the U.S. Constitution. Is it no wonder, then, that organizations like the Government Accountability Project have determined that we are today living in a "surveillance state" where "the enemy is the whistleblower"? In not acting to challenge U.S. officials' and some mass media commentators' predetermination of Snowden as a traitor, ALA stepped away from its stated commitments to the right to privacy, and in stepping away abandonment is not likely to be far off. As Louis Brandeis once wrote,

> Decency, security, and liberty alike demand that government officials shall be subjected to the same rules of conduct that are commands to the citizen. In a government of laws, existence of the government will be imperiled if it fails to observe the law scrupulously. Our government is the potent, the omnipresent teacher. For good or for ill, it teaches the whole people by its example. Crime is contagious. If the Government becomes a lawbreaker, it breeds contempt for the law; it invites every man to become a law unto himself; it invites anarchy [Dash 78].

Some ALA councilors claimed that the third resolved on the IFC/COL "substitute" resolution clearly covered ALA's commitment to the rights of whistleblowers:

> [ALA] urges the U.S. Congress and President Obama to provide authentic protections that prevent government intimidation and criminal prosecution of government employees and private contractors who make disclosures of wrongdoing in the intelligence community ... [Office].

One must ask, however, what is *inauthentic* about current whistleblower protections? Laws *already* provide authentic protection; what is missing is authentic *recognition and enforcement* of those laws. The situation we face is that some members of Congress, the President, and other interested parties *do not want* to treat Snowden as a whistleblower. They do not want to give Snowden the protection of already existing laws, because his actions exposed the "man behind the curtain" as a charlatan with respect to NSA's claim to being an agency that protects the public and abides by the law in doing so.

This resolved clause also acts as if the need for authentic protection is of merely theoretical rather than of immediate practical interest. Without explicitly stating that there is an existing, real, flesh-and-blood person named Edward Snowden who is not, right now, being protected from government intimidation and criminal prosecution, ALA is abandoning a human being whose case just might embody values and positions supposedly important to the association. And, more chillingly, the practice of carefully crafting language in order to avoid potential conflict with authority stands as an example of the sort of semantic game-playing that presents itself as sincere, authentic communication while actually being something else. The IFC/COL resolution is nothing more that political gamesmanship, grandstanding, and avoidance. Despite its reaffirmation of "unwavering support for fundamental principles ... including ... accountability ... transparency, and oversight," in the absence of any specificity regarding the situation that gave rise to the document (namely a discussion about Edward Snowden) it says much about nothing that anyone need act upon, it holds no one accountable, makes opaque with words what should be transparent, and protects no one, instead abandoning the oversight responsible citizens should exercise within a democracy when officials and agencies misuse and abuse positions of authority. It is a defense of writs of assistance cloaked in the language of democracy. John Adams surely lies agitated in his grave.

Moorman claimed that Council was in need of more information that would be provided by the IFA and COL. Neither was forthcoming with additional information about Edward Snowden's status as a whistleblower. Indeed, both basically ignored this matter altogether. And, what of Moorman's claim that work of the Washington Office would be hindered by a statement from ALA declaring Snowden a whistleblower? The Washington Office is supposed to *represent* ALA in dealings with legislators and legislation. If questions arose regarding ALA's position on Snowden, the Washington Office would be *obliged* to explain in a *positive* manner the will of Council in taking the position. Was the staff at the Washington Office unable or unwilling to do so? Either way it would be derelict in its duty as the lobbying arm of the association.

In the end, ALA Council completely succumbed into compliance with an authority more powerful than the collective conscience expressed on June 30th—abandoning an informed and principled decision when an elite appealed to fears of ALA Washington Office lobbyists "paralyzed" by a statement that challenged the federal government. What this incident says about the current state of librarianship as a "cornerstone of democracy" is that this image, this metaphor, is either just a fine façade or that the cornerstone is losing its integrity, cracked by fears of unintended consequences. When citizens are silent, fail to hold those in power accountable, or allow an elite to ensure that everyone speaks with one voice, we abandon the possibility of democracy, and along with it ... privacy.

Notes: 1. *Quoted in Dash, 78.* 2. *Quoted in Raber, 675.* 3. *Many thanks to Susan Maret for bringing to my attention the work of Sissela Bok.* 4. *ALA* **divisions** *include: American Association of School Librarians (AASL); Association of College and Research Libraries (ACRL); Association for Library Collections and Technical Services (ALCTS); Association of Library Services to Children (ALSC); Association of Specialized & Cooperative Library Agencies (ASCLA); Library Leadership & Management Association (LLAMA); Library & Information Technology Association (LITA); Public Library Association (PLA); Reference & User Services Association (RUSA); United for Libraries; and Young Adult Library Services Assn. (YALSA). ALA* **round tables** *(=RT) are: Ethnic & Multicultural Information Exchange (EMIERT); Exhibits (ERT); Federal and Armed Forces Libraries (FAFLRT); Games & Gaming (GAMERT); Gay, Lesbian, Bisexual, and Transgender (GLBTRT); Government Documents (GODORT); Intellectual Freedom (IFRT); International Relations (IRRT); Learning (LearnRT, formerly CLENERT); Library History (LHRT); Library Instruction (LIRT); Library Research (LRRT); Library Support Staff (LSSIRT); Map and Geospatial Information (MAGIRT); New Members (NMRT); Retired Members (RMRT); Social Responsibilities (SRRT); Staff Organizations (SORT); Sustainability (SustainRT); Video (VRT), and the Round Table Coordinating Assembly, a body that consists of officers of all the round tables. In addition to ALA's 50 state library association* **chapters***, which elect one councilor each, both Guam and the Virgin Islands (territories of the U.S.) also have one councilor each.* 5. *On 14 June 2014 The Washington Post and The Guardian (U.S. edition) were jointly awarded the Pulitzer Prize for reporting on the NSA scandal.*

6. Charting a New Course— ALA and Climate Crisis

In economic affairs the logic of facts will work itself out somewhat slowly.
—Albert Einstein, 1934

... survival is not an academic skill. It is learning how to stand alone, unpopular and sometimes reviled, and how to make common cause with those others identified as outside the structures in order to define and seek a world in which we can all flourish. It is learning how to take our differences and make them strengths. For the master's tools will never dismantle the master's house. They may allow us temporarily to beat him at his own game, but they will never enable us to bring about genuine change. And this fact is only threatening to those [people] who still define the master's house as their only source of support.
—Audre Lorde, 1979

Climate change is an extension of colonialism.
Sarra Tekola, 2015

In late January 2013, a resolution that would commit the American Library Association to divesting financial holdings of fossil fuel industry stocks was presented to Council. The initiative was inspired by the launch in Seattle the previous November of a divestment campaign by the organization 350.org.

350.org takes its name from data gathered and calculations made by scientists that 350 parts-per-million (ppm) of carbon dioxide (CO_2) in Earth's atmosphere is the uppermost limit the planet's ecosystems can absorb to maintain planetary temperatures that support the biosphere within which human life evolved. Concerns within the scientific community regarding the "greenhouse effect" of industrial, agricultural, and other releases of CO_2 into the atmosphere prompted Charles Keeling, working for the Scripps Institute of Oceanography, to began measuring CO_2 levels at the Mauna Loa Observatory in Hawaii. First measurements taken in 1958 indicated CO_2 levels of just under 320 ppm (co2now.org). When Bill McKibbon, 350.org's founder, came to Seattle to unveil this audacious campaign, atmospheric levels of CO_2 measured 396 ppm. As I write this chapter, in late 2015, levels surpass 402 ppm.

The idea behind the fossil fuel divestment campaign is that, in the face of decades of inaction by industry and government to meaningfully curb fossil fuel emissions, grassroots efforts by ordinary people must be made for a peaceful transition of our communities, societies, economies, and cultures into an era of planetary climate change—or, more accurately in terms of human civilization, climate *crisis*. In explaining why divestment was being proposed to pressure corporations and nations that refuse to constrain emissions, McKibbon informed the crowd,

> It's simple math: we can burn less than 565 more gigatons of carbon dioxide and stay below 2°C of warming—anything more than that risks catastrophe for life on earth. The only problem? Fossil fuel corporations now have 2,795 gigatons in their reserves, five times the safe amount. And they're planning to burn it all—unless we rise up to stop them [McKibbon].

The divestment launch took place in Seattle's beautiful and capacious music venue, Benaroya Hall, filled to the rafters that evening with people of all ages and colors, united in shared concern for the planet and all its life systems.

I was in the audience. Arriving in a cynical mood, expecting little more than cheerleading for actions requiring little effort, minimal sacrifices, in other words more of the predominant environmentalist argument that you can't ask U.S. consumers to give up anything. Or, maybe the message would be more of the financial shell-game of carbon offsets. I was shocked, therefore, when McKibbon announced a divestment campaign, a boycott of sorts—municipalities, colleges, unions, retirement funds were being asked to rid investment portfolios of holdings in fossil fuel industries. Roaring cheers and wild applause erupted when McKibbon announced that Seattle's Mayor McGinn had committed to sponsoring the divestment campaign in Seattle.

Archbishop Desmond Tutu was present also, via a video statement urging listeners to join in the divestment campaign:

> The divestment movement played a key role in helping to liberate South Africa. The corporations understood the logic of money, even when they were not swayed by the dictates of morality. Climate change is a deeply moral issue too, of course. Here in Africa we see the dreadful suffering of people from worsening drought, from rising food prices, from floods, even though they have done nothing to cause the situation. Once again we can join together as a world and put pressure where it counts [Tutu].

This, I thought, is a step in the right direction. Apparently, at least one environmental organization, 350.org, had the gumption to take a step toward doing what absolutely had to be done—put the fossil fuel industry out of business.

Leaving Benaroya with a flicker of hope in my heart, inspiration struck. ALA's upcoming midwinter meeting was being held in Seattle. Why not draft a fossil fuel divestment resolution, and send it on to the Councilors I still knew to see if they thought it worthwhile. After all, when I resigned from Council back in 2009, I'd promised to remain active in ALA in whatever manner I could. Here was an opportunity to make good on that promise.

Guilt trips and moral evolution

Long before any given behavior, be it murder or enslavement or tax evasion or the dumping of toxic waste into fertilizer, is determined to be objectionable, much less criminal, someone, somewhere, must feel in the quiet recesses of their heart that the behavior is wrong. The person might share their feelings and thoughts about questionable behaviors with others, and together they might join in common cause to persuade still others of their perspective, working collectively toward the prohibition or criminalization of behaviors deemed unacceptable. Movements for social change emerged from the brutalities of slavery, the subjugation of women, the economic exploitation of children, the closeted existence of homosexuals, and the institutional warehousing of the disabled, infirm, aged. In this manner, slavery was criminalized. Jim Crow segregation too, as was discrimination against women, the denial of marriage to same-sex couples, and smoking in public places. Throughout history, behaviors once considered acceptable, even moral, in the eyes of God and Man, have lost favor in the eyes of larger human communities, and those who insist on engaging in such behaviors come to be regarded as guilty of unacceptable, immoral, if not criminal, acts. This is the process through which rights are extended from one set of rights holders to others.

What one era considers moral, another, seeking to expand rights, determines immoral. One tactic found effective in this change process is the use of social pressure to make a person who engages in, condones, or allows the objectionable behavior to feel guilty, i.e., the guilt trip.

A current example comes from the animal rights movement.

"Animals have certain basic moral rights," says Tom Regan, a philosopher who has contributed greatly to the animal rights movement, "including in particular the fundamental right to be treated with respect" (Regan 237). One relatively recent example of still ongoing evolution in morality, can be seen in veganism. Putting the ethics of animal rights into practice are vegans, people for whom all products from animal sources are shunned. A vegan might consider a human who consumes fish, chickens, pigs, cows or animal byproducts—eggs, cheese, feathers, silk, honey—as the moral equivalent of the human who eats other humans.

I will never forget the expression on the face of a vegan librarian at a conference reception. Her gaze fell along a table laden with deviled eggs, cheese, shrimp, thinly sliced pig and cow flesh. Watching undetected, I saw signs of bile appear in her face. She walked away thoroughly disgusted, and I immediately felt guilty for finding pleasure (and sustenance) in some of these creatures, and found myself unable to eat anything at the reception.

Guilt of another sort caught up with me in 2009, brought on by information and experiences I'd been accumulating since 1970. What I had learned about climate science, and direct experience with what were most certainly manifestations of the consequences of global warming combined to "guilt trip" me into resigning from my at-large seat on ALA Council. Here's the story.

The first celebration of Earth Day was in 1970. I was an 8th grade student at Colin Kelly Junior High School in Eugene, Oregon. One of my teachers must have planned lessons in conjunction with the event, or maybe there was an Earth Day information fair put on by activist students. I've no recollection of what prompted my awareness, but I do remember two facts I'd learned and the harangues to which I subsequently subjected my parents.

The facts: First, the release of CO_2 into the atmosphere was causing a rise in the planet's temperature, something called the "greenhouse effect." Second, the release of chemicals called chlorofluorocarbons (CFCs) from aerosol spray cans was putting a hole the atmosphere's ozone layer.

The harangue: My family's house contained aerosol cans of hairspray, furniture polish, and insect repellent. Everytime anyone pushed the spray button they were contributing to the destruction of the ozone layer. Using these products was downright unconscionable, immoral, planet-destroying. My parents did not agree—the Earth is large, one household couldn't matter. As for a parallel harangue about CO_2 emissions, I somehow missed the connection between burning gasoline and global warming. Maybe I was being selective. Our Plymouth Fury station wagon was indispensable. Perhaps I just hadn't made that connection.

By the time 2009 rolled around, use of CFCs had long been banned in the U.S. (but stockpiles continue to be used), the ozone hole had shrunk (Handwerk), but CO_2 emissions were on the rise, and I had personally experienced two (two!) so-called one-hundred-year floods in a span of *three* years! Floods of this magnitude are considered to have only a 1 percent chance of happening in any given year. I'd left New York City in 2004, and was living in the small town of Snoqualmie, Washington, on the east side of King County (Seattle is on the west side) at the base of the western slopes of the Cascade Mountains, and my townhouse apartment was located in the flood plain of the Snoqualmie River. The most recent major floods of the Snoqualmie had occurred in February 1996, and November 1995.

Fortunately, the four-unit complex I lived in was built to 21st century specifications, which required that living quarters be at least 4-feet above ground level. In the early evening of November 6, 2006, two men came to my door informing me that everyone living in the flood plain was being advised to evacuate. Floodwaters of the Snoqualmie River were expected to crest at something like 2:00 a.m.

Dumb me thought "cresting" meant that the flood would come and go between the time I went to sleep and awoke the next morning. I thanked the men, and said I preferred to stay home. To which they replied that they *highly* recommended that I, at the very least, move my "rolling stock" to higher ground. Rolling stock? When I asked, one very politely said, "Your car, ma'am." The two kind emergency volunteers gave me a phone number in case I needed help, and wished me well.

I was new to car ownership, so I figured I actually should heed the rolling stock advice, and knew the perfect place. Just a block away, at the high school where I worked as librarian, there was a driveway for delivery trucks that was several feet higher than anywhere else around. I promptly got in the car and drove there, only to discover rolling stock of all sorts already parked—pick-up trucks, cars, motorcycles, a riding lawnmower. Fortunately, there was one spot left for me.

The river did, indeed, crest in the wee hours of the morning. Turns out, however, it can take *days* for a flooded river to return to its banks after it crests. Overnight my apartment building had become an island with Cascade mountain floodwaters, along with gasoline, and oil, and sewage, and garbage, and flotsam (maybe even jetsam) of all sorts floating by. When I opened the door to my apartment that morning, I was struck by the sickening odor of chemicals and gas, a thin sheen coating the river water, most likely picked up from asphalt, the Jiffy Lube half a block away, and gas stations "up river."

I hadn't expected that smell. It burned. A raccoon made his way along the upper branches of the hedge dividing my apartment from Highway 202. I supposed (never having previously given it a thought) that raccoons can't swim.

Of all I did that day—calling the emergency number to find out if and where I could vote (it being Election Day); discovering that riding a bike through water over a foot deep is a tricky proposition; feeling the earth shudder under the volume of water flowing over Snoqualmie Falls, the mist smelling of mud—the memory that stands apart is a feeling I experienced of invisibility.

Determined to vote, I got the bike out of my flooded garage, started to take off in water up to my knees, immediately fell over, not having anticipated the resistance water offers to pedaling a bike. I struggled up from the overgrown, flowing river, thoroughly drenched in mucky water. Fortunately, part of the cause of the flood, warm winds called the "Pineapple Express" that melt mountain snow rather quickly, plus getting my sea-legs on the bike, kept me relatively warm.

The invisibility descended at the firehouse where I voted, and then again when I decided a hot cup of coffee was in order. A firefighter and election day volunteer greeted me politely, making no mention of my bedraggled state. After voting, I rode the bike a couple miles uphill to Snoqualmie Ridge, a development of McMansions, which I figured still had electricity. Sure enough, lights were on, and a coffee shop was open and serving. In I went, still quite wet, but oh-so comforted by the fragrance of coffee, the normalcy of people coming and going, and to my joy, the presence of a fireplace. I sat for about an hour, slowly drying. People looked at me, but no one said a word.

Not until I'd returned home did I reflect on the experience at the firehouse and the coffee shop. There I was, a soaking wet, middle-aged woman on a bike, on a cloudy, but rainless morning. It should have been obvious that I'd come up from the old part of town which everyone knew (or should have known) was flooded, and not one person who saw me thought to ask if I was okay, how I'd gotten wet, whether my home had been flooded, nothing. Nada. This, I thought, must be how it feels to be a homeless person. A disquieting condition to be seen by others, but not acknowledged. All the people around me went about their business, with not a moment to pause and express concern, or even interest, in the obvious plight of another. It wasn't that I needed sympathy or assistance from any of these people, but I was struck by the absence of any acknowledgment. The thought was amplified as I further considered that Hurricane Katrina had hit the Gulf Coast a year earlier. I tried to imagine how invisible people of New Orleans and surrounding areas must have felt, and still be feeling, in the wake of *that* storm and flood. My situation was nothing compared to theirs, but I now had a personal experience that gave me a sense of how coldly disconnected "normal life" is from communities experiencing the impact of climate change. My capacity to empathize deepened that day, not that it had been shallow.

Four months before the Snoqualmie's Election Day flood, my sister Natalie and I, attending the 2006 ALA annual conference in New Orleans, had rented bikes and taken a self-guided tour of the Ninth Ward. We'd walked though the convention center wondering if the new carpets and scrubbed walls appeased the spirits of those flood refugees who'd lived and died there. We watched, outraged, as workers planted full-grown, imported palm trees along Canal Street, sprucing up the French Quarter, while more pressing needs went unmet. And, we rode through the Ninth Ward, block after block after block of devastation by wind, flood, bulldozer. Here were homes, clearly loved by those who had to flee for their lives. National guardsmen told us we weren't safe riding around, but we did anyway and met several very friendly, determined people. Signs on fences said "Save Our Neighborhood, No Bulldozing! Contact Acorn." Crosses and wreaths attached to houses spoke to the deaths of loved ones. Abandoned boats and book-returns, cars and couches, indicated the thoroughness of the disaster. Every few blocks a homeowner had returned with ladder, hammer, nails, and determination. Another sign, blue silk-screened fist and sunflower, demanded "Rebuild New Orleans from the ground up!" Another asked, "Saw Levee Break? Wanted: Witnesses, Photos/Video, call..." We talked with a man who'd saved his own life clinging to the top of a lamppost. A woman pleaded, "Bear witness to what you have seen."

Besides devastation, we witnessed resilience: an abandoned schoolyard become a field of sunflowers to leach toxins from the soil; people riding bicycles everywhere; candles flickering in windows during a blackout that didn't extend to the neighborhood a block away—the French Quarter remained sparklingly lighted.

The forces of resilience and care were powerfully evident, but, unfortunately, seemed to be no match for those responsible for the conditions that bred super-storm Katrina—apathy, greed, complacency, habit, denial, racism. A few years later, I read Dave Eggars' excellent book *Zeitoun*, an account of the experience of one New Orleans resident during Katrina. It is the story of that resilience, of the heroism of "ordinary" people. It is also the story of how militarized, emergency first-responders imprisoned and brutalized, for *months*, a man who had done nothing but be a victim of a horrific natural disaster and who had helped others with his rowboat and humanity.

Every climate-related disaster happens in a localized place—some large, some small. Levels of invisibility for the people living in those places vary considerably, depending on race, economic status, ability to make themselves heard. The people and ecosystems impacted desperately need to be acknowledged and helped, but it is so easy for the rest of us, those distant from the disaster, to go on with business as usual. Maybe we write a check, donate to a relief agency. Easy to spare a couple minutes and a few bucks. Or, perhaps one volunteers with a church group, medical clinic, or ALA to help cleanup, build a school, give dental care, all of which might take a few hours or days, maybe weeks or more of one's time and energy, but in the end, one returns to the comforts of one's home, job, routines, consumption, and CO_2 emissions. And for all of us living in industrialized countries, those routines dependent as they are on the burning of fossil fuels collectively combine to increase the strength of hurricanes, the frequency of 100-year floods, the record-breaking heatwaves, statewide forest fires. We donate money and time, we sign petitions and post on blogs, maybe we shop locally, buy and build green, but the basic structure of our daily routines keeps the systems that depend on the combustion of fossil fuels very much alive. Climate change manifests here and there, so it's easy not to treat it like the global, ever-present crisis it truly is.

Which brings me to the point of sharing these stories, the guilt trip that led to my resignation from Council.

At the end of the last Council session in June 2009, I stood at a microphone and asked for a point of personal privilege. Up to that day, I had attended every ALA meeting for the previous 20 years, mostly on my own dime. My involvement in ALA began in SRRT, where I was a member of several task forces, and, over the years, chair of the Library Union Task Force (1991–93); SRRT secretary (1996–99) and coordinator (2005–2007); co-chair of the International Responsibilities Task Force–SRRT (2002 to 2005); and representative on SRRT Action Council for the Progressive Librarians Guild (1991–2009). Outside of SRRT, I was an active member and co-chair of the ALA/AFL-CIO Joint Committee on Library Services to Labor Groups (1990–93); an intern, then member, of the ALA Committee on Organization (2001 to 2003); member of the ALA Committee on Education (2005–2007); and service as an elected, at-large member of Council in the years 1998–2005 and 2007–2009. I thrived in ALA.

However, the joy I found in contributing to the mission of my professional association began to be overshadowed by what I knew about climate change. Most years, attending ALA meant taking two round trip flights to Chicago or San Antonio or Orlando or wherever midwinter or annual happened to be. I always tried to get a window seat while flying, and as I looked out across great expanses of land, mountains, city, sky, a thought was ever present—this plane is spewing hundreds of tons of CO_2 directly into the upper reaches of the atmosphere, and my purchase of this ticket is contributing to those emissions. My life contributed in many ways to global warming, but my activity in ALA especially so. Questions clambered for attention—Am I being a responsible citizen of planet Earth while flying, knowing what I know about CO_2 emissions? Should I give up flying and stop attending ALA meetings?

Talking this dilemma over with friends and colleagues, some sympathized, others ridiculed my concern. I was a fool for thinking that my absence on a plane would make any difference. The plane would fly regardless of whether I was in the seat or somebody else. My activism in ALA was important enough to justify flights to conferences. I could buy carbon offsets. I could plant trees. Admitting that my own personal boycott of the airline industry would not make one iota of difference in CO_2 levels, I had to ask myself whether my contributions in ALA justified living with the growing feelings of guilt I had flying. Was the only arena in which I could contribute to librarianship a national one?

I've long lived in close proximity to airports. My father was in the Air Force, an uncle is a retired PanAm pilot who let me sit in the pilot's seat on a Boeing 747 one day. I will never forget "the Eagle has landed." As a teenager I made a model of the USS Enterprise and hung it from the ceiling in my room. While in New York City, I lived under flight paths going into and out of LaGuardia Airport. In Newark, I lived a couple of miles from Newark Airport. In Lynnwood, test runs of new planes from the Boeing plant south of Everett regularly flew overhead. And, today, in Seattle, planes landing at SeaTac fly directly over my neighborhood. Airports, planes, spaceships had long fueled my imagination, and now I conjured up images of all the airports in the world, big and small. I animated an imaginary map with little planes taking off every few minutes, contrails knotting a net around the globe, burning fuel, emitting CO_2...24/7, year-in, year-out. Forever. And ever?

Add to these images the koyaanisqatsi kaleidoscope of cars and trucks, urban traffic jams, round-the-clock coal-fueled powerplants, tar-sands extraction, trains hauling coal. Next to this my two round-trip flights to ALA were nothing. Just drops in the bucket.

But they were *my* drops in the bucket, and my heart said *that* made a difference.

With a group of people living in the Snoqualmie River valley who'd become my friends, I'd been engaged in reading study guides compiled by the Northwest Earth Institute. The unit "Global Warming: Changing CO_2urse" had us all thinking of ways we could personally reduce our "carbon footprints." The concept of a carbon footprint is that the daily activities of an individual produce a certain amount of CO_2 depending, in part, on that person's activities and on the country and state in which they live. Environmental organizations had come up with "carbon calculators" mounted on websites where one could enter information about driving a car, diet, electricity use, home heating, and … air travel.

At the same time as my internal debate over whether to quit air travel was taking place, way off in Great Britain, George Marshall, author and founder of the Climate Outreach Information Network, engaged in an "informal research project" in which he asked climate scientists and activists how they'd spent their holidays. These were people who fully recognized the burning of fossil fuels as a source of global warming, acid rain, melting glaciers and polar ice, strengthening storms, rising seas. Indeed, they made a living tracking these phenomena, and informing governments, industry, and the general public about the state of the planet.

Each person happily told Marshall about holiday plans—to Thailand, on ski trips, scuba diving in the Pacific, a family outing to Sri Lanka—all flying to vacation destinations. Marshall asked each whether s/he was concerned that CO_2 emissions for pleasure outings would contribute to global warming.

An atmospheric physics researcher "blithely" replied, "Of course," and went on to say that he believed the government would one day make such flights illegal. Another scientist engaged in a research project in Antarctica justified his ski trips saying, "my job is stressful." Another justified regular flights to South Africa by saying "my offsets help set a price in the carbon market." A journalist expressed resignation to climate change, "I can't see much hope," and so felt little compunction in taking the family on long-distance pleasure trips. And a Greenpeace activist raved what "a GREAT trip" the scuba diving had been (Marshall).

Marshall makes an observation that speaks volumes about the rut of inaction into which we've been stuck for the half-century+ that we've known about CO_2 emissions and global warming.

Intriguing as their dissonance may be, what is especially revealing is that every one of these people has a career that is predicated on the assumption that information is sufficient to generate change—an assumption that a moment's introspection would show them was deeply flawed (*ibid.*).

For more than fifty years, government, industry and people living industrial-nation lifestyles have done nothing but compound the problem. Between 1990 (when world governments convened to set CO_2 emission reductions) and 2013, emissions *increased* by 61 percent (Klein 11).

We talk, talk, talk. Scientists research and jet-set. Activists burn. Everybody buys more, more, more. Governments have not taken meaningful action. Industry has given us the climate denial "out." Environmentalists can't break out of the mold. So, what in the world is a librarian to do?

I calculated my personal contributions to planetary CO_2 emissions at the Nature Conservancy website.

	% of my CO_2 footprint		% of average U.S. CO_2 footprint
	No flights	*2 flights to ALA*	
Home energy	73.9%	43%	36.8%
Driving and flying	0%	41.9%	43.5%
Recycling & waste	8.7%	5%	4.4%
Food & diet	17.4%	10.1%	13.3%
TOTAL greenhouse gas	6 tons/year	10 tons/year	27 tons/year

Out of about 60 round-trip flights I've taken over the course of my life, over half have been to ALA conferences. Giving up flying would reduce my personal CO_2 emissions by nearly 42 percent. Whose side was I on?

At the microphone, I addressed my Council colleagues.

> I rise to a point of personal privilege to announce that I, too, am retiring from my position on Council even though I have one year left on my term. I made this decision last December because, as some of you probably read the piece I had in *American Libraries* last year concerning global warming, for many, many years I have, every time I've gotten into an airplane (even though I love to sit at the window and watch our beautiful country go by), I'm very cognizant of the pollution that airplanes spew into the atmosphere. Forty years ago, as a junior high school student, I learned about global warming, and I have tried to live my life in a way that contributed as little as possible to climate change. And even though I know that my absence on any airplane is not going to make much difference, I believe in what Gandhi said about being the change you wish to see in the world. So it is with great relief that, after many years of being troubled by traveling via airplane, I've made the decision to stop. And that requires that I can no longer attend the national conferences. I want to assure you all, however, that I will continue to be active in professional matters on a local and a regional level. It has been a tremendous pleasure, and privilege, and an honor to serve with you. Thank you [Gregory-Wood].

To myself I made another promise, a self-imposed quota—three roundtrip flights and then I was done forever with air travel. As of 2015, I have one flight remaining. My hope is that it will never be used, although love for family and friends exerts a certain pressure, a feeling of obligation that makes this a hope rather than a certainty, a phenomena George Monbiot calls "love miles."

In his book *Heat: How to Stop the Planet from Burning* (2006), Monbiot devotes an entire chapter to air travel, describing just how impossible this mode of transportation is without the use of fossil fuels, despite the wishful sci-fi scenarios and advertising the airline and tourism industries heap upon us. He estimates that if the world's countries are to realize the 90 percent reduction in CO_2 emissions required, one round-trip flight between New York and London would emit a year's worth of the average CO_2 quota (173). Monbiot recognizes that the reason many of us fly is for love. Love of family, love of friends, love of places. The problem is that our "love miles" produce greenhouse gases, and greenhouse gases are heating up the planet, which we also love. He writes that while it is easy for well-traveled people concerned about global warming

> ... to pour scorn on the drivers of sports utility vehicles, whose politics generally differ from ours, it is rather harder to contemplate a world in which our own freedoms are curtailed, especially the freedoms which shaped us [172].

Social and familial obligations are powerful forces of conformity, but the time has come when we must admit that the actions demanded of those obligations are now morally questionable.

Keeping a promise

Four years after my resignation from Council, while preparing the fossil fuel divestment resolution for presentation in January 2013, I conducted a little investigation into the question of the earliest date at which the general public was informed of CO_2 impact on global warming. Given that in 1970, I, an average 8th grade student, had learned about the greenhouse effect, surely there must have been widespread knowledge of the problem prior to the first Earth Day. From a little book by Mark Maslin, *Global Warming: A Very Short Introduction* (2004), I learned that the greenhouse effect was first theorized in 1896 by Svante Arrhenius, a Swedish scientist. He arrived at this theory mathematically.

Arrhenius' calculations, however, were not likely to have come to the attention of the general public. Maslin did say that all the science needed to understand the connection between greenhouse gas emissions and climate change was done in the 1950s and early 1960s. I was curious to know whether the general public had any idea that we had turned up the heat on the planet, so I went to a generally reliable, generally accessible source—*The New York Times*. Accessing the *New York Times Historical* database via my public library account from home, and using a series of date delimiters, I made two discoveries.

First, President Johnson established a Science Advisory Committee whose report in November 1965 prompted him to make several recommendations for federal legislation on multiple sources of air, water, and soil pollutants (Text). Second, the earliest article I found in the *New York Times* informing the general public of the connection between CO_2 emissions and global warming appeared five months before I was born.

On September 25, 1955, the *Times* carried a brief article "Why Earth Warms: Scientist Blames Man-Made Changes on Earth's Surface." The article reports the work of Dr. John G. Hutton, an engineer with General Electric, which he presented at a meeting of the American Institute of Electrical Engineers the previous week. Hutton's research suggested a connection between increased CO_2 emissions "by automobiles, trucks, trains and ships ... factories and refineries" and warming trends that "no meteorologist denies." The article goes on to describe changes scientists had been observing, "Glaciers are melting more rapidly and fish are caught off Greenland that were formerly seen only in waters farther to the south" (Why E11). The article ends noting that much more should be known about the "greenhouse effect" from research being conducted during the International Geophysical Year in 1958.

I was astounded. The general public had been informed of this problem *fifty* years ago and we were only making it worse. What was wrong with us?

I turned the PDF of "Why Earth Warms" into a bookmark—We can't say we didn't know: Help YOUR library's community transition to a fossil-fuel-free future! I left a stack on the Council literature table next to the resolution on fossil fuel divestment, and personally handed one to ALA Executive Director Keith Fiels. He tucked it into his shirt pocket with, it seemed to me, a sad smile.

The Resolution on Divestment of Holdings in Fossil Fuel Companies was placed on the agenda for Council III. On the previous Friday evening gathering in the Council Suite of members of the unofficial Progressive Council Caucus, I met with old friends and two new councilors who were very interested in the resolution, Ben Trapskin and Ann Crewdson, who decided to be the official mover and seconder. The draft was revised at the meeting, and I offered to submit it to the Resolutions Committee and to the Budget and Analysis Review Committee (BARC). Unbeknownst to me, however, the process had changed, and an electronic file was now required. Not thinking to ask if the process for submission was different, I simply walked hardcopies of the resolution to the ALA Office and place them in folders for committee members' review.

RESOLUTION ON DIVESTMENT OF HOLDINGS IN FOSSIL FUEL COMPANIES

WHEREAS in light of alarming evidence of the impact CO_2 emissions are having right now on climate change, and the fact that fossil fuel corporations claim to have 2,795 gigatons of CO_2 in their reserves (five times amount that can be burned to stay below a 2° C increase in global temperature that the international community agrees is the upper limit most life forms can tolerate) the organization 350.org has launched a fossil fuel divestment campaign, supported by individuals such as Bishop Desmond Tutu, who calls action on climate change the moral issue of our times;

WHEREAS in the 1980s the American Library Association joined in the divestment campaign against South African apartheid as a tool for non-violent political change;

WHEREAS floods, fires, droughts and storms connected to climate change and costing billions of dollars in damages have prompted organizations representing some institutional investors to call on governments to develop workable frameworks that will reduce climate risk and support low carbon investment;

WHEREAS around the globe libraries and their communities are already experiencing the negative social and economic impact of climate change, like those our own libraries suffered from hurricanes Katrina and Sandy, and devastating tornados such as those in Joplin, Missouri;

WHEREAS increasing numbers of people are joining 350.org's call to divest holdings in fossil fuel companies such as the mayor of Seattle who recently called on the city retirement board to divest, and college students across the country who are demanding that their institutions of higher learning divest their holdings in fossil fuel industries;

WHEREAS ALA's Strategic Plan 2011–2015 states that: "Libraries are widely recognized as key players in economic development, including strong and vibrant communities, and in sustaining a strong democracy"; and

WHEREAS ALA recognizes the role its financial investments can play in meeting the social responsibilities of the Association; now, therefore, be it

RESOLVED, that the American Library Association:
1. goes on record to publicly recognize that human generation of CO_2 is resulting in global climate change;
2. directs its endowment trustees to divest all holdings in the fossil fuel industry and invest in renewable energy initiatives;

3. renews relations with the Book Industry Environmental Council, the Green Press Initiative, and other partners in the publishing and information technology industries to explore how we can help our communities and nation transition away from a fossil fueled economy;
4. calls on President Obama to hold a White House Conference on Climate Change which libraries will assist in launching with a series of library-based local, state, regional, national, and international community conversations focused on planning and implementing a peaceful transition to a post-fossil-free fuel, sustainable human relationship with the planet; and
5. amend ALA Policy B.5.5 to state that libraries are urged, in addition to the collection and provision of information regarding the environment, to take steps in assisting communities transition to fossil-free, renewable, sustainable energy sources [Resolution 2013].

At Friday's Progressive Council Caucus meeting, my friends had insisted that, when the resolution came up for debate, a request should be made asking permission for me to speak. After all, I'd drafted the resolution, was a former member of Council, and had words to contribute to the conversation.

Ben Trapskin moved the resolution, and after he'd spoken to it requested that I be allowed to address the body. However, as a result of my not following the changed process for resolution submission, the propriety of anybody discussing the matter was quickly challenged by councilor Larry Romans on the grounds that BARC had not reviewed the resolution. Clearly it had fiscal implications, and so required BARC's input and recommendation.

In the midst of Larry Romans' attempt to rule the resolution out-of-order, when it became clear that the resolution was to be ruled out-of-order, Al informed the body that it was not likely that I'd be present at annual in Chicago and requested that I be invited to speak. The chair, whose initial ruling that debate was in order was challenged by Romans, the parliamentarian consulted, the chair's decision determined in violation of Sturgis, the debate ruled out-of-order, and then the chair asked the body if it would give consent allowing me to speak anyway. At that, a loud chorus of male voices spontaneously erupted into "Boo!"

I'd attended many Council meetings over the years, and this was the first time I'd heard boos *before* a person had even had a chance to speak. Pam Klipsch, immediately moved to the microphone and said, in a politely chastising manner, that Council should have the *courtesy* to give a former member an opportunity to speak. Whereupon, Council gave its consent, I was given two minutes (rather than the usual three), described where the idea had come from, why divestment was important, and ended by saying that I just might show up in Chicago to see how the resolution fared. And, sure enough, I did.

Taking Amtrak to Chicago the following June just after school let out, I was present to witness the debate that ensued over the resolution.

On July 1, 2013, the Resolution on Divestment of Holdings in Fossil Fuel Companies was on Council II's agenda. It followed on the heels of a resolution that thanked librarians for actions taken during recent weather-related disasters, which wasn't without its own share of controversy. The Resolution on Library Service to the Community in a Disaster named, as recipients of ALA's thanks, librarians in the states of New York, New Jersey, and Connecticut impacted by hurricanes Sandy and Irene. During debate two councilors noted that libraries in other states and the District of Columbia too had been impacted by these storms, suggesting that no mention of specific states be made in order to be inclusive of all. Council then moved on to discuss fossil fuels.

BARC reported the previous day that the fiscal implications of divestment would be onerous, limit the Endowment Trustees' ability to maximize investment returns, and negatively impact ALA's finances. Therefore much of the discussion focused on fiscal matters (Budget 1). Several councilors spoke to the urgency of taking action on climate change. Pam Klipsch, for instance said,

> Twenty or thirty years from now there will be people standing here in this Council and they will be dealing with the consequences of the decisions we are making here today. If you're talking about economic impact, environmental damage is impacting the social and economic stability of this country, of our lives, of this Association, it's impacting libraries, it's impacting salaries, it's impacting resources available to us to deal with the damage that we are causing because we are not confronting and not facing the consequences of this problem [Council].

Charles Kratz spoke of the divestment movement that was gaining steam across the country:

> I'm going to vote to support this resolution and even if this goes down to defeat I want to extend what I said last night in Council forum. With all due respect to the Executive Board, because I have served on the Executive Board, I understand the fiduciary responsibility of the Executive Board, and the endowment trustees, and even this Council, but this issue is not going to go away. It's being discussed all over the country at American universities and colleges, and so I think this is a small step, but even if this does not pass today, the board and this Council needs to look at this issue because this issue is going to come up over and over again and it's not going to go away. We have an obligation. On our campuses today this is not coming from people of my age, these issues are being raised by the students, and I don't see many students in this room, but the students are the future of this Association, and these are the people who are bringing this up on campuses today [*ibid.*].

And Karen Schneider suggested that ALA "take a look at its own carbon footprint and take an aggressive stance in several areas such as … looking to move to one single face-to-face meeting per year rather than two" (*ibid.*).

The question was soon called, and a vote taken. A show of hands was inconclusive and so a count was made with councilors standing to give their vote. The chair announced the resolution had failed, with 27 voting in favor, 79 opposed. Voices of concern were raised, and Charles Kratz went to the microphone to ask for a recount, saying that he'd witnessed many vote counts, and that there were certainly more than 27 people standing in favor of the resolution. On recount the resolution still failed, but the vote was 56 in favor, 82 opposed.

Divestment did receive support in one ALA venue, besides SRRT. The Executive Board of REFORMA urged by president-elect Isabel Espinal approved the resolution, noting that communities of color were those most impacted by climate change.

There is still time for ALA to join the divestment movement. According to 350.org's website, as of October 2015, 450 entities have agreed to divest stock in fossil fuel industries, and the estimated value of divestments to date is $2.6 trillion (Divestment). A list of divestors can be found at http://gofossilfree.org/commitments/. If these groups have found ways to divest, ALA can certainly also.

Fast forward two years: sustainability

In 2014, a new round table was established within ALA, the Sustainability Round Table (SustainRT). In previous years, efforts within ALA on environmental issues were based, almost exclusively, in SRRT's Task Force on the Environment (TfoE). While SRRT task forces have given birth to several of ALA's round tables—GODORT, EMIERT, GLBTRT—the SustainRT was not an outgrowth of SRRT, except, perhaps, as a reaction to perceptions SustainRT organizers might have had that a unit independent of SRRT was more likely to be effective in ALA. After all, SRRT had a longstanding reputation of raising "uncomfortable" issues that might prove problematic for the work in which SustainRT members wished to engage. I was concerned about the political implications of the establishment of a roundtable dedicated to environmental issues separate from SRRT, and expressed them to SustainRT organizers. The meaning of this development seemed indicative of two troubling possibilities. First, that the TFoE had not been a welcoming space for the new generation of environmentally-minded librarian activists. The second possibility was that the new generation preferred to distance themselves and their work from SRRT's political activism in an attempt to appeal more broadly to ALA, a tactic that might be fruitful, but then might also result in the political neutering of environmental issues. Most likely the impetus for independence was a combination of the two.

The mission of the Sustainability Round Table is "to provide resources for the library community to support sustainability through curriculum development; collections; exhibits; events; advocacy, communication, library buildings and space design" (Sustainability).

The first resolution sponsored by SustainRT, Resolution on the Importance of Sustainable Libraries, was brought to ALA's very first virtual membership meeting on June 4, 2015, and was met with success, both at the virtual meeting and a few weeks later at Council.

RESOLUTION ON THE IMPORTANCE OF SUSTAINABLE LIBRARIES

WHEREAS our communities are faced with economic, environmental and societal changes that are of great concern to our quality of life;

WHEREAS libraries are uniquely positioned and essential to build the capacity of the communities they serve to become sustainable, resilient and regenerative;

WHEREAS library leaders, and those who inspire future library leaders, have a mandate to ensure future access to economical library services;

WHEREAS libraries that demonstrate good stewardship of the resources entrusted to them can build community support that leads to sustainable funding;

WHEREAS the people who work in our libraries and those who access services in our facilities deserve a healthy environment in which to do so;

WHEREAS the Intergovernmental Panel on Climate Change (IPCC) has determined that: "Human influence on the climate system is clear.... Recent climate changes have had widespread impacts on human and natural systems";

WHEREAS the American Library Association has acknowledged in its 2015 Strategic

Plan that "Libraries are widely recognized as key players in economic development, in building strong and vibrant communities, and in sustaining a strong democracy" and launched the ALA Center for Civic Life (CCL) in 2010 in conjunction with the Kettering Foundation to promote community engagement and foster public deliberation through libraries; and

WHEREAS libraries that demonstrate leadership in making sustainable decisions that positively address climate change, respect and use natural resources, and create healthy indoor and outdoor environments will stabilize and reduce their long-term energy costs, help build more sustainable communities, and thereby increase community support for the library; now, therefore, be it

RESOLVED, that the American Library Association (ALA), on behalf of its members:

1. recognizes the important and unique role libraries play in wider community conversations about resiliency, climate change, and a sustainable future and begins a new era of thinking sustainably in order to consider the economic, environmental and socially equitable viability of choices made on behalf of the association;
2. enthusiastically encourages activities by itself, its membership, library schools and state associations to be proactive in their application of sustainable thinking in the areas of their facilities, operations, policy, technology, programming, partnerships and library school curricula; and
3. directs the ALA Executive Director to pursue sustainable choices when planning conferences and meetings and to actively promote best practices of sustainability through ALA publications, research and educational opportunities to reach our shared goal of vital, visible and viable libraries for the future [Resolution 2015].

Passage of the Resolution on the Importance of Sustainable Libraries is most welcome as it puts ALA on record as recognizing the need for action in regard to climate change, even stating in the sixth whereas clause that humans have influenced the climate.

That said, the resolution deserves a close look for two reasons. First, it is not clear from the resolution what, exactly, is meant by sustainable libraries. The second reason arises from the fact that the actual *cause* of this lack of clarity is that the word "sustainable" has come to mean very different things to very different people with very different interests in how, or whether, climate change should be addressed. Ambiguity in relation to sustainability is a slippery slope these days, as described by Adrian Parr in her 2009 book *Hijacking Sustainability*.

Parr investigates the phenomenon of "green washing"—the use of appeals to people's environmental concerns to sell everything from consumer products to entertainment to the military, and she warns that "The more the power of sustainability culture is appropriated by the mechanisms of State and corporate culture, the more it camouflages the darker underbelly of both—militarism and capitalism" (6).

This co-opting of the idea and language of effective efforts toward creating ways of life that sustain life, make problematic overly general appeals to sustainability like that in this resolution. Three points in the resolution, however, are crystal clear, and can act as a point of departure toward the clarity needed for action.

- Libraries are a place for community conversations about climate change, resiliency, and a sustainable future.
- ALA must decide what its responsibilities are in regard to climate crisis.
- Once those responsibilities are determined, ALA needs to plan its own actions

and promote throughout the profession new perspectives and best practices that reflect those responsibilities.

The resolution moved at the virtual ALA membership meeting by Rebekkah Smith Aldrich contained supplementary information provided to meet the requirements for resolution submission by ALA's Resolution Committee. For example, in describing how the resolution supports ALA's mission, and core values, its authors write,

> The resolution is designed to strengthen the mission and core values of the Association. "Sustainability" is defined as the "capacity to endure." Within the mission statement of ALA we see the words "development," "promotion," "improvement," and "ensure." All of these words speak to the need to be proactive as we think of the future of library service and our profession [ALA 2].

In regard to all the various matters related to sustainability that are addressed in the resolution, the question must be asked: What *exactly* is it that we want to endure, to sustain about

- the environment?
- the economy?
- society?
- libraries?
- ALA?

And the follow-up question: In what *manner* do we wish for these entities to endure?

- as they currently exist?
- or, differently?

The geophysical context within which decisions must be made about what aspects of the environment, economy, society, libraries, and ALA we want sustained is the following: Climate science models indicate that we humans have until 2017 to begin cutting CO_2 emissions by 10 percent per year in order to avoid warming above 2° C. As I began writing this chapter, the Meteorological Society of America released a report stating that warming of the oceans has reached a point where continued warming cannot be stopped (Kaufman). Any attempt to realistically proceed with implementation of Resolution on the Importance of Sustainable Libraries must be aimed at contributing to this annual target of 10 percent per year.

Let us take as a given that we want the environment—life on the planet—to endure. Human life and other life.

What about the economy do we want to endure? Large sectors of the economy are responsible for the climate crisis, do we want the fossil fuel industry to endure and sell to us its reserves of 2,795 gigatons of CO_2 emissions? Burning those gigatons will certainly make much of life (including human) unsustainable. Given this, one must conclude that we do NOT want to sustain the fossil fuel industry. This suggests that one of the first actions for ALA is to posthaste divest all fossil fuel industry holdings.

What about society do we want to endure? In the U.S. the fundamental characteristics of our society are: high levels of consumption of goods designed for quick disposability and replacement, produced in places far away that require the combustion of massive quantities of fossil fuel for their transport from place of manufacture to place of consumption/disposal; an ever growing gap in wealth and access to the fruits of society;

increasing levels of violence, with local police agencies becoming militarized; racism, sexism, and anti-immigrant sentiment; high levels of apathy, cynicism, and hopelessness among the citizenry, with increased rates of youth suicides as one measure. Do we treasure consumption so much that we want to sustain those aspects of society? Do we take cultural pride in huge disparities between rich and poor such that we want those disparities to continue to grow? Do industries that profit from weapons manufacture and that perpetuate psychological and political predilections to violence deserve to endure?

Libraries and ALA—as librarians we certainly want both to endure. Our communities need our libraries, and librarians need our professional association. The question becomes, What steps do libraries and ALA need to take to contribute to a global 10 percent reduction of CO_2 emissions next year? And the year after that, and the next, until CO_2 and other greenhouse gas emissions are brought into balance with the planet's ability to process it? Any action that does not contribute to that reduction level (or more) is not helpful. The reduction must be measurable.

Climate change—front and center, from now to eternity

As Naomi Klein wrote, climate change is not an *issue*. Climate change is now the *framework* within which all other issues must now be addressed.

In 2013, CO_2 emissions were 61 percent higher than in 1990 despite all international conferences, research, negotiations, LEED construction, green thises-and-thats. In 2012, the World Bank reported that at current rates of emission growth, the planet is "on track for a 4° C warmer world [by century's end] marked by extreme heat waves, declining global food stocks, loss of ecosystems and biodiversity, and life-threatening sea level rise.... [T]here is also no certainty that adaptation to a 4° C world is possible" (Klein 13). As for what a 4° C increase in planetary temperatures might mean, a former director of the Tyndall Centre for Climate Change Research in the United Kingdom says it is "incompatible with any reasonable characterization of an organized, equitable, and civilized community" (*ibid.*). And if we are to keep temperatures from going past 2° C, industrial countries must cut emissions by 8 to 10 percent per year. The International Energy Agency predicts a 6° C increase if greenhouse gas emissions are not brought under control by 2017. Past that, the momentum built up by rising temperatures is expected to make the target of 2° C impossible.

Since 1990, neoliberalism's self-regulating free market, the world's entrepreneurs, billionaires and government officials have had a quarter of a century to fiddle with fixes and market forces to reduce emissions. Instead, during this period emissions have grown by 61 percent.

Compounding the problem is the fact that, in the U.S., instead of increased demands from the public for action, we've seen the development of climate change denial. According to a 2007 Harris poll, 71 percent of people in the U.S. believed the burning of fossil fuels causes climate change. In 2009, that number had fallen to 51 percent. In 2011, it fell further to 44 percent.

Proving the quip made by activist and writer Upton Sinclair that a person's willingness to understand something is dependent on the source of their paycheck, other polls indicate that in Appalachia's coal country, for instance, 49 percent of Democrats believe that humans cause climate change, while in other areas of the country 72 to 77 percent of Democrats believe this. In Alberta, Canada, where tar sands extraction has boosted the local economy, 41 percent of the population believe humans cause climate change, whereas in Canada's Atlantic provinces the number is 68 percent. And, while 97 percent of climate scientists state categorically that human activities are responsible for global warming, only 47 percent of economic geologists do (economic geologists being the people whose work involves the economic exploitation of geological resources). As Klein puts it, "The bottom line is that we are all inclined to denial when the truth is too costly—whether emotionally, intellectually, or financially" (46).

Compounding the problem of people "not knowing" when self-imposed ignorance permits inaction, are two others—the nature and extent of information made available to the public, and the willingness of even those who know best—scientists and environmentalists—to take action.

A simple example of the availability of reliable information is the frequency with which the mainstream media has covered climate change news. According to Douglas Fischer's "Climate Coverage," in 2007 the three major media networks—ABC, CBS, NBC—carried 147 stories on climate change. In 2011 there were 11 stories. The numbers went up with 29 stories in 2012, and 30 in 2013 (34). During 2014, the number of news stories increased by 30 percent over the previous year (Fischer). Quantity does not necessarily reflect quality, but, for the most part, news outlets do provide enough reliable information to keep citizens reasonably well informed. But then, news programs and sources face stiff competition for public attention, awash as it is in a culture of distraction, entertainment, mindlessness.

What about those who are most well informed, highly educated people who do pay attention to climate science? What about the experts and policy makers?

In July 2015, a group of Britain's leading scientific and academic professional associations issued a joint Climate Communiqué in anticipation of the new round of climate talks held in Paris in November and December. Scanning the list of 24 signatory organizations, ranging from the granddaddy of them all, the Royal Society, to the British Academy for the Humanities and Social Sciences, to ZSL: Let's Work for Wildlife, I was struck by the absence of the Library Association. Perhaps ALA's sister organization was not invited to sign or, invited, passed up the opportunity—possibly for good reason.

The Communiqué states unequivocally,

> ... if we are to have a reasonable chance of limiting global warming in this century to 2°C relative to the pre-industrial period, we must *transition to a zero-carbon world by early in the second half of the century* [Climate; emphasis in the original].

In a footnote, "zero-carbon" is more specifically defined as "net zero global CO_2 emissions." What this means is *not* that all CO_2 emissions must cease, but they must be neutralized, balanced by something else's ability to absorb them. The "something" is usually Earth's natural processes, which we have overwhelmed. Some entrepreneurial scientists suggest "seeding" the seas and the stratosphere with iron or sulfur to produce

CO_2-eating algae or to reflect solar radiation. Playing god with our chemistry sets, however, is what we need to *stop* doing.

The Climate Communiqué, coming from 24 of Britain's leading professional organizations, is worth looking at for whatever guidance—or cautions—it might offer other professional associations, such as ALA, in addressing climate change. The one-page call to the world's climate negotiators lays out the *risks* of inaction, the necessity of *response*, and the *opportunities* the situation offers, and then ends with a call to action.

The diplomatic and logistical efforts needed to gather support for the Climate Communiqué from such a diverse group of organizations is admirable. Likewise, the unified public pronouncement of the climate crisis confronting humanity, and its call for action should spur climate negotiations to begin emission reductions immediately. Unfortunately, a close reading of the document reveals that it contains *nothing* that suggests any sort of departure from the actions chemists, physicists, engineers, academics, and even many environmentalists have already taken since 1990. Indeed, while the spirit of the Communiqué conveys deep concern, the actual language conveys a business-as-usual message expressing urgent need for:

- invention
- novel technological solutions
- sustained research
- entrepreneurship
- economic progress
- safeguarding the *services* that ecosystems provide [emphasis added].

Sustained research into the inventions that will supposedly lead to novel technological solutions that savvy entrepreneurs can market in the pursuit of economic progress (and profits) is exactly what is *not* needed in the face of the climate crisis. And the last phrase from the document especially indicates that the mindset of human domination over the natural world drives this call to action: "*Services* that ecosystems provide," as if the planet's ecosystems were subcontractors hired by one sector of humanity (namely, the privileged) to service appetites for plastic and copper and oil and water. The Communiqué is an unreflective, if heartfelt, expression of the technological mindset that it is the manifest destiny of some humans to be serviced by the natural world. This is the mindset that got us into, and has kept us in, the mess we face today. We've played around unremittingly with the chemistry of the atmosphere for going on two centuries. And this "playing chemistry" has happened at the command of profit-driven industries for sustained research, inventions, and patents *with the assistance* of members of some of these very organizations, and their associational predecessors.

Take, for example, the Royal Society, founded in 1660. Although early membership in the Society was open to nonscientists, many of the scientifically-minded and active members not only assisted in giving the world the miracles of modern science, but they also assisted in the colonization of other people's homelands for the express purpose of exploring for, and exploiting, natural (and human) "resources" of those lands. A Royal Society member, Thomas Savery, invented the steam engine in 1699. Savery's invention eventually led to the manufacture of mechanical devises used throughout industry for extraction, transportation, manufacture of materials from mines and plantations and factories throughout the British Empire—pumps and drills, steamships and trains, threshers and looms. After the development of the fossil-fueled internal combustion engine, trains, trucks, ships and planes began encircling the globe. All of which have carried in their wake the economic, and often brutal, exploitation of indigenous peoples, immigrants, peasants, workers, women, and children.

Not only have members of the Royal Society been partially responsible for processes leading to climate change, but they, along with members of fraternal associations in other industrial nations, have known about the relationship between CO_2 emissions and the greenhouse effect since the 1950s, and done virtually nothing to stop it.

If the organizations supporting this Climate Communiqué were to approach the climate crisis with wisdom, care, and a sense of professional accountability as to its origins and the current activities that are exacerbating the crisis, their message would be very different. An intellectually and spiritually powerful, game-changing communiqué on the climate crisis coming from these professions would include the following:

- acknowledgment of the associations' role, both historically and currently, in generating, contributing to, ignoring, compounding the climate crisis;
- a demand that exploration of fossil fuels cease and that extraction be curbed immediately;
- recognition that playing God with the climate via chemical, biological, or engineered additives is unacceptable to the scientific community because such processes are untestable and almost certain to result in unforeseen, unintended, and negative consequences;
- willingness to work with existing industries to retool and transition to the zero-carbon economy, and away from planned-obsolescence as an industrial practice;
- a call for a halt to transoceanic shipping of nonessential goods, with "essential" to be determined through community conversations globally;
- advocacy for changes in agriculture, away from fossil-fuel and chemical intensive practices;
- insistence that the transition to the zero-carbon economy be peaceful and planned; and
- a call for critical conversations on glorified violence in the mass media, racism, misogyny, and anti-immigrant sentiment, with an eye to establishing a social climate in which non-violent transition to a hotter planet is possible.

An honest communiqué would end with an apology, an acknowledgment, and an offer.

The apology would be extended to the indigenous peoples of the world, past and present, extinct and alive, for all harm done. The acknowledgment would be of the harm inflicted on indigenous, indentured, enslaved peoples, and otherwise exploited peoples, with a listing of the benefits elites accrued from harm inflicted. The offer would be to listen from a position of humility and care, and take action on the expressed needs of indigenous and poor and female and other historically oppressed peoples. The same apology, acknowledgment, and offer would be made to the flora and fauna of the planet, translated from human language into a change in the behavior of Homo sapiens.

A climate crisis communiqué with this sort of message would truly begin the long-term process of reparations, perhaps even redemption, for all the wrongs wrought by imperialist, colonizing, industrial nations.

Librarians and the climate crisis

> If we can shift the cultural context even a little, then there will be some breathing room for those sensible reformist policies that will at least get the atmospheric carbon numbers moving in the right direction. And winning is contagious so, who knows? [Klein 26].

When a crisis is at hand, people do not go about business-as-usual. Yes, the routines and habits of daily life during times of crisis offer comfort and a sense of stability, but they are sensed as luxuries, things not to be taken for granted. Such was the cup of coffee I savored while soaked to the bone on Election Day 2006.

The climate crisis must be addressed *as a crisis*, as a *present* and approaching crisis. We know enough about the general consequences of the crisis, if not the exact details, to take action. What we know clearly calls for immediate reductions of greenhouse gas emissions, with the understanding that past and present emissions have warmed the planet so much that the resulting release of methane from polar regions is accelerating and must be taken into consideration when calculating reductions over which humans have control.

What can an ordinary librarian do, what can ALA and our sister organizations around the globe do to immediately reduce greenhouse gas emissions?

First, we must realize that we've been mistaken to treat climate change as a technical and political challenge for experts alone to resolve. Leaving solutions in the hands of those who most often are beholden to corporate interests has been a grave mistake, because they've managed to do nothing but make the problem significantly worse. Many have pointed out that solutions to the problem of climate change are *ethical*, and that mega-storms, floods, heat waves, extinctions, fires are a wake up call, an alarm demanding a seismic shift in human thought, morals, priorities, and relationships.

Our knee-jerk burning of fossil fuel is not so much a technical problem, any more than spousal abuse is, as it is a moral one. We know what must be done—stop burning fossil fuels. The question becomes, how to extract our lives from what has become a deadly dependence?

The cultural shift Klein suggests is one of mindset, not technology. When an appeal to "sustainability" is made these days, what is usually meant is a tweak here and a tweak there to leave Western standards of living and culture relatively intact, little inconvenienced. Again, we come to the question of what constitutes a sustainable library/economy/community.

Thinking and writing about librarianship within the context of the environment is not new and neither is taking action at the places where the two intersect.

In a collection of essays, *Greening Libraries*, edited by Monika Antonelli and Mark McCullough, 29 authors describe green library buildings, energy audits, retrofitting and construction, green committees, outreach, services, programs, resources, and reflections on all these and other library greening initiatives. More recently, Occupy Wall Street activist librarian, Mandy Henk, authored *Ecology, Economy, Equity: The Path to a Carbon-Neutral Library*.

In *Greening Libraries*, Maria J. Jankowska outlines activities within ALA concerning the environment beginning in 1989 with the establishment of SRRT's Task Force on the

Environment (TFOE). She also mentions a project in which she was centrally involved as editor, *Electronic Green Journal*, founded in 1994 and published by the University of Idaho Library. In the same collection, authors Charles Forrest, Karen Munro, and Kate Zoellner describe planning and implementing green practices at ACRL's biennial conference in their essay "Toward Sustainable Conferences: Going Green at the 2009 ACRL 14th National Conference in Seattle." Forrest, Munro, and Zoellner confront the reality of CO_2 emissions within the context of a regular, ongoing, professional activity—organizing and attending conferences. Taking their work one step further is Dave Hudson's excellent *Greening Libraries* essay "Beyond Swag: Reflections on Libraries, Pencils, and the Limits of 'Green' Consumption." In *Ecology, Economy, Equity*, Henk extends the conversation, from what has mostly focused on the technical into the arena of ethics, and writes,

> Any attempt to define and implement a sustainable library or a vision of what sustainable librarianship should look like cannot be successful unless the challenges, both technical and ethical, that derive from the realities of carbon pollution are confronted head on [Henk 99].

Speaking directly to ethics, University of Illinois instructor, Maggie Kainulainen, in her essay "Saying Climate Change: Ethics of the Sublime and the Problem of Representation" offers a way toward the head on confrontation for which Henk issues her call, suggesting that when anyone considers proposals for addressing the climate crisis, what "must be considered are the visions of the world they support and what alternatives are silenced" (Kainulainen 115).

Kainulainen describes climate change as "a vast and strange object within which 'nature' and 'history' become intertwined and reciprocal." She unpacks the rhetoric that lays claim to "green" and "sustainable" for everyone from BP to Greenpeace in order to discover places where hegemonic control over debates on climate change can be destabilized. After all, for decades, despite the actions and protests and pleadings of grassroots groups and nongovernmental organizations, the debate (and inaction) has been controlled by elites, usually representing those with economic stakes in the status quo.

She quotes philosopher Kevin DeLuca, that climate change "provide[s] the opportunity to question and disarticulate Industrialism" (114). Such a disarticulation, cutting through the spin and sound-bytes of PR people and policy wonks, offers a way out of the maze of dis- and mis- and mal-information. Example: through a critical lens, the purchase of carbon offsets for an intercontinental jaunt becomes not an ethical choice (except under the questionable ethical standards of an industrial system that has no interest in abandoning fossil fuels), instead it is seen for what it is—a marketing device designed to protect profitability and make a buck off frequent flyers' feelings of guilt.

> To think as big as the ecological thought demands, to make conscious space for uncertainty, to accept uncomfortable interdependence with alien agents, human and nonhuman, this is thinking an impossible thought in the discursive field of neoliberalism; it requires that one become "open, radically open—open forever, without the possibility of closing again" [117].

Neoliberal thought has led to the reality of trucks parked along roads to Calais to haul off humans who have the audacity to try to enter Britain. Neoliberal thought leads to the reality of forests fenced off to the people who live in them so the CO_2 absorbed by the trees can be used as carbon offsets. Neoliberal thought leads to the reality of postponed and postponed and postponed reinforcement of levees in the Ninth Ward. Neoliberalism can tolerate, till kingdom come, LEED buildings and sustainable libraries and green swag, just as long as they don't interrupt the global flow of *stuff* (and profits). (See the short online video "The Story of Stuff.")

The question remains, how do librarians confront the challenge of climate crisis head on? How do we make a 10 percent cut in CO_2 emissions this year, and next, and the year after that until we've come to a place of net zero emissions? The United States, with about 4 percent of the world's population, produces 19 percent of global greenhouse gases, and whereas transportation globally accounts for 13 percent of emissions, in the U.S. the number is 27 percent (Global 2015). Reducing that number would be one place to start.

Every movement for change needs people willing to engage in dialogue and action. Librarians could contribute a spark that contributes to the change the planet now demands of humanity. Or, are we as a profession so content with the status quo maintained so tenaciously by the world's elites and their enforcers that we will simply go along to get along with the powers that be?

In what remains of this chapter, and this book, I offer a suggestion.

The suggestion is a simple one, just as burning gas is simple. Of course, the ripple effect of even simple acts reverberate throughout the social and the natural worlds in the way it is said that the flutter of a butterfly's wings might trigger a hurricane.

The suggestion flows from climate science estimates that CO_2 emissions must be cut by 8 to 10 percent per year to avert worse case global warming of more than 2 C°.

The suggestion is based on an historic precedent—the belt-tightening expected of every citizen and community, organization, and business during World War II.

The suggestion is offered because, after over 50 years of inaction by industry and government to act on the knowledge scientists had of the relation of CO_2 emissions to a warmer planet, I (and countless others) have no doubt that the courage for action, the disarticulation of neoliberal policies and practices, will only come from ordinary people taking extraordinary steps to confront the most sublime power humanity has ever met—the meeting of Human History with Mother Nature.

The suggestion flows from thinking about how to disturb, disrupt, disarticulate, and dismantle the systems and ways of thinking that have placed life on the planet in jeopardy. As Henk says, we need to confront the problem head on, thinking impossible thoughts, or as Adrian Parr, in his book *Hijacking Sustainability* (2009) says, "Putting the state of unimaginableness to work..." (165). It also flows from wondering how to wrest political power from today's elite, those who benefit so tremendously from the status quo that they seem willing to let global temperatures rise forever. Is this the way the 1 percent behave when a child is sick?

Describing an organization called Architecture for Humanity, Parr notes the work they do that focuses on making communities sustainable, and the approach they take that could be a powerful model for others, like librarians. The power of their model comes from taking an absolutely pragmatic leap into the abyss of unimaginableness to extract from it something that expresses the vitality of life and which can then be used to construct a sustainable way of life in the present and for the benefit of life in the future.... [I]t involves connecting communities to the creative life of matter and social energy. It is ... political because they engage, displace, and reorganize the very conditions that constitute the sustainability of design, pushing "architecture" into the background so that the vitality of social life can step up into the foreground.... [I]t is ethical because it does not negate the vitality of life; it affirms and is strengthened by life's vital and material dimensions [157].

At the heart of Architecture for Humanity's work are community conversations, the participation of all in decision-making for the benefit of all. Or, in the words of a friend and colleague, who, in describing the work of Spanish philosopher Paco Fernándes Buey, wrote, "politics must be understood as the ethics of the collective wisdom/action/knowledge/mind and ... must be democratic" (Plaza). Political power must be taken from the hands of those so far distant from communities of life that they destroy, like powaqqatsi or the "greedy parasites" in the song Solidarity Forever.

My pragmatic leap of unimaginable disruption is that ALA Council consider the following proposed resolution and call to action:

DRAFT—Resolution on the Immediate Reduction of CO_2 Emissions, and Call to Action

WHEREAS the world's climate scientists have informed humanity that CO_2 emissions by industrialized nations must be cut by 8 to 10 percent per year to minimize the possibility that global warming could exceed 2°C, temperatures about which Professor James Hansen says "It is not difficult to imagine that conflicts arising from forced migrations and economic collapse might make the planet ungovernable, threatening the fabric of civilisation" [Bagley 2015];

WHEREAS librarianship wishes for civilization to continue and the transition to a hotter planet be done peacefully, in a planned fashion;

WHEREAS efforts taken by government, industry, and the free market have to date failed to reduce CO_2 emissions;

WHEREAS history shows that movements for social justice and change always begin among ordinary people engaging in acts of moral courage;

WHEREAS historic precedent exists since World War II proving that citizens at the grassroots level can contribute greatly, positively, and peacefully to national efforts when faced with crisis conditions;

THEREFORE, be it resolved that the American Library Association

(1) takes immediate steps to reduce its own carbon footprint by canceling midwinter meetings and annual conferences until such time as the long distance travel the meetings necessitate can be fueled from renewable energy sources;
(2) calls on its employees, Association members, and all served by our profession to immediately reduce their nonessential long distance air travel;
(3) invites its affiliates, partners, publishers, vendors, and professional associations worldwide to join us in this action;
(4) sends this resolution and attached Call to Action to the library press, the mainstream press, the President of the United States, members of Congress, governors, convention bureaus, and all other interested parties.

Call to Action

The action of the American Library Association and those who join our call, in ceasing nonessential long distance air travel to help the United States meet a 10 percent reduction of CO_2 emissions by the end of this year, will reverberate throughout our communities, our society, the economy, and the political landscape. We anticipate the announcement of our action to generate both positive and negative reactions. Our action will directly impact the jobs of ALA employees, lives of family members, community relationships, the cities where ALA meets, and all the people and industries that facilitate conventions such as ours. We know that if this action becomes widespread the entire airline industry will be impacted. Ticket agents, baggage handlers, flight attendants, pilots and navigators, airport service workers, custodial crews, and the workers and subcontractors of airplane manufacturing industries will all be impacted. We know also, however, that these industries could be redirected for modes of transportation fueled with renewable energy sources. Workers can be retrained, physical plants retooled.

Although we know our actions might generate hostility, we also know that nonviolent actions such as we are taking must be made for the benefit of our and future generations. Just as Rosa Parks knowingly made herself vulnerable to a racist society in order to take a step forward in the struggle for the civil rights of black Americans, so we make ourselves vulnerable to those who might feel threatened by our action. We take this step knowing that the vast majority of people on the planet approve of the steps we are taking.

This is one step in a much larger journey that we as individuals, as members of the human family must take together.

Being proactive professionals, ALA members nationwide are launching an information campaign to explain our Call to Action. Librarians will go out into our communities to meet with community partners, friends of the library groups, city councils, legislators, parent/teacher/student associations, unions, religious groups, chambers of commerce, foundations, and others. Librarians will help facilitate community conversations designed to foster collective input on further steps to reduce CO_2 emissions, and to call on our collective wisdom in community to prioritize needs, assist the most vulnerable, brainstorm ideas, and put into action steps leading to a peaceful transition from the era of fossil fuels to a new era of renewable energy. We will work to reenergize and reimagine democracy from the ground up.

Additionally, as professionals we know we are living through the most momentous time humanity will probably ever experience, and we will engage in projects to document this time of transition, with the assistance of educators, students, and others in our local and regional communities.

We take these actions in the spirit of nonviolence that has led to great social transformations in the past. We cannot over emphasize the necessity of working for a peaceful, all-inclusive transition whatever the future holds. Already, the U.S. military and police forces are prepared for social disruption, tensions, and violence that could attend climate change if ordinary people do not take it upon ourselves to prepare and plan for a peaceful transition. We do *not* want to see our communities torn apart, collapsing into a desperate dog-eat-dog state of existence. We have no doubt that U.S. culture, as it exists today, could easily collapse into violent chaos. Therefore, we take this action and call for others to join us in order to avoid the chaos and conflict and inhumanity that will surely come if we continue along the suicidal course of prevarication and inaction on greenhouse gas emissions.

Immediate Steps for Units of ALA (examples)

- inform convention sites with which ALA already has signed contracts that ALA will host regional conferences in their facilities, and as soon as all currently signed contracts have been honored, ALA staff will postpone all future midwinter and annual until humans have achieved net zero CO_2 emissions;
- we will partner with vendors in conversations about retooling, restructuring their products and services toward the elimination of the need for long-distance, CO_2 emitting transportation;
- the Committee on Legislation will draft legislation calling on national protections for individuals who lose jobs due to climate change mitigation actions, the ALA Washington Office will assist;

- the Library Administration and Management Association will draft policies on job sharing, income equity, and income redistribution the purpose of which will be the creation of new jobs and the reduction of income disparities in the workplace;
- the Association of College and Research Libraries and the Association of Research Libraries will work with information technology industries and providers to stop the practice of planned obsolescence for the transition period; they will also work with educators and agriculture to transition to local, organic agriculture; and
- YALSA, AASL, and ALSC will work with educators and publishers on the climate change transition documentation project, and in rethinking schools in light of the changing climate. Education for the 21st century must move well beyond STEM and STEAM to embrace ways of knowing and skills that our system of education has so far refused to acknowledge, much less consider.

To those who say that the above Resolution and Call to Action are an extreme, unnecessary course of action, I have found myself incapable of any response … except for a plea.

Yes, this proposal for ALA and librarianship suggests an extreme step. It is, and isn't. The crisis of World War II that last put ALA meetings on hold, will stand as nothing compared to the climate crisis.

Some will respond that geotechnologies, seeding the stratosphere, salting the seas will fix the problem. They won't. Unless, of course, the "problem" is defined as insufficient funding for research and development, for the class of professionals, investors, manufacturers, and camp-followers whose predecessors and contemporaries, funders and customers, have failed to stop CO_2 emissions sooner than now. Further tinkering with the planet's chemistry will *not* fix ecosystems, and will most certainly make matters worse. The technological mindset that has driven climate change must stand aside, as a way of thinking centered on healing social and environmental ills is given the opportunity to step forward to guide us in changing our wasteful way of life.

My plea to you is that you read what remains of this chapter with an open mind, a calm heart, and a willingness to stand in the shoes of someone you don't know.

Several years ago, I read one of those lists—If the world consisted on 100 people, X percent would have A and Y percent would have B. One item on the list stuck with me. It was something like this: If the world population consisted of 100 people, 2 of them would have flown on an airplane at least once in their life.

Now, step into the shoes/sandals/footprints of the remaining 98 percent of the planet's population, and ask yourself the following two questions:

- What *entitles* 2 percent of the world's population to continue using a mode of transportation that produces an estimated 2 to 3 tons of CO_2 per passenger on a cross-country roundtrip flight, keeping in mind that jumbo-jets are highly unlikely to ever fly using renewable energy sources (*See*, for example, Rosenthal 2010).
- Given the imperative of reducing CO_2 emissions immediately, shouldn't the use of jet fuel be limited to absolutely essential needs? In the face of *global* climate *crisis*, just how essential are ALA midwinter meetings and annual conferences? How essential are spring break jaunts to Hawaii, Paris, Sri Lanka? How essential are weekend ski trips? How essential is the transport of tulips from Holland, salmon from Alaska, lousy Kindle cases from China? How is essential defined? Who does the defining? Stand in the shoes of 98 percent of people who have never flown and will never fly, and ask yourself how does what the

2 percent consider essential compare with what the 98 percent might define as essential? Furthermore, in any consideration of essential, what is *fair*?

As is clear from these questions regarding what activities and products might actually justify CO_2 emissions, were air transportation to be limited to absolute necessities many sectors of economies around the globe—the airline industry, tulip growers, tourism, etc.—would be impacted just as, for instance, Detroit was in the 1980s when auto industry CEOs decided to take jobs and factories elsewhere, usually to places where pollution was not regulated and wages were nearly nothing compared to those of United Auto Workers union members.

Nobody wants their livelihoods threatened. I know. I've lost two jobs to budget cuts since the bankers cast us all into a recession in 2008. Who knows what the future holds for anyone on the employment front.

One thing we can know for certain is that if a sector of the economy will be hard hit as we transition to a fossil-fuel free future, we can *plan* for it. Secretive, self-serving decisions made in corporate boardrooms to maximize profits for the 1 percent can instead be turned into open discussions between everyone, using that "d" word librarians regard so highly—democracy. If the U.S. government can bail out the banking industry, it can assist others transition and retool too. Boeing workers could make trains that run on electricity generated from sunshine instead of long dead micro-organisms. Members of communities across the country could engage in conversations to prioritize needs—fuel for recreational or emergency vehicles; plastics for more Lego sets or medical instruments; water for organic farms or golf courses?

Consider the other option—*not planning* for the transition to a hotter planet.

What happens if we, the people, simply let boardroom bigwigs and their buddies in office "take care" of the climate crisis?

History and recent experience suggest that they will:

- put profits before people;
- act as if they alone have all the answers, as if they are God when it comes to the planet's ecosystems and inhabitants;
- call in the national guard, the Pinkertons, and the Blackwaters if workers or environmentalists or just plain worried folks get "out of hand";
- continue using the mass media to incite racist, anti-immigrant sentiment throughout the plugged-in populace;
- turn off water spigots to the homes of people who can't pay because they've got no income;
- build even bigger gates, mount newer security gadgets, hire armed mercenaries to protect their "private property";
- do nothing to prevent famine, which is always preventable; and
- turn our children into Enders and Katnisses—good kids become mass murderers at the whim of adults.

Sound outlandish?

Consider this, and then I'm done.

A couple of generations ago, some talented, thoughtful writers looked around, got a sense of the direction the social/political/technological winds were blowing, and wrote some cautionary tales: *Fahrenheit 451, Brave New World, 1984, Animal Farm*. These literary works fueled the imaginations of librarians, helping us to become ardent defenders of intellectual freedom and opponents of censorship. Rightfully so.

Unfortunately, neither Bradbury, Huxley nor Orwell figured climate change into their stories. Sexism and racism didn't enter into their pictures either. Librarianship needs new literary guides for the times ahead. Maybe Nancy Pearl could be called upon to work her magic—*Cautionary (and Inspirational) Tales for a Time of Climate Crisis*, or something along those lines. If she did, I'd be happy to recommend four titles by talented and prescient authors (every bit the equals to the literary heroes named above):

- Margaret Atwood (2003, 2009, 2013). *Oryx and Crake, Year of the Flood,* and *Maddaddam*
- Naomi Klein (2014). *This Changes Everything: Capitalism versus Climate*
- Pope Francis (2015). *Encyclical on Climate Change and Inequality*
- Dr. Seuss (1971). *The Lorax*

Sorry...I can't resist two more—offered for both your entertainment and edification, more along the inspirational, rather than cautionary, line. Parts guaranteed to make you laugh, cry, challenge your thinking:

- Colin Beavan (2010) *No Impact Man: Adventures of a Guilty Liberal Who Attempts to Save the Planet, and the Discoveries He Makes About Himself and Our Way of Life in the Process*
- Walter Mosley (2008) *The Right Mistake: the Further Philosophical Investigations of Socrates Fortlow*

Atwood, because she tells us metaphorically where we're headed; Klein, because she uses facts to do the same; the Pope et al., because they, unlike many U.S. environmentalists, know (and are willing to say it out loud in public) that the rich must make some sacrifices; Dr. Seuss, because he speaks to children; Beavan because he has gone where no 21st century white, middle class man in New York City has ever gone before; Mosley, because he knows that *everyone must be present* at the table, and that systems of justice in communities committed to democracy *can* work, but only if we listen deeply to one another and act in the interests of all.

Librarians could host community conversations aimed at prioritizing needs as society takes on the task of reducing CO_2 emissions to net zero. Creative, life-affirming challenges to curent, mindless consumerism might give everyone the *time* needed for dialogues about what is truly important. Nonviolent actions like boycotts, job sharing, demands for income equalization and full employment in jobs that heal the planet should be considered.

We must choose a peaceful, planned transition in which the needs of all are expressed and play determining roles in decision making. Or the choice that has already been made by elites and experts to continue more-or-less with business-as-usual will drag us all further down the road toward social chaos and environmental collapse.

The big question now for librarianship, indeed for everyone, is—Which side are you on?

Works Cited

Introduction

"About ACRL." Association of College and Research Libraries, 2015. Web. 7 Sept. 2015. http://www.ala.org/acrl/aboutacrl.

"About ALA." American Library Association, 2015. Web. 4 Sept. 2015. http://www.ala.org/aboutala/.

"About ALSC." Association of Library Services to Children, 2015. Web. 4 Sept. 2015. http://www.ala.org/alsc/aboutalsc.

"About YALSA." Young Adult Library Services Association, 2015. Web. 7 Sept. 2015. http://www.ala.org/yalsa/aboutyalsa.

"ALA Committee on Legislation, Charge." American Library Association, 2015. Web. 7 Sept. 2015. http://www.ala.org/groups/committees/ala/ala-lg.

ALA Policy Manual, Section A: Organization and Operational Policies. American Library Association. 27 Jan. 2013. Web. 7 Sept. 2015. http://www.ala.org/aboutala/governance/policymanual/.

Chaplin, Ralph. "Why I Wrote 'Solidarity Forever.'" *Industrial Workers of the World.* n. d. Web. 3 October 2015. http://www.iww.org/history/icons/solidarity_forever/1.

"Committee on Organization, Charge." *American Library Association*, 2015. Web. 7 Sept. 2015. http://www.ala.org/groups/committees/ala/ala-coo.

"Council Composition and Charge." *American Library Association*, 2015. Web. 19 Sept. 2015. http://www.ala.org/aboutala/governance/council.

"Council Roster." *American Library Association*, 2015. Web. 19 Sept. 2015. http://www.ala.org/aboutala/council-roster.

Edwards, Margaret A. *The Fair Garden and the Swarm of Beasts: The Library and the Young Adult.* New York: Hawthorn Books, 1969. Print.

"Gay, Lesbian, Bisexual, and Transgender Round Table." *American Library Association*, 2015. Web. 19 Sept. 2015. http://www.ala.org/glbtrt/.

"Government Documents Round Table, Mission." *American Library Association*, 2015. Web. 7 Sept. 2015. http://www.ala.org/godort/.

"Intellectual Freedom Committee, Charge." *American Library Association*, 2015. Web. 7 Sept. 2015. http://www.ala.org/groups/committees/ala/ala-if.

"International Relations Committee, Charge." *American Library Association*, 2015. Web. 7 Sept. 2015. http://www.ala.org/groups/committees/ala/ala-ir.

Josey, E. J. *The Black Librarian in America.* Metuchen NJ: Scarecrow Press, 1970. Print.

Kagan, Alfred. *Progressive Library Organizations: A Worldwide History.* Jefferson NC: McFarland, 2015. Print.

Leckie, Gloria J., Lisa M. Given, and John E. Buschman. *Critical Theory for Library and Information Science: Exploring the Social from Across the Discipline.* Santa Barbara CA: Libraries Unlimited, 2010. Print

"Our History." *Black Caucus of the American Library Association, Inc.*, 2015. Web. 4 Sept. 2015. http://www.bcala.org/index.php/about-us/our-history.

"PLG's Commitment." *Progressive Librarians Guild*, 2015. Web. 7 Sept. 2015. http://www.progressivelibrariansguild.org/.

Raber, Douglas. "ACONDA and ANACONDA: Social Change, Social Responsibility, and Librarianship." *Library Trends*, vol. 55, no. 3. Winter 2001, p. 675. Print.

Samek, Toni. *Intellectual Freedom and Social Responsibility in American Librarianship, 1967–1974.* Jefferson NC: McFarland, 2001. Print.

"Social Responsibilities Round Table." *American Library Association*, 2015. Web. 7 Sept. 2015. http://www.ala.org/srrt/home.

"Sustainability Round Table." *American Library Association*, 2015. Web. 7 Sept. 2015. http://www.ala.org/sustainrt/.

Chapter 1

Bailey, Tom, et al. "Shockley and Free Speech." *Harvard Crimson.* 6 November 1973. Web. 16 May 2015.

Berry, John N., III. "The Debate Nobody Won." *Library Journal*, 102.14 (Aug. 1977): 1573–1580. Print.

Biblo, Mary. "Re: ALA to screen The Speaker in Las Vegas." Message to alacoun@ala.org. 5 June 2014. E-mail.

"Bill of Rights." *Charters of Freedom.* National Archives. N.d. Web. 3 October 2015. http://www.archives.gov/exhibits/charters/bill_of_rights_transcript.html.

Black Caucus. "Past President Clara Stanton Jones reads the Statement Signed by 25 Members and Endorsed by the Black Caucus of the ALA, p. 25–31." *American Library Association*, 21 July

2014. Web. 3 October 2015. http://www.ala.org/tools/speaker. PDF file.

Cohen, Stanley. *States of Denial: Knowing About Atrocities and Suffering*. Cambridge: Polity, 2001. Print.

Collins, Patricia Hill. *Black Feminist Thought: Knowledge, Consciousness, and the Politics of Empowerment*, 2d ed. New York: Routledge, 2000. Print.

Goldsby, Richard. *Race and Races*. New York: Macmillan, 1977. Print.

Goldsby, Richard. "RE: question re 1976 Mississippi State debate." Message to author. 17 May 2015. E-mail.

Haiman, Franklyn S. "How Much of Our Speech Is Free?" *The Speaker: A Film About Freedom: A Discussion Guide*. Chicago: ALA, 1977. PDF file.

Harvard Black Law Student Association. "Text of Black Law Students' Statement." *Harvard Law Record*, 57.4 (19 October 1973): 9. Print.

Holmes, J. "Abrahms v. United States, Dissenting Opinion." *Legal Information Institute*. 10 November 1919. Web. 3 October 2015. https://www.law.cornell.edu/supremecourt/text/250/616#writing-USSC_CR_0250_0616_ZD.

Honma, Todd. "Trippin' Over the Color Line: The Invisibility of Race in Library and Information Studies." *Interactions: UCLA Journal of Education and Information Studies*, 1.2 (2005): Article 2. Web. 24 Sept. 2015. http://escholarship.org/uc/item/4nj0w1mp.

Horn, Zoia. *Zoia! Memoirs of Zoia Horn, Battler for the People's Right to Know*. Jefferson NC: McFarland, 1995. Print.

Jones, Barbara M. "The Speaker Controversy in the 21st Century." *American Libraries*, 45.6 (June 2014): 13. Print.

Jones, Clara S. "Reflections on *The Speaker*." *Wilson Library Bulletin*, 52 (September 1977): 55. Wilson-Web.

Jones, Clara Stanton. "E. J. Josey: Librarian for All Seasons." *E. J. Josey: An Activist Librarian*, edited by Ismail Abdullahi. Metuchen NJ: Scarecrow Press, 1992. Print.

Josey, E. J., ed. *The Black Librarian in America*. Metuchen NJ: Scarecrow Press, 1970.

Kubitz, Kermit. "Debate on Genetics Cancelled by Forum." *Harvard Law Record*, 57.4 (19 Oct. 1973): 1. Print.

Lincoln, Abraham. "Lincoln-Douglas debates." *Wikipedia*. 22 Sept. 2015. Web. 3 October 2015. http://en.wikipedia.org/wiki/Lincoln%E2%80%93Douglas_debates.

McMullin, Florence, and Judith F. Krug. "Preface." *The Speaker: A Film About Freedom: A Discussion Guide*. Chicago: ALA, 1977. PDF file.

Morehart, Phil, and George M. Eberhart. Resurrecting *The Speaker*. *American Libraries—The Scoop*, 1 July 2014. Blog. 4 Oct. 2015. http://www.americanlibrariesmagazine/blogs/the-scoop/resurrecting-the-speaker.

Offord, Jerome, Jr. "Black Caucus of the ALA Statement on 'The Speaker' Sponsorship." *OIF Blog*. 12 June 2014. Web. 3 October 2015. http://www.oif.ala.org/oif/?p=5028.

Pearson, Lois R. "*The Speaker*: Step or Misstep into Filmmaking?" *American Libraries*, 8.7 (July/Aug. 1977): 371–373. Print.

Reed, Steven. "Princeton Picks Up Harvard Reject." *Harvard Crimson*, 17 Nov. 1973. Web. 16 May 2015.

Sacks, Albert M. "Dean Sacks' Statement on Forum Debate." *Harvard Law Record*, 5.5. (2 Nov. 1973): 13. Print.

Scheurich, James Joseph. *Anti-Racist Scholarship: An Advocacy*. Albany: State University of New York Press, 2002. Print.

Schuman, Patricia Glass. "Resurrecting The Speaker." Message to Karen Downing, forwarded to alacoun@ala.org. 23 May 2014. E-mail.

"Shockley's Rights." Letter to editor. *Harvard Crimson*, 27 Oct. 1973. Web. 16 May 2015.

States, David J. "Shockley's Racism Circus Comes to Yale." *The Crimson*. 23 April 1975. Web. 16 May 2015. http://www.thecrimson.com/article/1975/4/23/shockleyes-racism-circus-come-to-yale.

"Viewing and Speaking About "The Speaker" at ALA Annual Conference." *OIF Blog*, 22 May 2014. Web. 24 Sept. 2015. http://www.oif.ala.org/oif/?p=4985.

Wedgeworth, Robert. "The Seeds of Prosperity: ALA in the 1970s, Part II." *American Libraries*, 34.2 (Feb. 2003): 47–51. Print.

Weker, Jonathan L. "Yale Suspends 11 for Halting Debate for Alleged Role in Shouting Down Shockley." *Harvard Crimson*, 13 May 1974. Web. 16 May 2015. http://www.thecrimson.com/article/1974/5/13/yale-suspends-11-for-halting-debate/.

Chapter 2

"1960 Summer Olympics." *Wikipedia*, 30 Sept. 2015. Web. 19 April 2014. http://en.wikipedia.org/wiki/1960_Summer_Olympics.

AAP Resolution on South Africa, Adopted Unanimously by the AAP Board of Directors, January 14, 1988. Washington, D.C.: Association of American Publishers, 1988. Print.

Africa: Selected Readings. Edited and annotated by Fred Burke. Boston: Houghton Mifflin, 1974. Print.

African National Congress. "Position paper on the Cultural and Academic Boycott Adopted by the National Executive Committee of the ANC, 28 May 1989." *African National Congress*, 2011. N.d. Web. 29 July 2014. http://www.anc.org.za/show.php?id=6870.

American Committee on Africa. "We Say NO to Apartheid: A Declaration of American Artists [1965]." *African Activist Archive*, n.d, Web. 19 April 2014. http://africanactivist.msu.edu/document_metadata.php?objectid=32-130-FC3.

"Anniston Library Desegregates Following Beating of Ministers." *Library Journal*, 88, 1 November 1963. Print.

"Announcements." *American Library Journal*, vol. 1, no. 7, 31 March 1899. New York: F. Leypoldt Publisher.

"Apartheid." *Wikipedia*, 17 April 2014. Web. 19 April 2014. http://en.wikipedia.org/wiki/Apartheid.

Atlanta-Fulton Public Library System. "100 Years of Library Service." N.d. Web. 19 August 2015. http://www.afpls.org/history/166-100-years-of-library-service#top.

Barry, H.D. "Apartheid." *ALA Bulletin*, 58, no. 1. January 1964. Print.

Bartlett, Vernon. *Struggle for Africa*. New York: F. A. Praeger, 1953. Print.

Berman, Sanford. "Getting to It: A Guest Editorial." *American Libraries*, vol. 8, no. 2, February 1977.

Berninghausen, D. K. "Antithesis in Librarianship: Social Responsibility vs. The Library Bill of Rights." *Library Journal*, 97.20 (15 Nov. 1972): 3675–3681. Print.

"Berninghausen Debate." *Library Journal* 98.1 (1 Jan. 1973): 25–41. Print.

Berry, John N., III. "Major Owens." *Library Journal*, 2013. Web. 30 July 2014. http://lj.libraryjournal.com/ 2013/12/opinion/john-berry/major-owens-years-in-politics-but-always-a-librarian-blatantberry/#_.

Blackston, Jeanette. "African American Authors Represented on the ALA Notable, Newbery, and Caldecott Book Lists." *Handbook of Black Librarianship*, 2d edition, edited by E.J. Josey and Marva L. DeLoach. Lanham MD: Scarecrow Press, 2000. Print.

"Canada Lee." *Wikipedia*, n.d. Web. 14 July 2014. http://en.wikipedia.org/wiki/Canada_Lee.

Coan, Stephen (2013) "Acclaimed SA academic's Nazi Secret." *The Witness*. 2013. Web. 20 July 2014. http://www.witness.co.za/index.php?showcontent&global[_id]=101061.

Cockburn, Andrew. "A Loophole in U.S. Sanctions Against Pretoria." *New York Times*, Late Edition (East Coast). 13 Oct. 1986: A19. ProQuest. Web. 4 Oct. 2015.

Cunningham, J. "Negro Segregation." *Library Journal*, 61.13 (July 1936): 515. Print.

Congress of South African Writers. "Fax to Progressive Librarians Guild," 20 June 1990. Courtesy of the University of Illinois Archives. Robert Doyle Papers, 1983–1994, 70/1/22.

"Defiance Campaign." *South African History Online: Towards a People's History*. N.d. Web. 19 April 2014. http://www.sahistory.org.za/topic/defiance-campaign-1952.

Dick, Archie L. *The Hidden History of South Africa's Book and Reading Cultures*. Toronto: University of Toronto Press, 2013. Print.

Dimensions of the Struggle Against Apartheid: A Tribute to Paul Robeson, Held Under the Auspices of the United Nations Special Committee Against Apartheid (10 April 1978). New York: African Heritage Studies Association, 1978. Print.

Doyle, Robert P. "Fact Sheet—South Africa." Chicago: American Library Association, [1989].

"Editorial: ALA and the Segregation Issue." *ALA Bulletin*, 55.6 (June 1961): 485–486. Print.

"Editorial Forum." *Library Journal*, 54.14 (Aug. 1929): 660. Print.

"Editorial Forum." *Library Journal*, 54.22 (15 Dec. 1929): 1028. Print.

Elder, S. "IFLA Comes to the United States." *American Libraries*, 6.2 (1975): 74.

Esquith, Stephen L. *The Political Responsibilities of Everyday Bystanders*. University Park: Pennsylvania State University Press, 2010. Print.

Goodman, Jordan. *Paul Robeson: A Watched Man*. London: Verso Press, 2013. Print.

"Grace South African plants may cost Baker & Taylor." *American Libraries*, 17.10 (Nov. 1986). JSTOR, Web. 20 July 2014.

"Guidelines for Librarians Interacting with South Africa." *SRRT Newsletter*, 93 (Sept. 1989): 7–9. Print.

Handbook of Black Librarianship, 2d ed. Edited by E. J. Josey and Marva L. DeLoach. Lanham MD: Scarecrow Press, 2000. Print.

Hanlon, Joseph, and Roger Omond. *The Sanctions Handbook: For or Against?* Harmondsworth, UK: Penguin, 1987. Print.

"Houston Exempts Library from South Africa Ban." *American Libraries*, 18.11 (Dec. 1987). JSTOR. Web. 20 July 2014.

Intellectual Freedom Committee. "Minutes, 1990 Midwinter Meeting, Chicago." Courtesy of the University of Illinois Archives. Robert Doyle Papers, 1983–1994, 70/1/22.

International Federation of Library Associations. "IFLA Executive Board, Brussels, December 18–20, 1973, Summary report." *IFLA News*, 47 (Feb. 1973). Print.

International Federation of Library Associations. "Summary Report of the Meeting of the Executive Board Held in the National Diet Library, Tokyo, May 27–30, 1974." *IFLA News*, 49 (Aug. 1974). Print.

Kagan, Alfred. "An Alternative View on IFLA, Human Rights, and the Social Responsibility of International Librarianship." *IFLA Journal*, 34.3. (Oct. 2008). Print.

Kagan, Alfred. *Progressive Library Organizations: A Worldwide History*. Jefferson NC: McFarland, 2015.

Kgositsile, Keorapetse W. "To Fanon." *A Broadside Treasury*, edited by Gwendolyn Brooks. Detroit: Broadside Press, 1971. Print.

Kolbe, V. S. Letter to John Bruce Howell and Alfred Kagan, 7 June 1990. Photocopy. Courtesy of the University of Illinois Archives. Robert Doyle Papers, 1983–1994, 70/1/22.

Liebaers, Herman. "From the President." *IFLA News*, 39 (Feb. 1972). Print.

Liebaers, Herman. "IFLA's Answer to UNESCO's Director General about the inquires on the activities of its branch in South Africa with regard to apartheid." *IFLA News*, 40 (May 1972). Print.

Liebaers, Herman. "The Dutch Tea Party of IFLA in the Seventies—a quick flack back of forty five years before the Dutch Tea Party." 68th IFLA Council and General Conference, August 18–24, 2002. *IFLA—History*. Web. 20 July 2014.

Luthuli, A. J. *Let My People Go*. New York: McGraw-Hill, 1962. Print.

Malan, Rian. *The Lion Sleeps Tonight: And Other Stories of Africa*. New York: Grove, 2012. Print.

Marquess, Eliza Bruckner. "Understanding America's Race Problem. " *Library Journal*, 69. 5 (1 Sept. 1944). Print.

McElfresh, Mona Harrop. "To Secure These Rights Governments Are Instituted Among Men." *ALA Bulletin*, 42,2 (Feb. 1948): 74–75. Print.

"Members reject free-access document as aiding apartheid." *American Libraries*, 18.7 (Jul–Aug. 1987). JSTOR. Web. 20 July 2014.

Mezerik, A.G., editor. *Apartheid in the Republic of South Africa: Bantustans—Boycotts—UN Action*. New York: International Review Service: Analysis and Review of International Problems, 1964. Print.

Nixon, Rob. *Homelands, Harlem and Hollywood: South African Culture and the World Beyond*. New York: Routledge, 1994. Print.

"Notable Books of 1953." *ALA Bulletin*, 48, 3 (Mar. 1954). Print.

Owens, Major R. "American Library Association Guidelines on South Africa." *Congressional Record—Extensions of Remarks, 17 Nov. 1989*. Washington, D.C.: U.S. Government Printing Office, 1989. Print.

"Position Paper on the Cultural and Academic Boycott, adopted by the National Executive Committee of the African National Congress, Lusaka, May 1989." (2011). *African National Congress: South Africa's National Liberation Movement*, 2011. Web. 21 Aug. 2015. http://www.anc.org.za/show.php?id=6870.

Progressive Librarian. Libraries and Sanctions: A Special Issue on South Africa. New York: Progressive Librarians Guild, 1990. Print.

Proudfoot, Merrill. "Censorship Noose Tightens Around Librarians in South Africa." *American Libraries*, 6.8 (Sept. 1975). JSTOR. Web. 24 June 2014.

"Race Relations Honor Roll for 1942." *Library Journal*, 68.5 (Mar. 1943).

Ranganathan, S. R. "IFLA: What It Should Be and Do." *Libri: International Journal of Libraries & Information Services*, 5.2 (1954): 182–189. Print.

Reeves, Ambrose. *Shooting at Sharpeville: The Agony of South Africa*. Boston: Houghton Mifflin Co., 1961. Print.

"Resolution: Access/South Africa, MBRN#8, 1987." Photocopy. Courtesy of the University of Illinois Archives. Robert Doyle Papers, 1983–1994, 70/1/22.

"S. African Library Association Affirms Support of Apartheid." *Library Journal (1876)*, 88 (1 Nov. 1963): 4180. Library and Information Science Source. Web. 3 Oct. 2015.

Seidman, Ann and Neva (1978). *South Africa and U.S. Multinational Corporations*. Westport CT: Lawrence Hill, 1978. Print.

Shearar, Jeremy. *Against the World: South Africa and Human Rights at the United Nations, 1945–1961*. Pretoria: UNISA Press, 2011. Print.

Sink, Bob. "Ernestine Rose (1880–1961)." *NYPL Librarians* [Blog]. March 19, 2011. Web. 19 August 2015. http://nypl-librarians.blogspot.com/2011/03/ernestine-rose-1880-1961.html.

Snow, E. N. "A Suggestion." *Bulletin of the American Library Association*, 30.7 (1936): 571. Print.

"South African Librarians Renounce Apartheid." *American Libraries*, 11 (Apr. 1980). Print.

The Starvation of Young Black Minds: The Effect of Book Boycotts in South Africa, Report of a Fact-Finding Mission to South Africa—May 18–28, 1989. [New York:] Association of American Publishers and the Fund for Free Expression. Print. Courtesy of Al Kagan.

Steyn, Carol. *The Medieval & Renaissance Manuscripts of the Grey Collection Catalogued*. Art Historical Work Group of South Africa, 2010. Print.

Swan, John, and Noel Peattie. *The Freedom to Lie: A Debate about Democracy*. Jefferson NC: McFarland, 1989. Print.

Thomison, Dennis. *A History of the American Library Association, 1876–1972*. Chicago: American Library Association, 1978. Print.

UNESCO, Executive Board. "Resolutions and Decisions Adopted by the Executive Board at its 88th Session (Paris, 6 October–2 November 1971)." 88/EX/Decisions 6.5. p. 30–40. Print.

United States, Department of State Archive. "The End of Apartheid." N.d. Web. 29 July 2014. http://2001-2009.state.gov/r/pa/ho/time/pcw/98678.htm.

Yust, William F. (1913). "What of the black and yellow races?" *Bulletin of the American Library Association*, 7.4. (1913): 158–170. JSTOR. Web. 24 June 2014. http://www.jstor.org/stable/25685168.

Chapter 3

"ALA Council Voting Record, 1992 Annual Conference." *American Libraries* (Oct. 1993): 857–8. Print.

"ALA Council Voting Record, 1993 Midwinter Meeting." *American Libraries* (Oct. 1993): 853–4. Print.

Abdulhadi, Rabab. "Activism and Exile: Palestinianness and the Politics of Solidarity" in *Local Actions: Cultural Activism, Power, and Public Life in America*, edited by Melissa Checker and Maggie Fishman. New York: Columbia University Press, 2004. Print.

Action Council, Social Responsibilities Round Table. "Draft Resolution on Israeli Censorship." *SRRT Newsletter*, 103 (Mar. 1992): 3–4.

Action Council, Social Responsibilities Round Table. "On Israeli Censorship." *SRRT Newsletter*, 105 (Sept. 1992): 2–3.

Action Council, Social Responsibilities Round Table. "On Omar al-Safi." *SRRT Newsletter*, 105 (Sept. 1992): 4.

American-Arab Anti-Discrimination Committee. *The Bitter Year: Arabs Under Israeli Occupation in 1982*. Washington, D.C.: American-Arab Anti-Discrimination Committee, 1983. Print.

American Library Association. "Reaffirmation of Freedom of Expression of Foreign, Nationals. adopted by the ALA Council, June 27, 1984 at Dallas." Photocopy. Courtesy of the University of Illinois Archives. Robert Doyle Papers, 1983–1994, 70/1/22.

Anti-Defamation League. "About the ADL." *Anti-Defamation League*, n.d. Web. 1 September 2014. http://www.adl.org/about-adl/.

Article 19. *Information Freedom and Censorship: World Report 1991*. Chicago: American Library Association, 1991. Print.

Bennoune, Karima. *Israeli Censorship in the Occupied Territories (Preliminary Report)*. Chicago: DataBase Project on Palestinian Human Rights, 1990. Print.

Benvenisti, Meron. *Israeli Censorship of Arab Publications*. New York: Fund for Free Expression, 1983. Print.

Berman, Sanford. Letter to Editor. *American Libraries*, 23.5 (May 1992): 363. Print.

The Bitter Year: Arabs Under Israeli Occupation in 1982. Washington, D.C.: American-Arab Anti-Discrimination Committee, 1983. Print.

Blankfort, Jeffrey. "An Act of Censorship: American Library Association Becomes Another Israeli Occupied Territory." *JR's Rare Books and Commentary*. N.d. Web. 30 November 2014. http://www.jrbooksonline.com/adl/adl/adl-controls-american-library-association.htm.

Boyle, Kevin, ed. *World Report 1988: Article 19 Information, Freedom, and Censorship*. Burnt Mill, Essex, UK: Longman, 1988. Print.

Brenner, Lenni. *Zionism in the Age of the Dictators*. Westport CT: Lawrence Hill, 1983. Print.

Chandler, Adam L. "American Library Association Buries Israel Censorship Issue." *Washington Report on Middle East Affairs*, Sept/Oct 1994. Web. 17 August 2014. http://www.wrmea.org/1994-september-october/pro-israel-mccarthyism-american-library-association-buries-israel-censorship-issue.html.

Chomsky, Noam. *The Fateful Triangle: The United States, Israel, and the Palestinians*. Boston: South End, 1983. Print.

Claiborne, William. "Israel Penalizes Reporter for Violating Censorship." *Washington Post*, 25 February 1980. A7. Proquest. Web. 17 August 2014.

Council, American Library Association (1974). Policy on Abridgment of the Rights of Freedom of Expression of Foreign Nationals, July 12. Courtesy of the University of Illinois Archives. Robert Doyle Papers, 1983–1994, 70/1/22.

Council, American Library Association. "Implementation Report," [1991]. Courtesy of the University of Illinois Archives. Robert Doyle Papers, 1983–1994, 70/1/22.

Council, American Library Association (1992a). Resolution on Israeli Censorship, July 1. Courtesy of the University of Illinois Archives. Robert Doyle Papers, 1983–1994, 70/1/22.

Council, American Library Association (1992b). Resolution on the Deportation of Bir Zeit University Librarian Omar al-Safi, July 1. Courtesy of the University of Illinois Archives. Robert Doyle Papers, 1983–1994, 70/1/22.

Doyle, Robert P. "Fact Sheet: Israeli Censorship Controversy." Chicago: ALA, 1993. Photocopy. Courtesy of the University of Illinois Archives. Robert Doyle Papers, 1983–1994, 70/1/22.

Elizur, Yuval. "Wider Censorship Sought in Israel." *Washington Post* (19 Jan. 1976): A12. *Proquest*. Web.

Fine, Sara. Correspondence to E. J. Josey, 17 May 1990. Photocopy. Courtesy of the University of Illinois Archives. Robert Doyle Papers, 1983–1994, 70/1/22.

Flagg, Gordon, et al. "ALA's 112th Annual Conference: Upbeat and Hopeful in New Orleans." *American Libraries* (Jul/Aug. 1993): 613+. *Academic OneFile*. Web. 6 Dec. 2014.

Friedman, Robert I. "Israeli Censorship of the Palestinian Press." *Journal of Palestine Studies*, 13.1 (Autumn 1983): 93–101. Print.

Friedman, Robert I. "The Jewish Thought Police: How the Anti-Defamation League Censors Books, Intimidates Librarians, and Spies on Citizens." *Village Voice* (27 July 1993): 33–39. *ProQuest*. Web. 5 Aug. 2014.

Greenberg, J. L. Letter to Peggy Sullivan, Executive Director, ALA (13 Jan. 1993). Courtesy of the University of Illinois Archives. Robert Doyle Papers, 1983–1994, 70/1/22.

Hansen, Allen C. *USIA: Public Diplomacy in the Computer Age*, 2d edition. New York: Praeger, 1989. Print.

Henry, William A., III, and Leroy Aarons. "A Double Standard for Israel?" *Time*, 120.2 (1982): 85. *Academic Search Complete*. Web. 5 August 2014.

Horn, Zoia. "Why Doesn't ALA Act on Israeli Censorship?" *American Libraries*, 23 (Jan. 1992): 92. *Library and Information Science Sources*. Web. 3 Oct. 2015.

John, Nancy. "Summary for the ALA Executive Board, ALA International Relations Committee, Fall Orientation/Planning Meeting, Saturday, October 17, 1992." Photocopy. Courtesy of the University of Illinois Archives. Robert Doyle Papers, 1983–1994, 70/1/22.

Kniffel, Leonard. "Not the Big One: ALA's 111th Annual Conference." *American Libraries*, 23.7 (Jul/Aug. 1992): 554–564. *Library and Information Science Sources*. Web. 3 Oct. 2015.

Kniffel, Leonard. "Spending Dollars, Making Sense: The Executive Board's Autumn Effort." *American Libraries*, 23.11 (Dec. 1992): 963–967. *Library and Information Science Sources*. 3 Oct. 2015.

Lewis, Anthony. "Looking the Other Way." *New York Times* (15 Mar. 1982): A17. *New York Times Historical*. Web. 15 Nov. 2014.

Long, James M. "Israel Masks 'Foreign Legion.'" *Washington Post* (6 Feb. 1949): B2. *ProQuest Historical Newspapers: Washington Post (1877–1997)*. 15 Nov. 2014.

Masalha, Nur. *The Palestine Nakba: Decolonizing History, Narrating the Subaltern, Reclaiming Memory*. London: Zed Books, 2012. Print.

Oberdorfer, Don. "U.S. to Remain Out of UNESCO: Mismanagement, Bias Cited." *Washington Post* (18 Apr. 1990): A28. Courtesy of the University of Illinois Archives. Robert Doyle Papers, 1983–1994, 70/1/22.

Powell, Faye (1992). "Letter to Editor." *American Libraries* (Jul/Aug. 1992): 552. Print.

"Presidential Special Task Force on the Conduct of Meetings and ALA Values." *ALA Council Document #62, 1992-93*. Photocopy. Courtesy of the University of Illinois Archives. Robert Doyle Papers, 1983–1994, 70/1/22.

"Resolution on David Langlois Williams and His Position Within the Social Responsibilities Round Table of ALA," *SRRT Newsletter*, 113 (Sept. 1994): 4. Print.

"Resolution on Israeli Censorship." *SRRT Newsletter*, 96 (June 1990): 2–3. Print.

"Resolution on the Task Force on Israeli Censorship and Palestinian Libraries." *SRRT Newsletter*, 109 (Sept. 1993): 7. Print.

Rodinson, Maxime. *Israel and the Arabs*. Translated from the French by Michael Perl. Harmondsworth, UK: Penguin Books, 1970.

Rogoff, Shulamit. Letter to Peggy Sullivan [Executive Director], ALA. December 28, 1992. Photocopy. Courtesy of the University of Illinois Archives. Robert Doyle Papers, 1983–1994, 70/1/22.

Rokach, Livia. *Israel's Sacred Terrorism: A Study Based on Moshe Sharett's Personal Diary and Other Documents*. Belmont MA: Association of Arab-American University Graduates, 1980. AAUG Information Paper Series: No. 23. Print.

Said, Edward. *After the Last Sky: Palestinian Lives*. New York: Pantheon, 1986. Print.

Selfa, Lance. *The Struggle for Palestine*. Chicago: Haymarket Books, 2002. Print.

Silver, Matthew M. *Our Exodus : Leon Uris and the Americanization of Israel's Founding Story*. Detroit: Wayne State University Press, 2010. Print.

Stillwell, Stephen. "From the Coordinator." *SRRT Newsletter*, 117 (Sept. 1995): 1. Print.

Stillwell, Stephen. "Israeli Censorship Issue, Updated: A Message from the Coordinator." *SRRT Newsletter*, 111 (Mar. 1994): 6. Print.

Sullivan, Peggy. Memo dated 19 January 1993, to ALA Council Members (1992–93), re: Resolution on Israeli Censorship and the Resolution on the Deportation of Bir Zeit University Librarian Omar Al-Safi. Photocopy. Courtesy of the University of Illinois Archives. Robert Doyle Papers, 1983–1994, 70/1/22.

Timerman, Jacobo. *The Longest War: Israel in Lebanon*. Translated from the Spanish by Miguel Acoca. New York: Alfred A. Knopf, 1982. Print.

Turki, Fawaz. *The Disinherited: Journal of a Palestinian Exile*. New York: Monthly Review Press, 1972.

Wackerman, Ellie, et al. Letter to Marilyn L. Miller, President, ALA, 16 June 1993. Photocopy. Courtesy of the University of Illinois Archives. Robert Doyle Papers, 1983–1994, 70/1/22.

Warren, James. "Activist librarian: David Williams Bites the Hand That Feeds Him and a Good Many Others Too." *Chicago Tribune* (Aug. 22. 1993): 5.2. Photocopy. Courtesy of the University of Illinois Archives. Robert Doyle Papers, 1983–1994, 70/1/22.

"United States Information Agency." *Wikipedia*. 5 Nov. 2014. Web. 27 Nov. 2014. http://en.wikipedia.org/wiki/United_States_Information_Agency

Williams, David. Letter to E. J. Josey, 27 December 1989. Courtesy of the University of Illinois Archives. Robert Doyle Papers, 1983–1994, 70/1/22.

Williams, David. "Israeli Censorship Issue at ALA." *SRRT Newsletter*, 97 (Sept. 1990): 5–6. Print.

Williams, David. "International Human Rights Task Force." *SRRT Newsletter*, 99 (March 1991): 2–3. Print.

Williams, David. "International Human Rights Task Force." *SRRT Newsletter*, 100 (June 1991): 3–4. Print.

Williams, David. "International Human Rights." *SRRT Newsletter*, 102 (Dec. 1991): 3. Print.

Williams, David. "ALA Goes on Record Against Israeli Censorship," *SRRT Newsletter*, 105 (Sept. 1992): 7–8. Print.

Williams, David. "Israeli Censorship Issue Revisited." *SRRT Newsletter*, 109 (Sept. 1993): 7–9. Print.

Yizhar, S. *Hirbet Hizah* [1949] quoted in *Our Exodus: Leon Uris and the Americanization of Israel's Founding Story*, by Matthew M. Silver. Detroit: Wayne State University Press, 2010. Print.

Zyroff, Ellen. Letter to Hardy Franklin, President Elect, ALA, 1 June 1993. Photocopy. Courtesy of the University of Illinois Archives. Robert Doyle Papers, 1983–1994, 70/1/22.

Chapter 4

"The Abusers, State-by-State." *Washington Times* (20 May 1991). *NewsBank Database*. Web. 14 Feb. 2015.

ALA Organizational Self Study Committee. Memo to ALA Council, Phase I Report, 9 June 1994. Photocopy. Courtesy of the American Library Association Archives at the University of Illinois. Record Series 1/1/1.

"ALSC Advisory Committee to the Boy Scouts of America." American Library Association, Council Document 56 (2 June 1994). Photocopy. Courtesy of the American Library Association Archives at the University of Illinois. Record Series 24/2/6.

Association of Library Services to Children (1992a). Minutes. Board of Directors, 1992 Midwinter Meeting. Courtesy of the American Library Association Archives at the University of Illinois. Record Series 24/1/1.

Association of Library Services to Children (1992b). Minutes. Board of Directors, 1992 Annual Meeting. Courtesy of the American Library Association Archives at the University of Illinois. Record Series 24/1/1.

Association of Library Services to Children (1993). Minutes. Board of Directors, 1992 Midwinter Meeting. Courtesy of the American Library Association Archives at the University of Illinois. Record Series 24/1/1.

Association of Library Services to Children (1994). Major Actions of the ALSC Board, 1993 Annual Conference Highlights. Courtesy of the American Library Association Archives at the University of Illinois. Record Series 24/1/1.

Baden-Powell, Robert. *Scouting for Boys: The Original 1908 Edition*. Cambridge, UK: Oxford University Press, 2004. Print.

Barron, James. "Will Hire: Scouts Affiliate in City Defies Ban on Gays." *New York Times*, Late Edition (East Coast). 3 Apr. 2015. *ProQuest*. Web. 3 Oct. 2015.

Berry, John N., III (1993). "Wasteful Efforts at ALA Midwinter." *Library Journal*, 118. 3. (15 Feb. 1993): 104. Print.

Berry, John N., III (1998). "Boy Scout Values." *Library Journal*, 123.17 (15 Oct. 1998): 6. *Library and Information Science Sources*. Web. 3 Oct. 2015.

Boy Scout Handbook, 7th ed. New Brunswick NJ: Boy Scouts of America, 1966. Print.

Boy Scout Handbook, 11th ed. Irving TX: Boy Scouts of America, 1998. Print.

Boy Scouts Honor ALA. *ALA Bulletin*, 55. 2 (Feb. 1961): 197. *Library and Information Science Sources*. Web. 3 Oct. 2015.

"Boy Scouts of America Amend Adult Leadership Policy." (2015). *Boy Scouts of America*. Scouting Newsroom Blog. 27 July 27 2015. Web. 30 August 2015. http://scoutingnewsroom.org/blog/boy-scouts-of-america-amends-adult-leadership-policy/.

Caywood, Carolyn (1998). "Learning Experiences." *School Library Journal*, 44.12 (Dec. 1998): 49. *Library and Information Science Sources*. Web. 3 Oct. 2015.

Committee on Organization. "Report to Council, 1994 Annual Conference, Miami Beach. 1993–94 CD#22.1." American Library Association. Courtesy of the American Library Association Archives at the University of Illinois. Record Series 1/1/1.

"Council Minutes, 1993 Midwinter Meeting." American Library Association (Jan. 1993): 38. Courtesy of the American Library Association Archives at the University of Illinois. Record Series 1/1/1.

"Council Minutes 1994 Midwinter Meeting." (1994a). American Library Association (4–10 Feb. 1994). Courtesy of the American Library Association Archives at the University of Illinois. Record Series 1/1/1.

"Council Minutes 1994 Annual Conference." (1994b). American Library Association (23–30 June 1994). Photocopy. Courtesy of the American Library Association Archives at the University of Illinois. Record Series 1/1/1.

"Council Minutes, 1998 Annual Conference." American Library Association (25 June–1 July 1998): 9. Courtesy of the American Library Association Archives at the University of Illinois. Record Series 1/1/1.

"Council Minutes, 1999 Midwinter Meeting." American Library Association (29 Jan.–3 Feb. 1999): 15–16, 28–29. Courtesy of the American Library Association Archives at the University of Illinois. Record Series 1/1/1.

Duberman, Martin. *The Martin Duberman Reader: The Essential Historical, Biographical, and Autobiographical Writings*. New York: New Press, 2013. Print.

Flagg, Gordon. "A Dangerous Liaison?" *American Libraries*, 29.6 (June/July 1998): 88. *Library and Information Science Sources*. Web. 3 Oct. 2015.

Garrison, Paul E. "Library Outreach to the Boy Scouts." *American Libraries*, 17 (Feb. 1986): 140–141. Print.

Gaughan, Thomas M. "The Last Socially Acceptable Prejudice." *American Libraries*, 23 (Sept. 1992): 612. *Library and Information Science Sources*. Web. 3 Oct. 2015.

Gerhardt, Lillian. "A Rocky Time in Denver." *School Library Journal*, 39.3 (March 1993): 124–129. Print.

Giroux, Henry A. "The Plague of American Authoritarianism." *TruthDig*, 24 Aug. 2015. Web. 25 August 2015. http://www.truthdig.com/report/item/the_plague_of_american_authoritarianism_20150824.

"'Good Book Week'—What It Is." *The Publishers' Weekly*, 90.16 (14 Oct. 1916): 1273–1274. Print.

Gordon, Ruth I. Letter to Anitra Steele (8 Feb. 1988): 1. Photocopy. Record Series 24/2/6, Courtesy of the American Library Association Archives at the University of Illinois.

Handbook for Boys, 5th ed. New Brunswick, NJ: National Council, Boy Scouts of America, 1955. Print.

Hurt, Huber Williams. "The Library and Boy Scouts." *ALA Bulletin*, 33.10 (Oct. 1939): 688. Print.

Jenkins, Christine. "1985 Gay Book Award for *Another Mother Tongue: Gay Words, Gay Worlds." *SRRT Newsletter*, 79 (March 1986): 4. Print.

Kniffel, Leonard. "ALA Council Actions." *American Libraries*, 26.7 (July/Aug. 1995): 676–679. Print.

Kniffel, Leonard. "ALA Council: Postponements, Referrals, Routines Outpace Actions." *American Libraries*, 29.7 (Aug. 1998): 96–98. Print.

Larson, John W. Letter to Susan Roman, Executive Director, ALSC, May 17, 1988. Photocopy. Courtesy of the American Library Association Archives at the University of Illinois. Record Series 24/2/6.

Interpretations of the *Library Bill of Rights*. American Library Association, 2 July 2008. Web. 23 Sept. 2015. http://www.ala.org/advocacy/intfreedom/librarybill/interpretations/accesslibrary.

Manual for Chaplain Aides and Chaplains. "Declaration of Religious Principle." *Boy Scouts of America*, 2015. Web. 29 Aug. 2015. http://www.scouting.org/scoutsource/Media/Relationships/ManualforChaplainsandAides.aspx.

Mathiews, Franklin K. "Books as Merchandise and Something More." *The Publishers' Weekly*, 15 May 1915. Print.

Mathiews, Franklin K., ed. *The Boy Scouts Yearbook*. New York: D. Appleton, 1932. Print.

Newman, Lesléa. "The More Things Change..." *Publishers Weekly*, 19 Oct. 2009. Print.

Olson, Reneé. "Debate Reignites Over Link to Boy Scouts." *School Library Journal*, 44/5, May 1998. Print.

"On Corporate Sponsorship Issues." *SRRT Newsletter*, 107 (March 1993): 3–4. Print.

"Remarks by ALA President Marilyn Miller at the Beginning of the Rally Protesting Colorado Amendment 2, 25 January 1993." *SRRT Newsletter*, 107 (March 1993): 3. Print.

Rockefeller, John D., Jr. "Character and Business," in *The Boy Scouts Yearbook*, edited by Franklin K. Mathiews. New York: D. Appleton, 1932.

Roman, Susan. Memo to Mary Ghikas, 5 June 1998. "RE: ALSC and the Boy Scouts." Photocopy. Courtesy of the American Library Association Archives at the University of Illinois. Record Series 24/2/6.

Rosenthal, Michael. *The Character Factory: Baden-Powell and the Origins of the Boy Scout Movement*. New York: Pantheon Books, 1986.

Rosenzweig, Mark (2001). "Many Voices, One goal: note towards a critique of the 'One Voice' policy for ALA." *SRRT Newsletter*, 135 (May 2001). Web. 29 Aug. 2015. http://www.libr.org/srrt/news/srrt135.pdf.

Schuster, S. L. *Love Is for All*. Mountlake Terrace WA: Schuster-Isaacson Family Productions, 1974.

"SRRT, ALSC, and the Boy Scouts." *SRRT Newsletter*, 113 (Sept. 1994): 7–8. Print.

Scout Field Book. New York: Boy Scouts of America, 1948: 464.

Sokol, Chris. "Review, The Bread Book." *SRRT Newsletter*, 102 (Dec. 1991): 11. Print.

St. Lifer, Evan. "Fostering External Relationships." *Library Journal*, 123.10 (1 June 1998): 12–13. Print.

Steele, Anitra T. Letter to Committee Members, May 16, 1988. Photocopy. Courtesy of the American Library Association Archives at the University of Illinois. Record Series 24/2/6.

Steele, Anitra T. Memo to ALSC Organization and Bylaws Committee, June 28, 1988. Photocopy. Courtesy of the American Library Association Archives at the University of Illinois. Record Series 24/2/6.

Stillwell, Stephen J., Jr. "From the Coordinator." *SRRT Newsletter*, 109 (Sept. 1993): 1. Print.

Stillwell, Stephen J., Jr. "From the Coordinator." *SRRT Newsletter*, 113 (Sept. 1994): 1–2. Print.

Together Is Better... Let's Read—American Library Association National Reading Program, Program Guide Chicago: American Library Association, 1992. Photocopy. Courtesy of the American Library Association Archives at the University of Illinois. Record Series, 12/1/10.

"Voting Record, 1993 Midwinter Meeting." *American Libraries*, 24.9 (Oct. 1993): 849–860. Print.

"Voting Record, 1994 Annual Conference." American Library Association. Photocopy. Courtesy of the American Library Association Archives at the University of Illinois. Record Series 1/1/1.

West, James E. and William Hillcourt. *Scout Field Book*. New Brunswick NJ: National Council, Boy Scouts of America, 1954. Print.

"When Sex is the Question." *SRRT Newsletter*, 105 (Sept. 1992): 9. Print.

Wiegand, Wayne. "This Month, 10 Years Ago." *American Libraries*, 33.7 (Aug. 2002): 104. Print.

Whitwell, Stuart C. A. "This Is Not Going to Be Easy." *American Libraries*, 26.7 (July/Aug. 1995): 689–692. Print.

"Young Adult Library Services Association." *School Library Journal*, 39.3 (Mar. 1993): 128–129. Print.

Young, Gay & Proud! Boston: Alyson, 1980. Print.

Chapter 5

ALA Policy Manual. American Library Association, 10 Aug. 2010. Web. 14 April 2014. http://www.ala.org/aboutala/governance/policymanual.

American Library Association. "40.2 Code of Professional Ethics for Librarians." *ALA Handbook of Organization 2008-2009: An Annual Guide to Member Participation*. Chicago: ALA, 1995. Print.

Bok, Sissela. *Secrets: On the Ethics of Concealment and Revelation*. New York: Pantheon, 1982. Print.

"Charters of Freedom, Bill of Rights." *National Archives and Records Administration*. N.d. Web. 19 Sept. 2015. http://www.archives.gov/exhibits/charters/bill_of_rights_transcript.html.

Chomsky, Noam. *Pirates and Emperors, Old and New: International Terrorism in the Real World*, new edition. Cambridge MA: South End, 2002. Print.

Cole, David. "Can Privacy Be Saved?" *New York Review of Books*, 6 March 2014. Web. 4 Oct. 2015.

http://www.nybooks.com/articles/archives/2014/mar/06/can-privacy-be-saved/

Committee on Legislation (2004). "Resolution on Securing Government Accountability through Whistleblower Protection." *American Library Association*, 2004. Web. 26 May 2014. http://www.ala.org/offices/sites/ala.org.offices/files/content/wo/reference/colresolutions/PDF/000002-CD20.7.pdf.

Council I. Audio recording of meeting on 30 June 2013. *American Library Association*, 2013. Web. 14 April 2014. http://www.ala.org/aboutala/governance/council/councilaudio. MP3.

Council II. Audio recording of meeting on 1 July 2013. *American Library Association*, 2013. Web. 14 April 2014. http://www.ala.org/aboutala/governance/council/councilaudio. MP3.

Council III. Audio recording of meeting on 2 July 2013. *American Library Association*, 2013. Web. 14 April 2014. http://www.ala.org/aboutala/governance/council/councilaudio. MP3.

Dash, Samuel. *The Intruders: Unreasonable Searches and Seizures from King John to John Ashcroft*. New Brunswick NJ: Rutgers University Press, 2004. Print.

Eisler, Peter, and Susan Page. "3 NSA Veterans Speak Out on Whistle-Blower: We Told You So." *USA Today*. 16 June 2013. Web. 14 April 2014. http://www.usatoday.com/story/news/politics/2013/06/16/snowden-whistleblower-nsa-officials-roundtable/2428809/.

Esquith, Stephen L. *The Political Responsibilities of Everyday Bystanders*. University Park: Pennsylvania State University Press, 2010. Print.

Gellman, Barton, and Laura Poitras. "U.S., British Intelligence Mining Data from Nine U.S. Internet Companies in Broad Secret Program." *Washington Post*. 6 June 2013. Web. 14 April 2014.

Government Accountability Project (2013) "GAP Statement on Edward Snowden and NSA Domestic Surveillance." *GAP Government Accountability Project: Truth be told*. N.d. Web. 14 April 2014. http://www.whistleblower.org/press/gap-statement-edward-snowden-and-nsa-domestic-surveillance.

Greenwald, Glen, et al. (2013a) "Edward Snowden: The Whistleblower Behind the NSA Surveillance Revelations." *Guardian*, 9 June 2013. Web. 5 Nov. 2013.

Harger, Elaine. "Abandoning Snowden…and Privacy? Hegemony at Play in ALA." *Progressive Librarian*, 42, Summer 2014. Print.

Horn, Zoia. *Zoia! Memoirs of Zoia Horn, Battler for the People's Right to Know*. Jefferson NC: McFarland, 1995. Print.

Kagan, Al. "SRRT Councilor Report." *SRRT Newsletter*, 184. September 2013. Web. 20 Sept. 2015. http://libr.org/srrt/news/srrt184.php.

Kranich, Nancy. "Smart Voting Starts at Your Library." *Libraries: the cornerstone of democracy—Presidential Initiative*. American Library Association, 2000. Web. 14 April 2014. http://www.ala.org/aboutala/governance/officers/past/kranich/demo.

Office of Intellectual Freedom. "Resolution on the Need for Reforms for the Intelligence Community to Support Privacy, Open Government, Government Transparency, and Accountability." *American Library Association*. 2013. Web. 30 Sept. 2013. http://www.oif.ala.org/oif/?p=4803.

Polletta, Francesca. *Freedom Is an Endless Meeting: Democracy in American Social Movements*. Chicago: University of Chicago Press. 2002. Print.

Raber, Douglas. "ACONDA and ANACONDA: Social Change, Social Responsibility, and Librarianship." *Library Trends*, vol. 55, no. 3 (Winter 2001): 675. Print.

Resolution in Support of Whistleblower Edward Snowden." *American Library Association*. 29 June 2013. Web. 3 Oct. 2015. PDF file. http://www.ala.org/aboutala/sites/ala.org.aboutala/files/content/governance/council/council_documents/2013_annual_council_docs/cd_39_edward_snowden-%28ff%29.pdf.

Scott, Shane. "Leaker Charged with Violating Espionage Act." *New York Times*, Late Edition (East Coast) ed. 22 June 2013. ProQuest. Web. 12 Apr. 2014.

Sennett, Richard. *Authority*. New York: W. W. Norton, 1993, c1980. Print.

United for Libraries (2011) "Sample Whistle Blower Policy." *Sample Policies for Trustees. American Library Association*, 12 Dec. 2011. Web. 29 Sept. 2013. www.ala.org/united/sites/ala.org.united/files/content/trustees/orgtools/policies/whistleblower.doc.

Whistleblowing. "Poster of United States Office of Special Counsel." *Wikipedia*, 2013. Web. 9 Nov. 2013. http://en.wikipedia.org/wiki/File:Whistleblowing.pdf.

Chapter 6

Antonelli, Monika, and Mark McCullough, eds. *Greening Libraries*. Los Angeles: Library Juice Press, 2012.

Atwood, Margaret. *MaddAddam Trilogy: Oryx and Crake* (2003), *The Year of the Flood* (2009, MaddAddam* (2013). New York: Doubleday.

Bagley, Katherine. "New Study Says Even 2 Degrees of Warming 'Highly Dangerous.'" *Inside Climate News*. 21 July 2015. Web. 25 August 2015. http://insideclimatenews.org/news/21072015/new-study-says-even-2-degrees-warming-highly-dangerous.

Beavan, Colin. *No Impact Man: The Adventures of a Guilty Liberal Who Attempts to Save the Planet, and the Discoveries He Makes About Himself and Our Way of Life in the Precess*. New York: Picador, 2009.

Brown Donald A. *Climate Change Ethics: Navigat-*

ing the Perfect Moral Storm. London: Routledge, 2013. Print.

Budget Analysis and Review Committee. "Divesting Fossil Fuel Holdings in the ALA Endowment Fund." *American Library Association*. 22 May 2013. Photocopy.

Carson, Rachel. "Humbling the Human," excerpt from *Silent Spring*, quoted in *The Green Reader: Essays Toward a Sustainable Society*, edited by Andrew Dobson. San Francisco: Mercury House, 1991.

"Climate Communiqué." *Royal Society*. 21 July 2015. Web. 25 August 2015. https://royalsociety.org/policy/publications/2015/climate-communique/ Accessed co2now.org. Earth's CO_2 Home Page. http://co2now.org/.

Council II. Audio recording of meeting on 1 July 2013. *American Library Association*, 2013. Web. 14 April 2014. http://www.ala.org/aboutala/governance/council/councilaudio.MP3.

"Divestment Commitments." *Fossil Free*, n.d. Web. 12 Oct. 2015 http://gofossilfree.org/commitments/.

Eggars, Dave. *Zeitoun*. New York: Vintage, 2010. Print.

Einstein, Albert. Letter to Upton Sinclair, quoted in *I, Candidate for Governor, and How I Got Licked*. Berkeley: University of California Press, 1994. Print.

Fergusson, G. J. (1958). "Reduction of Atmospheric Radiocarbon Concentration by Fossil Fuel Carbon Dioxide and the Mean Life of Carbon Dioxide in the Atmosphere." *Proceedings of the Royal Society: Series A Mathematical and Physical Sciences*, 1235.1 (11 Feb. 1958): 243. Print.

Fischer, Douglas. "Back in the headlines: Climate coverage returns to its 2009 peak." *The Daily Climate*, 2 January 2015. Web. 2 October 2015. http://www.dailyclimate.org/tdc-newsroom/2015/01/climate-change-coverage-2014.

Francis, Pope. *Encyclical on Climate Change & Inequality: On Care for Our Common Home*. Brooklyn: Melville House, 2015.

"Global Greenhouse Gas Emissions Data." *Environmental Protection Agency, Climate Change*, 11 Sept. 2015. Web. 11 Oct. 2015. http://www3.epa.gov/climatechange/ghgemissions/global.html.

Global Warming: Changing CO_2urse. Portland OR: Northwest Earth Institute, 2008.

Gregory-Wood, Lois Ann. Message to the author, re: Greetings from Seattle and request. 4 Sept. 2015. E-mail.

Handwerk, Brian. "Whatever Happened to the Ozone Hole?" *National Geographic News*, 7 May 2010. Web. 23 Aug. 2015. http://news.nationalgeographic.com/news/2010/05/100505-science-environment-ozone-hole-25-years/.

Henk, Mandy. *Ecology, Economy, Equity: The Path to a Carbon-Neutral Library*. Chicago: ALA Editions, 2014. Print.

Kahn, Brian. "A Global Milestone: CO_2 Passes 400 PPM." *Climate Central*. 6 May 2015. Web. 2 Aug. 2015. http://www.climatecentral.org/news/co2-400-ppm-global-record-18965.

Kainulainen, Maggie. "Saying Climate Change: Ethics of the Sublime and the Problem of Representation." *Symploke*, 21.1 (2013): 109–123. *Project MUSE*. Web. 3 Oct. 2015. https://muse.jhu.edu/.

Kaufman, Donald (2015). "U.S. Scientists: No Way to Stop Warming of Oceans." *TruthDig*, 16 July 2015. Web. 17 July 2015.

Klein, Naomi. *This Changes Everything: Capitalism vs. Climate*. New York: Simon & Schuster, 2014. Print.

Lorde, Audre. *Sister Outsider: Essays & Speeches*. Trumansburg NY: Crossing Press, 1984. Print.

Marshall, George. "Why We Still Don't Believe in Climate Change." *Climate Change Denial*, 24 July 2009. Web. 16 July 2015. http://climatedenial.org/2009/07/24/why-we-still-dont-believe-in-climate-change/.

Maslin, Mark. *Global Warming: A Very Short Introduction*. New York: Oxford University Press, 2004. Print.

McKibbon, Bill. "Do the Math Tour." *350.org*. N.d. Web 23 Aug. 2015. http://math.350.org/.

Miller, Kathryn. *Public Libraries Going Green*. Chicago: American Library Association, 2010. Print.

Monbiot, George. *Heat: How to Stop the Planet from Burning*. [Toronto]: Doubleday, 2006. Print.

Mosley, Walter. *The Right Mistake: The Further Philosophical Investigations of Socrates Fortlow*. New York: Basic Civitas Books, 2008. Print.

Parr, Adrian. *Hijacking Sustainability*. Cambridge MA: MIT Press, 2009. Print.

Plaza, Sara. Personal message to author, re: news, comments, greetings from Bustarviejo. 10 Sept. 2015. E-mail. 10 Sept. 2015.

Regan, Tom. "The Case for Animal Rights," from *The Green Reader: Essays Toward a Sustainable Society*, edited by Andrew Dobson. San Francisco: Mercury House, 1991.

"Resolution on Divestment of Holdings in Fossil Fuel Companies." *American Library Association*. 28 November 2013. Web. 3 Oct. 2015. PDF file. http://www.ala.org/aboutala/sites/ala.org.aboutala/files/content/governance/council/council_agendas/2013mw_an_agendas/cd_35_fossil%20fuel%20resolution.pdf.

"Resolution on the Importance of Sustainable Libraries." *American Library Association*. 28 June 2015. Web. 3 Oct. 2015. PDF file. http://www.ala.org/aboutala/sites/ala.org.aboutala/files/content/governance/council/council_documents/2015_annual_council_documents/cd_36_substainable_libraries_resol_final.pdf

Rosenthal, Elisabeth. "Toward Sustainable Travel: Breaking the Flying Addiction." *Yale Environment 360*. 24 May 2010. Web. 5 Sept. 2015. http://e360.yale.edu/feature/toward_sustainable_travel/2280/.

Seuss, Dr. *The Lorax*. New York: Random House, 1971. Print.

"Sustainability Round Table." *American Library Association*. N.d. Web. 23 August 2015. http://www.ala.org/sustainrt/.

Tekola, Sarra. sHell No! Inquiry into the Complexities of Activism [Lecture]. Seattle, Town Hall, July 29, 2015.

"Text of President Johnson's Message to Congress on Conservation and Pollution." *New York Times (1923–Current file)*: 20 (24 Feb. 1966). *ProQuest*. Web. 3 Oct. 2015.

Tutu, Desmond. "Archbishop Desmond Tutu on Divestment." *350.org*, 26 April 2013. Web. 22 July 2015. https://www.youtube.com/watch?v=SR-xBzs09D8.

"Why Earth Warms." *New York Times, 1923–Current file* (25 Sept. 1955): E11. ProQuest 3 Oct. 2015.

Index

AAP *see* Association of American Publishers
AAP Report *see* "Starvation of Young Black Minds: The Effect of Book Boycotts on South Africa"
ABA *see* American Booksellers Association
ABC news 81-2, 192
abuse: cycle of 88; sexual 126-8, 208
abuse of authority 142, 147-50, 153, 161, 165, 170, 173
academic freedom 84-5, 87
access 2
Access to Public Libraries 58
accountability 87, 95, 146-152, 161-2, 172-3, 194, 210-11
achievement gap 33
acknowledgment vi, 3, 6, 15, 23, 32, 33, 37, 38, 42, 44, 70, 154, 156, 179-80, 194, 200
ACONDA *see* Activities Committee on New Directions in ALA
ACLU *see* American Civil Liberties Union
ACRL *see* Association of College and Research Libraries
activists 3, 9, 12, 48, 51, 58, 61, 63, 72, 76, 83, 88-9, 92, 96, 150-1, 177, 182, 188, 191, 195, 204, 208
Activities Committee on New Directions in ALA (ACONDA) 9, 141, 203, 211
Ad Hoc Activities Committee on New Directions (ANACONDA) 9, 203, 211
Adams, John 142, 173
advertising 103, 112-4, 116-8, 183; *see also* commercialization; marketing
Affordable Care Act 145-6
Africa, American Committee on 54
African Affairs, Council on 51
African National Congress (ANC) 11, 50-1, 54, 63-4, 66-70, 72, 204, 206; Defiance Campaign 51, 54, 205; *see also* anti-apartheid movement; boycott; Freedom Charter; sanctions: South Africa; SRRT Guidelines
African Studies Association, Archives-Libraries Committee of the 66
Afrikaners 60

After the Last Sky: Palestinian Lives 88, 208
Against the World: South Africa and Human Rights at the United Nations, 1945-1961 53, 206
age 8
Ahmed, Juniad 68-9
airline industry 181-3, 198-201
ALA *see* American Library Association
ALA/AFL-CIO Joint Committee on Library Services to Labor Groups 181
ALA Bulletin 47, 48, 50, 59, 123
ALA Chapters *see* chapters of ALA
ALA Council *see* Council
ALA Graphics 114-5, 117
ALA Handbook of Organization 112, 135, 210
ALA Policy Manual 10, 131, 147, 210
al-Safi, Omar 97-8, 100, 207-8
Alabama 32, 58
Alexander, Michelle 73
Al-Fajr (newspaper) 84
ALSC *see* Association of Library Services to Children
American-Arab Anti-Discrimination Committee 84
American Booksellers Association 10, 111, 118-22
American Civil Liberties Union 28
American Heritage Dictionary 76
American Libraries 15, 18, 20, 50, 58-9, 61-2, 64, 95, 98, 101, 103, 107-8, 111, 115, 117, 123-4, 136, 138, 150, 157, 183, 204-10
American Library Association 10; annual and midwinter attendance 92; bureaucracy 96, 151; constitution and bylaws 10-11, 99-100, 108, 112, 131-3; external relations 136; *see also* Activities Committee on New Directions in ALA (ACONDA); Ad Hoc Activities Committee on New Directions (ANACONDA); ALA/AFL-CIO Joint Committee on Library Services to Labor Groups; Association of College and Research Libraries (ACRL); Association of Library Services to Children (ALSC); Black Caucus (BCALA); Budget Analysis and Review Committee (BARC);

chapters of ALA; *Code of Professional Ethics for Librarians*; Committee on Legislation (COL); Committee on Organization (COO); core values; corporate partnerships; Council; Endowment Trustees; Ethnic Materials and Information Exchange Round Table; Executive Board (EMIERT); Federal and Armed Forces Libraries Round Table (FAFLRT); Government Documents Round Table (GODORT); Intellectual Freedom Committee (IFC); Intellectual Freedom Round Table (IFRT); International Relations Committee (IRC); Jewish Librarians Caucus; Library Bill of Rights; Library/Book Fellows Program; Library History Round Table (LHRT); membership meetings; Office of Intellectual Freedom (OIF); "one voice policy"; Organizational Self Study Committee (OSSC); policies; Policy Monitoring Committee; REFORMA (National Committee to Promote Library & Information Services to Latinos and the Spanish Speaking); Resolutions Committee; Social Responsibilities Round Table (SRR); *The Speaker: A Film About Freedom*; Sustainability Round Table (SustainRT); United for Libraries; Washington Office; Young Adult Library Services Association (YALSA)
American Library Journal 44
American Program Bureau 23
American Psychiatric Association 128
American Revolution 17, 142
Amnesty International 92
Amtrak 186
ANACONDA *see* Ad Hoc Activities Committee on New Directions in ALA
anarchist librarians 4
Anderson, Mary Jane 115, 132, 137
Animal Farm 202
animal rights 177, 212
anti-apartheid movement 3, 5-6, 12, 41, 43, 46, 48, 51-2, 54-5, 58; *see also* African National Con-

215

gress; boycott, cultural; Defiance Campaign; Pan-African Congress; sanctions; Sharpeville; South Africa; South African Indian Congress
anti-colonial movements 43, 52, 59, 91, 121, 142, 175
Anti-Defamation League 75–7, 94, 106, 207; censorship activity 76–7; spying activity 76–7
anti-gay legislation 98–9, 129–31, 210
anti-racist activism 43
Anti-racist Scholarship 6
anti-Semitism 36, 52, 76–7, 88, 101, 107
anti-war movement 28–9, 150
Antonelli, Monika 195, 211
AOL 147
apartheid in libraries 47
Apple 147
Aptheker, Herbert 49
Arab people 75, 78–80, 84, 88–91, 93, 95, 97, 207–8
Architecture for Humanity 197
Arendt, Hannah 139
Argentina 55
Arledge, Roone 82
Arrhenius, Svante 184
Article 11 53; *see also* Universal Declaration of Human Rights
Article 19 83, 87, 93, 95–7, 105, 207; *see also* free speech; intellectual freedom; Universal Declaration of Human Rights
Aruri, N. 92
Associated Press 78
Association of American Publishers (AAP) 5, 6, 10, 15, 42, 59, 65, 67, 68, 69, 71, 72, 205
Association of Arab-American University Graduates 90
Association of College and Research Libraries (ACRL) 10–11, 66, 166, 168, 173, 196, 200, 203
Association of Library Services to Children (ALSC) 11, 113–7, 123–5, 128, 130–2, 135–6, 138, 173, 200, 203, 209–10; Advisory Committee to the Boy Scouts of America 123–5, 132, 135, 209; Liaison with National Organizations Serving the Child Committee 124–5
atheists 6, 118, 135, 138
Atlanta (GA) 47
Atwood, Margaret 202
Auerback, Rita 137
Aunt Lute 111
Australia 55
authority 7, 17, 22, 34, 116–7, 119–20, 122, 133, 135, 138–9, 142, 151, 152, 160, 165–6, 172–3
Authority 160, 211
Avneri, Uri 89–90
awareness 44

Baden-Powell, Robert 118–21, 123, 125–6, 209; *see also* Boy Scouts Beyond the Seas; Scouting for Boys; Yarns for Boy Scouts;

Baez, Joan 57
Baker, James A., III (secretary of state) 95
Baker & Taylor 62–3, 65, 69, 205
banning (people, books, organizations) 34, 45, 49, 51, 54–5, 61–2, 71–2, 75, 80, 85–6, 93, 97, 109, 171,
BARC *see* Budget Analysis and Review Committee
Barry, H. D. 47
Barstow, Barbara 114
Bartlett, Vernon 50
BBC news 72
BCALA *see* Black Caucus
Beavan, Colin 202
behavior 24, 43, 76, 78, 101, 108, 121, 127, 176–7, 194
Beirut 81–3
Belafonte, Harry 57
Belgium 46
Bell, Derrick 21
Benaroya Hall 176
Benedict, Ruth 48
Bennoune, Karima 87
Benvenisti, Meron 80, 84, 207
Berger, Patricia 107
Berman, Sanford 62, 98, 103, 114, 205, 207
Berninghausen debate 42
Bernstein, Leonard 57
Berry, John N., III 27–32, 35, 39, 42, 115, 136, 203, 205, 209
Biblioteca Mexicana 44
Biblo, Herb 65, 98, 108
Biblo, Mary 15, 158–9, 164, 170, 203
bicycles 92, 179–80
Bikila, Abebe 55
Biko, Steve 61
Bill of Rights *see* First Amendment; Fourth Amendment; United States Constitution
Binney, William 148–9, 158
biodiversity 191
The Bitter Year: Arabs Under Israeli Occupation in 1982 84, 207
Black, Hugo L. (supreme court justice) 28
Black Caucus 5, 11, 15, 16, 26, 31–5, 38, 66, 203–4
Black Feminist Thought 6, 17, 204
Black Law Student Association (BLSA) 21, 22, 24, 36
Black Librarian in America 4
black librarians 4, 11, 17, 25–6, 32–3, 58, 203, 205
Bliquez, Pat 1
BLSA *see* Black Law Student Association (Harvard)
Boas, Franz 48
Bobbsey Twins 129
Bobker, Lee 20, 24, 26, 27; *see also The Speaker*; Vision Associates
Bodleian Library 44
Boeing 181, 201
Boer War 119
Bok, Sissela 7, 143–4, 173, 210
book awards 122, 126, 129, 138, 144,

209; *see also* Caldecott; Coretta Scott King; Newbery; Stonewall
"book boycott" 6, 41–3, 59, 62, 67, 206
book burning 45, 54, 71, 130
Book Industry Environmental Council 186
book recommendations 48, 49, 62, 116, 118, 122–3, 138, 202
Booz-Allen Hamilton 146
Bork, Robert 21; *see also* Watergate
Boston 24, 128, 142
Boy Scout Handbook 119, 127, 209; *see also Scout Field Book; Scouting for Boys*
Boy Scouts Beyond the Seas 119
Boy Scouts of America (BSA) 3, 6, 11, 111–2, 117–139; court rulings 124; jamborees 123–4, 132, 135; lawsuits against 123, 126; Library Commission 122; motto 118; New York City Council 138; reading merit badge 123, 135–7; religious belief 137–8; Scout Law 119–20; sex abuse 126; and sexuality 126–7; women 124; *see also* Association of Library Services to Children; gay scouts;
Boy Scouts Yearbook 120, 210
boycott, cultural 42, 51, 56–7, 63, 66, 68, 206; ANC modifications to 66–70, 72, 204
boycott, consumer 54, 63, 65–6
Boycott, Divestment and Sanctions Movement 107
boycott, economic 55–6 58
boycott, homophobic legislation 131
boycott, sports 55, 63, 68, 72, 98
boycotts 3, 55, 58–9, 62–3, 84, 98, 176, 181; *see also* "book boycott"; Montgomery Bus Boycott
Boyle, Francis 92
Boyle, Kevin 87, 207
Bradbury, Ray 202
Bragg, Billy 1
Brandeis, Louis (supreme court justice) 141, 172
Brave New World 202
Braverman, Miriam 27, 29, 30, 35
Brenner, Lenni 88, 207
Brinkley, David 88
British Academy for the Humanities and Social Sciences 192
British Mandate for Palestine 78–80
British Museum 44
British Press Ordinance 79
Brodart 63
Broderick, Dorothy 31
Brooklyn Public Library 42
Brown v Louisiana 58
Brubeck, Dave 57
Brutus, Dennis 92
BSA *see* Boy Scouts of America
Bucknell University 149
Budget Analysis and Review Committee (BARC) 11, 158, 185–7
Budlong, Tom 136
Buey, Paco Fernandes 198
bulldozers 89, 99, 180

Index

Buschman, John 7, 8
business-as-usual 65, 72, 193, 195
Bynum, Mollie 113–4, 116–7
bystanders 6, 43–5, 205

Caldecott award 122, 205
Cape Town (South Africa) 44, 60
capitalism 51
carbon dioxide (CO_2) 175–8, 180–5, 190–4, 196–201, 212; offsets 176, 181–2, 196–7; *see also* airline industry; carbon footprint; climate change; climate crisis; greenhouse gas emissions; net-zero carbon emissions; transportation
carbon footprint 181–3, 187, 198, 200
Cardinale, Christopher 2
Caribbean 55
Carnegie, Andrew 47
Carnegie libraries 44
Carroll, Dianne 57
Carter, Jimmy (president) 62
Castro, Fidel 20
Caywood, Carolyn 136–7, 209
CBS news 79, 81–2, 88, 192
censorship 3, 6, 8, 12, 15, 18–9, 22, 25–6, 35–9, 42, 49, 59, 61–2, 66, 71, 75–109, 112–3, 125, 131, 133, 139, 202, 206–8; Catholic Church 84; news broadcasts 81–3; *see also* book burning; British Press Ordinance; Editors Committee; military censor
Center for Civic Life 189
Central Intelligence Agency (CIA) 63–4, 76, 146
Chafee, Zechariah 28
Chafets, Ze'ev 82
Chaney, James 32
Chapin, James 98
Chaplin, Ralph 1
chapters of ALA 10–1, 173
character building 118–22, 210
chastisement 100, 106, 116, 138–9, 161, 186
Chelton, Mary K. 31
Chicago 10, 12, 18, 63, 80, 92, 134, 145–6, 150, 154, 181, 186; McCormick Place Convention Center 144
Chicago Public Library (CPL) 76–7, 80, 87
Chicago Sun Times 76
child labor 38, 119, 177
children 1–4, 11, 38, 44, 54, 56, 89, 90, 112–3, 122–3, 125, 127–9, 135, 141, 177, 194, 201–2
chilling effect 35, 133, 171–2
Chinese Bibliography 44
chlorofluorocarbons (CFCs) 178; *see also* ozone layer
Chomsky, Noam 7, 88, 154, 165, 170, 207, 210
Christianity 43
CIA *see* Central Intelligence Agency
Cincinnati Public Library 49

citizens 19, 24, 29, 36, 52, 64–5, 77–9, 81, 91–2, 96, 104, 106, 121–2, 129, 138, 141–3, 145–6, 149–50, 156, 161, 165–6, 170, 172–3, 181, 191–2, 197–8
Civallero, Edgardo vi
civil disobedience 51, 53, 96
Civil Rights, Committee on 49
civil rights activists 32, 58
civil rights movement 32, 42–3, 51–2, 55, 58, 59, 69, 76, 129, 199
civil war 45
civilization 175, 198
Clarion-Ledger (newspaper) 88
Clark, Geraldine 30, 31
class, social 2, 4, 8, 42, 44, 51, 91, 121, 130, 200, 202
Clay, Cassius 55
Cleaver, Eldridge 4
Cleveland Public Library 31
climate change 4, 7, 8, 175–202; media coverage 192; negotiations 191, 193; *see also* carbon dioxide; carbon footprint; climate crisis; collapse; curriculum; energy sources; greenhouse effect; greenhouse gas emissions; Intergovernmental Panel on Climate Change; sustainability; transition, peaceful
Climate Communique 192–4, 211
climate crisis 7, 175, 189–90, 193–7, 200–2; technological solutions 193, 195, 200
Climate Outreach Information Network 182
CO_2 *see* carbon dioxide
coal 182; miners 1–3, 192
Coatsworth, John 76–7
Cockburn, Andrew 63–4, 205
Code of Professional Ethics for Librarians 148, 152, 162, 210
coersion 22
CogNotes 145
Cohen, Stanley 5, 6, 33
Cold War 52, 72
collapse, social and environmental 9, 72, 90, 198–9
collection development 8, 33, 67, 93
Collins, Patricia Hill 6, 17, 204
Columbia University Libraries 32
Columbia University School of Library Service 4, 27, 42, 67, 88
Comito, Lauren 159
commercialization 12, 114, 116–7, 131; *see also* advertising; marketing
commitment 2, 19, 24, 61, 64, 77–8, 95, 97, 103, 119, 127, 130, 132, 137, 141–3, 150–1, 156, 170, 172, 203, 212
Committee on Israeli Censorship 92
Committee on Legislation (COL) 11, 146, 155, 158, 161, 164, 170, 199
Committee on Organization (COO) 11, 108, 131, 181, 203, 209
community conversations *see* conversation
complicity 3, 37, 64

CompUSA 102
Conable, Gordon 69–70, 137
confidentiality 2, 7, 143–4, 148, 150, 152–3, 162; mandatory reporters 143; *see also* privacy; secrecy
Congress of Racial Equality (CORE) 20
Congress of South African Writers 68
Conkling, Diedre 158–9, 170
consumer society 65, 88, 176, 180, 189–91, 196
conversation 2, 7, 9, 31, 35, 42, 89, 91, 107, 112, 134, 151–4, 186, 189, 194, 198–9, 201–2; *see also* dialogue
COO *see* Committee on Organization
CORE *see* Congress of Racial Equality
core values 2, 3, 151, 164, 190; *see also* access; confidentiality; democracy; diversity; education; intellectual freedom; lifelong learning; preservation; privacy; professionalism; public good; service; social responsibility
Coretta Scott King Award 129
"cornerstone of democracy" 112, 134, 137, 173, 211
corporal punishment 160
corporate partnerships 3, 6, 113–4, 116–7, 210
Council 3–7, 5, 9–11, 31, 103–6; Access/South Africa 64–5, 70, 206; on ALA partnership with McDonalds 115; on ALA relations with the Boy Scouts 135–8; Censorship in the Middle East Including Library Closures in the Occupied Territories 94–6; forum 11–2, 152–3, 155, 187; on GLBTQ issues 128, 130–2; listserv 3, 15, 149, 155; motions to reconsider 154–6, 158–61, 163, 166; motions to rescind 85–6, 105–6; 1984 resolution on censorship in the Occupied Territories 85–6; 1915 resolution on Boy Scout book initiative 118, 122; Privacy, Open Government, Government Transparency, and Accountability 161–3; Reaffirmation of Freedom of Expression of Foreign Nationals 83, 85–6, 97, 104, 207; Resolution in Support of Whistleblower Edward Snowden 6, 152–3; Resolution on Divestment of Holdings in Fossil Fuel Companies 185–6; Resolution on Government Intimidation 149–50; Resolution on Israeli Censorship 77, 96–8, 99–103, 105–6, 112–3, 133–4; Resolution on Library Service to the Community in a Disaster 186; Resolution on Securing Government Accountability Through Whistleblower Protection 147–8; Resolution on

the Deportation of Bir Zeit University Librarian Omar al-Safi 98–100; Resolution on the Importance of Sustainable Libraries 188–9; Resolution on the Need for Reforms for the Intelligence Community to Support on resolution process 9–11; Resolutions Committee 164, 185; segregated library associations 58; on South Africa 62; on *The Speaker* 16, 31–2; 24-hour rule 155–6; Units Which Violate ALA Policy 131–3; votes 15, 32, 34, 99–100, 154, 160–1, 163
courage 24, 39, 171, 197–8
Cox, Archibald 20, 21, 26, 36; *see also* Black Student Law Association; Harvard Law School; *The Speaker*; Vision Associates
CPL *see* Chicago Public Library
Crewdson, Ann 151, 185
Crismond, Linda 98
critical theory 5, 7–8
#critlib-Seattle 39
Croneberger, Robert 69, 71
Cronkite, Walter 88
cult of expertise *see* expertise
curriculum, climate change 12, 188
Cry the Beloved Country 51

Daddy's Roommate 129
Daily Show 129
Darling, Pamela 32
databases 6, 65, 67, 99, 102
Davis, Sammy, Jr. 57
De Beers Corporation 62
de Klerk, F.W. 72
de Klerk, J. 47
deliberation, due 155–6, 159, 161
DeLuca, Kevin 196
Delzell, Robert 20, 24, 25, 26, 27
democracy 2, 5, 10, 19, 28, 30, 37, 50, 66, 68–9, 71, 77–9, 81–2, 87, 91, 95–7, 102, 104, 112, 122, 131–2, 134–5, 139, 142, 151, 164–6, 172–3, 185, 189, 199, 201–2, 206, 211
Democratic Front for the Liberation of Palestine 97
demolition of homes 55, 75, 77, 89, 99, 180
denial 15, 17, 32–3, 35–7, 49–50, 78, 83–4, 130, 177, 180, 183, 191–2, 203, 212
DePaul University 92
deportation 75, 97–8, 100, 207
Derech Hanitzotz/Tariq al-Sharara (newspaper) 97
DeSantis, John 166
Dewey, Melville 4
Dewey, Thomas 48
Dheshieh refugee camp 80, 89–90
Dialog 102
dialogue 3–5, 10, 26, 37, 43, 97, 139, 151–3, 158, 162–3, 197; *see also* conversation
diamond mines 44, 65
Dick, Archie L. 71
diplomacy 13, 53, 56, 79–80, 88–9, 91, 95, 102, 104–5, 125, 162, 193, 207
disarticulate industrialism 196–7
discrimination 4, 46, 49–50, 52, 58–60, 91, 123, 129–30, 132, 137–8, 177
diversity 2, 4, 103, 130, 132, 137; *see also* biodiversity
divestment 4, 7, 63, 107, 155, 175–6, 185–7, 190, 212
domestic violence *see* violence
Dominion Library Associates 155
Donnell Library (NYPL) 123
Doyle, Robert 59, 84–5, 94, 102–3, 205, 207
Drake, Thomas 148
Drew, Lisa 42, 67–9
Drum (journal) 55
D'Souza, Frances 95
DuBois, W.E.B. 47
Dunlap, Connie 31
Durban (South Africa) 54
Dutch East India Company 60

Earth Day 177, 184
EB *see* Executive Board
eco-librarians 4
Ecology, Economy, Equity: The Path to a Carbon Neutral Library 195, 212
economic geologists 192
ecosystems 175, 180, 191, 193, 200–1
Editors Committee 79
education 2
educational films 27–9
Edwards, Margaret A. 4
Eggars, Dave 180, 212
Egypt 91, 95
Einstein, Albert 175, 212
Eisberg, Barbara 20, 24, 26, 27; *see also The Speaker*; Vision Associates
Elder, Shirley 59
elites 2, 38, 46, 153–4, 165–6, 170, 173, 194, 196–7
Elizur, Yuval 79
Elon, Amos 84
emergency responders 179–80, 201; militarization of 180
Emerick, Tyrone 30
Emerson, Thomas 28
EMIERT *see* Ethnic Materials and Information Exchange Round Table
Empire State College, State University of New York 1
Encyclical on Climate Change and Inequality 202
endowment funds 62, 185, 187, 211
Endowment Trustees 185, 187
endurance 190–91
energy sources 183, 185–6, 189, 195, 199–200; renewable 185–6, 198–200
England *see* Great Britain
environmentalists 176, 182–3, 193
epidemics 45
epistemological racism 6, 15, 17, 37
Espinal, Isabel 187

Espionage Act of 1917 146, 148–9, 154, 158
Esquith, Stephen L. 6, 42–4
Estes, Rice 58
Ethnic Materials and Information Exchange Round Table 11, 93, 188
ethnicity 8
Eubanks, Jackie 150
Eugene Register-Guard (newspaper) 88
eugenics 17, 20, 23, 33, 36, 129; *see also* racism; Shockley, William
Eurocentrism 57
eviction 75
exclusion 44, 55, 58, 138
Executive Board 7, 11, 17–9, 25–7, 33, 83, 98, 100–1, 103, 105–7, 115, 124–5, 131–3, 135–6, 150, 154–5, 157, 159–61, 164, 166, 169, 187, 207–8
Exodus 88, 208
expertise 2, 11, 22, 68, 84, 91, 160, 165–6
exploitation 3, 6, 43–4, 177, 192, 194
extreme violence *see* violence

Facebook 147, 151–2, 157, 159
FAFLRT *see* Federal and Armed Forces Libraries Round Table
Fahrenheit 451 202
The Fair Garden and the Swarm of Beasts 4, 203
famine 45, 73, 201
Farrell, Maggie 166, 168
fast food 3, 112–5
The Fateful Triangle: The United States, Israel, and the Palestinians 88, 207
FBI *see* Federal Bureau of Investigation
fear 2, 30, 45, 102, 112, 128, 131, 135, 139, 141, 143, 173
Federal and Armed Forces Libraries Round Table (FAFLRT) 147
Federal Bureau of Investigation (FBI) 76, 143, 148, 150, 153
Feinman, Valerie 166
feminism 6, 12, 17, 204
"fighting words" 8
Fine, Sara 93
fires 180, 185, 195
First Amendment 8, 12, 16, 17, 19–22, 24, 26–9, 31, 33, 34, 36–9, 64–5, 130, 149; interpretations 28, 31; *see also* free speech; freedom of association; freedom of the press; intellectual freedom; public platforms; *The Speaker: A Film About Freedom*
Flagg, Gordon 136, 207, 209
floods 176, 178–80, 185, 195, 202
Fonda, Henry 57
Ford Motor Company 56
Forrest, Charles 196
fossil fuel 4, 195, 212; divestment 7, 155, 175–6, 184–7; resolution 5, 211
Fourth Amendment 7, 142–3, 148, 150, 165, 211; *see also* National Se-

curity Agency; privacy; writs of assistance
France 46, 54–5
Francis, Pope *see* Pope Francis
Frank, Reuven 82
Frankfurt School 7
Franklin, Robbie vi
"free flow of information" 6, 57, 64–6, 69–71, 103, 105, 162
free speech 8, 18–20, 22–4, 28–9, 31, 34, 36, 65, 77, 81, 95, 147, 152–3, 158, 162, 170, 203–4; *see also* First Amendment; speech without ideas; symbolic speech
Freedman, Maurice 134, 137
Freedom Charter 55
Freedom House 84
freedom of association 77, 153
freedom of the press 38, 77, 79, 85, 93, 158
Freedom to Read Foundation 64, 144
Friedman, Robert I. 75–6, 207

Gaiman, Neil 145
Gaines, Ervin 30, 31
Gale Publishing Company 42, 92
Gandhi, Mahatma 58, 183
Garcia, Ed 149
Garner, Nancy 145, 154, 166
Garrison, Paul E. 123–4, 209
Gaughan, Tom 111–2, 126, 209
Gay, Lesbian, Bisexual and Transgender Round Table (GLBTRT) 10, 173, 203; *see also* Gay, Lesbian, Bisexual Task Force
Gay, Lesbian, Bisexual Task Force (GLBTF) 10–12, 111–2, 124–6, 130
gay librarians 4
gay scouts 4, 123–4; *see also* Association of Library Services to Children; Boy Scouts of America
Gaza 81, 84, 87, 91, 96–7, 105
gender identity 8, 130–1
General Electric 184
genocide 21, 23–4, 45; cultural 77–8, 80, 106
gentrification 33
Georgia 32, 49, 52, 58; Walton County 49
geotechnology 200
Gerhardt, Lillian 115, 209
Germany, West 46
Ghana 54–5
Ghikas, Mary 135, 210
Giroux, Henry 139, 209
Glasby, Jane 159, 164, 170
glastnost 41
GLBTF *see* Gay, Lesbian, Bisexual Task Force
GLBTQ librarians 4
GLBTRT *see* Gay, Lesbian, Bisexual and Transgender Round
global temperatures 177, 185, 191, 197–8
global warming *see* carbon dioxide; climate change; climate crisis; greenhouse effect; greenhouse gas emissions

Global Warming: A Very Short Introduction 184, 212
GODORT *see* Government Documents Round Table
Goedert, Paula 101–2
golden arches 113, 115–6
Goldsby, Richard 23, 204
Golrick, Michael 117–8, 135–7
Gonzalez, Mario 157, 159, 166
"Good Book Week" 122
Goodman, Andrew 32
Google 147
Gordon, Ruth I. 98, 124, 135–7
Gordon, William 137
Government Accountability Project (GAP) 149, 172, 211
Government Documents Round Table (GODORT) 12, 146–7, 173, 188, 203
government watchdog groups 149
Gramsci, Antonio 72
Grapes of Wrath 49; *see also* Library Bill of Rights
Great Britain 46, 54–5; *see also* British Mandate for Palestine
Great Depression 120
Green Press Initiative 186
"green washing" 189
Greenfield, Dror 94
greenhouse effect 175, 177, 183–4, 191, 194–5, 197, 199, 212; *see also* carbon dioxide; climate change; climate crisis
greenhouse gas emissions 175–6, 178, 180–5, 191–3, 194–201, 212; *see also* net-zero carbon emissions
Greening Libraries 195
Greenland 184
Greenpeace 182, 196
Grey Collection 44
The Guardian (newspaper) 146, 153, 173, 211
Guidelines for Librarians Interacting with South Africa *see* SRRT Guidelines
guilt 85, 100, 121, 171, 176–7, 180–1, 196, 202

Ha'Aretz (newspaper) 84
The Hague (Netherlands) 60
Haiman, Franklyn S. 28, 29
Hamash, Jamal 80
Hammarskjold, Dag 54
Handbook of Black Librarianship 58
Hanlon, Joseph 63
Harger, Natalie 179
Harger, Richard 23
Harlem 48; Librarians Section, City Wide Citizens' Committee on 48, 49
Harris, Julie 57
Harry Van Arsdale, Jr., School of Labor Studies 1
Harvard Crimson (newspaper) 22
Harvard Law Forum 20, 21, 22, 23
Harvard Law Record (newspaper) 21, 22
Harvard Law School 6, 20, 21, 26

Harvard Medical School 22
hate speech 8, 36
Hattiesburg (MS) 24
Heat: How to Stop the Planet from Burning 183, 212
heat waves 195
Heather Has Two Mommies 129
hegemony 3, 6–7, 9, 35, 141, 144, 171, 196, 211
Henk, Mandy 195–7, 212
Herman, Edward 77
heterosexuality 120
Hidden History of South Africa's Book and Reading Cultures 71
hierarchy in librarianship 12, 92
Hijacking Sustainability 189, 212
Hilyard, Nann Blain 152–3, 155
Hirbet Hizah (Israel) 75
history 1–4, 6, 10, 41–4, 47, 78, 126–7, 138, 142, 177, 196–8, 201, 208, 211
Hitler, Adolf 7, 24, 125, 139
Hitler Youth 125
Ho, Dara 154
Holiday, Billie 49
Holley, Edward G. 107
Holmes, Oliver Wendell, Jr. (supreme court justice) 28, 29
holocaust 21, 24; denial 36
Homelands, Harlem and Hollywood: South African Culture and the World Beyond 55
homophobia 111–2, 126, 128–9, 138
The Homosexual in America 127
Honma, Todd 6, 15, 37, 39, 204
"Honor Role of Race Relations" 48
Horn, Zoia 26–7, 29, 35, 69, 95, 149–50, 204, 207, 211
Horrocks, Norman 108, 132
Houston (TX) 64, 205
Hovsepian, Nubar 94
Howell, John Bruce 69, 72, 205
Huddleston, Trevor 51
Hudson, Dave 196
Hug-a-Homosexual 126
Hughes, Langston 48
human rights 12, 36, 42, 44, 46, 52–3, 61–2, 64–5, 69–71, 81, 83, 87, 94–7, 100, 130, 132, 137, 139, 205–8
hunger 12, 45
Huntley, Chet 88
Hurley, David 169
hurricanes 179–80, 185, 187, 197
Hussein, King of Jordan *see* King Hussein of Jordan
Hutton, John G. 184
Huxley, Aldous 202
H.W. Wilson Company 98

Iacono, Frank 132
identity 4, 8, 87, 130, 131, 143
ideology 6–7, 38–9, 43, 46, 64–5, 77, 86, 89, 91, 119, 121–2
IFC *see* Intellectual Freedom Committee
IFLA Journal 60
IFRT *see* Intellectual Freedom Round Table

IHRTF *see* International Human Rights Task Force
image control 77–8, 82, 99, 102, 115, 135, 173
imperialism 78, 80, 120–2, 194;
imprisonment 6, 44, 53, 56, 61, 63, 71–3, 79–80, 85, 90, 95, 97–8, 125, 180; solitary confinement 98
incarceration 33, 73, 191
India 5
indigenous peoples 43, 78, 194
Industrial Workers of the World (IWW) 12, 24
industrialized countries 12, 57, 175, 180, 182, 191–2, 194, 196, 198, 203; *see also* disarticulate industrialism
inequality 9, 202
Information Freedom and Censorship: World Report 1991 94
information literacy 88, 165
Innis, Roy 20, 21
Innis-Shockley debate 21, 22, 36
intellectual freedom 2, 8, 12, 15–6, 19–20, 31, 35, 42–4, 61, 70–1, 76, 84–7, 93, 97, 106, 130, 141, 143, 150, 152, 162, 202
Intellectual Freedom and Social Responsibility in American Librarianship, 1967–1974 9, 203
Intellectual Freedom Committee (IFC) 6, 12, 17, 19, 26–7, 29, 69–70, 80–1, 83, 86, 95, 106, 130, 147, 155–6, 158–9, 161, 170, 203, 205; *see also* Krug, Judith; *The Speaker: A Film about Freedom*
intellectual freedom purists 4, 6, 8, 42, 71
Intellectual Freedom Round Table (IFRT) 12, 64, 93
intention 25–6, 37–9, 144; *see also* unintended consequences
Intergovernmental Panel on Climate Change (IPCC) 188
internal combustion engine 194
International Federation of Library Associations (IFLA) 57–62, 97, 105
International Geophysical Year 184
International Human Rights Task Force (IHRTF) 12, 75–6, 91, 93, 94, 96, 98, 100
International Relations Committee (IRC) 12, 59, 66, 69, 72, 80–87, 91, 93–6, 100–6; Subcommittee on the Alleged Banning of Palestinian and Arab Books in the Israeli Occupied Territories as It Related to Article 19 as Adopted by the American Library Association Council in 1989 93
International Relations Round Table (IRRT) 66, 93, 173
internet 4, 141, 143–4, 146, 153, 162, 171; service providers 147
intimidation 3, 19, 75–6, 106, 126, 147, 149–51, 156, 163, 165, 170, 172, 207; defined 76; government 150

intolerance *see* tolerance
invisibility 34
IPCC *see* Intergovernmental Panel on Climate Change
IQ (intelligence quotient) 17, 21, 23
IRC *see* International Relations Committee
Ireland 55
IRRT *see* International Relations Round Table
Ismail, Noha 94
Israel 3, 6, 75–109; democracy in 78, 87, 88, 96, 102; *see also* British Mandate for Palestine
Israel and the Arabs 88, 208
Israel Library Association 84, 93
Israeli Censorship in the Occupied Territories (Preliminary Report) 87, 207
Israeli Censorship of Arab Publications: A Survey 80–1
Israeli Defense Forces 76, 84; air force 78
Israeli Ministry of Justice 79
Israel's Sacred Terrorism 88–90, 208
Italy 46, 55
IWW *see* Industrial Workers of the World

Jackson, Jesse 63
Jackson State University 23
Jacobsen's Index of Objectionable Literature 61
Jankowska, Maria J. 195
Japan 46, 56, 119, 146
Jefferson, Julius 16
Jenkins, Christine 111, 209
Jerusalem 79–80, 84, 90
Jewish Librarians Caucus 93
Jewish people 21, 76, 78–9, 88–91, 93, 97, 100, 107, 129, 207
Jewish Workers Trade Unions 91
Jim Crow 17, 24, 32, 43–5, 47–8, 51–2, 58, 72–3, 112, 138, 177, 191; compared to apartheid 52; *see also* "new Jim Crow"
Johannesburg (South Africa) 54
John, Nancy 101, 103–6, 207
Johns, Sara Kelly 154
Johnson, Lyndon (president) 184, 212; Science Advisory Committee 184
Jones, Barbara M. 15, 16
Jones, Clara Stanton 15, 17, 19, 25, 27, 30, 31, 33
Jordan 79, 85, 91, 95
Josey, E. J. 4, 18, 31, 32, 58, 65, 72, 86, 98, 101, 203–5, 207–8
Justinian (Roman emperor) 142
Juvenile Book Week 118, 121–3

Kagan, Al vi, 9, 60, 69, 72, 98, 108, 149, 155, 158, 163, 170–1, 203, 205
Kainulainen, Maggie 196, 212
Kaley, Dianne Chen 157–8
Kansas City 61
Keeling, Charles 176
Kellum-Rose, Nancy 31

Kennedy, John Fitzgerald (president) 46
Kgositsile, Keorapetse W. 41
kibbutz 88–9
King, Martin Luther, Jr. 8, 36, 37
King Hussein of Jordan 79
Klein, Naomi 7, 191–2, 195, 202, 212
Klipsch, Pamela 70–1, 186–7
Knesset 89
Kolbe, Vincent 69, 71–2
Kranich, Nancy 136, 165–6, 211
Kratz, Charles 157, 187
Krug, Judith 16, 18–9, 24–9, 37
Ku Klux Klan 8, 52, 76
Kuhn, Jim 149, 151, 156

Labor College 1, 2
labor history 1, 2
labor unions 1–3, 12, 49, 72, 91, 120, 139, 181
Larson, John W. 124, 210
Lebanon 80–1, 88, 90–1, 95, 208
Leckie, Gloria 7, 8
Lee, Canada 51
LEED construction 191
Legi-Slate 102
Let My People Go 54, 206
Levy, Leonard 28
Lewis, Anthony 80, 208
Lexis Nexis 102
LHRT *see* Library History Round Table
Library Association 192
Library Bill of Rights 12, 49, 128, 130–1, 152, 162, 205, 210
Library/Book Fellows Program (ALA/USIA) 59, 102–3, 105; *see also* United States Information Agency
Library History Round Table (LHRT) 15, 35
Library Journal 27, 35, 44, 46–8, 57, 115–7, 136
Library of Congress 16, 92; subject headings 62, 112
Library Union Task Force (LUTF) 181
Libri (journal) 57
Liebaers, Herman 59–61, 205–6
lies 8
lifelong learning 2
lifestyle 182
Lincoln, Abraham 24
Linda, Solomon 41
LIS curricula 7
London 67
Long, James M. 78
Long, Sarah 137
The Longest War: Israel in Lebanon 88, 90, 208
The Lorax 202
Lorde, Audre 175, 212
Louisiana 32, 58
Love Is for All 127, 210
"love miles" 183
loyalty 33, 99, 119–22, 138
Lusaka statement 68; *see also* boycott, cultural

LUTF *see* Library Union Task Force
Luthuli, Albert 54, 56, 206
Lynch, Beverly 16, 100, 103
lynching 33, 49
Lyon, George Ella 2

Maalouf, Maddoud 95
Maddaddam 202
Madison Square Garden 51
Malan, D.F. 53
Malan, Rian 41, 206
Malinconico, Michael 132
Mandela, Nelson 51, 63–4, 72
Manley, Will 98–9
manliness 119, 121–2, 127
Manning, Bradley [Chelsea] 149, 151, 155, 163, 166, 168
maps, confiscation of 81, 85
Maret, Susan vi, 173
Margolis, Bernard 108, 137, 156
marketing 102, 114, 196; *see also* advertising; commercialization
Marlin, Mike 149, 166
Marshall, A.P. 35
Marshall, George 182, 212
Maslin, Mark 182, 212
Mass Democratic Movement (South Africa) 12, 63, 66–9, 70
mass extinctions 195
mass media 22, 24, 28, 81, 83, 88–9, 139, 165, 192, 172, 194, 201
Mathiews, Franklin K. 118–22, 210
Mauna Loa Observatory 175
McCallon, Mark 16, 30, 39
McCook, Kathleen de la Peña vi
McCullough, Mark 195, 211
McDonald's (fast food) 3, 6, 111–7, 125, 133; *see also* corporate partnerships
McElfresh, Mona Harrop 49
McKibbon, Bill 175–6, 212
McMullin, Florence 19, 24, 25, 26, 27, 29
MDM *see* Mass Democratic Movement
Meeropol, Abel 49
Meiklejohn, Alexander 28
Melcher, Frederic G. 122
membership meetings, ALA 9, 15, 27, 29–31, 58, 64, 96, 98–9, 100, 105–7, 109, 112, 131–3, 144, 150–3, 158–9, 163, 188, 190; quorum 112, 131–2; virtual 188, 190
mercenaries 78
Merensky Library 61
MERIP *see* Middle East Research and Information Project
Meteorological Society of America 190
methane *see* greenhouse gas emissions
Meyer, Eugene 24
Mezerik, A. G. 46
Miami Beach (FL) 58
Michener, James 89
Microsoft 147
Middle East 75–6, 78, 82, 87–8, 91–2, 94–6, 99–100, 207

Middle East Report 88
Middle East Research and Information Project (MERIP) 88
Middle East Watch 92
militarism 121, 189
military censor 79–82, 84–5
military forces 9, 54, 56, 78–82, 84–7, 89, 91, 96–7, 99, 105–6, 121, 129, 162, 168, 189, 199
military training 121
Miller, Arthur 57
Miller, Marilyn L. 107–8, 115, 130, 132, 208, 210
mindsets 7, 53, 121, 139, 193, 195, 200
Minudri, Regina 107–8
Mississippi 23–4, 32, 52, 58
Mississippi Library Association 32
Mississippi State University 23–4
Monbiot, George 183, 212
Montagu, Ashley 57
Montclair (NJ) 30
Montgomery Bus Boycott 55
Moorman, John A. 155–7, 159–60, 166, 170, 173
morality 21, 36–7, 43, 45, 65–6, 70–2, 77, 82, 90, 98, 138–9, 141, 146, 154, 176–8, 184–5, 195, 198, 211
Morrison, Samuel F. 76
Mosley, Walter 202
Munro, Karen 196
Mussolini, Benito 57, 125, 139

NAACP 21, 49
namasté vi
Nancy Drew 129
Nathan, Avie 96
National Association for the Advancement of Colored People *see* NAACP
National Commission on Libraries and Information Science (NCLIS) 103
National Committee to Promote Library & Information Services to Latinos and the Spanish Speaking *see* REFORMA
National Lawyers Guild 92
National Liberation Movement (South Africa) 68
National Library (South Africa) 60, 62
National Library Week 32
National Reading Program 113–4, 116–7, 210
National Review 23
national security (as reason for censorship) 28, 81, 87, 94, 139, 147, 162–4, 166
National Security Agency (NSA) 4, 12, 64, 138, 144, 146–9, 153, 158, 162, 165–6, 168, 171–3, 211
Native Son 49
Nazis 7, 21, 30, 60–2, 70, 76, 79, 88, 130, 205
NBC news 81–2, 88, 192
Neal, Jim 154
Negro Slave Revolts in the United States, 1526-1860 49
neoliberalism 23, 191, 196–7

net-zero carbon emissions 192, 194 197, 199
Netherlands 46, 60
neutrality 3, 7, 8, 37
New Haven (CT) 24
"new Jim Crow" 17, 73, 191
New Orleans (LA) 64, 106, 179–80, 207; Ninth Ward 179–80; *see also* hurricanes
New York 26
New York City (NY) 1, 41, 138, 178, 181, 202
New York City Board of Education 30, 122–3, 129
New York Public Library 48, 92
New York Times (newspaper) 63, 184
New Zealand 55
Newbery award 122, 205
Newman, Bobbie 157
Newman, Leslea 129, 210
Newman, Paul 88
news Beirut 79, 81–3, 99; *see also* military censors
news broadcast companies *see* ABC news; BBC news; CBS news; NBC news
1984 (novel) 80, 202
Nixon, Richard (president) 20–1; *see also* Watergate
Nixon, Rob 55, 57, 206
No Impact Man: Adventures of a Guilty Liberal Who Attempts to Save the Planet, and the Discoveries He Makes About Himself and Our Way of Life in the Process 202
Nobel laureate 17, 20, 22
Nobel Peace Prize 56, 63
nonviolence 8, 54, 58, 63, 97, 199; *see also* civil disobedience
normalization 33, 69
Northrop, Herbert R. 49
Northwest Earth Institute 182
Northwestern University 28
Notable Books 49, 50–2, 206; *see also* book recommendations
November 29th Coalition 89, 91
NSA *see* National Security Agency
nuclear weapons 57, 79, 89
Nyquist, Corinne 69–70

Obama, Barack (president) 145–6, 149, 151, 163, 170, 172, 186
obedience 119–21
objectivity 7
Occupation: Israel Over Palestine 92
Occupied Territories *see* Palestine; *see also* British Mandate for Palestine
oceans 190, 212
Odetta 57
Office for Intellectual Freedom (OIF) 3, 5, 15–6, 18–9, 22, 25, 26, 32, 34–5, 37, 39, 171; *see also* Jones, Barbara M.; Krug, Judith; *The Speaker: A Film about Freedom*; "Speaking about *The Speaker*"
Office of Literacy and Outreach Services (OLOS) 35

Offord, Jerome, Jr. 34, 35
OIF *see* Office of Intellectual Freedom
OLOS *see* Office of Literacy and Outreach Services
Olson, Renee 135, 210
Olympic games 55, 204
Omond, Roger 63
"one voice policy" 6, 122, 134–5
oppression 2–3, 37, 44, 46, 70, 76, 88
Orange, Satia 35
Organizational Self Study Committee (OSSC) 12, 99, 112, 131, 134, 208
Organized Labor and the Negro 49
Orwell, George 80, 202
Oryx and Crake 202
OSSC *see* Organizational Self Study Committee
ostracism 2, 56–8
Othello 48
Otis, James 142
Outlook (magazine) 122
outreach services 8
Overseas Development Council 102
Owens, Major R. 41, 42, 67, 72, 98, 205–6
ozone layer (atmosphere) 178, 212; *see also* chlorofluorocarbons

PAC *see* Pan-African Congress
Pace, Andrew 164
Pakistan 55
Palestine 3, 6, 75–109, 131; library closings 94, 96–7; *see also* British Mandate for Palestine
Palestine Human Rights Campaign 92
Palestine Liberation Organization (PLO) 96, 100
The Palestine Rules and Laws 81
Palestine Solidarity Committee 92
Palestinian/Israeli Conflict: A Select Bibliography 76–7, 80, 87
Palestinian people 75–78, 80–1, 85–94, 96–7, 99, 207
Palestinian Women's Club 81
PalTalk 147
Pan-African Congress 54
Paris 59
Park College 61
Parks, Rosa 199
parliamentary procedures 6, 10, 30, 132, 155; point of personal privilege 181, 183
Parr, Adrian 189, 197, 212
pass laws (South Africa) 44, 53–4
paternalism 52
Paton, Alan 51
patriotism 78, 142, 146
Peace Information Exchange Task Force 125
Pearl, Nancy 202
Pearson, C. Arthur 123
Peattie, Noel 42, 206
people of color 8, 43, 187
perestroika 41

Pérez de Cuéllar, Javier 95
persuasion 5, 22, 36–7, 76, 85, 152, 161
Phillips, Utah 1
Phinazee, Annette Hoage 58
Pick, Josepha 94
picket line 1
Plaza, Sara Moreno vi, 198, 212
PLG *see* Progressive Librarians Guild
PLO *see* Palestine Liberation Organization
Poitier, Sidney 51, 57
police forces 9, 47, 54–6, 61, 64, 76, 139, 143, 150, 191, 199; militarization of 191
police state 139
policy, ALA 3, 5, 9–10, 12, 32, 69, 86, 117, 131–3, 135–6, 144, 147, 149–50, 186, 210
Policy Monitoring Committee 147
political prisoners 51, 61, 64, 56, 149, 151
Political Responsibilities of Everyday Bystanders 6, 43, 44
poll taxes 49, 72, 87, 89, 176
Pope Francis 202
Porter, Michael 169
poverty 12, 45
power 2–3, 7–9, 24, 37, 41, 45–6, 49, 52, 61, 66, 68, 69, 79, 87, 91, 102, 105, 131, 133, 139, 144, 149–50, 160–1, 173, 184, 189, 194, 197–8
Pratt Institute 122
Preminger, Otto 88
preservation 2
Pretoria (South Africa) 54
priorities 7, 44, 71, 89, 195, 199, 201
PRISM 147, 153, 162
prisons *see* imprisonment; incarceration
privacy 2, 6–7, 77, 141–173, 210–11; rights 141, 143, 148, 150, 152, 162–4, 172; *see also* confidentiality; secrecy
privilege 3, 33, 37, 47, 71, 120, 181, 183, 193; *see also* white privilege
professionalism 2, 77
profit 3, 46, 72, 114, 193, 196–7, 201
Progressive Council Caucus 12
Progressive Librarian 41, 163
progressive librarians 4
Progressive Librarians Guild 5, 12, 41, 68, 88, 92, 181, 203
Progressive Library Organizations: A Worldwide History 9, 72, 203
propaganda 66, 76, 90, 100, 102–3, 105
protests 23, 33, 51, 54, 72, 196
Proudfoot, Merrill 61
public good 2
public librarians 31, 122
public opinion 21, 24, 91
public platforms 16, 21–23, 35–6, 38
Publishers' Weekly 122, 210
publishing industry 119, 123, 186

Raber, Douglas 9, 203, 211
Rabin, Yitzhak 79

race 8, 15, 17, 21, 23, 25, 31–2, 34, 37, 44, 46–8, 50, 52–4, 58, 60, 62, 90, 132, 180, 204, 206; discrimination 49; equality 19, 36, 48; *see also* "Honor Role of Race Relations"
"raceologist" *see* eugenics
racism 5, 6, 8, 15–7, 20, 21 23–6, 31–3, 34, 35–7, 39, 41–4, 46–52, 55–6, 58, 70, 73, 91, 138–8, 180, 191, 194, 202, 204; *see also Access to Public Libraries*; epistemological racism; eugenics; segregation
Ramallah 80
Ranganathan, S. R. 57–8, 206
Raphael, Molly 157–9, 164–6, 168
Rather, Dan 83
Raviv, Dan 79
Reagan, Ronald (president) 63
The Real Terror Network 77
recommended reading lists *see* book awards; book recommendations; "Honor Role of Race Relations"; Juvenile Book Week; Notable Books
Reed, Sally Gardner 136–7
REFORMA 187
refugee camps *see* Dheshieh; Sabra and Shatila
reparations 17, 32, 37, 194
resilience 180
Resni, Ed 115
resolutions *see* Council; Social Responsibilities Round Table
Richardson, Elliot 21; *see also* Watergate
Richmond (VA) 48
Ridler, Elizabeth 164, 169–70
The Right Mistake: The Further Philosophical Investigations of Socrates Fortlow 202
Robbins, Jerome 57
Robeson, Paul 48–9, 51–2, 57, 73, 205
Rockefeller, John D., Jr. 120, 210
Rodinson, Maxime 88, 91, 208
Rokach, Israel 90
Rokach, Livia 88–90, 208
Rom, Pat 150
Roman, Susan 124, 135, 164, 210
Romans, Larry 164, 166, 169, 186
Roosevelt, Eleanor 48
Rose, Ernestine 48, 206
Rosenfeld, Joel 98
Rosenthal, Michael 111, 121, 210
Rosenzweig, Mark vi, 88, 92, 98, 134–7, 210
Royal Society 192–4, 211
Ruckelshaus, William 21; *see also* Watergate
Rudolph, Wilma 55
Rusher, William 23

Sabra and Shatila refugee camps 90
Sacks, Albert M. 22, 24, 204
Said, Edward 88, 208
SAILIS *see* South African Institute for Librarianship and Information Science

Saint, Eva Marie 88
SALA *see* South African Library Association
Samek, Toni 9, 203
San Francisco 26, 77, 96, 109, 111-2, 211
San Francisco Examiner 77
San Francisco Public Library 63, 111
sanctions 5, 6, 42-44, 51-2, 54-9, 62-70, 72, 79, 84, 107, 133, 205-6; legislation 62-5
Sanctions Handbook 63, 205
Sandifer, Eddie 23
Sandstrom, John 166
Saturday Night Massacre *see* Watergate
Savery, Thomas 193
Scheurich, James Joseph 6, 204
Schneider, Karen 164, 187
Schomberg Center for Research in Black Culture 48
Schuman, Pat 15, 204
Schuster, S. L. 128-9, 210
Schwerner, Michael 32
school librarians 30, 31
School Library Journal 115-7, 135-5
Schottlander, Brian 157, 166
Schwartz, Michel 97-9
Scout Field Book 127, 210
Scouting for Boys 119, 126, 209; *see also* Baden-Powell, Robert; *Boy Scout Handbook;* Boy Scouts of America; *Scout Field Book*
Scribner, Charles 119-20
Scripps Institute of Oceanography 175
SDS *see* Students for a Democratic Society
SEA *see* Seattle Education Association
sea levels 191
search warrants *see* Fourth Amendment
searches and seizures *see* Fourth Amendment
Seasholes, Craig 1-2
Seattle (WA) 2, 39, 143, 175-6, 178, 181, 185, 196, 212
Seattle Education Association (SEA) 1
secrecy 7, 127, 137, 141, 143-4, 146, 149, 162-3; *see also* confidentiality; privacy
sedition 101
Sedney, Frances V. 115
seeding (atmosphere and oceans) 192, 200; *see also* geotechnology
Seeger, Pete 57
segregation 17, 24, 45, 55, 70, 177, 205; ALA policy opposing 32, 48, 50, 58-9, 159; in libraries 47, 58; library associations 32, 58; *see also* apartheid in libraries
Seidman, Ann and Neva 46
self-governance 28
semantics 104, 136, 172; *see also* violence, semantic
Sennett, Richard 7, 160-1, 211

service 2
Sessions, Judith 107-8
settlers, Israeli 76, 89
Seuss, Dr. 202
Sever, Shmuel 98
severe violence *see* violence
sexual orientation 8, 127-8, 130-2, 137; *see also* gay librarians; gay scouts; homophobia
Shakespeare, William 48
shame 27, 44, 128, 132, 136, 160-1, 164
Sharett, Moshe 89-90, 208
Sharett, Yakov 90
Sharpeville (South Africa) 54-5, 206
Shearar, Jeremy 53, 206
Shelkrot, Elliott 29
Shields, Gerald 31
Shields, Gregg 135
Shockley, William 17, 19-21, 22, 24, 29, 31, 36-7; *see also* eugenics; Harvard Law School; racism; Voluntary Sterilization Bonus Plan
silence 18, 24, 34, 37, 44-5, 50, 72, 86, 90, 124, 126, 131, 134, 135, 139, 160-1, 170-1, 173, 196
Silicon Valley 20
Simone, Nina 57
Sinclair, Upton 191-2, 212
60 Minutes (TV news show) 26
Skype 147
Slocum, Grace 27
Smith, Lillian 49
Smuts, Jan 52-3
Snoqualmie Valley (WA) 178-9, 182
Snow, Edith N. 48
Snowden, Edward 4, 6-7, 141, 143-61, 163-6, 168-173, 211
social change 2, 9, 42, 77, 177
social media 151, 157
Social Responsibilities Round Table (SRRT) 5, 6, 9-13, 31-2, 34, 42, 66, 69-72, 80, 87-8, 91, 94, 96-8, 100-1, 105-9, 111-7, 124-6, 130-4, 136, 139, 146, 149-50, 155, 158, 181, 187-8, 195, 203, 206-8; Action Council 12, 80, 87-8, 91, 96, 107-9, 114-6, 125, 181, 206-7; Library Union Task Force; On Corporate Sponsorship Issues 113-6, 210; Resolution on the ALSC/Boy Scouts Relationship 113; *see also* Gay, Lesbian, Bisexual Task Force; International Human Rights Task Force; Peace Information Exchange Task Force; SRRT Guidelines for Librarians Interacting with South Africa; Task Force on Israeli Censorship and Palestinian Libraries; Task Force on the Environment
social responsibility 2, 3, 8, 15
socialism 51
soil 180, 184
Sokol, Chris 111, 210

"Solidarity Forever" (song) 1, 198, 203
Somerville, Mary 136
songs 1, 2, 41, 49, 88, 198, 203
Sophiatown 51, 55
The Source 89
South Africa 3, 41-73; Parliament 53; trade 46; *see also* African National Congress; anti-apartheid movement; "book boycott"; Congress of South African Writers; Pan-African Congress; pass laws; South African Indian Congress; South African Library Association; SRRT Guidelines; Suppression of Communism Act; United Nations resolutions against South Africa
South Africa and U.S. Multinational Corporations 46
South African Indian Congress 51
South African Institute for Librarianship and Information Science (SAILIS) 62
South African Library Association (SALA) 47, 60, 62, 206
South African Student Association 61
Soviet Union 52, 72, 91
Soweto (South Africa) 61
The Speaker: A Film about Freedom 3, 5, 15-39; ALA "imprimatur" 18, 27; Black Caucus response (1978) 33, 34, 38; budget 17; consultation with IFC members 26; discussion guide 16, 18, 25, 27-30, 32; IFC subcommittee 18, 22, 27, 38; OCLC record 18; original proposal 19, 27; perspective on First Amendment 33, 34, 37; preview screenings 18, 27; script 18, 26, 27; summary 19; survey 30; *see also* "Speaking About *The Speaker*"
"Speaking About *The Speaker*" 15, 25, 30, 34, 35, 39
"speaking with one voice" *see* "one voice policy"
speech without ideas 28; *see also* First Amendment; free speech; symbolic speech
Spinsters 111
Spokane (WA) 24
sports *see* boycotts, sports; Olympic games
spying 76, 158, 171
Sri Lanka 55
SRRT *see* Social Responsibilities Round Table
SRRT Guidelines for Librarians Interacting with South Africa 41-2, 66-7, 69-70, 72, 205-6
Stars and Stripes (newspaper) 88
"Starvation of Young Black Minds: The Effect of Book Boycotts on South Africa" 42, 59, 67-9, 72, 206
State University of New York-Buffalo 31

States, David J. 23
States of Denial: Knowing About Atrocities and Suffering 5, 33
steam engine 193
Steele, Anitra R. 124–5, 209–10
Steinbeck, John 49
Stephenson, James 113, 115–6
stereotypes 19, 27, 30–1, 33, 38, 44, 52, 139
Sterling, Claire 77
Stewart, Jon 129
Stillwell, Stephen 75, 88, 101, 107, 115, 125, 131–2, 208, 210
Stonewall 127
Stonewall Children's and Youth Literature Award 138
"Story of Stuff" 197
Stoss, Fred 149
Strange Fruit 49; *see also* Library Bill of Rights
strikes, labor 1 ; South Africa 51
Struggle for Africa 50
Students for a Democratic Society (SDS) 21, 22, 24
subject headings 8, 62, 112
Suess, Eric 164
suffering, human 3, 5, 17, 33, 35, 203; *see also* bystanders; exploitation, oppression; racism; torture; violence
suicide 119–20, 138, 191
Sullivan, Ed 57
Sultzberger, Arthur Hayes 49
Sunnyvale (CA) 27
Suppression of Communism Act (South Africa) 51
surveillance 81, 146, 149–53, 158, 162–3, 172, 211
sustainability 4, 7, 12, 188–91, 195, 197, 212; *see also* Sustainability Round Table (SustainRT)
Sustainability Round Table (SustainRT) 5, 12, 188, 203, 212
SustainRT *see* Sustainability Round Table
swag, beyond 196
Swan, John 42, 206
Swan/Peattie debate 42
symbolic speech 28; *see also* First Amendment; free speech; speech without ideas

tar-sands 182, 192
Task Force on Israeli Censorship and Palestinian Libraries 96, 101, 107, 109, 208
Task Force on the Environment (TFoE) 12, 188, 196
taxes 72, 87, 89, 176; *see also* poll taxes
teen librarians *see* YA librarians
Tekola, Sarra 175, 212
Tel Aviv (Israel) 78
Tel Aviv University 94
telephone 4
television 57; *see also* ABC news; BBC news; CBS news; censorship; NBC news; *60 Minutes*
The Terror Network 77

textbooks 71, 85
TFoE *see* Task Force on the Environment
This Changes Everything: Capitalism vs Climate 7, 202, 212
Thomas, Sherry 111
350.org 175–6, 185, 187, 212
Time (magazine) 81, 83
Timerman, Jacobo 88, 90, 208
"Together is Better…Let's Read!" 113–4, 116, 210
tolerance 17, 19, 25, 28–9, 32–3, 35–7, 50, 52, 62, 120, 129, 132, 142, 185, 197
torture 6, 56, 61, 149, 163
totalitarianism 139
tourism 183, 201; *see also* "love miles"
trade embargoes 63
trade unions *see* labor unions
Trade Unions Council (Britain) 54
transition, peaceful 175, 185–6, 192, 194, 198–201
transportation 183, 193, 197, 199–201; *see also* airline industry; bicycles; carbon dioxide; carbon footprint
Trapskin, Ben 185–6
Truman, Harry 49
Trump, Donald 139
trust 9, 17–8, 23, 33, 83, 119, 133, 141, 143, 145, 154, 165, 169, 188
truth-and-reconciliation 37
Turock, Betty 101
Tutu, Desmond 63, 176, 185, 212
24-hour rule *see* Council
Twiss, Tom 146, 148–50
Tyndall Centre for Climate Change Research 191

unemployed 120
UNESCO 59–61, 102–3, 205–6, 208
unintended consequences 5, 157, 159–60, 173, 177, 187, 194
"Union Maid" (song) 1
unions *see* labor unions; Seattle Education Association; Trade Unions Council; United Auto Workers
United Auto Workers 201
United for Libraries 148, 211
United Kingdom *see* Great Britain
United Nations 46, 52–4, 56, 83, 87, 95, 97, 105, 205–6; Charter 52–56; resolutions against South Africa 54, 56
United Nations Educational, Scientific, and Cultural Organization *see* UNESCO
United States Constitution 7, 12, 18, 28, 38, 64, 77, 82, 142–3, 146, 148–9, 165, 172; *see also* First Amendment; Fourth Amendment
United States Congress 16, 24, 41–2, 62–3, 67, 72, 129, 147–8, 151, 153, 159, 163, 165, 170, 172, 198
United States Department of Health and Human Services 145, 154; *see also* Affordable Care Act
United States Department of State 51, 54, 80, 83, 95, 97, 102–3, 105, 206
United States Information Agency 12–3, 102–3, 105, 207, 208; *see also* diplomacy; Library/Book Fellows Program; propaganda
United States Office of Special Counsel 165–6, 167
United States Supreme Court 28–9, 58, 138
United States trade with South Africa 46
Universal Declaration of Human Rights 53, 61, 83, 95, 97; *see also* Article 11; Article 19
University of Chicago 76
University of Delhi 57
University of Idaho 196
University of Illinois 92
University of Pittsburgh 31, 146
University of Pretoria 61
University of Utah 88–9, 91
Uris, Leon 88, 208
USA Today (newspaper) 148–9, 158, 211
USAPATRIOT Act 152–3, 162–3
USIA *see* United States Information Agency

values 2, 8 *see also* core values; morality; priorities
vegans 177; *see also* animal rights; morality
Verwoerd, Hendrik 57
violence 3, 6–9, 33, 37, 42, 56, 58, 61, 77, 139, 154, 160–1, 191, 194, 199; defined 45; material 45; semantic 45, 50; severe 6, 42–6, 51, 65, 71, 77; *see also* nonviolence
Vision Associates 20, 26, 36
Vleeschauwer, Herman De 60–2
Voluntary Sterilization Bonus Plan (VSBP) 17, 23, 24; *see also* eugenics; racism
VSBP *see* Voluntary Sterilization Bonus Plan

Wallach, Eli 57
war criminals 61–2
Washington Office, ALA 144, 156–8, 163–4, 173, 199
Washington Post (newspaper) 78–9, 82, 146, 153, 173, 207–8
Washington Report on Middle East Affairs 75
Watergate 20, 21; *see also* Cox, Archibald
Watson, Elizabeth 135
Wedgeworth, Robert 16–8, 30, 37, 42, 67–9, 72, 204
Weiner, Karl 30
Which Side Are You On? The Story of a Song 2
whistleblowers 4, 6, 146–154, 156–161, 163–168, 171–3, 210–11; retaliation 167; Sample Whistleblower

Index

Policy 148; *see also* Binney, William; Drake, Thomas; National Security Agency; Snowden, Edward; Wiebe, J. Kirk
white librarians 17, 19, 32–3
white privilege 33, 37–8, 71, 120; *see also* privilege
white supremacy 33, 34, 36–7, 43, 52–3, 62, 64
Whitney, Karen 108
Whitten, Sam 31
Whitwell, Stuart C. A. 134, 210
Wiebe, J. Kirk 148
Wijnstroom, Margreet 60–1
WikiLeaks 149, 151; *see also* Manning, Bradley
Wilding, Tom 125, 169
Wilkins, Roy 21
Willhoite, Michael 129
William Morrow and Company 42, 67
Williams, Avery 31
Williams, David 76–7, 80, 83–4, 86–7, 91, 93–4, 96, 98–101, 104, 107–8, 133, 208
Williamsburg Regional Library 155

Wilson Library Bulletin 25, 98
Wilsonline 102
Wobbly *see* Industrial Workers of the World
Woods, Donald 61
working class 4, 44, 51
working class librarians 4
World Council of Churches 55–6
World Report 1988: Article 19 Information, Freedom, and Censorship 87, 207
World Report 1991 94–5, 97, 207
World War I 29, 91, 121–2
World War II 7, 24, 43, 52, 60, 78, 91, 197–8, 200
W.R. Grace 63, 65, 69, 205
Wright, Bob 31
Wright, Richard 49
writs of assistance 142, 173; *see also* Fourth Amendment; privacy

YA (young adult) librarians 4
Yahoo 147
Yale University 23, 24
Yankee Book Peddler 63
Yarns for Boy Scouts 119
Yates, Ella 30, 32, 33

YALSA *see* Young Adult Library Services Association
Year of the Flood 202
Yizhar, S. 75, 208
Young Adult Library Services Association (YALSA) 13, 115, 130, 138, 200, 203, 210
Young Adult Services Division 26
Young Americans for Freedom 23, 24
Young, Gay & Proud! 128, 210
Your Fatwa Does Not Apply Here 87
YouTube 1, 5, 16, 18, 32, 37, 147

Zeitoun 180, 212
"zero carbon" *see* net-zero carbon emissions
Zionism 76, 78, 88, 90–1, 112, 207
Zionism in the Age of the Dictators 88, 207
Zoellner, Kate 196
Zoia! Memoirs of Zoia Horn, Battler for the People's Right to Know 150, 204, 211
zoo 64
ZSL: Let's Work for Wildlife 192
Zulu 41

www.ingramcontent.com/pod-product-compliance
Ingram Content Group UK Ltd.
Pitfield, Milton Keynes, MK11 3LW, UK
UKHW050531150426
5217IPUK00026B/1883